"THE BEAUTY *of* LIFE"

WILLIAM MORRIS & THE ART OF DESIGN

"THE BEAUTY *of* LIFE"

WILLIAM MORRIS & THE ART OF DESIGN

Edited by DIANE WAGGONER

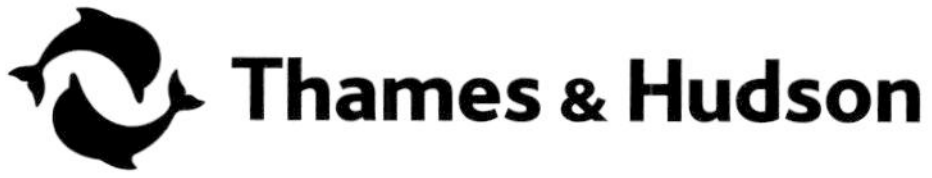

On p. 2
1 Designed by William Morris for Morris & Company

Jasmine wallpaper, first issued 1872 (detail)

Block-printed in distemper colours, printed by Jeffrey & Company, London, whole piece 42 x 23 (106.7 x 58.4)

NOTE
In captions, unless otherwise stated, objects are in The Huntington collections. Dimensions are given in inches followed by centimetres.

This book is published to coincide with the exhibition *"The Beauty of Life": William Morris and the Art of Design*, organized by The Huntington Library, Art Collections, and Botanical Gardens, San Marino, California.

Exhibition dates

The Huntington Library, Art Collections, and Botanical Gardens, San Marino, California
8 November 2003–4 April 2004

Yale Center for British Art, New Haven, Connecticut
14 October 2004–2 January 2005

First published in paperback in the United States of America in 2003 by Thames & Hudson Inc., 500 Fifth Avenue, New York, New York 10110

thamesandhudsonusa.com

Library of Congress Catalog Card Number 2003103603

ISBN 0-500-28434-2

Printed and bound in Singapore by C.S. Graphics

CONTENTS

FOREWORD 6
EDITOR'S ACKNOWLEDGMENTS 6
DONORS TO THE WILLIAM MORRIS ACQUISITION 7

INTRODUCTION — DIANE WAGGONER 8

WILLIAM MORRIS: A LIFE IN DESIGN — PAT KIRKHAM 20

THE FIRM: MORRIS & COMPANY — PAT KIRKHAM 32

STAINED GLASS & CHURCH DECORATION — DIANE WAGGONER 64

THE DECORATION OF HOUSES — DIANE WAGGONER 76

THE ART OF THE BOOK — DIANE WAGGONER 88

JOHN HENRY DEARLE — DIANE WAGGONER 98

THE THINGS THAT MIGHT BE: BRITISH DESIGN AFTER MORRIS — GILLIAN NAYLOR 108

TWO SIDES OF THE RIVER: MORRIS & AMERICAN ARTS AND CRAFTS — EDWARD R. BOSLEY 134

NOTES 169
SELECT BIBLIOGRAPHY 173
INDEX 174
CONTRIBUTORS 176

FOREWORD

'The Beauty of Life': William Morris and the Art of Design, published on the occasion of the exhibition of the same title at The Huntington, celebrates the acquisition of a major collection of materials relating to William Morris and to his firm, Morris & Company. At a stroke, this collection makes The Huntington one of the leading world centres for the study of the European design revolutions of the mid-nineteenth century.

For Morris is one of the giants of the nineteenth century, a man who greatly influenced both his contemporaries and succeeding generations in architecture, interior decoration, pattern design, typography and book design, illustration—all the arts, in short, whose growth and transformation were motivated at this time by the industrialization of production in advanced economies, and by doubts about the effects of these great changes on the quality of society and the possibilities of human happiness. Morris's writing and lecturing on the relationship between art and society constitutes a major contribution to the non-Marxist lineage of radical thought in the nineteenth century, a tradition which, since the 1920s, has been much obscured. This book, a contribution to the history of design, seeks to engage nonetheless with the wider issues. Like The Huntington's collection, it covers the entire span of Morris's achievement and the operations of Morris & Company, dealing with the technicalities and economics of design and production, as well as with Morris's socialism. In related essays, the authors consider Morris's life and examine his legacy in the history of design in the twentieth century in Britain and America. In this way, the acquisition of the Morris collection, together with this book and exhibition, help to fulfill The Huntington's longstanding commitment to the study of the European roots of much Southern Californian culture and domesticity. Very simply, it is much easier to understand the originality of Charles and Henry Greene in Pasadena if we can see from where they started. And the same is true of other great names of American art and design in the twentieth century.

We list in the Acknowledgments the donors who made this acquisition possible. It is our pleasure to offer all these individuals and foundations our warmest thanks.

John Murdoch,
Director of the Art Collections

David S. Zeidberg,
Avery Director of the Library

EDITOR'S ACKNOWLEDGMENTS

First and foremost I am grateful to the Andrew W. Mellon Foundation for supporting me as a Curatorial Fellow at The Huntington during the development of this book and exhibition. Among my colleagues, great thanks are due to Shelley Bennett for her enthusiastic support throughout all stages of this project, and to Anne Mallek, who has devoted three years to cataloguing and researching the Morris collection. Anne's unflagging enthusiasm and intellectual curiosity have enriched this project in countless ways. Guilland Sutherland, our expert editor, has been remarkable for patience and sagacity. Pat Kirkham, Gillian Naylor, and Ted Bosley were wonderful colleagues who taught me much about the subject. Linda Parry of the Victoria & Albert Museum has shared her time and expertise to enrich our knowledge of the collection. Thanks are also due to Peter Cormack and Norah Gillow of the William Morris Gallery, Walthamstow, for answering questions, and to Alan Crawford for his advice and encouragement.

Diane Waggoner

DONORS TO THE WILLIAM MORRIS ACQUISITION

The Ahmanson Foundation
Mr and Mrs Daniel E. Biles
Mr and Mrs Theodore G. Congdon
Mrs Sidney F. Brody
Marilyn and Don Conlan
The Ida Hull Lloyd Crotty Foundation
Elsie de Wolfe Foundation, Inc.
Betty and Brack Duker
The Frances C. Dyke Bequest
Mr and Mrs Robert F. Erburu
The Essick Foundation, Inc.
Mr and Mrs Stanley F. Farrar
Mr Michael H. Finnell
The Fletcher Jones Foundation
Frances & Sidney Brody Charitable Fund
J. Paul Getty Trust
The Hillcrest Foundation
Mrs Natalie A. Howard
W. M. Keck Foundation
Mr and Mrs Jon Lovelace
Mr and Mrs Kenneth S. McCormick
Frank and Toshie Mosher
Alfred C. Munger Foundation
Mr and Mrs Charles T. Munger
The Ralph M. Parsons Foundation
The Richards Family Foundation
Mrs J. Randolph Richards
Mr and Mrs Jud O. Roberts
Mr and Mrs James F. Rothenberg
Mr and Mrs E. L. Shannon, Jr
Mr Stewart R. Smith and Ms Robin A. Ferracone
Mr and Mrs Alan G. Stanford
Mr and Mrs John A. Sturgeon
Mr and Mrs L. Sherman Telleen
Mr and Mrs Charles B. Thornton, Jr
The Thornton Foundation
Mr and Mrs Robert E. Wycoff
Mr and Mrs E. Eugene Yeager

SOCIALIST LEAGUE

HAMMERSMITH BRANCH

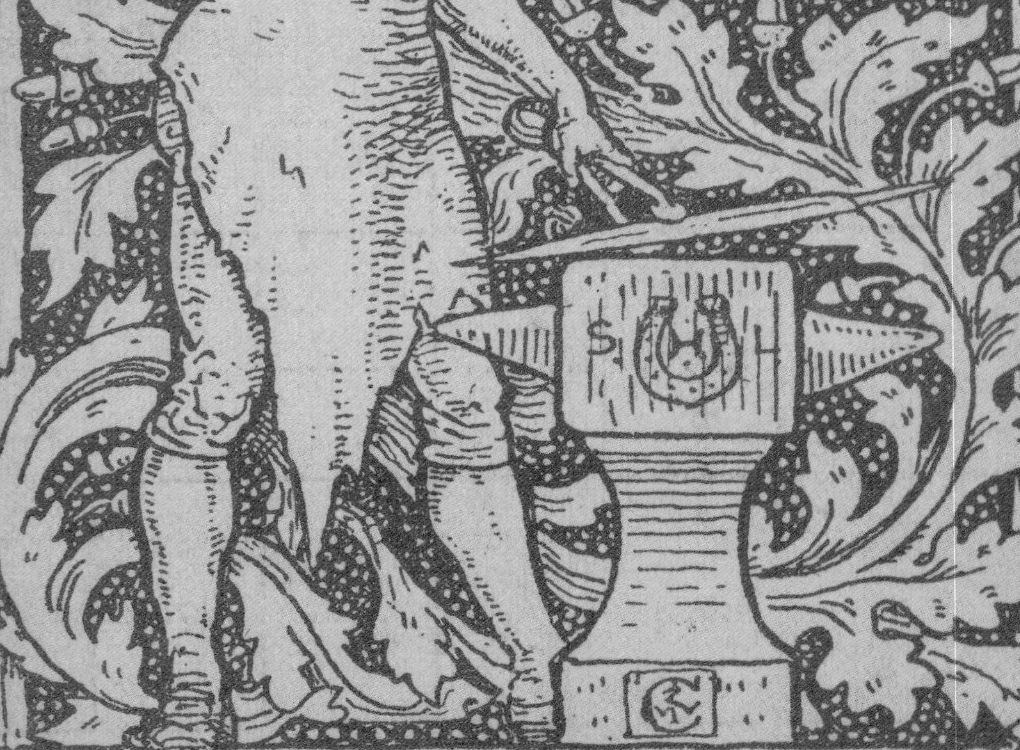

BRANCH SECRETARY. Emery Walker

TREASURER. William Morris

INTRODUCTION

DIANE WAGGONER

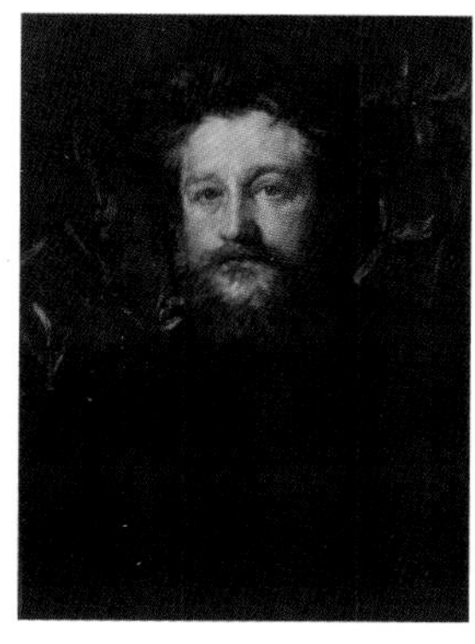

3 Malcolm Osborne after a painting by G. F. Watts

William Morris, 1910

Mezzotint, 12½ x 9 (31.8 x 22.9)

In his lecture 'The Beauty of Life' delivered in 1880, William Morris (1834–96) defined art and beauty together as integral to life itself: 'beauty, which is what is meant by *art*, using the word in its widest sense, is, I contend, no mere accident to human life, which people can take or leave as they choose, but a positive necessity of life, if we are to live as nature meant us to; that is, unless we are content to be less than men.'[1] Morris's lecture had a double refrain: first, he preached that art in the medieval period had been 'made by the people for the people as a joy for the maker and the user'; and second, he hoped that this art could be reclaimed in life by his golden rule, 'Have nothing in your houses which you do not know to be useful or believe to be beautiful.' In his own life Morris devoted himself to the decorative arts as the head of the internationally successful Morris & Company ('the Firm'), which he ran for over thirty years. He looked to the past as inspiration for the present and for the future, and he discovered a deep fulfilment in the daily work of craftsmanship and creation.

This book contains a series of essays that examine the life and work of Morris and of Morris & Company, and also the legacy of Morris and the Firm in the late nineteenth and twentieth centuries on both sides of the Atlantic. It celebrates The Huntington's Morris collection as a vehicle for this study. Morris was a man of tremendous energies, his accomplishments astonishing in their range and depth. He became successively a poet, embroiderer, pattern designer, calligrapher, dyer, weaver, translator, architectural preservationist, socialist and book printer and publisher. His lifelong friend and collaborator, the artist Edward Burne-Jones, whose talents as a painter and figure designer for the Firm complemented Morris's, summed up the trajectory of Morris's life in his catalogue of the arts and crafts that Morris variously adopted and mastered:

2 Hammersmith Branch Socialist League membership card for Henry Halliday Sparling, 1890

4½ x 3 (11.4 x 7.6)

Signed by Emery Walker and William Morris.

> When I first knew Morris nothing would content him but being a monk, and getting to Rome, and then he must be an architect, and apprenticed himself to [G. E.] Street, and worked for two years, but when I came to London and began to

> paint he threw it all up, and must paint too, and then he must give it up and make poems, and then he must give it up and make window hangings and pretty things, and when he had achieved that, he must be a good poet again, and then after two or three years of Earthly Paradise time, he must learn dyeing, and lived in a vat, and learned weaving, and knew all about looms, and then made more books, and learned tapestry, and then wanted to smash everything up and begin the world anew, and now it is printing he cares for, and to make wonderful rich-looking books – and all things he does splendidly – and if he lives the printing will have an end – but not I hope, before *Chaucer* and the *Morte d'Arthur* are done; then he'll do I don't know what, but every minute will be alive.[2]

Morris was known in his own lifetime as both writer and decorator, or as Henry James dubbed him the 'poet and paper-maker',[3] but it is his philosophy of design that most influenced the twentieth century. He accomplished his revolution in design through Morris & Company. Established initially with his coterie of friends, the Firm was founded as Morris, Marshall, Faulkner & Company in 1861 by a group of ambitious and somewhat inexperienced young men who, in addition to Morris, included the painters Ford Madox Brown, Dante Gabriel Rossetti and Edward Burne-Jones, and the architect Philip Webb, as well as Peter Paul Marshall and Charles Faulkner. It would be reorganized as Morris & Company in 1875 under Morris's sole direction. While the Firm made its first splash with stained glass for church decoration, it was domestic decoration that most inspired Morris. He summed up his belief in the importance of the home in his memorable words, 'If I were asked to say what is at once the most important production of Art and the thing most to be longed for, I should answer, A beautiful House.'[4] Morris's love of houses and home can be traced throughout his life, in his letters and writings and his life's work as a designer, and in his love for his own homes, Red House in Kent (which he moved into in 1860), Kelmscott Manor in Oxfordshire (taken in 1871 and kept until his death in 1896) [4], and

4 William Morris for the Kelmscott Press

Pasted-up proof for *News from Nowhere*, *c.* 1892

Graphite and ink, full sheet $11\frac{5}{8}$ x $8\frac{3}{8}$ (29.5 x 21.3)

The house, drawn by C. M. Gere for Morris, is Kelmscott Manor, the sixteenth-century home in Oxfordshire that Morris rented from 1871 until the end of his life. Jane Morris would eventually purchase it after his death.

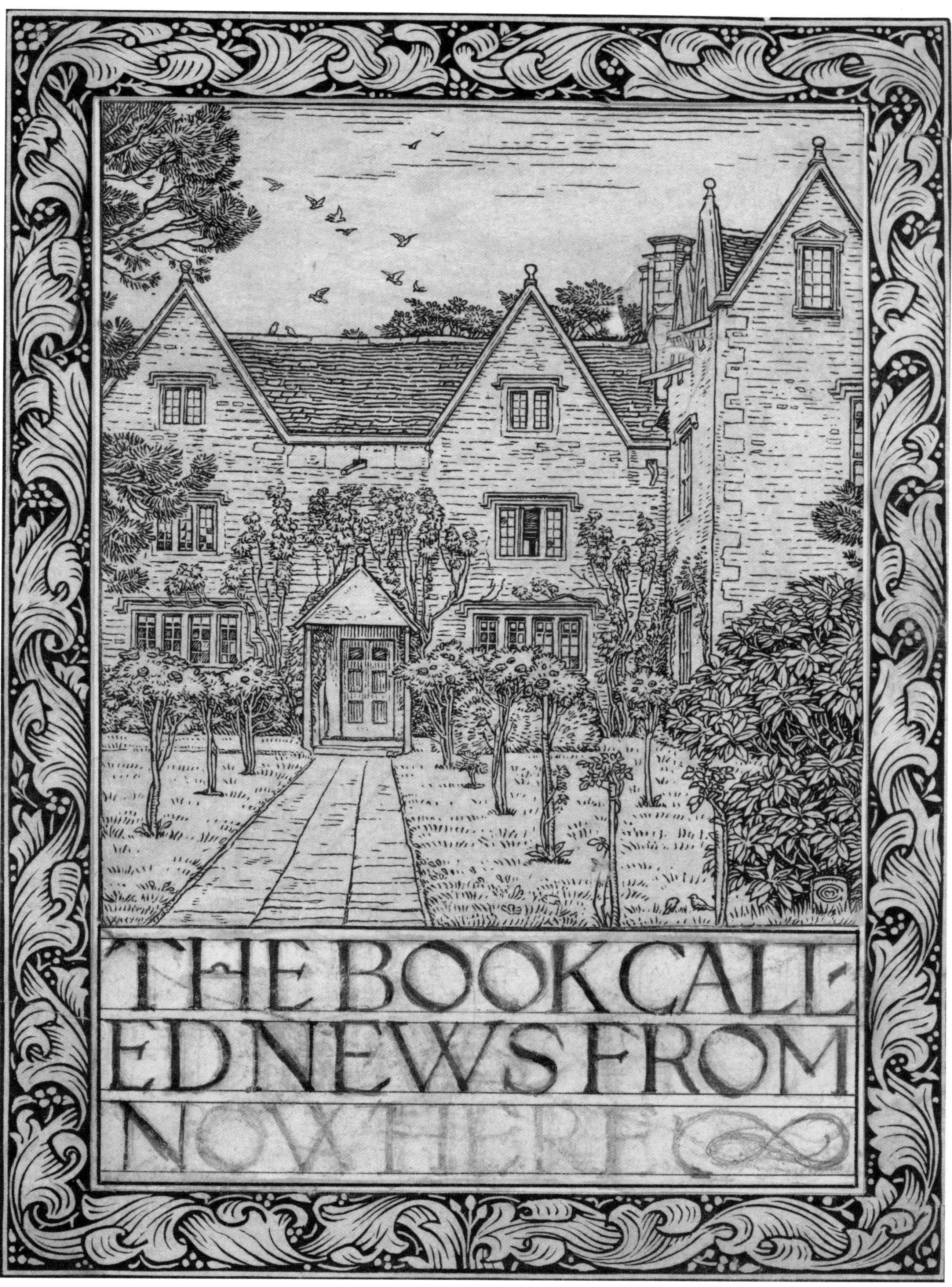
THE BOOK CALL
ED NEWS FROM
NOWHERE

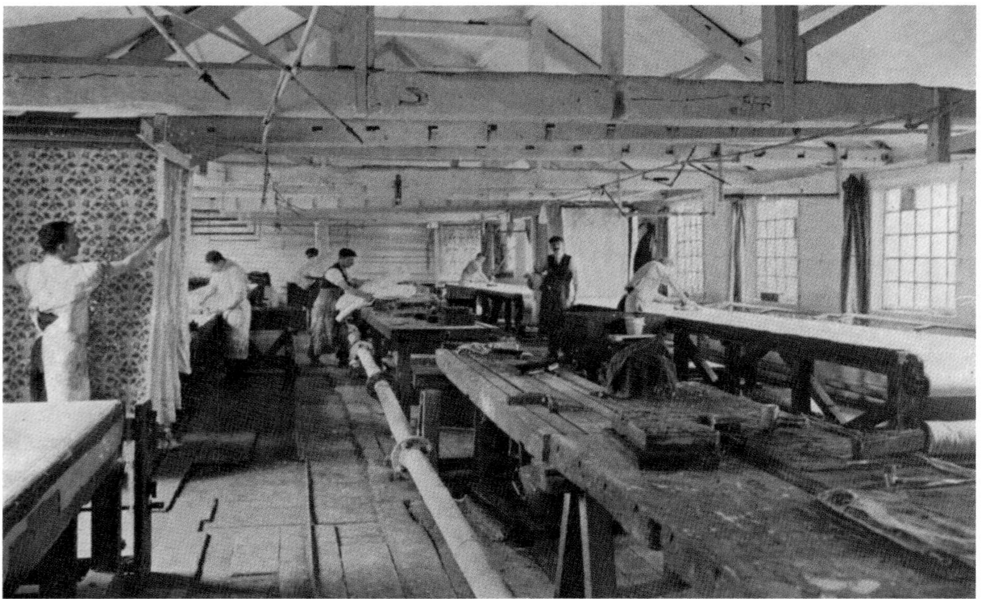

5 Workers block-printing cotton at Merton Abbey, Surrey

From *A Brief Sketch of the Morris Movement* (London: privately printed for Morris & Company, 1911)

Kelmscott House, Hammersmith (from 1878). In his most idealistic writing, the utopian novel *News from Nowhere*, he wrote of his beloved Kelmscott Manor as the ideal home, picturing its façade in the frontispiece to the book [4]. He was an innovator in interior design, not only as a pattern designer but also for the simplicity and quality of goods that he advocated. For Morris, beauty, as embodied in the home, and the creative labour that went into producing beautiful things had the power to improve the lives of individuals and nations.

In all of his various activities, Morris endeavoured to unify art and craftsmanship, mind and hand. He railed against what he perceived as the loss of this ideal in the industrial revolution:

> In almost all cases there is no sympathy between the designer and the man who carries out the design. ... I know by experience that the making of design after design – mere diagrams, mind you – without oneself executing them, is a great strain upon the mind. It is necessary, unless all workmen of all grades are to be permanently degraded into machines, that the hand should rest the mind as well as the mind the hand. And I say that this is the kind of work which the world has lost, supplying its place with the work which is the result of the division of labour.[5]

Morris's hopes for art eventually led him into the political arena. He had written to a friend in his early twenties that 'I can't enter into politico-social subjects with any interest, for on the whole I see that things are in a muddle, and I have no power or vocation to set them right in ever so little a degree. My work is the embodiment of dreams in one form or another.'[6] Although he began his creative life with this embrace of art only, his experiences in the world as the head of his own company guided him to espouse the political as inextricable from the aesthetic and creative life. He was not always content that the Firm, in order to be a viable business, often decorated the home of the privileged aristocrat rather than of the average worker. He hoped to set the world right when he became a committed socialist and in the 1880s he worked tirelessly as a political activist. Believing that social reform was an extension of aesthetic reform, Morris felt that the state of the decorative arts in England had been degraded by mass production. Again and again he advocated that not only must the designer understand the medium for which he or she designs and be true to its materials but there must also be pleasure in the labour that produces the goods, as he believed had been the case in the medieval period. The past was always a place of inspiration for Morris, whether he looked at the structure of society or the traditional techniques of producing stained glass or dyeing fabric, which he worked to revitalize and preserve. At the same time that he sought to make the home beautiful, he hoped to make the world a better place. Morris's ideals were to have a deep impact on succeeding generations of designers, artists and craftsmen. This book pays tribute to Morris's life and his legacy.

With the recent acquisition of the William Morris collection of Sanford and Helen Berger, The Huntington houses the largest collection of material associated with Morris in North America and is now a major centre for the study of William Morris and of Morris & Company. Prior to the acquisition, Morris the writer had already been well represented in the collections, with one of the most significant collections of manuscripts for Morris's published writings, many of them purchased by Henry E. Huntington himself. This material includes the seven-volume manuscript of Morris's most famous poem, *The Earthly Paradise,* and the manuscripts for several of Morris's other poems, prose romances, and translations of classical literature and Icelandic sagas. The Huntington also houses manuscripts of Morris's socialist essays and speeches, material related to the Society for the Protection of Ancient Buildings, all the books printed at the Kelmscott Press, designs by Morris and proofs for Kelmscott Press ornamentation, and over fifty letters from Morris to various friends.

The Huntington's collection also ranges beyond Morris to related areas, including Pre-Raphaelitism and the Arts and Crafts movement. The British holdings consist of letters and drawings by artists of the Pre-Raphaelite circle and other associates of Morris.[7] These include Burne-Jones, Rossetti, Walter Crane, Charles Fairfax-Murray, William Holman Hunt, John Everett Millais, Algernon Charles Swinburne and John Ruskin. On the American side, the Arts and Crafts movement is represented by works by the southern Californian architects Greene & Greene, such as the full dining room from the Robinson house. Moreover, the archives relating to Greene & Greene are on deposit in the Art Collections and are available to scholars courtesy of The Gamble House and the University of Southern California School of Architecture. The Library also has significant holdings in the archive of the printer, illustrator, and typographer Will Bradley and the corporate archive of Daniel Berkeley Updike's Merrymount Press.

The major acquisition of the Bergers' collection builds on the strengths of The Huntington's collection and expands it into whole new areas, particularly focusing on Morris & Company. The Bergers, architects who had met at the Harvard Graduate School of Design and studied there with Walter Gropius, had first become intrigued by Morris when they acquired a facsimile of the Kelmscott Chaucer in 1965. Sandy

1/2" Scale

Design for West Window
St. Stephen's Church: Guernsey
By Messrs Morris, Marshall, Faulkner & Co

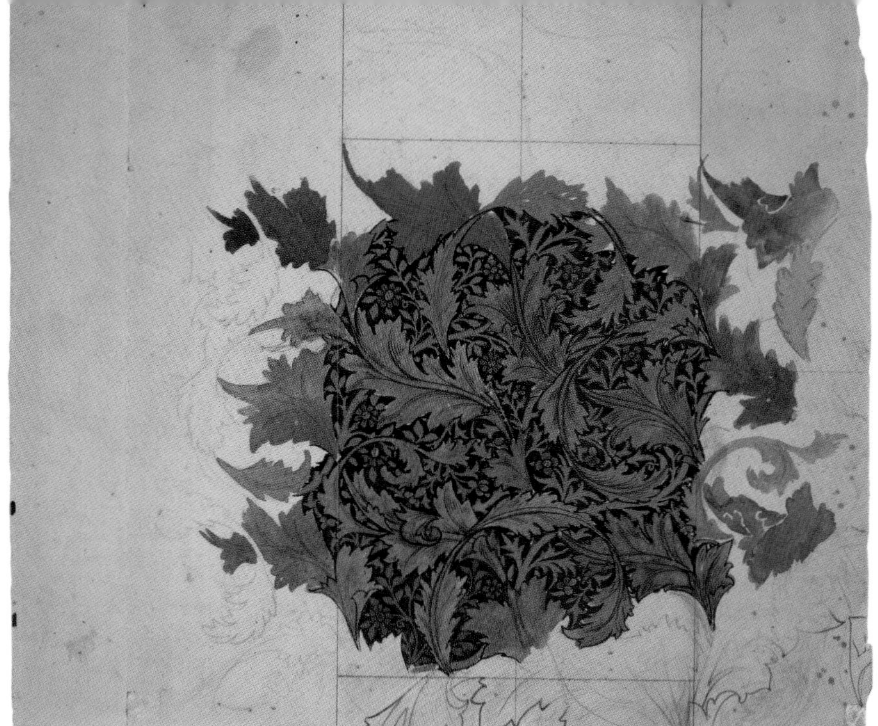

7 J. H. Dearle for Morris & Company

Design for *Granville* wallpaper, *c.* 1896

Watercolour, graphite and ink, 13¾ x 11 (34.9 x 27.9)

Berger recalled that 'It was a modest copy, not even full size, but there was something totally magnetic about it.'[8] Their collecting began in earnest with the acquisition of a full set of books published by the Kelmscott Press, many with presentation inscriptions. In 1968, they were given the rare opportunity of purchasing the re-mainder of the Morris & Company archives from the estate of Duncan Dearle, the son of John Henry Dearle. J. H. Dearle had been Morris's chosen successor as artistic director of the Firm, who shaped its fortunes in the twentieth century. Duncan Dearle had taken over the reins of Morris & Company at his father's death in 1932 and had saved the archive of designs when the Firm was liquidated in 1940. Among the material are over one thousand sketch designs [6] and full-scale cartoons for stained glass, a large archive of photographs of stained glass cartoons, and seminal archival documentation of the Firm's business history. These include the original Minute Book of Morris, Marshall, Faulkner and Company (1862–74) [21], the two ledgers of Morris & Company stained glass commissions – the 'Catalogue of Designs used for Windows Executed' (1876–1916) and its continuation (1916–40) – and the Merton Abbey dye book, a notebook of the dye recipes used for printed textiles in the workshops at Merton Abbey, Surrey, that the Firm occupied from 1881 [56]. The collection also includes hundreds of designs for wallpaper [7], printed and woven textiles, carpets, tapestry, and embroidery. While the stained glass material covers the entire chronological history of the Firm, most of the pattern designs are from the 1880s onward and showcase the work of J. H. Dearle. In addition, the collection includes Morris's portfolio of over one hundred figure drawings, by far the largest extant collection [8]. Before the founding of the Firm, when Morris had hoped to be a painter, he made a large number of these drawings, experimenting with different poses and costumes for both the male and female figure. Later figure drawings were executed as studies for the Firm's 1860s stained glass, painted decoration and embroidery commissions. Morris returned to these drawings throughout the rest of his career, re-using poses several times for the Firm's stained glass.

6 Philip Webb for Morris, Marshall, Faulkner & Company with the designs of William Morris, Edward Burne-Jones, Dante Gabriel Rossetti, and Ford Madox Brown

Tree of Jesse, sketch design for the west window of St Stephen's, Guernsey, Channel Islands, *c.* 1864

Watercolour and ink, full sheet 12⅜ x 8¼ (31.4 x 21)

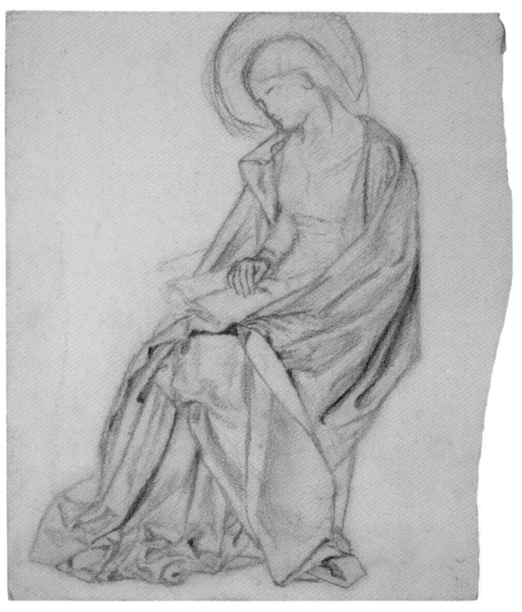

8 William Morris

Mary Virgin, figure drawing, between 1857 and 1865

Graphite, 12½ x 9⅞ (31.8 x 25.1)

Other pieces were acquired individually by the Bergers: a complete stained glass window of ten lights and thirteen tracery panels, 18 feet (5.5 metres) high, from the demolished Unitarian Chapel in Heywood, Lancashire, and accompanying figure cartoons by Edward Burne-Jones [9, 10], a Hammersmith carpet, samples of wallpaper and textiles, and so on. The Bergers also embarked on an ambitious project to photograph extant Morris & Company stained glass windows, and The Huntington now has their fine study collection of 12,000 slides of windows from all over the world. Added to this material are a significant reference library, multiple editions of Morris's published literary works, including several inscribed copies that Morris gave to friends and family, such as his mother, Burne-Jones and Robert Browning, Morris's socialist pamphlets and other socialist ephemera [2], and over one hundred letters, mostly from Morris to his friend Aglaia Coronio and the embroiderer Catherine Holiday. There are also dozens of letters from Morris's associates. Sandy and Helen Berger were devoted to their study of William Morris. Sandy Berger once said, 'A day doesn't go by that William Morris doesn't somehow command my full attention.'[9] The Bergers were also very generous to scholars in sharing their collection. The collection's new home at The Huntington will enable this tradition to continue, as the material will be preserved together for future scholars.

As it is primarily a collection of works on paper, The Huntington's material enables the study of design and process. In his lecture 'Art and the Beauty of the Earth', delivered at an art school, Morris instructed his audience always to 'think your design out in your head before you begin to get it on the paper. Don't begin by slobbering and messing about in the hope that something may come out of it. You must see it before you can draw it, whether the design be of your own invention or Nature's. Remember always, form before colour, and outline, silhouette, before modelling; not because these latter are of less importance, but because they can't be right if the first are wrong.'[10] In The Huntington's collection, the mind and hand of Morris and his associates can be studied at work, as the design is visualized and then

9 Edward Burne-Jones for Morris & Company

Liberty, cartoon for a window at Manchester College Chapel, Oxford, *c.* 1896

Black and white chalk, full sheet 54½ x 18½ (138.4 x 47)

This design was re-used for the Unitarian Chapel, Heywood, Lancashire (see ill. 10). Throughout the Firm's history Morris & Company adapted earlier designs of figures and backgrounds for subsequent commissions.

10 Designed by Edward Burne-Jones for Morris & Company

Liberty, stained glass from the Unitarian Chapel, Heywood, Lancashire, 1898

75$\frac{7}{16}$ x 19 (191.6 x 48.3)

This is one light from a multiple-light window depicting ten allegorical figures representing virtues.

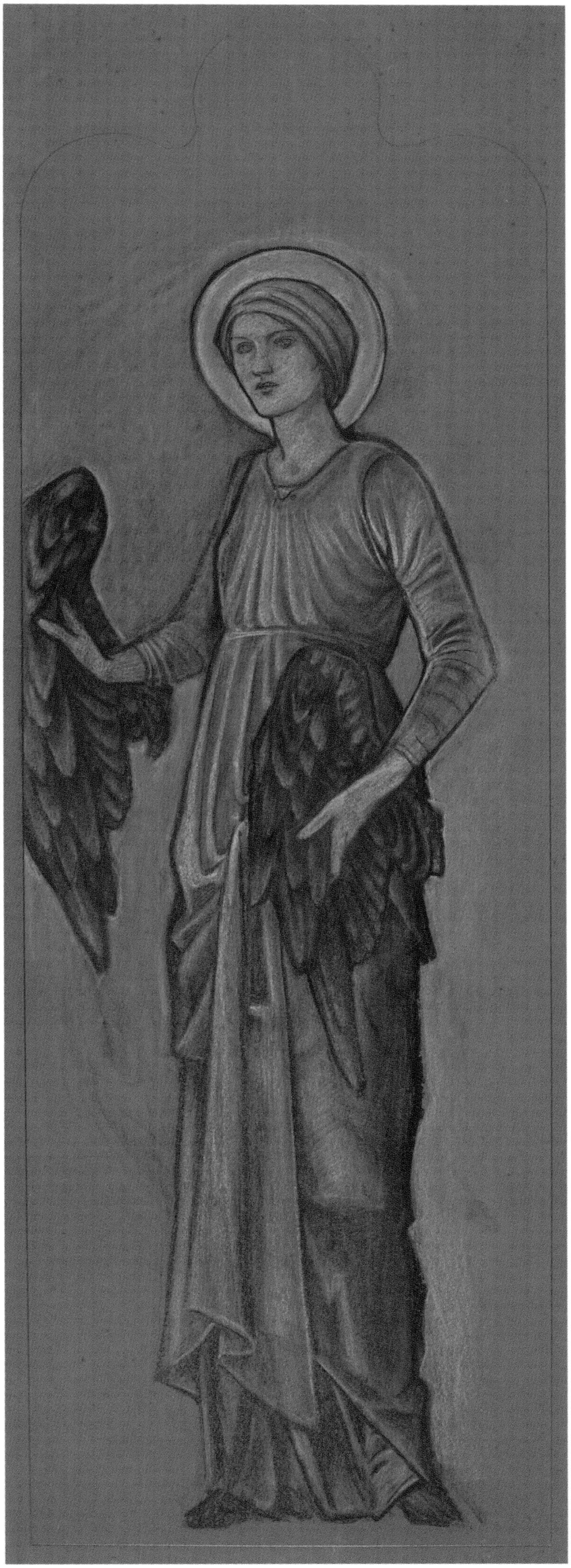

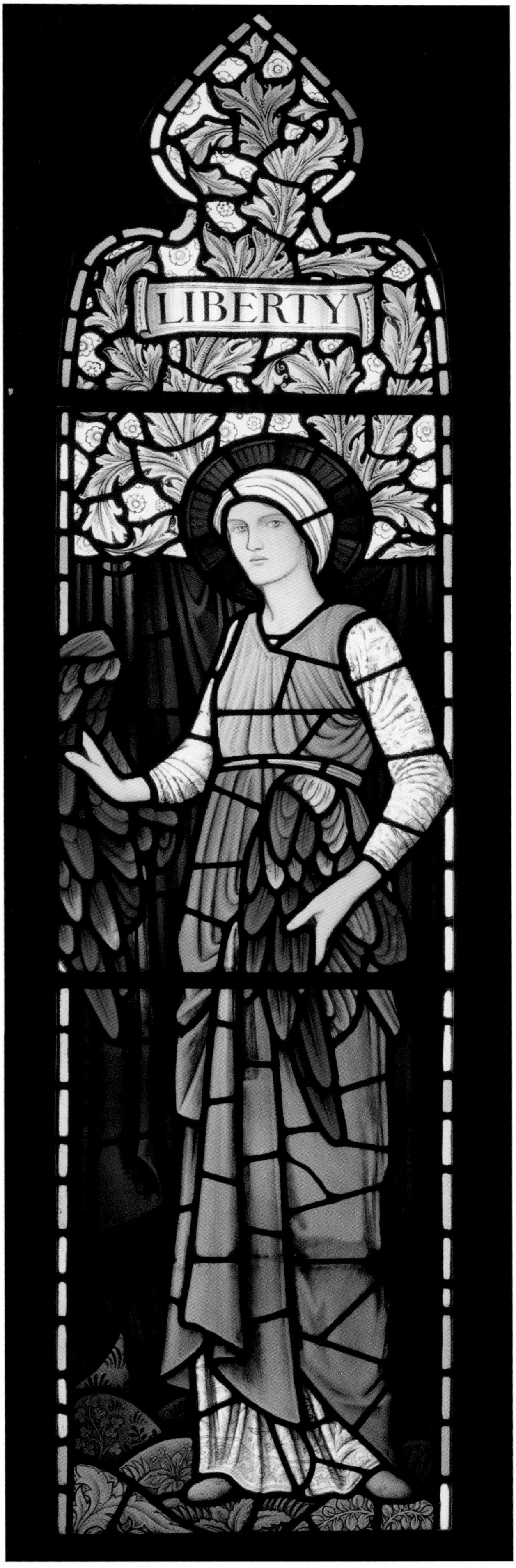

LIBERTY

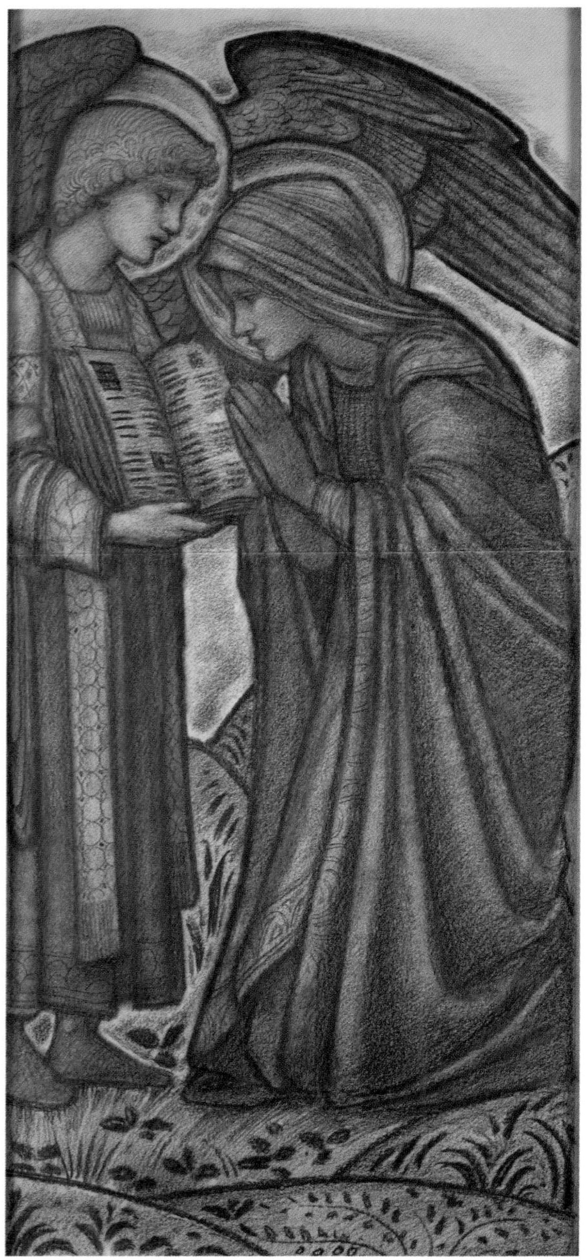

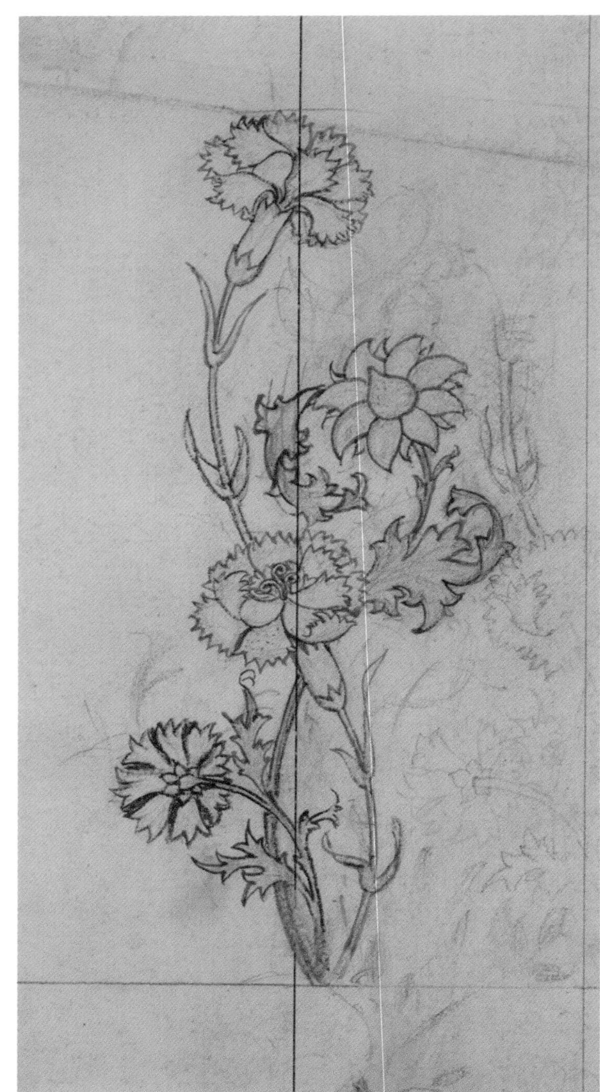

11 Edward Burne-Jones for Morris & Company

St Frances, cartoon for stained glass at St James's, Weybridge, Surrey, 1887

Charcoal and graphite, 31½ x 14 (80 x 35.6)

12 William Morris for Morris & Company

Preliminary design for *Pink and Rose* wallpaper, *c.* 1890 (detail)

Graphite, red pencil and ink, full sheet 11¼ x 7⅞ (28.6 x 20)

See ill. 29 for one of the woodblocks used to print this wallpaper.

13 William Morris for the Kelmscott Press

Design for a marginal ornament (detail)

Graphite and ink, full sheet 3⅝ x 10 (7.6 x 25.4).

committed to paper [12, 13]. Indeed, many of the designs are purely experimental and were never put into production. Others include instructions to the craftsmen who would be responsible for translating the design on paper into a piece of stained glass, a completed embroidery, or a handprinted wallpaper or textile.

The collection also allows the study of Morris & Company as a business. The 1860s entries in the Morris, Marshall, Faulkner & Company Minute Book [21] describe a group of young men meeting and making jokes, but slowly evolving into a professional business, with some of the aches and pains that come with that growth. The

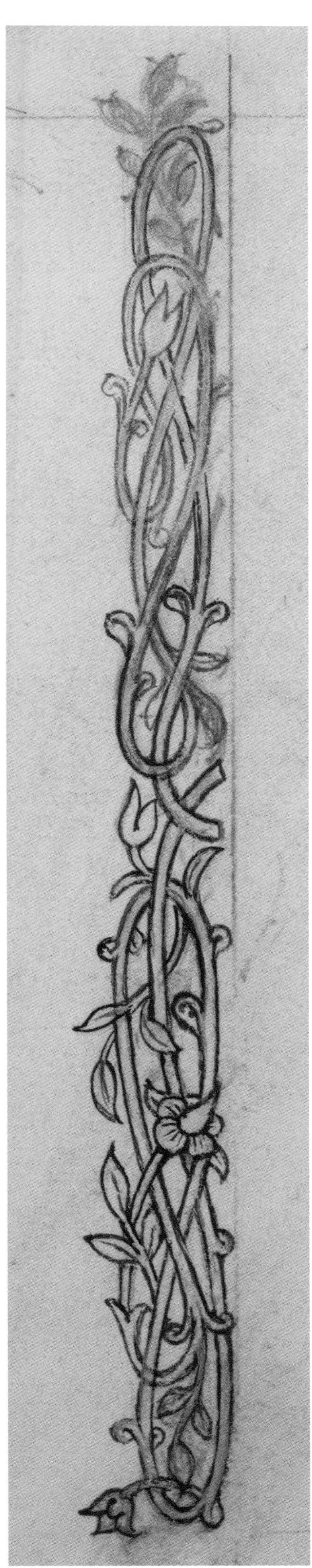

early designs for stained glass show the collaboration between the various members and, indeed, the Minute Book records that one of the very first motions passed by the members, in 1863, was that the designs were not to be credited to individual artists. The entries from 1874, however, demonstrate the painful dissolution of the original Firm as the members took sides against each other. A new professional era began for the Firm when it reorganized as Morris & Company. The 'Catalogue of Designs used for Windows Executed' ledger opens in 1876 and demonstrates Burne-Jones's ascension to chief figure designer. From this point in its history the Firm shifted towards trading on the increasingly famous names of William Morris and Edward Burne-Jones. The ambitious expansion of Morris & Company in 1881 to workshops at Merton Abbey, where Morris was able to produce goods on a much larger scale than theretofore and to his own standards of quality, allowed the production not just of stained glass and embroidery, under Morris's direction and supervision, but also of printed and woven textiles, carpets, and, finally, tapestry. The Merton Abbey dye book [56] represents this ambitious growth by detailing the printed textile patterns that Morris produced by the traditional dyeing techniques that he resurrected. Finally, the range of designs shows the expansion of Morris & Company's empire throughout England and elsewhere, with the hundreds of stained glass windows that Morris & Company executed, the ambitious interior decoration schemes commissioned from the Firm, and the dozens of wallpaper and textile patterns produced by the Firm for sale at their Oxford Street shop and through their agents in other countries.

This book consists of four essays and four shorter pieces focusing on designs in The Huntington's collection. Pat Kirkham's contribution is in two parts. Her opening essay chronicles Morris's life as a designer and his accomplishments, while her second recounts the history of Morris & Company. Complementing her studies are my own four pieces that examine objects in order to illuminate Morris and the Firm through representative works from The Huntington collection. The first two of these examine designs for church and house decoration, charting the evolution of the Firm's stained glass designs and its designs for goods to furnish the home. The third considers material related to Morris as a writer and book printer, and the last focuses on the designs of J. H. Dearle, to highlight Dearle's often overlooked contribution to the history of the Firm. The two essays by Gillian Naylor and Edward R. Bosley look at Morris's legacy. Naylor considers Morris's influence on British designers in the late nineteenth and early twentieth centuries, while Bosley investigates Morris's profound impact on the Arts and Crafts movement in America in the same time period, each examining designers of stained glass, textiles, and books and typography. Morris wrote to the American poet Emma Lazarus in 1883 after her visit to Merton Abbey, 'I am really glad that you were pleased with your visit to so small & imperfect an establishment as our works are: a place which hangs doubtful between the past and present, & is, I more than fear, going to be of no influence on the future – However we must try our best, & at any rate be pleased that it pleases us.'[11] As both Naylor and Bosley demonstrate, Morris's fears were unwarranted. His 'small and imperfect' company, which gave him so much pleasure in life, would influence and inspire generations of designers, now into the twenty-first century.

WILLIAM MORRIS:

HAVE NOTHING IN YOUR HOUSES THAT YOU DO NOT KNOW TO BE USEFUL OR BELIEVE TO BE BEAUTIFUL.[1]

William Morris, 'The Beauty of Life', 1880

A LIFE IN DESIGN

PAT KIRKHAM

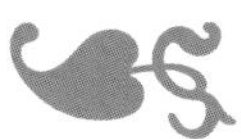

William Morris is mainly remembered as a British designer of wallpapers and chintzes, and as a 'founding father' of the Arts and Crafts movement, but he was much, much more. One of the most famous figures of his day, he was a poet, novelist, translator, socialist activist, environmentalist, entrepreneur and designer of a wide range of objects, including embroidery, tapestry, furniture, carpets, stained glass, tiles, textiles, wallpaper, books and type. He 'recovered' a host of 'lost' craft techniques and, before he espoused socialism, it was as a *maker* of things – someone who got his hands dirty – that he most vigorously challenged contemporary expectations of the occupations, preoccupations and passions of a middle-class educated man.

One of the most popular poets of the second half of the nineteenth century, he achieved fame with *The Earthly Paradise* (published in four parts, 1868–70) [63], a homage to Geoffrey Chaucer. Some of his long, lyrical, sensuous, and sometimes sublimely autobiographical poems ran to several editions. Set in imagined pre-industrial societies, his narratives often feature quests through lovingly depicted terrains and run the gamut of human emotions, particularly love and despair. Oscar Wilde believed Morris's poetry to be without comparison 'in the literature of our country'.[2] Morris was asked to stand for election as Professor of Poetry at Oxford University (he refused) and was a serious contender to succeed Alfred, Lord Tennyson as Poet Laureate. His translations ranged from the *Aeneid* and the *Odyssey* to Old French romances, *Beowulf* (with A. J. Wyatt) and Icelandic sagas (with Eiríkr Magnússon [15]). The latter inspired Morris's *Sigurd the Volsung and the Fall of the Niblungs* (1876), regarded by George Bernard Shaw as the 'greatest epic since Homer'.[3] His love of literature and design came together in the Kelmscott Press – a publishing venture of the 1890s that produced books of extraordinary beauty and set standards for artistic hand-printed books thereafter [70] – and in calligraphy and illuminated manuscripts. The beauty of the latter led John Ruskin, the preeminent champion of Gothic architecture, design, and craftsmanship, to declare Morris to be 'as great as any thirteenth century draughtsman' in terms of illumination [61].[4]

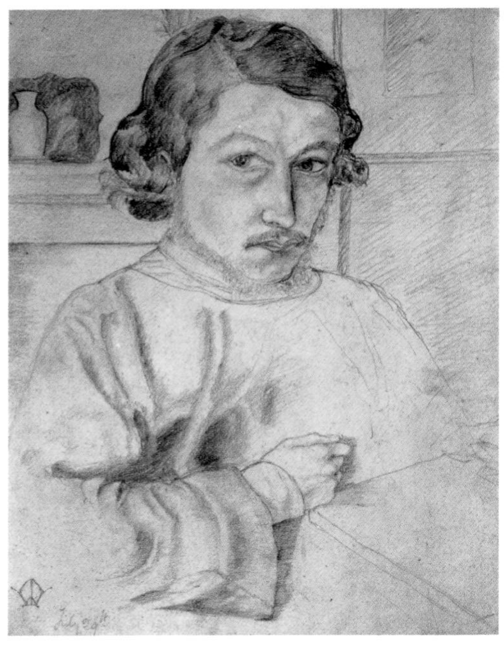

14 William Morris
Self-Portrait, 1856
Graphite, $11\frac{1}{5} \times 8\frac{7}{10}$
(28.5 x 22.1)
Victoria & Albert Museum Picture Library, London

15 *Volsunga Saga: The Story of the Volsungs and Niblungs*, translated from the Icelandic by Eiríkr Magnússon and William Morris, and edited by Henry Halliday Sparling (London: F. S. Ellis, 1870)

A page with decorative illumination and the initials 'EBJ' for Edward Burne-Jones, by an unknown hand.

Many consider Morris to be Britain's greatest designer. He was certainly one of the most impressive pattern designers of the nineteenth century. He was widely known as the head of a successful interior design and furnishings firm and by the mid-1880s 'Morrisonian' and 'Morrisian' were established trade terms.[5] A vast repository of knowledge about decorative arts, design and handicraft traditions in a wide range of countries from the medieval period onwards, Morris was considered as something of a national asset and advised London's South Kensington Museum, now the Victoria & Albert Museum, on acquisitions. As both designer and maker he inspired by example; his lectures on art and society became the basis of the central tenets of the Arts and Crafts movement and elevated the status of the decorative arts (then also known as the 'lesser arts'), as did the business that bore his name. He was also a passionate campaigner against pollution and founded the Society for the Protection of Ancient Buildings (SPAB), a powerful conservation lobby that campaigned against the excesses of the contemporary 'restorers' of ancient buildings and spawned a 'school of rational builders'.[6]

Morris was able to conjure up imaginary worlds and convey them to others but he was far from the woolly-minded dreamer that he is often made out to be. This dreamer was also a doer. It proved a powerful combination. Morris's overarching passions – a love of beautiful things and a hatred of contemporary society – were closely intertwined. The one emphatically positive, the other aggressively negative, each stimulated him to action. They played a part in the setting up of Morris, Marshall, Faulkner & Company (known as 'the Firm'), and in his eventual turn to political activism. There was a wholeness about the various endeavours of William Morris whose many activities and beliefs added up to much more than the sum of the parts. Taken together, they constitute an impressive attempt to regenerate art for the greater good and, when Morris deemed that to have failed, to fight for the regeneration of the wider society of which art was a part.

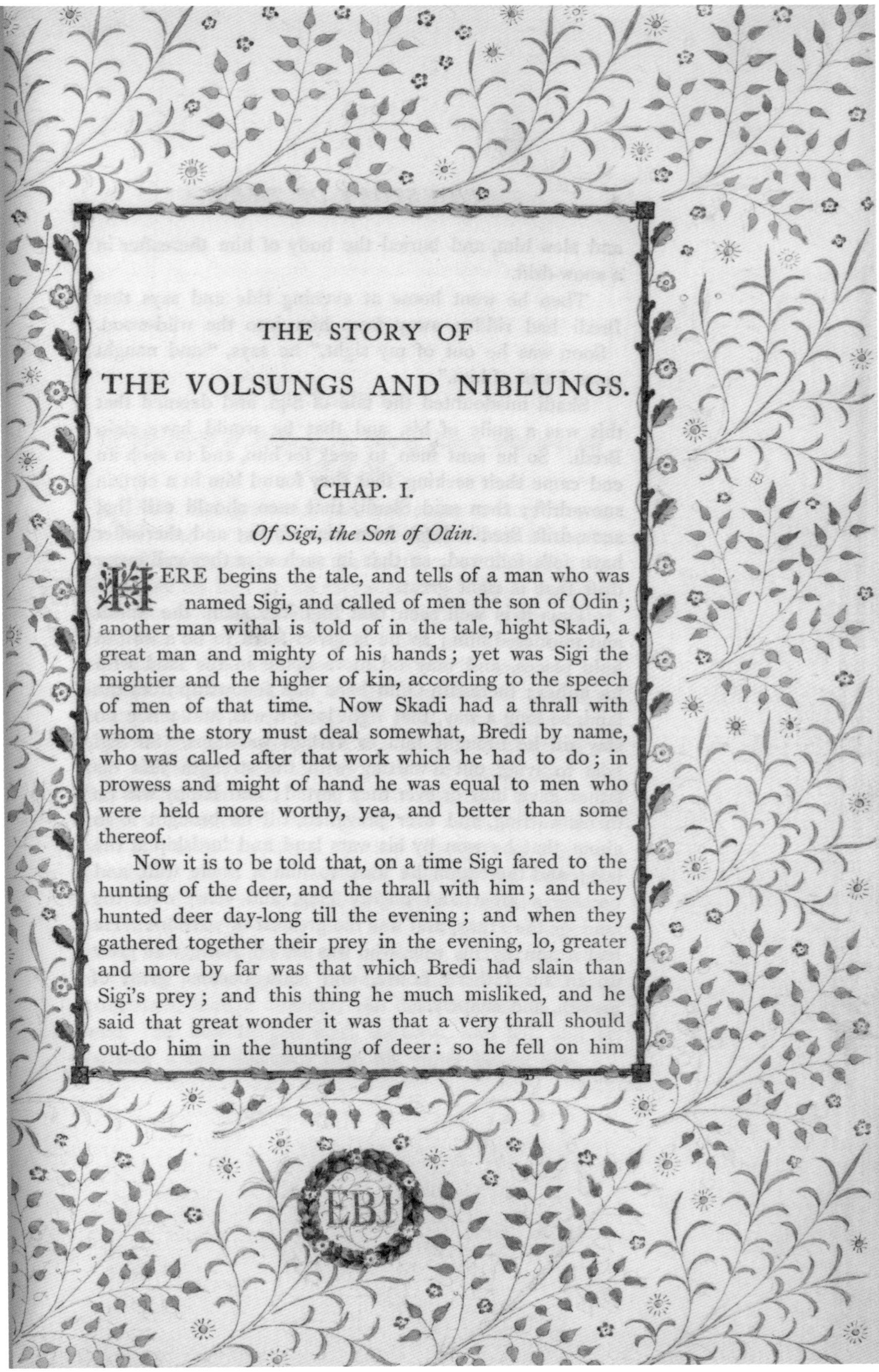

THE STORY OF

THE VOLSUNGS AND NIBLUNGS.

CHAP. I.

Of Sigi, the Son of Odin.

HERE begins the tale, and tells of a man who was named Sigi, and called of men the son of Odin; another man withal is told of in the tale, hight Skadi, a great man and mighty of his hands; yet was Sigi the mightier and the higher of kin, according to the speech of men of that time. Now Skadi had a thrall with whom the story must deal somewhat, Bredi by name, who was called after that work which he had to do; in prowess and might of hand he was equal to men who were held more worthy, yea, and better than some thereof.

Now it is to be told that, on a time Sigi fared to the hunting of the deer, and the thrall with him; and they hunted deer day-long till the evening; and when they gathered together their prey in the evening, lo, greater and more by far was that which Bredi had slain than Sigi's prey; and this thing he much misliked, and he said that great wonder it was that a very thrall should out-do him in the hunting of deer: so he fell on him

His prodigious energies, passion, insatiable curiosity, were poured into each and every project he took up. The marks of his integrity and deep moral convictions were everywhere. Contemporaries commented on his ability to work on multiple projects, and on his seemingly endless capacity to engage with new enterprises. So many activities were undertaken on the same day, or in the same week or month, that merely to follow his movements is both exhausting and exhilarating. One has to marvel at the energy and focus of a man who achieved more by mid-morning than most of us would in a day or week. In the case of handicrafts he often passed on the execution of his designs to others, but only after an intense period of research and development into appropriate materials and techniques.

Morris was truly a 'Renaissance man' but he was also a 'Victorian'. Born in 1834, three years before Victoria became Queen of England, he died in 1896, one year before her Diamond Jubilee. Like many contemporaries, however, he was deeply disturbed by aspects of the world around him. His ideas and work need to be considered within the context of the social and economic upheavals caused by the rapid industrialization and urbanization experienced in nineteenth-century Britain, and of the Romantic movement that looked to compensatory worlds, often in the real or imagined past. It was Romanticism rather than the blinding inequalities of Victorian Britain that had most impact on Morris as a boy. His appreciation of Gothic architecture and design as well as the social fabric of medieval society was undoubtedly rooted in the Romantic movement's fascination with the 'primitive' – with art that predated Raphael, religion that predated the Reformation, and cultures that predated capitalism and industrialization – but that appreciation was fed in different ways at different times of his life. From early boyhood, when his masculinity was shaped by the chivalrous tales of Walter Scott, and his undergraduate days when he read Ruskin, Morris's 'exotic other' was located mainly in an imagined Europe of the Middle Ages. It was not until his trips to Iceland in 1871 and 1873 that he found another 'primitive' culture that made such an impact upon the ways in which he conceptualized how the world might be.

Morris first developed what would become a highly tuned love of history, nature, and Gothic architecture within a *nouveau-riche* household that adopted a pseudo-medieval coat of arms. It comes as little surprise that the child who rode his Shetland pony wearing a suit of armour, and had read Walter Scott's Waverley Novels at the age of four, should fall in love with Canterbury Cathedral at the age of eight.[7] He had his own garden and spent a great deal of his time in Epping Forest that bordered on Walthamstow, Essex, where he lived. His days as an English public schoolboy were less idyllic. He hated Marlborough College, one of several institutions established to train middle-class youth in gentlemanly ways, where he felt he learned nothing because 'next to nothing was taught'.[8] In later years he became an outspoken advocate of children's rights and de-schooling. His dislike of the school notwithstanding, he read books, told and wrote stories, and revelled in the local countryside and medieval buildings. By the age of fifteen, his need 'to see, to categorize, to date, and above all to know *how* things had been done' was remarkable.[9]

He also soaked up the Anglo-Catholic ethos of the school. The groundswell of religious revivalism in Britain at that time tended towards the polarities of evangelical Protestant fundamentalism on the one hand and an admiration for 'Popery' on the other. A few brave souls converted to Roman Catholicism, including the Gothic Revival architect and designer A. W. N. Pugin, whose argument that the morality of architecture and design related to the morality of the culture that produced it, and insistence that there should be 'no features about a building which are not necessary for convenience, construction or propriety', were to influence Morris, Ruskin and the Arts and Crafts movement.[10] For the most part conversion was not necessary because, within the established Church of England, 'High Church' (Anglo-Catholic) clergy allowed worshippers to go as far as they wished along the road to Catholicism, short of swearing allegiance to Rome. Moved by the ineffable beauty of the rituals, music, vestments and decoration, the young Morris repudiated his family's middle-of-the-road Protestantism in favour of a richer cerebral and aesthetic mix.

He went to Oxford University in 1853 intending to dedicate his life to God, as did Edward Burne-Jones, who recognized Morris's talents and declared he would become a 'star'. They became close friends. It was through Burne-Jones, the son of a gilder from Birmingham, and other friends from that city, that Morris learned in detail of the miseries of working-class life in one of Britain's largest cities. His reading of Ruskin sharpened his social critique while intensifying his love of the Gothic. A key text for Morris's generation was Ruskin's *The Stones of Venice* (3 vols, 1851–53), especially 'The Nature of Gothic' in volume 2, a moral *tour-de-force* that 'explicitly associated the political collapse and artistic withering of Venice with a loss in the moral fiber of the people' and predicted a similar fate for Victorian Britain.[11] Ruskin judged the arts by the freedom of expression allowed to the workman. He considered the imperfections of medieval products evidence of the essential humanity of the work process; by contrast, the perfections of antique handwork and modern machine production were considered the products of different types of 'slave' labour.

Reading 'The Nature of Gothic' was a turning point for the young Morris and Burne-Jones. It 'seemed to point out a new road on which the world should travel' and

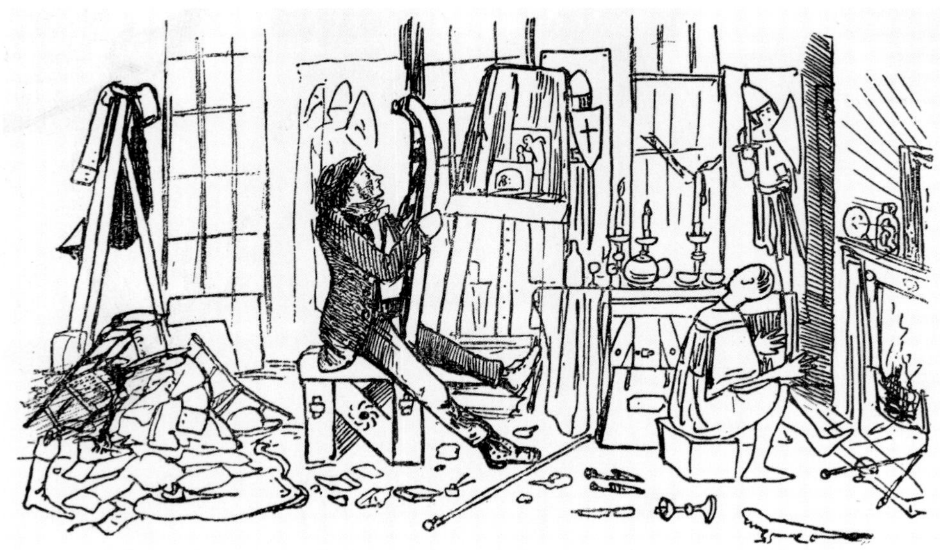

16 Edward Burne-Jones

Caricature of himself in the studio at 17 Red Lion Square

From Georgiana Burne-Jones, *Memorials of Edward Burne-Jones* (London: Macmillan & Co., 1904)

Burne-Jones shows himself seated backwards on a tall chair in the flat that he and Morris shared after their student days, from 1856 to 1859. Morris, Rossetti wrote, was 'having some intensely mediaeval furniture made – tables and chairs like incubi and succubi. He and I have painted the back of a chair with figures and inscriptions in gules and vert and azure...'

the pair abandoned the Church for art.[12] Morris said that he might have done something then about those 'socio-political ideas which would have developed but for the attractions of art and poetry'.[13] Morris was not the only young man to put art before politics; indeed it was two much more politically sophisticated friends, the Pre-Raphaelite painters Dante Gabriel Rossetti (who introduced Morris to Continental radicalism) and Ford Madox Brown (a staunch democrat), who encouraged Morris and Burne-Jones to view taking up art and crusading against the philistinism of the age as a 'sacred duty'. Burne-Jones became a painter and Morris began to train as an architect in the office of G. E. Street, a leading Gothic Revivalist. Under Rossetti's sway, Morris abandoned architecture for painting, but from the late 1850s he focused on decorative arts. In 1859 Morris married Jane Burden (1839–1914), daughter of an Oxford stablehand whom Morris first encountered when she posed for Rossetti. With Jane, he had two daughters, Jenny (1861–1935) and May (1862–1938).

Morris took Ruskin's concept of 'Joy in Labour' and expanded upon it in a series of lectures on art and society from 1877 onwards. It was through these, particularly *Hopes and Fears for Art* (1882), that the notion of joy in handwork permeated the Arts and Crafts movement and came to be embedded in objects as well as institutions and individual endeavours, Romantic or not and regardless of historical accuracy. 'Joy in Labour' had a strong impact on discourses of work and alienation at a time when work was increasingly sub-divided and machine production was replacing hand production. Although Morris cited examples of handcrafted objects as proof of alternative ways of approaching work, Arts and Crafts historian Alan Crawford has pointed out that, while applicable to decorative arts production, his comments had little direct relevance to office workers, chambermaids, or steelworkers.[14] As Morris turned to socialism in the 1880s, however, work was identified less and less with art and more and more with wider social issues. For Morris himself 'Joy in Labour' remained a fundamental reason for his handicraft activities and the concept continues to inform craft practices today.

Morris dedicated himself to the design and production of beautiful, well-made items for over twenty years, but by the early 1880s he could no longer regard it as a 'sacred duty'. Morris & Company was a fashionable and profitable firm, and could have been more so had Morris been willing to yield on certain points of principle, but he felt increasingly uncomfortable with the contradictions that arose from trying to reform art through a single enterprise. Far from ushering in a new period of 'free' art expressive of joy in labour and supplying objects dependent on 'taste' rather than money, as its founders had hoped, the Firm ended up mainly supplying expensive items for a particular middle- and upper-class taste that it had shaped. The paradoxical situation in which Morris found himself was articulated as early as 1866 by Warington Taylor, who then managed the Firm. In connection with the prestigious commission to redecorate St James's Palace, Taylor told the partners not to underprice their work, commenting: 'Just remember we are embezzling the public money now.' At the same time, however, he asked 'what business has any palace to be decorated at all?'[15] Such questions niggled away at Morris who, when advising on decorative schemes at Rounton Grange for Sir Isaac Lowthian Bell, lost his temper and told his client that he did not like spending his life 'ministering to the swinish luxury of the rich'.[16]

His interest in Old Norse literature [15] proved a 'good corrective to the maundering side of medievalism',[17] and his visits to Iceland focused his priorities and pushed him further along the path from 'Romantic to Revolutionary':[18] 'I learned one lesson there, thoroughly I hope, that the most grinding poverty is a trifling evil compared with the inequality of classes'.[19] Morris wrote in 1883 that

> in spite of all the success I have had, I have not failed to be conscious that the art I have been helping to produce would fall with the death of the few of us who really care about it, and that a reform in art which is founded on individualism must perish with the individuals who have set it going. Both my historical studies and my practical conflict with the philistinism of modern society have *forced* on me the conviction that art cannot have a real life and growth under the present system of commercialism and profit-mongering.

This view he described as 'Socialism seen through the eyes of an artist'.[20]

Morris had found a new cause. Aged forty-nine and frustrated with the established party of reform, the Liberal Party, which he had joined during an anti-war campaign and then abandoned over its Imperialist policies, he became a member of one of the first revolutionary socialist groups in Europe, the Democratic Federation (later the SDF, the Social Democratic Federation). Many friends and admirers were shocked. Tennyson was horrified, as was the increasingly conservative Burne-Jones, whose abhorrence of his friend's politics introduced an unspoken but profound intellectual difference into their lifelong friendship. William De Morgan, the pottery designer and manufacturer, who had been active in anti-war campaigns with Morris, stood aside, but other close friends such as architect Philip Webb, Oxford mathematician Charles Faulkner, and designer Walter Crane, together with a few employees, followed him into the socialist movement. Some biographers

THE SOCIALIST PLATFORM.—No. 2.

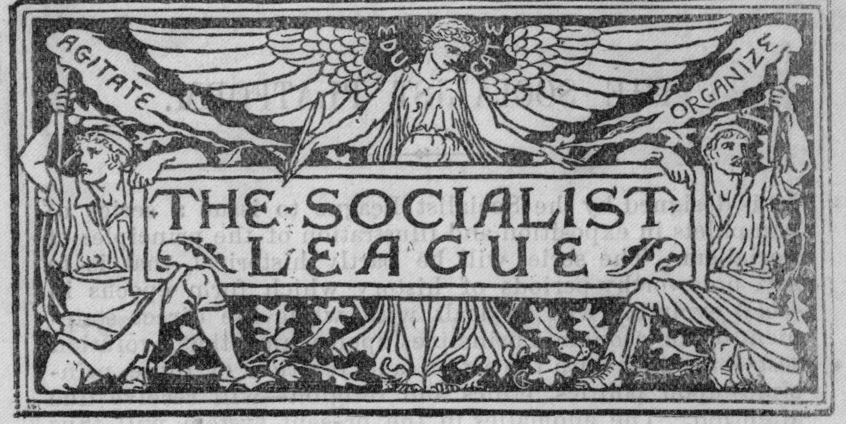

USEFUL WORK
v.
USELESS TOIL

BY
WILLIAM MORRIS.

PRICE ONE PENNY.

LONDON:
SOCIALIST LEAGUE OFFICE,
13 FARRINGDON ROAD, HOLBORN VIADUCT, E.C.

1885.

17 William Morris
Useful Work v. Useless Toil (London: printed and published by William Morris and Joseph Lane, 1885)

have tried to explain away Morris's political convictions as an aberration, but today most Morris scholars acknowledge the interconnections between the various 'causes' taken up by this prodigiously talented man who cared passionately about the world around him. Morris saw things as a whole; the present and future as informed by the past. For him the reform of art and design was part and parcel of broader social and economic reform, and vice versa. His most recent and comprehensive biographer, Fiona MacCarthy, using previously unavailable private letters, has pointed to the grand inevitability of Morris's journey from Victorian entrepreneur to vanguard activist.[21]

As a poet who turned to politics, Morris stands in the tradition of Blake, Shelley, Byron and Yeats. His ideas were informed by Ruskin and the stringent critiques of British society expressed by Carlyle, Dickens and Kingsley, but also by his experience as an employer and producer of beautiful objects. By the mid-1880s he was a supporter of women's rights and a committed Marxist. He remained so until his death, refuting any suggestion otherwise.[22] He read Marx in French before English translations were available, and his much used copy of *Das Kapital* had to be rebound at least twice. His view of history as related to the present and the future meant that he was receptive to Marx's historical and dialectical frameworks. Together with his knowledge of 'pre-modern' societies and hatred of contemporary 'civilization', this led to an acceptance of the Marxist thesis/antithesis/synthesis ('pre-modern'/capitalism/socialism or barbarism) schema of change. But Morris's socialism was never schematic; it was brim full of passion and human concerns. His emphasis on hope was utopian, while the more spontaneous and libertarian elements of his politics were closer to the anarchism of his friends the exiled Russian revolutionaries Sergius Stepniak and Peter Kropotkin.[23]

Given his interest in 'Joy in Labour' it is not surprising that Morris has been described as 'Britain's greatest diagnostician of alienation'.[24] He may have looked to the past for examples of non-alienated labour, but his understanding of what it is to be estranged from one's work has a modern ring to it, as do his comments on commodification. Although he loved beautiful objects, he saw the pursuit of good *per se* as a mechanism central to the perpetuation of capitalism, the very system he wanted to abolish. His thought-provoking tract on consumption and waste, *Useful Work v. Useless Toil* (1885) [17], raises the issue of production for production's sake, from the manufacture of all manner of shoddy goods including foods from which nutritional value has been removed – 'the much praised cheapness of our epoch' – to 'articles of folly and luxury ... which no sane man could desire'.[25] Morris set high moral and ethical standards for the revolutionary socialist movement and recognized more clearly than many, then and since, that the measure of any successful revolution is the happiness, at work and home, of each and every member of the society created by it. This socialism with a truly human face features in his uplifting novel *News From Nowhere* (1890) [4], set in the post-revolutionary future.

Just as Morris used inherited money to further the reform of art and design, he also used it to support political campaigns, magazines and newspapers. In the embryonic socialist movement he took on leadership roles but he never shirked the mundane tasks associated with political agitation, from selling newspapers in the streets in all weathers to travelling throughout the country, addressing meetings, conferring with comrades, and debating the way forward. His socialist writings retain a freshness and immediacy. Plainspoken, they are eloquent in their language of hope. Morris invoked education and offered visions of the future to infuse discontent with political understanding, confidence and the will to organize, fight and win. Not the best of public speakers, he was at his most eloquent, incendiary, passionate and compassionate in 1887 when, moved by the dignity, suffering and anger of Northumbrian miners faced with a huge wage cut, he addressed an audience of six thousand, amongst whom he noted many women.

As he fought on many fronts to make the world a better place in which to live, his environmental work became part and parcel of his socialism.[26] Just as he supported workers in their day-to-day struggles against their 'masters' while arguing for more long-term solutions to the problems of capitalism, he campaigned to save particular buildings or parts of the countryside while formulating policies for the safekeeping of the countryside and the material heritage. He was a ceaseless campaigner, fighting against the despoliation of buildings and places many thought insignificant (such as small parish churches and his beloved Epping Forest) as well as such renowned ones as Canterbury Cathedral or St Mark's, Venice.[27] His last public act before his death in 1896 was to lend his not inconsiderable weight to a new cause, protecting the countryside from unsightly advertising, at the first meeting of the Society for Checking the Abuses of Public Advertising (SCAPA). Like the Levellers, he preached that the earth was a common treasure, arguing that those of us who live on it have no right to interfere with buildings or objects conceived and constructed by those who went before us; we are but custodians for future generations.[28]

Although in extremely poor health from 1895, he continued to attend as many meetings as possible. He last spoke in the open air, in the rain, at Stepniak's funeral, together with Eleanor Marx and Keir Hardie. When he addressed the SDF's 1896 New Year meeting it was clear to all, himself included, that his health was failing fast. He set about finishing poems and novels, and worried that he might not see to completion the Kelmscott Chaucer [70, 71], a project that brought him much joy in the last few years of his life and a renewed closeness with Burne-Jones [18]. He mustered what strength he had left to write a May Day call-to-arms denouncing Imperialism, which he believed would lead to world wars and set workers of one country against those of another. He urged opposition to a system based on greed for

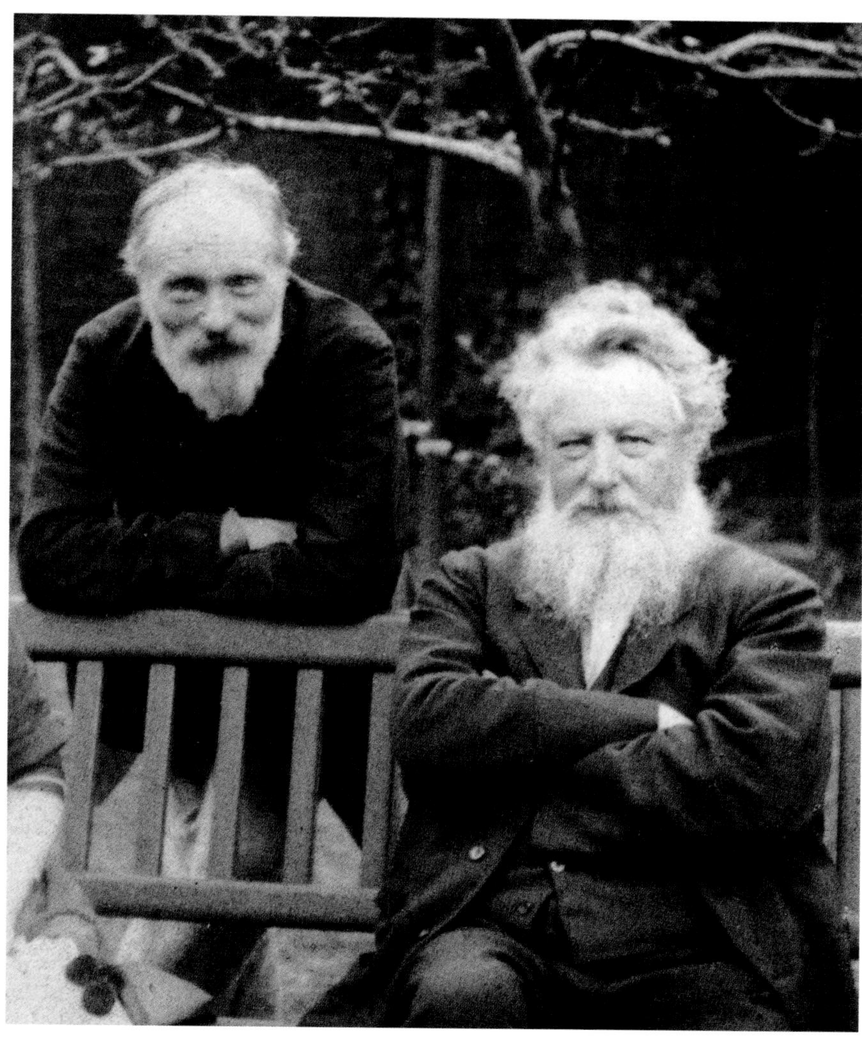

18 Frederick Hollyer

Edward Burne-Jones and William Morris in the garden of Burne-Jones's home, The Grange, Fulham, 1890

Photograph

William Morris Gallery, London

new markets, increased profits, and 'fresh opportunities for *waste;* the waste of our labour and our lives', and called for the building of one based on production for '*use,* for *happiness,* for LIFE'.[29]

When he died on 3 October 1896, one of his physicians attributed his death to 'simply being William Morris, and having done more work than most ten men'.[30] Tributes poured in from all over the world, many referring to his human qualities as well as his genius and notable achievements. Fellow socialist Robert Blatchford ended his with the comment, 'Strike at him where you would, he rang true.'[31] Morris inspired many people in each and every undertaking with which he was associated – before and after his death. Today his novels are rarely read, whereas his designs enjoy considerable popularity. The beautiful Kelmscott Press editions continue to delight those who behold them, as do the magnificent stained glass windows found in buildings all over the world. His tender poems continue to touch the heart, while his lectures and example as a political and environmental activist still have much to offer those interested in making the world a better place in which to live.

THE FIRM:

THE GROWTH OF DECORATIVE ART IN THIS COUNTRY . . . HAS NOW REACHED A POINT AT WHICH IT SEEMS DESIRABLE THAT ARTISTS OF REPUTATION SHOULD DEVOTE THEIR TIME TO IT.

Morris, Marshall, Faulkner & Company, *Prospectus*, 1861

MORRIS & COMPANY

PAT KIRKHAM

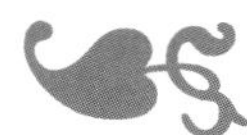

Morris, Marshall, Faulkner & Company was established in 1861 in London, the richest city in the richest country in the world, at a time when Britain was known as 'the workshop of the world'. If a firm selling expensive, well made and well designed goods of esoteric appearance had a chance of surviving anywhere it was there. The economic importance of 'art manufactures' – the self-conscious input of 'art' into products – was acknowledged at government level; a Select Committee of 1835 inquired into ways of improving British competitiveness in this sector.[1] It was not new for artists to be employed as designers by individual firms, but neither was it common. 'Art manufactures' was a buzz term in the 1840s and the founders of Morris, Marshall, Faulkner & Company must have been aware of Summerly's Art Manufactures, a scheme that connected manufacturers with artists and 'the best Art with familiar objects in daily use'.[2]

The lowly status of the 'lesser arts', as the decorative arts were known, was challenged by those who believed there was no hierarchy of the arts in the Gothic period, when embroidery and carving were as highly regarded as painting and sculpture. Morris, Marshall, Faulkner & Company aimed to restore the decorative arts to their former glory, and the high public profiles of two of the founders, Pre-Raphaelite painters Dante Gabriel Rossetti and Ford Madox Brown, lent considerable weight to this. The other five partners were Burne-Jones (painter), Webb (architect), Morris (not then settled on his future occupation), Peter Paul Marshall (surveyor, sanitary engineer and amateur painter), and Charles Faulkner (an Oxford mathematician, then training as a civil engineer, who kept the accounts) [21]. The firm – 'the Firm' to its familiars – became one of the most successful 'art manufacture' enterprises of the nineteenth century.

The idea of a firm of 'art workmen' had been on Morris's mind since his Oxford days, but several factors precipitated its formation. The growing friendship between Morris and Burne-Jones on the one hand and Rossetti and Brown on the other was crucial, as was Ruskin's befriending Morris and Burne-Jones in the late 1850s. The

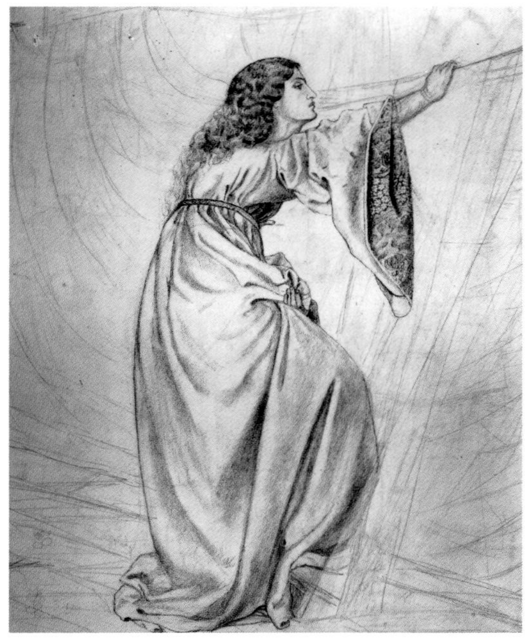

19 William Morris

Iseult Boarding the Ship, 1857–60

Pencil and ink, 20 x 16 (51 x 41)

William Morris Gallery, London

Morris's drawing for an uncompleted wall painting depicts Jane Burden, soon to be his wife, as the tragic heroine Iseult.

personal connection with Ruskin and the impact of his latest diatribe against class and culture, *Unto This Last* (1860), reinforced the young disciples' determination to undertake projects worthy of their hero. When the Firm was founded five of the partners had experience of product design, some of it on a commercial basis. Burne-Jones, Rossetti and Brown had designed stained glass; Brown, Morris and Webb furniture; Rossetti, Morris and Burne-Jones murals; Morris, Webb, Rossetti and Brown embroidery; while Webb had designed table glass.

The 'intensely mediaeval' furniture that Morris designed for the rooms he shared in London with Burne-Jones [16], among the first examples of a vogue for a medieval style of painted furniture, predates the foundation of the Firm by five years. Burne-Jones, who with Rossetti painted some of it, remarked that 'when we have painted designs of knights and ladies upon them they will be perfect marvels'.[3] In 1857 Rossetti, who thought the time ripe for an English School of mural painters,[4] included Morris and Burne-Jones in a group of artists commissioned to create coloured frescoes based on Thomas Malory's *Morte d'Arthur* (*c.* 1470) for the newly completed Oxford Union Debating Hall. The sense of brotherhood and camaraderie experienced there continued during the decorating and furnishing of Red House in Kent (1859–60), designed by Webb for Morris and his new wife Jane Burden [19] (a working-class 'stunner' discovered by Rossetti and Swinburne). Webb designed furniture and metal candlesticks, grates and fire irons, as well as a gothicized horse-drawn coach in which the Morrises and their guests could explore the countryside.[5] Burne-Jones's contributions included a tempera mural of a wedding feast (Jane and William were Queen and King) and allegorical stained glass for the windows. The Morrises worked embroidered hangings [20] and painted the drawing room ceiling.

This feeling of brotherhood was a feature of the early years of Morris, Marshall, Faulkner & Company, and it was but a small step from the varied interests of the partners to a firm of 'Fine Art Workmen in Painting, Carving, Furniture, and the Metals'

20 William Morris

Daisy curtain, worked by Jane Morris, Bessie Burden and others, early 1860s (detail)

Wool ground embroidered in wools in couched stitches, complete curtain 65¾ x 117¾ (167 x 299)

Reproduced with the permission of the Society of Antiquaries of London

One of five curtains embroidered for the master bedroom at Red House. The design is taken from an illustration in a late fifteenth-century manuscript of Froissart's *Chronicles*. This motif of floral clusters appears again and again in Morris's work.

that included mural decoration, stained glass, architectural carving, stamped leather, jewelry and embroidery in its prospectus.[6] In the first few years demand was greatest for stained glass, followed by furniture and furnishings (mainly for churches), but hand-painted tiles, embroideries, table glass, metalwork, wall hangings, and wallpapers were also offered. The partners were paid for designs according to the type of work and their respective skills. Morris was the only partner extensively involved with making, and supervised all production. Some items were made within the Firm: there was, for example, a kiln at the premises it took at the outset at 8 Red Lion Square. George Campfield made much of the early stained glass work, while women members of the partners' families painted tiles and worked embroideries.

Each partner held one £20 share, of which only £1 was called up. Business commenced with £100 borrowed from his mother by Morris, who was business manager with a salary of £150 per annum. All the partners played an active role during the first two or three years, but the Firm only remained afloat because Morris sold inherited shares to meet the annual deficits. The publicity gained by showing their work at the International Exhibition of 1862, where the stained glass and embroidery won two medals, enhanced their public profile. A few 'progressive' artists commissioned domestic interiors in the 1860s, and some of the commissioned items were reproduced and sold from the showroom attached to the larger premises taken at 26 Queen Square in 1865. Despite two major public commissions in the 1860s, however, the product base remained narrow, a fact highlighted during the economic depression of the late 1860s when it became clear that survival depended on diversification.

The Firm would not have got off the ground without the talents and contacts of Rossetti, Brown, Webb and Burne-Jones, but by the late 1860s Morris was the lynchpin. The others were involved with their respective careers; 'shopkeeping', as he liked to call it, became Morris's. Faced with a rapidly diminishing share income, he needed the Firm as much as it needed him. He was not as good a businessman then as he later became, but he learned quickly. He added a host of wallpapers and chintzes to the product range in the 1870s and persuaded Burne-Jones to step up his output of cartoons for stained glass. These developments ensured that the business became quite profitable. Frustrated with making profits for sleeping partners, in 1874 Morris announced he wanted sole proprietorship. Webb, Burne-Jones and Faulkner backed him, but Rossetti (whom Morris had treated more than decently, given Rossetti's open affair with Jane Morris), Marshall (whose input was minimal) and Brown objected. They were compensated, but not before a bitter wrangle.[7] The band of brothers had fallen apart.

From 1875 the business was known as Morris & Company, and in 1877 show-rooms were opened at 449 Oxford Street. Production increased after 1881, when a semi-rural site at Merton Abbey near Wimbledon suitable for textile production was acquired [5], and from 1890 when the furniture-making workshop of Holland & Son was taken over.[8] The Firm went from strength to strength financially, despite the failure of a Manchester branch in the 1880s, and its international reputation grew by leaps and bounds. Goods were sold abroad through agents, particularly in Germany

21 Minute Book for Morris, Marshall, Faulkner & Company, 10 December 1862 to 23 October 1874

These pages show the minutes of the first meeting of the firm, with all partners present except Peter Paul Marshall.

and the United States, from the late 1870s, and the widespread circulation of Morris's writings in the 1880s made him and his designs famous. From the time of his socialist involvement in the early 1880s, Morris delegated much of the day-to-day running of the business to his assistant, John Henry Dearle, while his daughter May supervised the embroidery section. Morris remained sole proprietor until 1890, when the managers of the Oxford Street showrooms, Frank and Robert Smith, were taken on as partners with a view to Morris's further diminishing his input. His role thereafter was mainly that of a consultant, but he remained closely involved with what had become the most famous decorating firm in the world.

The vast majority of the Firm's production was by hand. Morris has been attacked for a Luddite-like hatred of machines, but this was not entirely the case.[9] He was not against machines as such. Machinery was used within the Firm when appropriate, as were semi-mechanized tools such as the Jacquard loom that involved the weaver working with a punch-card system. When on one occasion George Bernard Shaw observed that a machine would as well do a certain process, Morris promptly replied that one was already on order. Morris's position was clear. He was in favour of all machines that eliminated or alleviated heavy laborious work, or that saved human beings from work that required them to act like machines or as cogs in a machine. He was equally clear that, under capitalism, the fundamental importance of the profit motive meant that machines were used to increase production rather than to save labour, and history has borne him out on this.[10]

Morris hated the proliferation of cheap shoddy goods turned out by acute divisions of labour, whether by machine or by hand. His personal preference was for handwork; he found it richly rewarding. He also believed that handwork and undivided labour were essential to 'Joy in Labour' and the regeneration of the decorative arts. At the same time, he recognized that using high-quality materials and tools, as well as hand labour, meant that most products would be expensive. Like many designers before and since, he was not prepared to trade off quality, either of design or production, for cheapness of product.

For the most part, the question of whether or not to use machines within the Firm was not a pressing one because in many handicraft trades there simply were no machines that could substitute for hand labour, skilled or unskilled.[11] Most of the types of manufacture undertaken by the Firm were not industrialized when it was established, nor did they become so during Morris's lifetime. The exception was the production of certain textiles and wallpapers, and in both those cases the question of machinery was linked to issues of quality. Although Britain was the most industrialized country in the world in the mid-nineteenth century, only half of its factories and workshops were mechanized.[12] There was little incentive to do so in many sectors. Adult labour was cheap, and that of children even cheaper (children were used in the shoddy end of many trades, including furniture and fancy box making). There was no machine production of stained glass, embroidery or furniture. Where machinery was available, as in the case of wood carving, it was only economically viable when enormous quantities of repetitive carving on flat wood were required, and even then considerable hand finishing was needed. In the case of wallpapers, Morris tried both hand and machine production. The Firm sold a few cheaper lines,

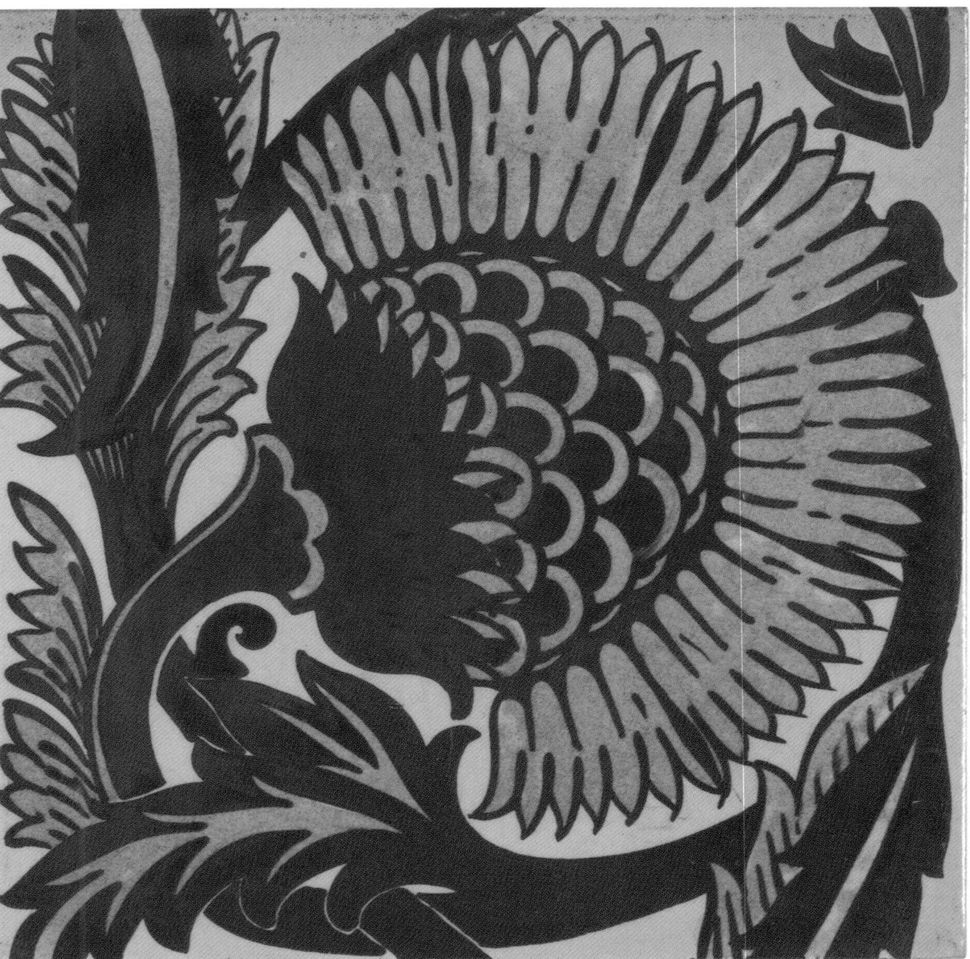

22 Designed by William De Morgan

B.B.B. tile, *c.* 1880

Stencilled in red lustre on an English earthenware blank, 6 x 6 (15.3 x 15.3)

The initials are those of the ornamental ironfounders Bishop, Barnard and Bishop, for whom many of these tiles were produced for use in fireplaces.

although he never found them as aesthetically pleasing, colourfast or durable as hand-printed ones. He designed for the four main types of machine-produced carpets then commercially available. He did so with the machine process in mind, but again found them less beautiful than hand-knotted ones. His designing linoleum and exploring the possibility of introducing a line of cheap dress-cottons are proof that he was not against inexpensive goods *per se*.[13] Let there be no doubt about the main object of his hatred in terms of manufactured goods: it was not machinery but shoddy products, whether made by hand or machine. Many agreed with him then, as many do today.

The main activities of the Firm – interior design, furniture, wallpapers, textiles and stained glass – are outlined in the sections that follow, and amplified, with particular reference to The Huntington's Morris holdings, in Diane Waggoner's contributions (pp. 64–107). I shall discuss interior design first because it was at the heart of the enterprise embarked upon in 1861. In a short chapter such as this it is not possible to consider every type of object or activity with which the Firm was involved. Painted tiles, for instance, for wall and fireplace decoration, were produced in-house in the 1860s, but thereafter they came from William De Morgan's firm, with De Morgan designing most of them [22]. Webb's designs for table glass were realized by James Powell & Sons, the company that also supplied the glass for the

Morris firm's stained glass work. From the 1880s William Benson designed (and his firm produced) most of the metalwork sold by Morris & Company, including large quantities of light-fittings.

Interiors

'If I were asked to say what is at once the most important production of Art and the thing most to be longed for, I should answer, A beautiful House.'[14] The creation of complete rooms, as at Red House, was at the heart of the partners' ambitions in 1861, but the design and supply of the panoply of individual objects necessary to such work was not easily achieved. The expansion into wallpapers and a wider range of textiles did more than anything to make this possible. The Firm offered a 'look' that was taken up not only by rich clients, who could afford to have entire rooms or houses 'made over', but also by middle-class householders, who were able to choose from a wide variety of items at prices ranging from very expensive to relatively cheap. For some a 'Morris' look was achieved with little more than wallpaper, portiere, firescreen or cushion cover (sold already embroidered or in kit form to complete at home). As Walter Crane remarked in 1911,

> The great advantage and charm of the Morrisian method is that it lends itself to either simplicity or splendour. You might almost be as plain as Thoreau, with a rush-bottomed chair, a piece of matting, an oaken trestle table; or you might have gold and lustre (the choice ware of William De Morgan) gleaming from a sideboard, and jewelled light in the windows, and the walls hung with arras tapestry.[15]

Most first-generation Morrisian interiors tended towards splendour. The early domestic commissions came about through personal contacts. Artists such as Myles Birket Foster and Spencer Stanhope had their homes decorated by the Firm in the 1860s, as did Aldham Heath, a Yorkshire textile manufacturer who had patronized the Pre-Raphaelites and whose contacts led to several important commissions, including stained glass for Bradford Cathedral.[16] Little remains of these early interiors, but a tile panel suggests the flavour of one element of the Birket Foster commission [52]. More is known about two contemporary public commissions (1866–69) that were more bold and theatrical than the domestic ones. The reception room later known as the Green Dining Room [23] at the South Kensington Museum was sufficiently 'domestic' to ensure that visitors felt 'at home' in a public space, and sufficiently different, novel and colourful to make the experience memorable. The panels of figurative designs and compositions of branches, leaves and berries set at eye level into the blue wood dado suggest an art gallery display. Above the blue panelling comes a contrasting green wall overlaid with a light pattern of leaves and branches, modelled in gesso, that link it to the panels. Further lightness of touch comes in the windows decorated with garlanded women and in the pale, delicately patterned and gilded ceiling, while the dog-chasing-hare theme of the bright painted frieze adds a touch of lightheartedness. The scheme for the Armoury and Tapestry Room in St James's Palace was equally eye-catching but far more solemn, regal and densely decorated.[17] The gold stylized floral decoration against black woodwork

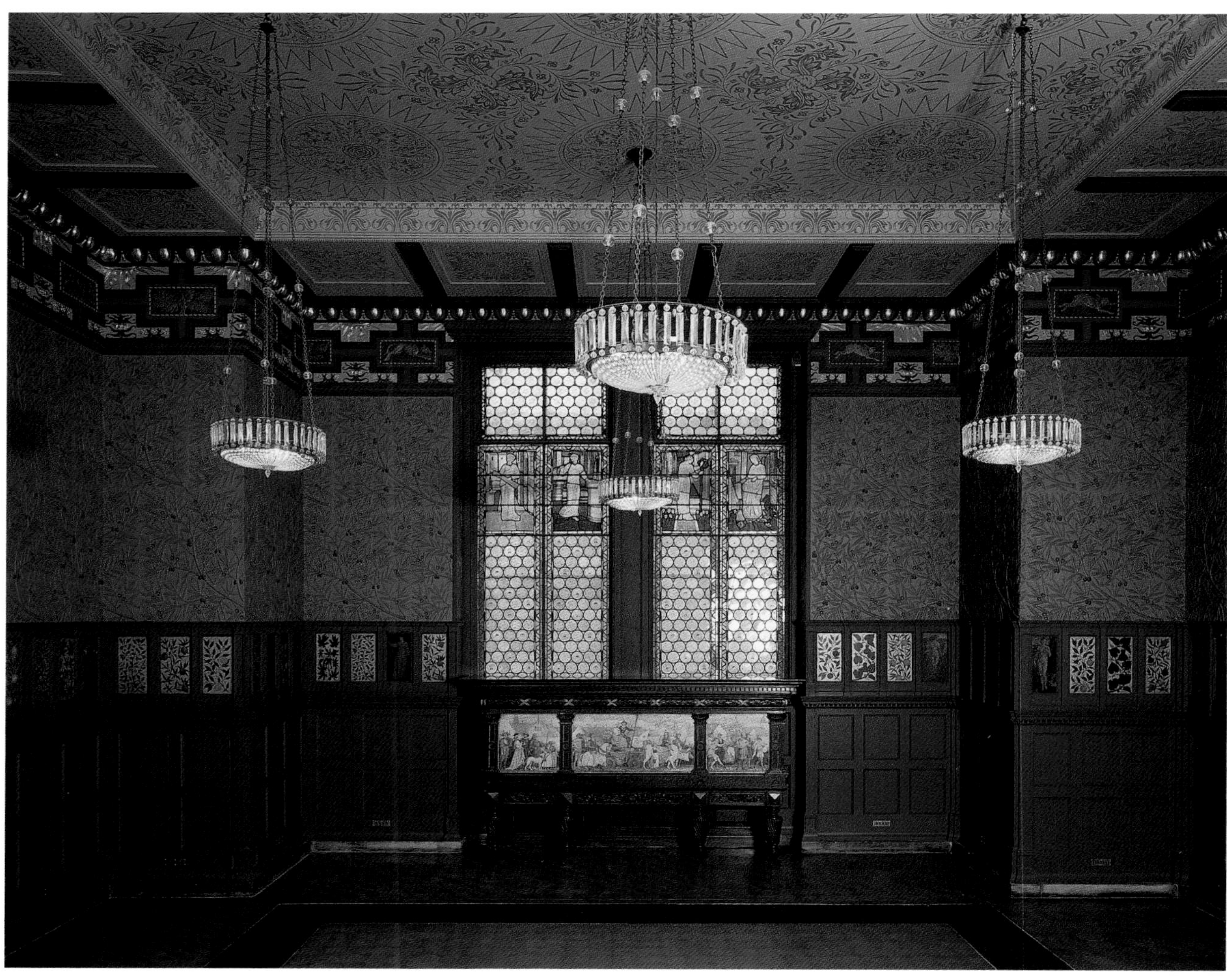

suggests an early example of Aesthetic movement design, but the use of gold and other bright colours was more an attempt to capture the brilliance of those medieval interiors which had in earlier times housed armour and tapestries.

The prestigious commission for the interior decoration of the dining room at 1 Palace Green (1880–88) [24] came by way of Webb from his client George Howard, Earl of Carlisle. The elaborate gilded and wood panelling was specially designed to incorporate Burne-Jones's *Cupid and Psyche* paintings. Thirty years after its completion, *The Studio* commented, 'It would be a rash statement to affirm of the decoration of any single apartment, that it was absolutely the best example of the style it obeyed. Yet if ever it were safe to speak thus unreservedly, it might be concerning the beautiful dining-room at the Earl of Carlisle's House, Palace Green, representing as it does the united efforts of Burne-Jones, William Morris, and Philip Webb.'[18] In 1882 Morris and Webb advised on furnishings for Castle Howard, the Howard family seat in Yorkshire, for which large quantities of wallpapers, textiles and furniture were supplied, including fifty-four Sussex chairs [27] for the dining room.

The grandest commissions of the 1880s and 1890s were for 1 Holland Park (1880–88) for Alexander Ionides, and Stanmore Hall, Middlesex (1888–96), for William Knox D'Arcy. For the former, Webb supervised the structural alterations

23 Designed by Philip Webb, William Morris and Edward Burne-Jones for Morris, Marshall, Faulkner & Company

The Green Dining Room, South Kensington Museum, now Victoria & Albert Museum, London, 1866–67

Victoria & Albert Museum Picture Library, London

24 Designed by William Morris and Edward Burne-Jones, with Walter Crane, for Morris & Company

The dining room of 1 Palace Green, Kensington, London, 1880–88

From the catalogue *Morris & Company Decorators*, 1907

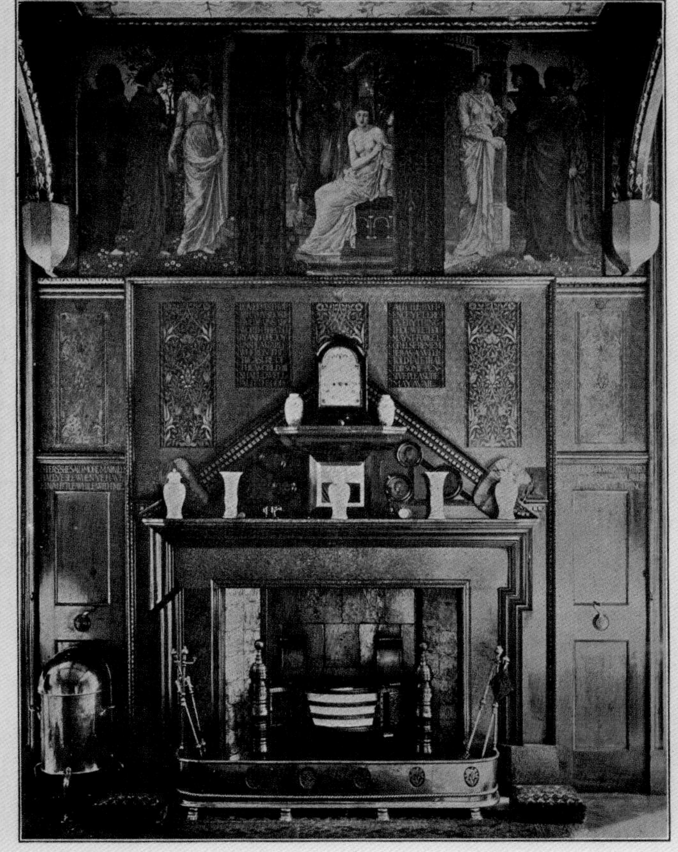

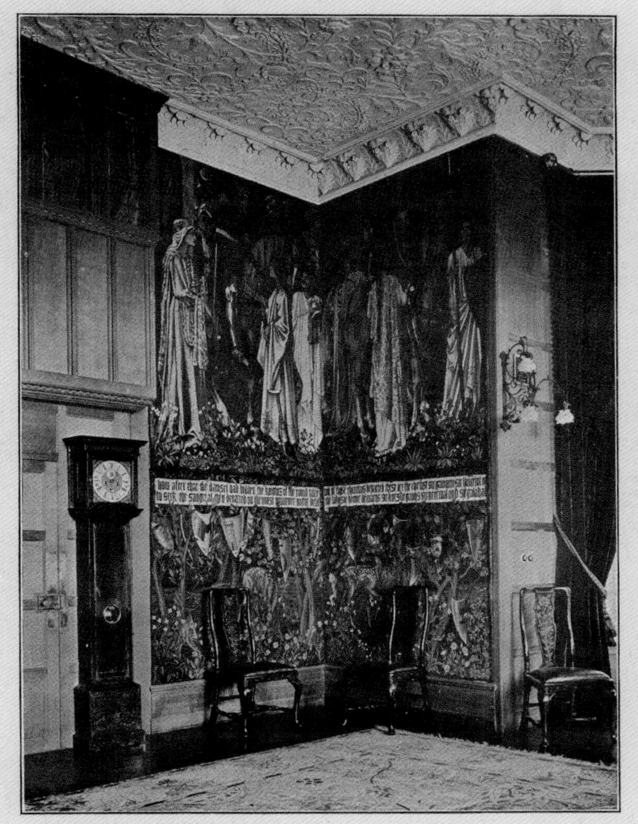

25 Designed by William Morris, Edward Burne-Jones and J. H. Dearle for Morris & Company

The dining room of Stanmore Hall, Middlesex, showing the tapestry *The Arming and Departure of the Knights of the Round Table on the Quest for the Holy Grail*, 1890

From the catalogue *Morris & Company Decorators*, 1907

while Morris masterminded the interior. Heavy silk hangings adorned the walls, windows and furniture, and the Firm supplied two magnificent hand-knotted Hammersmith carpets (*Carbrook* and *Holland Park*, both Morris designs), *The Forest* tapestry (1887, designed by Morris, Webb and Dearle) and a stained oak Broadwood piano (1884–85, designed by Burne-Jones and decorated with gold and silver gesso on a dark ground by Kate Faulkner). At Stanmore Hall [25, 59] – the last major commission before Morris's death and the largest and most extravagant undertaken by the Firm – Morris left the supervision to Dearle, who also designed mosaic floors, wall paintings, carpets, and the woven silk fabrics that hung on the walls in several rooms. Dearle's inexperience and lack of flair for interior design probably account for the dullness of the overall scheme, despite the inclusion of some memorable objects such as the stunning tapestries based on the Arthurian legend of the Holy Grail designed by Morris, Burne-Jones and Dearle for the walls of the dining room [25]. This room also housed a set of Georgian Revival dining chairs designed by George Jack, Webb's assistant.

In the 1880s Morris's anxieties about the failure of the Firm's original aim of 'good taste at the price as far as possible of ordinary furniture' led to his involvement in a very different interior design scheme.[19] In 1884, soon after he declared himself a socialist, he was approached by philanthropist Thomas Horsfall to create model interiors for workers' housing, to be exhibited in the Queen's Park art gallery, Manchester.[20] Morris was not comfortable with trying 'to make a poor man's art for the poor while we keep a rich man's art for ourselves: not to say, there, that suits your condition, I wouldn't have it myself but 'tis good enough for you', believing that 'what furniture a workman can buy should be exactly the same (if his room be large enough) as a lord buys'.[21] He had been 'aghast' at the cost of his own fairly crudely made pieces 'such as what would have been found in a yeoman's stead of old' and estimated that simple but 'well made instead of ill made' furniture for a workman's cottage would cost twenty times as much as the prices charged by firms supplying the working-class market.[22] Nevertheless, he was persuaded to contribute to the scheme. The issue of how to live, cook and look after children in one room (taken up by women in the labour movement in the early twentieth century) is ignored in Morris's 'Cottage Sitting-room', a 'Simple Life' cottage interior that the Arts and Crafts movement has ensured remains entrenched in the popular imagination. Surviving illustrations show a simple table, a wicker chair, a dresser with pretty china, prints on the walls, a high dado with wallpaper below, beams and panelling and niches on the fireplace wall. Instead of a wood and tile fireplace, as in a more expensive home, a cooking and heating range is neatly tucked into the spot where such an item would be. It seems unlikely that Morris believed that adding a working-class stove to a middle-class sitting room, or using cheaper Morris & Company products in rooms exhibited in an art gallery, would lead to that happy state where most workers would be able to afford such a room. The exercise probably intensified his conviction that this was not the way to reform design or society. Whatever the case, he did nothing else like it.

Furniture

The 'good citizen's furniture' described by Morris in 'The Lesser Arts of Life' (1877) was 'solid, and well made in workmanship', and in design had 'nothing about it that is not easily defensible, no monstrosities or extravagances'. Morris envisaged two categories: 'necessary work-a-day furniture', and more elegant and elaborately decorated 'state furniture' – 'blossoms of the art of furniture' – for the most important rooms.[23] Over the years there was a considerable variety in the appearance and cost of what was sold by the Firm. Morris did not design furniture (other than that for his own use in the late 1850s) but he took a keen interest in the Firm's activities. At first production was contracted out, but from 1865 Morris supervised it in-house.

The earliest furniture produced by the Firm was of relatively simple construction and for the most part highly decorated. The first pieces shown in public, at the International Exhibition of 1862, were 'state furniture' at its most exotic. They looked like what they were: furniture by artists. A low cabinet on a stand, painted black, red and gold with panels depicting the legend of St George, was designed by Webb and painted by Morris [26]. The degree to which this furniture challenged the hierarchy of the arts by deliberately reducing fine art to decoration confused and disconcerted many visitors to the exhibition. Even the trade publication *Building News* thought it sacrilegious – to 'art' – to include door handles within the painted picture that constituted each door and suggested purging such 'studied affectation of truthfulness'.[24]

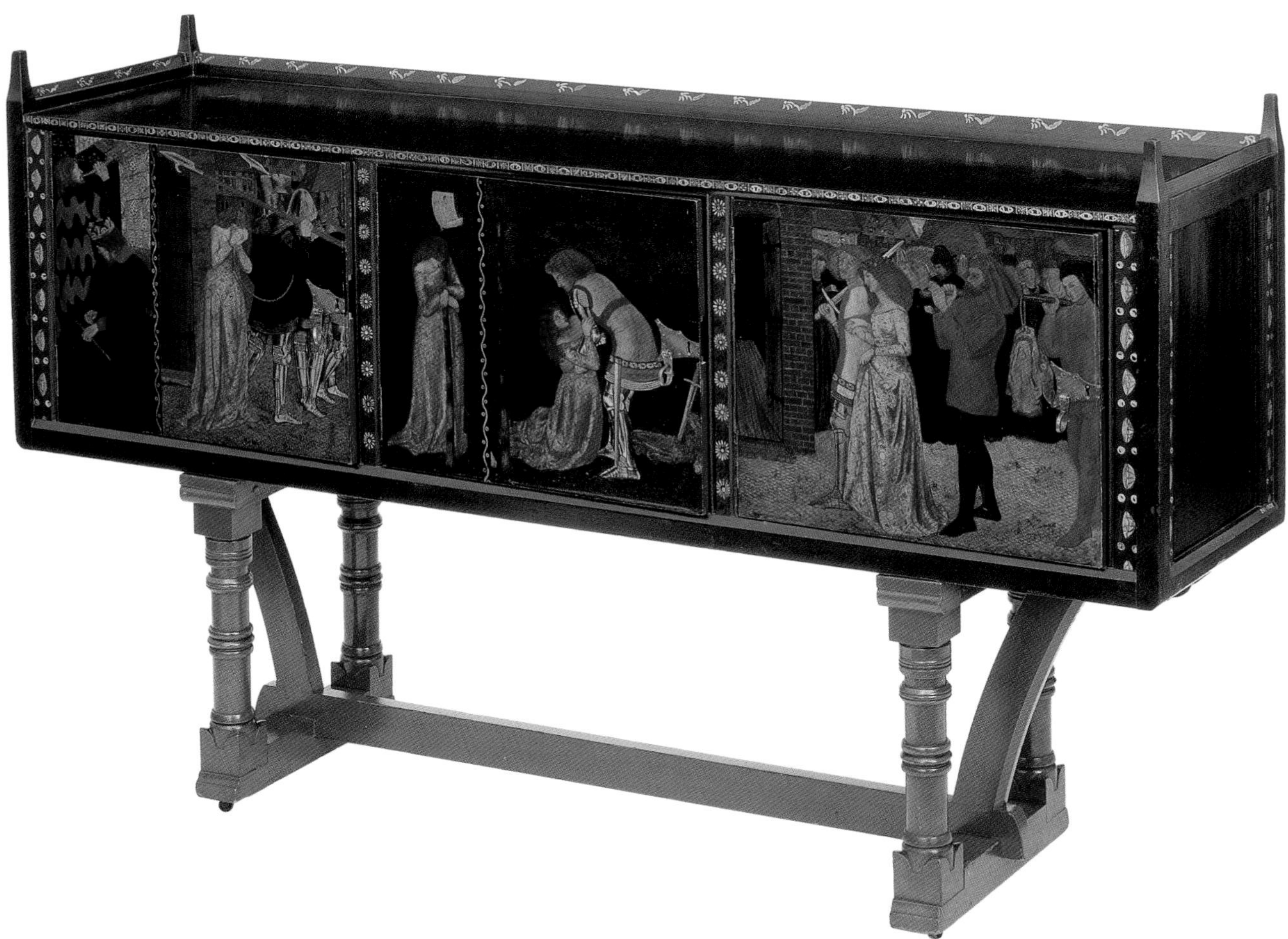

26 Designed by William Morris and Philip Webb for Morris, Marshall, Faulkner & Company

St George Cabinet, 1861–62

Mahogany, oak and pine, painted and gilded, copper handles, 37¾ x 70 x 17 (95.9 x 177.7 x 43.2)

Victoria & Albert Museum Picture Library, London

Rossetti's elegantly 'primitive' sofa with red serge covers, the wood frame of which was decorated in stripes of black and white, was regarded as very strange. Supposedly Egyptian in style, it had strong Japanese overtones – the simplicity and lightness of the frame and fans that stood behind some of the uprights – that would then have appealed only to a small group of devotees to a taste that gained in popularity as a result of Japanese goods shown in the same exhibition.[25] Today it is seen as an elegantly harmonious and sophisticated essay in the exoticism of the 'other'.

Rossetti's sofa had the lightness of Aesthetic movement art furniture and signalled the 'Sussex' seating range produced soon afterwards [27]. These relatively cheap rush-seated, turned-wood chairs and settles proved extremely popular. Made in batches of four to five dozen at a time, they remained in production into the twentieth century. Sussex chairs were based on a country prototype reputedly found by Brown, but it is not clear whether the partners thought they were reviving a rural or an urban vernacular, or whether they thought the original dated from the eighteenth century or the early nineteenth century.[26] Webb is credited with the armchair version of the Sussex chair and Brown with the round-seated version with triple top rail, while Rossetti is associated with an armchair based on early nineteenth-century French country models. The rehabilitation of outmoded lightweight chairs seems to have caught the imagination of all three. The Sussex range is a long way from the solid Gothic pieces of only a few years earlier. It had many levels of appeal, combining durability with lightness of form and weight, vernacular with modern, past with present, and low cost with good workmanship and high aesthetic value.

Warington Taylor recognized that much of its appeal lay in the 'poetry of simplicity'.[27] His description of this furniture as 'essentially gentlemanly with a total absence of ex-tallow chandler vulgarity' suggests that this aestheticization of the everyday was a romanticized one, more reminiscent of the genteel *cottage ornee* than a commonplace rural or urban vernacular. The qualities that Warington Taylor recognized as absent relate to class – lower-class connotations were missing; upper-class ones in place – while 'gentlemanly' suggests a masculinity somewhere between the robust and the effete. At a time when rooms, and a great deal of the furniture that went in them, were strictly coded as either 'feminine' (the drawing room) or 'masculine' (the dining room or library),[28] the Sussex range's lack of a specific, polarized gender ensured its use in a wide variety of settings.

It is difficult to say exactly what furniture Brown designed for the Firm, apart from a bookcase with amber curtains, incised decoration and pictorial panels shown at the 1862 exhibition.[29] He is usually credited with a group of cottagey bedroom furniture of the 1860s, some of which he used in his own home.[30] Webb, who in 1867 was appointed manager of the furniture section, designed both highly decorated items, such as chests and sideboards with painted decoration and panels of stamped leather, and plainer items including tables, mirrors on stands and music stands, some of which were ebonized or turned. It was he who designed the popular adjustable-back chair (*c.* 1866), originally sketched by Warington Taylor from one in a carpenter's workshop in Sussex.[31] In the United States it became known as 'the Morris Chair', even when produced in wicker [111].

In the 1880s George Jack designed several beautiful pieces of marquetry furniture in a late seventeenth- and early eighteenth-century manner, influenced by the 'Queen

27 Morris & Company

Sussex rush-seated chairs and settee

From the Morris & Company catalogue *Specimens of Upholstered Furniture*, between 1905 and 1917

THE SUSSEX RUSH-SEATED CHAIRS

MORRIS AND COMPANY

DECORATORS, LIMITED

449 OXFORD STREET, LONDON, W.

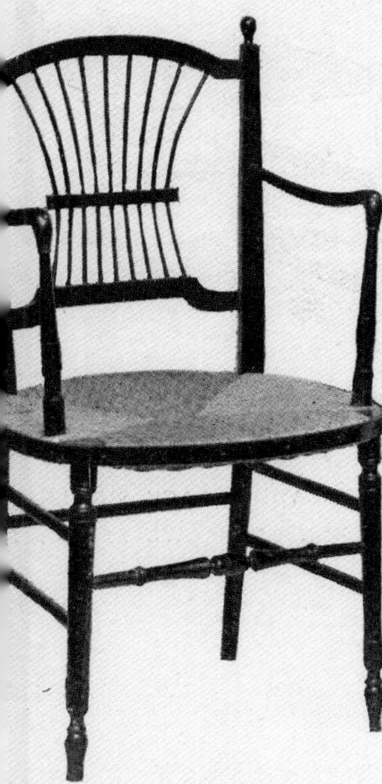

"ROSSETTI" ARM CHAIR
IN BLACK: 16/6.

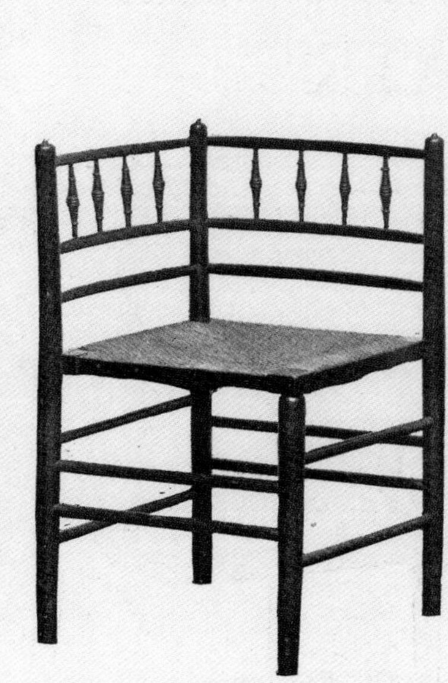

SUSSEX CORNER CHAIR
IN BLACK: 10/6.

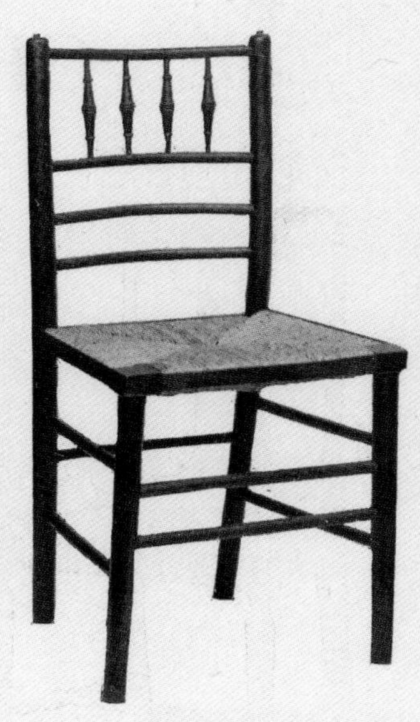

SUSSEX SINGLE CHAIR.
IN BLACK: 7/-

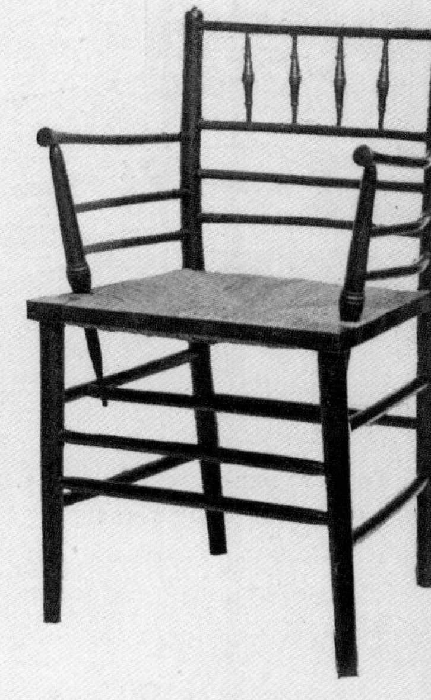

SUSSEX ARM-CHAIR.
IN BLACK: 9/9.

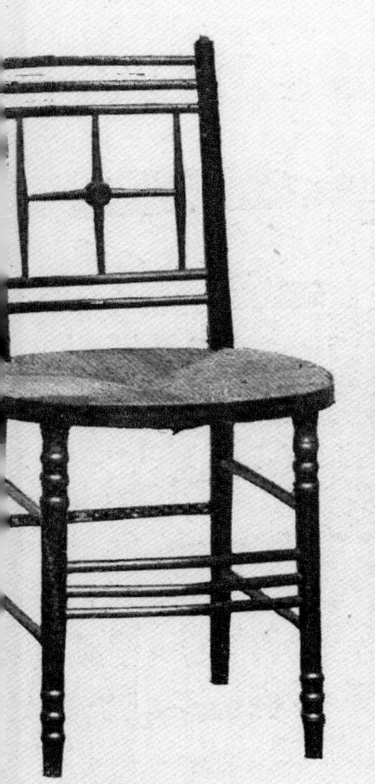

ROUND-SEAT CHAIR.
IN BLACK: 10/6.

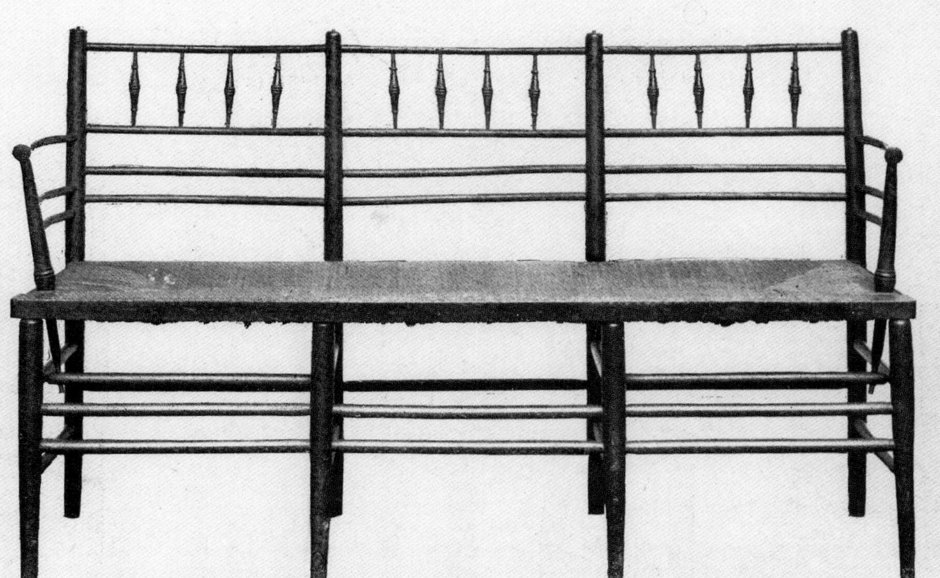

SUSSEX SETTEE, 4 FT. 6 INS. LONG.
IN BLACK: 35/-

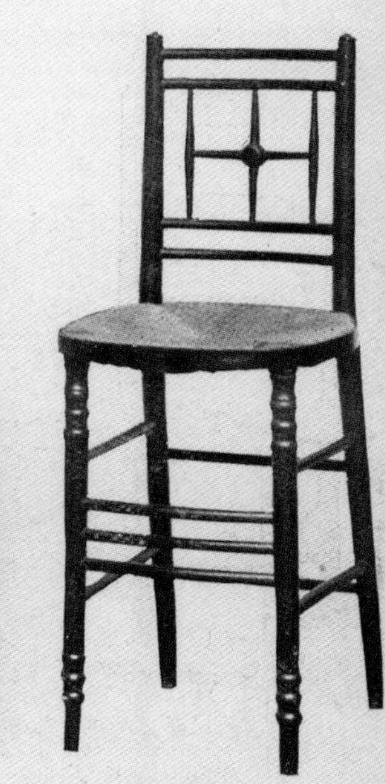

ROUND-SEAT PIANO CHAIR.
IN BLACK: 10/6.

"Of all the specific minor improvements in common household objects due to Morris, the rush-bottomed Sussex chair perhaps takes the first place. It was not his own invention, but was copied with trifling improvements from an old chair of village manufacture picked up in Sussex. With or without modification it has been taken up by all the modern furniture manufacturers, and is in almost universal use. But the Morris pattern of the later type (there were two) still excels all others in simplicity and elegance of proportion."

"Life of William Morris": By Prof. J. W. Mackail.

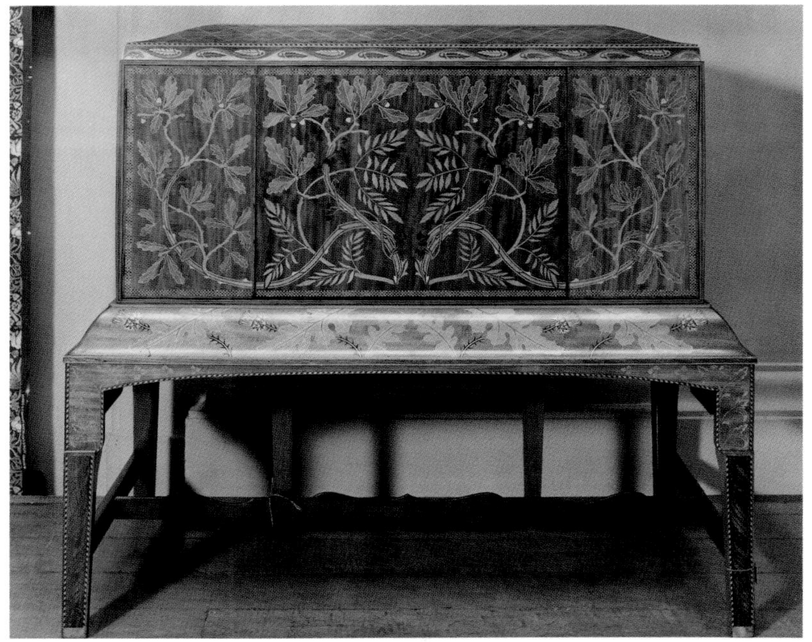

28 Designed by George Jack for Morris & Company

Secretaire, *c.* 1893

Sycamore with marquetry of various woods, 51½ x 55½ x 27 (130.8 x 140.9 x 68.5)

Victoria & Albert Museum Picture Library, London

Anne' style then popular in architecture and design.[32] His secretaire in sycamore with assorted wood marquetry (*c.* 1893) [28], first shown at the 1889 Arts and Crafts Exhibition, was generally praised, although one critic called it 'an exaggerated inlaid tea-caddy on a clumsy stand'.[33] His elegant bergere armchair in mahogany with cane seat (*c.* 1893), by contrast, drew from the design traditions of a century later, the English Regency period of the early nineteenth century. More substantial than the Sussex armchair, it was similar in that it was light, elegant, relatively plain, and could be used in more than one room. It was one of several to reflect the revival of late eighteenth- and early nineteenth-century designs generally referred to as 'Sheraton' and 'Regency', and remained in production into the twentieth century.

Wallpapers

Morris considered paper a cheap, 'quite modern and very humble' alternative to the more expensive wall hangings he so dearly loved.[34] Wallpapers were hugely popular at every level of the home furnishings trade, and those produced by the Morris firm slotted into an existing market which the company then began to shape. Morris designed the vast majority of wallpapers produced during his lifetime. His pupils, Kate Faulkner, May Morris and J. H. Dearle, also designed a few, mainly in a 'Morris' mode. Some of Dearle's of the 1890s are so similar to designs by Morris that, until recently, they were wrongly attributed [30]. Most papers produced by the Firm were hand-printed because machine printing, in which all colours were applied at once, necessitated the use of quick-drying colours that were thin and faded fast. Although a few papers were produced by machine, the more expensive, more durable hand-printed ones sold best. The latter involved mechanical reproduction by hand, with separate woodblocks [29] for each colour; *Acanthus* (1874) used fifteen. Each colour was applied separately and the process repeated until the roll was completed. Geometry and nature feature strongly in most of the designs. Morris loved nature, but as a pattern designer he stylized and abstracted it for visual effect. Much of

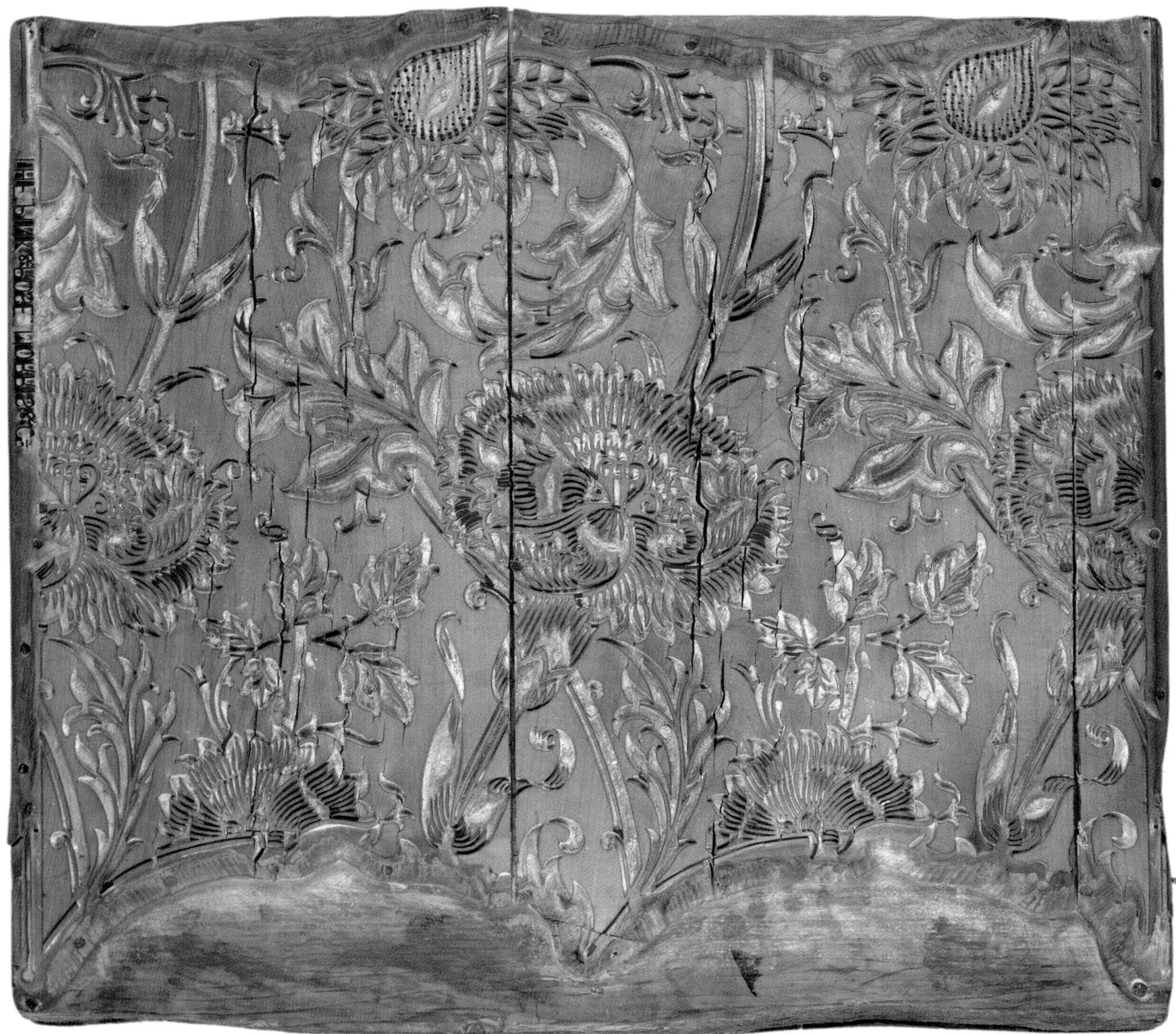

29 Designed by William Morris for Morris & Company

Woodblock for *Pink and Rose* wallpaper, *c.* 1890

Pearwood with brass pins, cut by Barrett's, London, 21¼ x 22⅜ x 2 (54 x 56.8 x 5)

One of the woodblocks used to print *Pink and Rose.* For Morris's preliminary design for this wallpaper, see ill. 12.

the English flora, foliage, animals and birds is readily recognizable but the reverse or mirror-image technique used in some designs emphasizes their non-realist, non-representational nature.

None of the partners had prior experience of wallpaper manufacture. The first attempts proved so problematic that production was put out to Jeffrey & Company, with Morris supervising the colour quality. So satisfactory was this arrangement that Jeffrey & Company was used until 1927, when it ceased business and production was taken over by Sanderson & Sons Ltd. The *Daisy* wallpaper (1864) came after Morris had designed an eponymous embroidery (for Red House [20]) and tile.[35] Familiar flowers were an ideological as well as an aesthetic choice, epitomizing the 'simple life' and reflecting a concern for the commonplace. *Daisy*'s simplicity resulted in part from Morris's lack of experience at pattern making, but the variety and delicacy of colour and form in the flowers and leaves distract the viewer from the plodding repeat.

It sold steadily until 1914. *Trellis* (1862, but not produced until 1864) was inspired by medieval-style rose trellises in the Red House gardens. The trellis serves as a grid for the pattern repeats while birds add extra interest. Morris remained fond of this design, using it in his bedroom at Kelmscott Manor, Oxfordshire. In *Fruit* (1866, also known as *Pomegranate*) diagonally placed branches that creep from one section of the pattern to another aid rhythm and disguise repeats.

In the 1870s the designs became more complex, with subtly interweaving naturalistic yet stylized backgrounds and foregrounds that added strength, movement and rhythm to the composition without overwhelming one another. *Jasmine* wallpaper (1872) [1] illustrates the changes.[36] The background of gently meandering hawthorn branches, with leaves and flowers, is overlaid with a delicately scrolling jasmine plant. In *Vine* (*c.* 1873), a grape-bearing vine grows over stylized willow leaves. The effect is one of density and unbroken colour. *Pimpernel* (1876) and *Acanthus* (1874) are three-dimensional in their density and held together by robust, visceral curves as crisp as medieval carvings.

The 1880s saw more historicist designs, some influenced by examples of patterns collected by Morris or seen at the South Kensington Museum. By 1880 the Firm offered 32 patterns in 125 colourways. The cheaper machine-printed papers cost 2*s.* 6*d.* per roll, but the hand-printed papers, competitively priced for their market niche at between 3*s.* and 16*s.*, sold best. So successful were Morris & Company wallpapers that they raised the international reputation of British wallpapers in general.[37]

30 Designed by J. H. Dearle for Morris & Company

Compton wallpaper, first issued 1896 (detail)

Block-printed in distemper colours, printed by Jeffrey & Company, London, full piece 26¾ x 20⅔ (68 x 52.5)

Textiles

Morris designed a wide range of textiles, from embroideries and tapestries, with close connections to painting, to printed and woven fabrics and carpets that showcased his talents as a designer of repeating patterns [31]. In 1863 the Firm claimed it could supply 'all kinds of embroidered hangings both for domestic and ecclesiastical purposes in linen, cotton, wool[len] silk or velvet' from the simplest line embroidery to elaborate needlework tapestry of figures and subjects.[38] Burne-Jones, Webb, Brown and Morris all designed medieval-style embroideries in the early 1860s but it was Morris who investigated past design and craft traditions, and who himself learned to embroider at a time when it was considered a womanly pastime.

The revival of interest from the 1830s onwards in medieval embroideries was part and parcel of the Gothic Revival in architecture and design. Morris and Webb became aware of embroidery when working for Street, one of the first architects to use medieval-style embroideries in Gothic Revival buildings; the others came to it through the Pre-Raphaelite interest in an art form that, in the Middle Ages, rivalled if not outshone painting. By the nineteenth century, however, embroidery was considered the lowliest of the decorative arts, not least because of its role in inculcating and shaping contemporary ideas of femininity.[39] By associating with an activity considered trivial and 'women's work', Street and other male embroidery designers breached a powerful gender divide while upholding the unity of the arts.

The pattern of the first embroidery designed and made by Morris, *If I Can* (1856–57), features fruit trees with birds in flight inspired by Froissart's *Chronicles.*[40] Its density and richness are missing from the self-consciously naive *Daisy* for Red

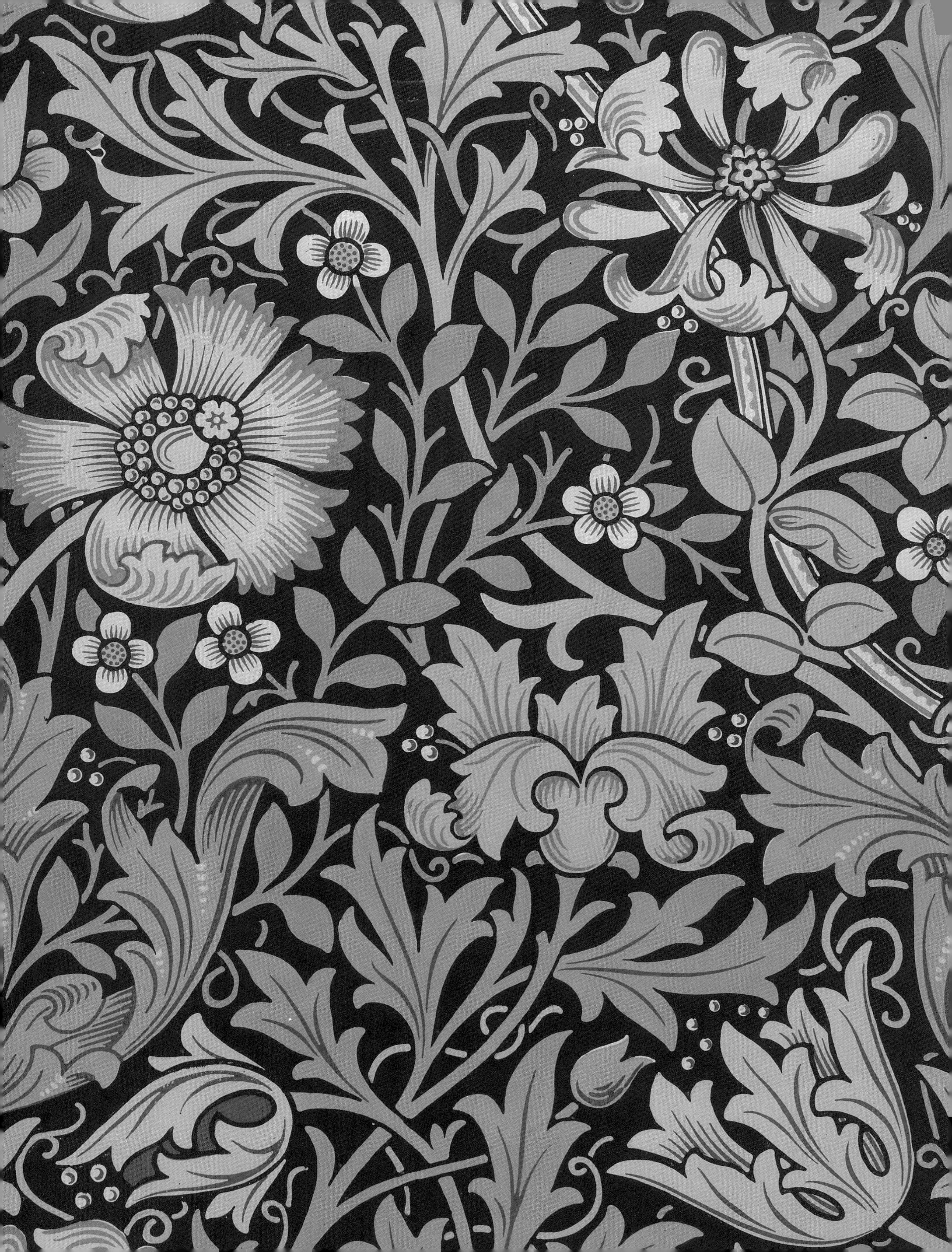

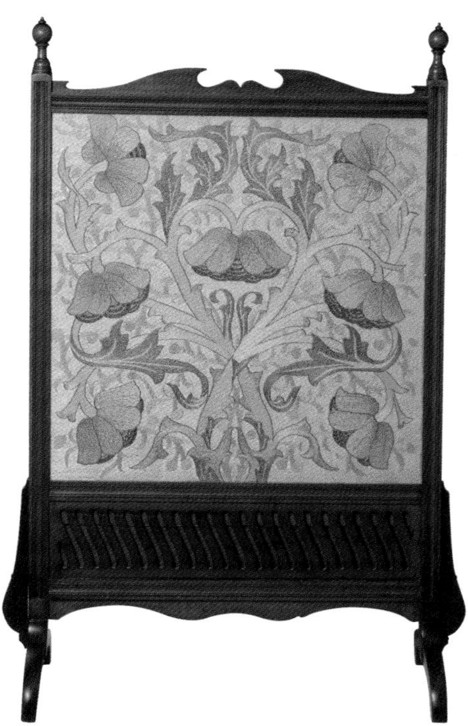

32 Morris & Company

Cheval screen with embroidered panel, *c.* 1880

Cotton embroidered in silks, mahogany frame and stand, 21¼ x 21 x 11¼ (54 x 53.3 x 28.6)

House [20], the conception as well as execution of which may possibly have been a collaboration between Morris and his wife. Once again, after spending enormous amounts of time reviving 'lost' handicraft traditions and developing appropriate natural dyes, Morris left the execution of his designs to others. Embroidery was one area in which women were better trained than men, and it was the women in the Firm's immediate circle who undertook such work. Jane Morris proved to be very talented, as did her sister, Bessie Burden (who supervised the production of many embroideries), and both her daughters, Jenny and May.[41] Morris's admiration of the skills of Catherine Holiday, an embroiderer who worked on a freelance basis for the Firm, can be seen in his correspondence to her.[42] Later embroideries include *The Musicians* (*c.* 1875, designed by Burne-Jones and Morris) and *Honeysuckle* (1876, designed by Morris); the former was worked at the Royal School of Art Needlework (RSAN), the latter worked by Jane and Jenny Morris and sold through the RSAN, with which the Morris firm appears to have had a business arrangement.[43] The late 1870s and 1880s saw the production of a number of large embroidered coverlets or wall hangings, with large-scale formal pattern repeats reminiscent of the Eastern silks studied by Morris at the South Kensington Museum, as well as a host of small items from firescreens [32] to cushion covers.

Tapestry, a different and more expensive way of making pictures and telling stories with threads, was not undertaken until the early 1880s when Morris's 'bright dream' of a tapestry works materialized at Merton Abbey.[44] Morris considered tapestry 'the noblest of the weaving arts' because there was nothing mechanical about it.[45] Again, he learned the art before teaching it to others. Using an eighteenth-century French manual, he wove his first tapestry in 1879. The Firm's first large-scale tapestry incorporating figures was based on Walter Crane's *Goose Girl* (1881), but most designs thereafter were supplied by Burne-Jones, using draped figures similar to those in his cartoons for stained glass. Morris considered his friend the only man alive who could produce pictures 'at once good enough and

31 Designed by J. H. Dearle for Morris & Company

Cherwell wall hanging, first issued 1887 (detail)

Block-printed velveteen, printed at Merton Abbey, full piece 85½ x 68 (217.2 x 172.7)

suitable for tapestry'.[46] His own design input became restricted to backgrounds and borders that evoked those of the late Gothic period.[47] As with other collaborations between these two, the figurative and decorative elements work well together.

The tapestries produced during Morris's lifetime include the paired *Flora* and *Pomona* (1883–85) and *Angeli Laudantes* [33] and *Angeli Ministrantes* (1894, designed by Dearle using figures originally drawn by Burne-Jones for stained glass windows at Salisbury Cathedral in the 1870s). The most popular design was *The Adoration* (1888, Burne-Jones, Morris and Dearle), presented by Morris and Burne-Jones to their alma mater, Exeter College, Oxford. Weavings in the 1890s included ones for Wilfred Scawen Blunt, Manchester Corporation and Eton College. In the 1900s versions went to Germany (Museum für Kunst und Gewerbe, Hamburg), Australia, Russia and France, as well as to Roker Church, Sunderland, and Carrow Hall, Norfolk, home of the Colman mustard family. The last tapestry collaboration between Burne-Jones and Morris, the *Holy Grail* series [25], harked back to their early interest in Arthurian legend. Like the Kelmscott Chaucer, these hand-woven tapestries were realizations of boyhood and adolescent dreams.

There are strong similarities between Morris's designs for printed wallpapers and those for printed textiles (chintzes). Geometry and nature dominated both and similar shifts in composition can be observed. Producing hand-printed textiles, however, proved much more difficult than hand-printed wallpapers. Two techniques were used: hand block printing, with multiple colours printed from separate blocks onto a self-coloured fabric; and indigo-discharge printing [35, 55, 95, 128], where the whole cloth was dyed dark blue and images printed by bleaching out particular patterns to full-tone (white) or half-tone (pale blue). Both methods were complicated and involved repetitive hand work and high levels of skill, and there was no well-established company to which production could be entrusted.

33 Designed by Edward Burne-Jones and J. H. Dearle for Morris & Company

Angeli Laudantes tapestry, 1894

Wool, silk and mohair on a cotton warp, woven at Merton Abbey, 93½ x 79½ (237.5 x 202)

Victoria & Albert Museum Picture Library, London

The majority of Morris's printed textiles date from between 1874 and 1885. Commercially available dyes were used on his first printed cotton, but he hated the results and began studying dyeing techniques. Chemical dyes had first been introduced in the early nineteenth century; Morris's pet hate, a bright purple coal-tar dye, dates from the 1850s, by which time the natural dyes used in Europe from the sixteenth century to the eighteenth were no longer available. Morris experimented with various materials in a small dye house at Queen Square while working with Thomas Wardle, proprietor of a hand-dyeing and printing firm at Leek in Staffordshire. By 1878, when he exhibited Morris designs on printed silks at the Paris Exposition Universelle, Wardle was printing fourteen patterns for the Firm. This continued after Morris started production of printed textiles at Merton Abbey in 1881–82 [5]. Without the pioneering work undertaken with Wardle the production of saleable items would not have been possible, but Morris was never quite satisfied with the artistic supervision at Wardle's premises. It was only after operations began at Merton Abbey that the quality and consistency he desired were achieved, particularly with indigo-discharge printing.

Some of the simpler printed cottons, such as *Marigold* and *Tulip* (both 1875), feature a single flower head with simple leaves in a flat composition, whereas more complex ones, such as *Columbine* [34] or *Honeysuckle* (1876) [85], with their riot of

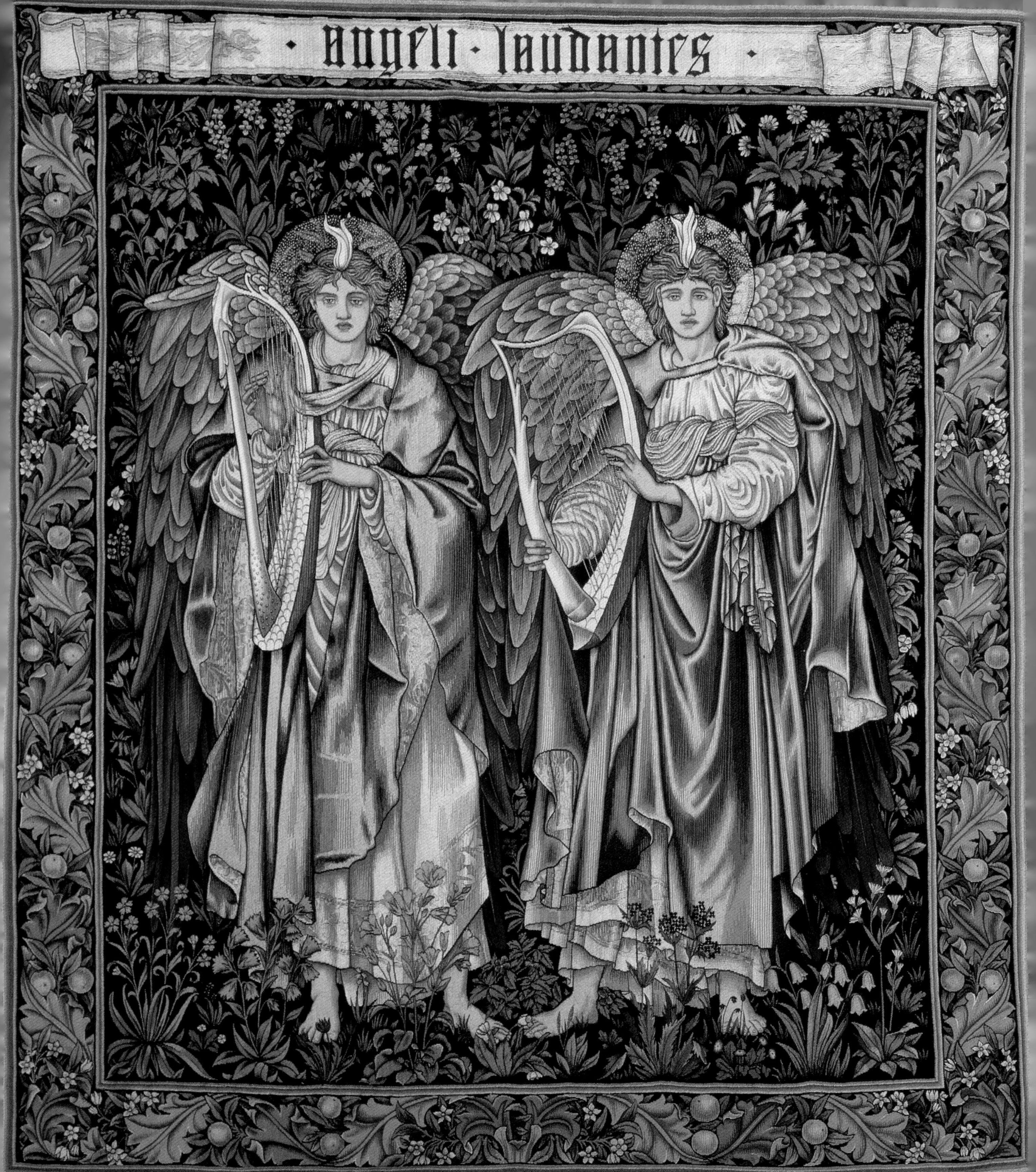
· Angeli · laudantes ·

34 Designed by William Morris for Morris & Company

Columbine printed fabric, first issued 1876 (detail)

Block-printed cotton and linen, printed by Thomas Wardle, Leek, Staffordshire, full piece 25½ x 36¼ (64.8 x 92.1)

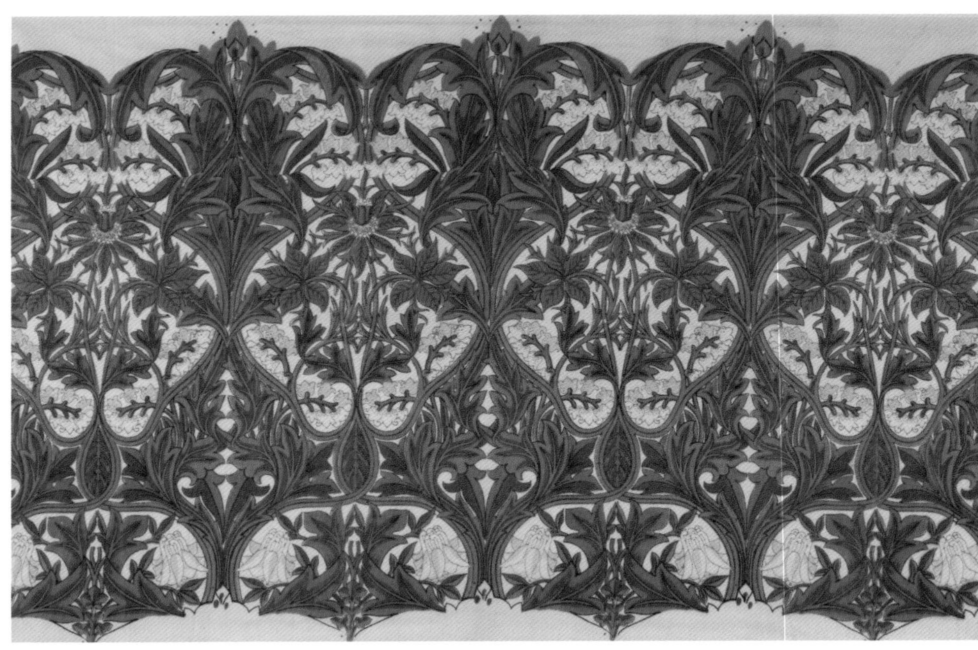

intertwining stems, background growth and flower heads, are more three-dimensional in effect. The latter's large-scale turnover repeat reflects Morris's preoccupation with Italian woven silks of the sixteenth and seventeenth centuries. Morris's best-known woven design, *Bird* (*c.* 1878), was produced shortly afterwards in wool, a cosier and cheaper material than silk and regarded as more 'English' [36]. Of the textiles produced by the indigo-discharge method, the furnishing fabrics *Brother Rabbit* (1880–81) and *Strawberry Thief* (1883) [35] are the best known. The former was made in both full-tone and half-tone, and also printed using red dye instead of indigo. *Strawberry Thief* was more ambitious: red and yellow were added to achieve green, purple, and orange. Despite its being expensive for a cotton (the fabric had to be dried after every stage of a risky process) it proved one of the Firm's best sellers.[48]

35 Designed by William Morris for Morris & Company

Strawberry Thief printed cotton, first issued 1883 (detail)

Indigo-discharged and block-printed cotton, printed at Merton Abbey, full piece 18⅝ x 38½ (47.3 x 97.8)

Until the 1870s, antique Persian carpets were Morris's preferred choice for floor coverings. In 1877, however, when studying Eastern carpets at the South Kensington Museum, he was so impressed by a sixteenth-century Persian example (it 'fairly threw me on my back. I had no idea that such wonders could be done in carpets')[49] that he began to experiment with the manufacture of hand-knotted carpets. Those produced thereafter by the Firm capture something of the rich colour and distinctive patterns of repeat, contrast and symmetry of antique Persian carpets. In typical Morris fashion he thought big, aiming 'to make England independent of the East for carpets which may be claimed to be considered works of art'.[50] The handmade rugs and carpets designed by Morris [58] and by Dearle [79] (mainly independently but sometimes in collaboration) were expensive: it took one day to weave 2 inches (50 mm) on a loom and a 16 x 13 foot (4.9 x 4 m) carpet cost over £100. Morris also designed machine-woven carpets, including Wiltons [37] – 'the very best kind of machine-woven carpets. ... If well made the material is very durable, and by skilful treatment in the designing, the restrictions as to colour are not noticeable'[51] – and the cheaper Kidderminsters, which he helped popularize.

36 Designed by William Morris for Morris & Company

Bird woven fabric, first issued *c.* 1878 (detail)

Wool double cloth, hand-loom Jacquard woven at Queen Square and later at Merton Abbey, full piece 82 x 47¾ (208.3 x 121.3)

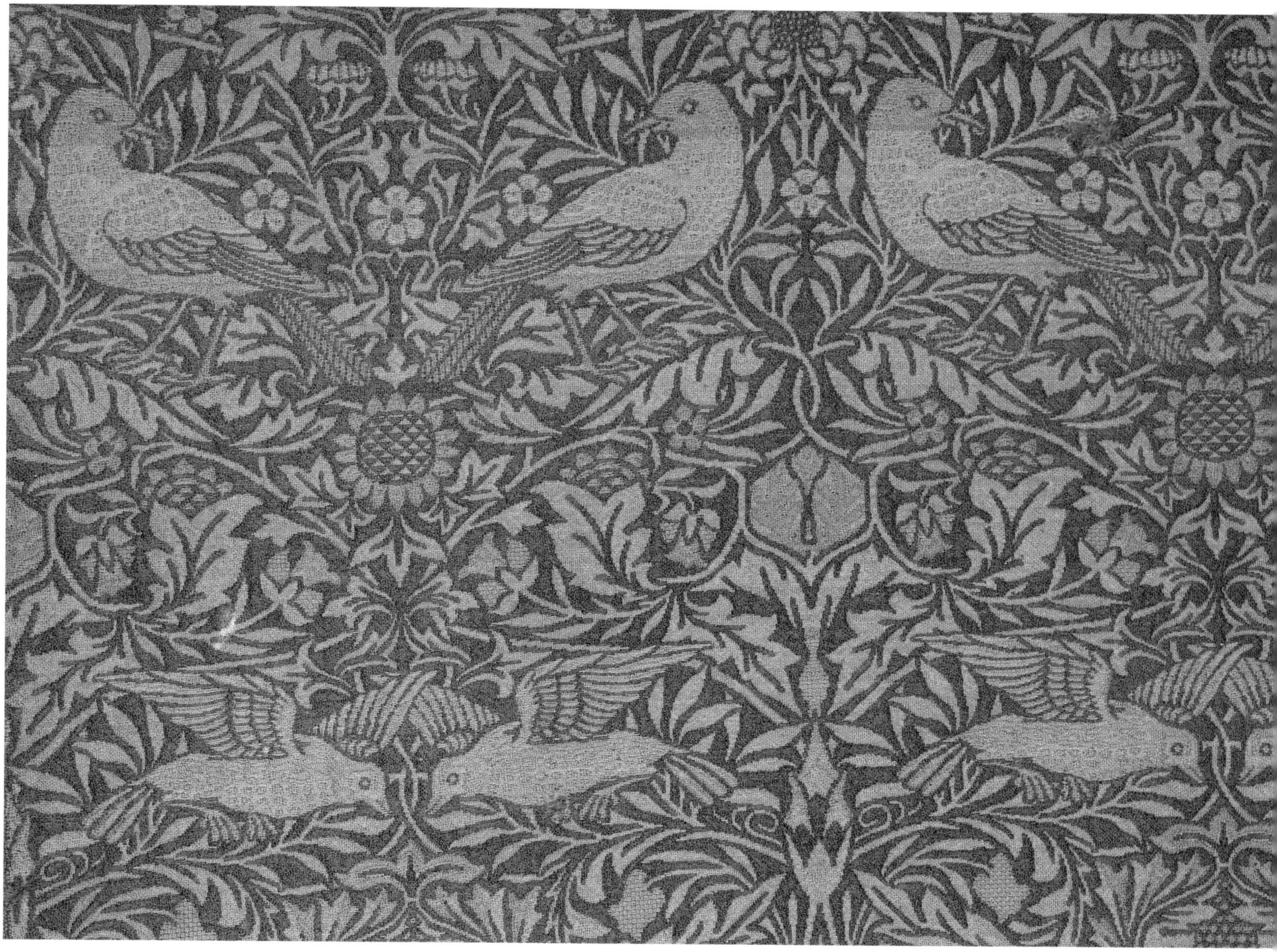

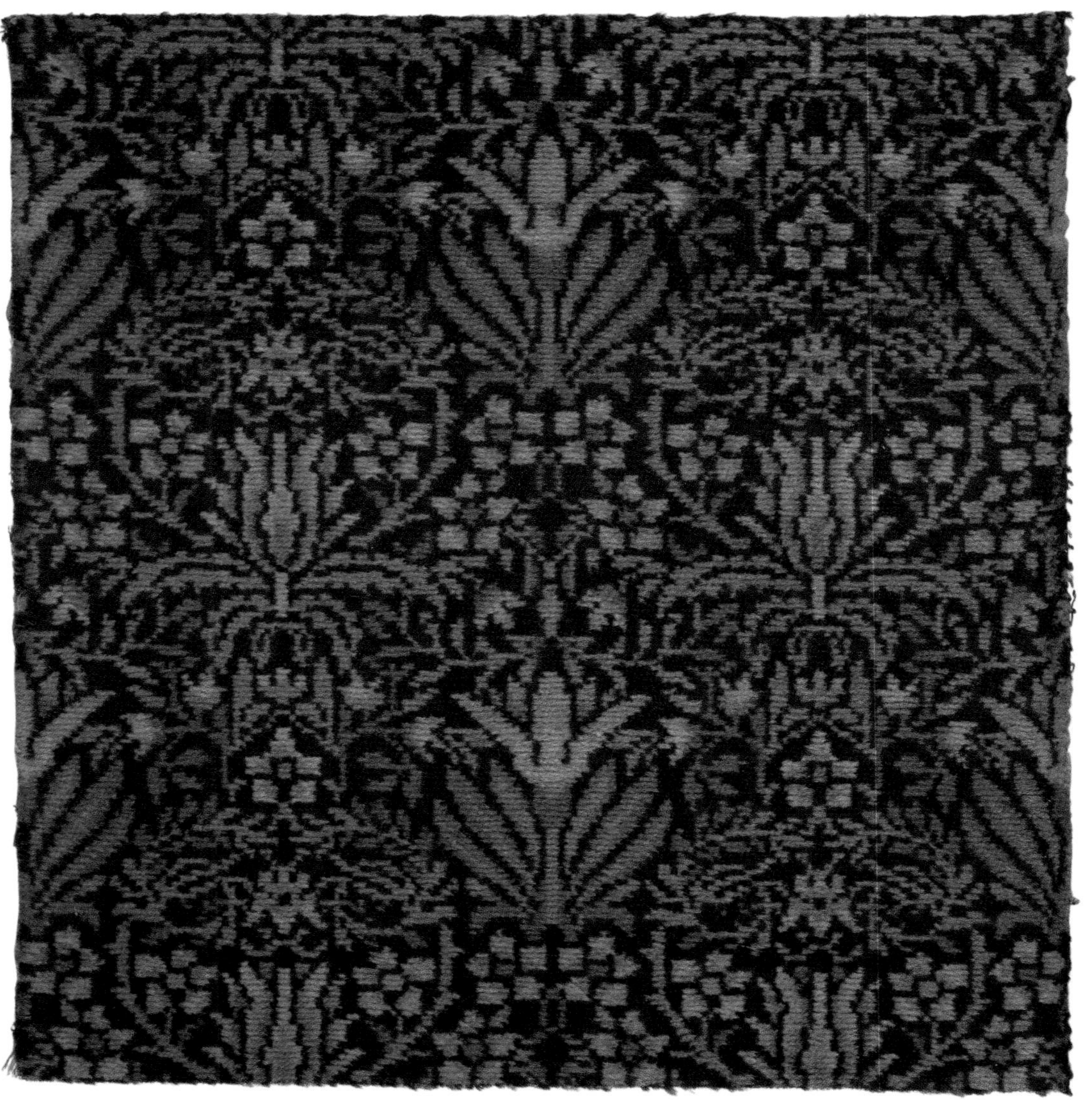

37 Designed by William Morris for Morris & Company

Lily machine-woven carpet, first issued *c.*1875

Wilton pile machine-woven on a Jacquard loom, manufactured by the Wilton Royal Carpet Factory, Wiltshire, 18¾ x 18 (47.6 x 45.7)

Surviving examples show a concern for designs appropriate to machine work, with similarities to the artful lack of complexity of the simpler wallpapers. *Lily* (*c.* 1875) [37], featuring black and green flower heads on bands of white and yellow, was a woollen-pile jute-backed Wilton, while *Tulip and Lily* (*c.* 1875) was a three-ply woollen-weave Kidderminster.[52]

Stained Glass

The Firm produced stained glass from 1861 until the 1930s. Morris and Burne-Jones fell in love with the 'sweet mellowed stained glass'[53] of the cathedrals of Northern France during a walking tour of 1854, by which time a revival of interest in medieval stained glass was well under way. Pugin's window designs were influential, as was the technical work undertaken by Charles Winston for James Powell & Sons, the firm from which Morris, Marshall, Faulkner & Company would buy its glass.

Religious revivalism and a population explosion had fuelled a boom in church building, and such was the level of demand for windows that the partners gambled on being able to break into this market – not least because, between them, they possessed a wealth of talent. Burne-Jones and Rossetti already had experience of working for Powell & Sons, and commissions were forthcoming from a Gothic Revival church architect, George Frederick Bodley. Despite the fact that in the 1860s stained glass constituted approximately three-quarters of its sales, the Firm's place in the market was not secure nor was the income from stained glass sufficient to sustain the business. Several architects and other potential clients chose rival firms instead, and sometimes clients of the Firm went elsewhere for subsequent work. The Firm's prices tended to be higher, its colours and shapes bolder and clearer, and its treatments less archaeologically inspired than those of other companies. Webb, Rossetti and Brown were influential in shifting Morris's aesthetic towards something less clearly defined as 'medieval', and several scholars have commented on the 'secular' feel to much of the Firm's ecclesiastical work and an 'anti-pietistic treatment of religious themes'.[54] The partners were agreed in eschewing imitation and so the Firm missed out on commissions from architects, clerics and laity who preferred work in a more orthodox Gothic Revival mode.

Glass was bought in, but Morris, an inveterate researcher, collaborated with Powell & Sons to try to improve quality and colour. He even fantasized about establishing his own glass manufactory, so that he could exercise the same sort of control he had achieved with textiles once dyeing and printing were undertaken within the Firm. As it was, he was in charge of colouring from the beginning. He selected all the glass from Powell & Sons, scrutinizing each piece against the light for brilliance and tone and developing the distinctive palette of rich rubies, golden yellows, muted blues and earthy greens, often offset against white, for which the Firm came to be known. In the first two or three years, all the partners with the exception of Faulkner designed for this painterly applied-art medium. For the most part each designer undertook the placing of lead lines on his work, but Rossetti was somewhat cavalier about the process and some of Brown's more irregular and jagged markings proved unrealizable in practice.[55] Lead-lining therefore also passed to Morris who, like Webb, had a sound grasp of the medium.

At first Webb and Morris were responsible for the overall designs, using quarries (square or lozenge-shaped pieces of clear glass), foliage canopies and other devices to adapt individual figures or rectangular, square and roundel-shaped designs into compositions that fitted the particular windows for which they were meant [38]. It was they who 'integrated the individual styles of the figure cartoonists – Rossetti's vigour, Brown's expressiveness, Burne-Jones's fluent elegance and modernity, Morris's own simple narrative directness – into a coherent entity'.[56] By the mid-1870s Morris was solely responsible, and most of the stained glass was designed by Burne-Jones, whose prodigious talents played a major role in establishing the international standing of the Firm. From the 1870s, Burne-Jones was the Firm's greatest asset after Morris himself. Morris restricted himself to designing backgrounds, which he adapted as Burne-Jones's style changed from a Rossetti-influenced Pre-Raphaelitism towards a more heavily Italianate pictorialism in the 1870s, only to take on Byzantine influences in the 1880s.[57] During the 1870s and 1880s certain employees became so well versed in carrying out Morris's background treatments and leading that, on occasions and subject to his approval, some decisions were made in the studio in his

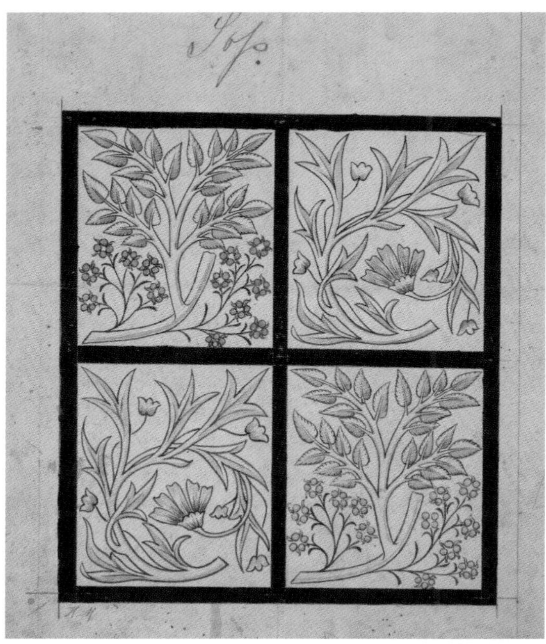

38 Morris & Company

Design for stained glass quarries, after 1890

Pen, ink, watercolour and wash, 14 x 10⅞ (35.6 x 27.6)

absence. The mid-1870s also saw the first use by the Firm of photographs to help rescale designs to fit different-sized windows. The camera took much of the tedious work out of this process.

The story of stained glass design for churches, which accounted for the bulk of the Firm's output, is covered further by Diane Waggoner later in this book (pp. 64–75). Although stained glass was advocated for domestic interiors, relatively little was commissioned. What is known dates mainly from the 1860s. It includes *King René's Honeymoon*, a series of panels designed in about 1863 for the home of the artist Myles Birket Foster; designed by Burne-Jones (*Painting* and *Sculpture*), Rossetti (*Music*) and Brown (*Architecture*), they were based on episodes from Walter Scott's *Anne of Geierstein* describing the king's love of the fine arts.[58] About the same time the Firm produced Rossetti's series of six panels that constituted *The Legend of St George.* One of the panels, reputedly made for a domestic setting, was shown at the 'Exhibition of Stained Glass, Mosaics. Etc.' held in 1864, at which Burne-Jones's *Penelope* (1864), a popular domestic design, was also shown. Rossetti's small, dark and dense panels stand in direct contrast to the light, delicate and large windows designed only a few years later as part of Webb and Morris's scheme for a public reception room at the South Kensington Museum [23]. Another secular commission was for glass for the Combination Room of Peterhouse College, Cambridge (*c.* 1874). The *Homer* window – the figure by Burne-Jones, the quarries probably by Morris – was first used there, but the design was re-used on later occasions. The *Minstrel* window (also known as *Woman Playing Lute, c.* 1874) features one of Morris's simplest but most effective draped figure designs. Eminently suitable for domestic use, it also appeared on painted tiles. With the addition of wings, to transform the minstrel into a Pre-Raphaelite angel, it was also used in ecclesiastical commissions.[59]

Although Morris admired mosaic-style leading, much of the Firm's distinctive style before the 1880s comes from lead that outlines relatively large pieces of glass. Some of the later glass, however, features small mosaic-like pieces and more emphatic leading [49, 50]. This reflects the growing interest of Morris, De Morgan, Street, Burne-Jones and others in mosaics, and in Byzantine design in general. In 1881 Street had commissioned Burne-Jones to work on mosaics at the church of St Paul, Rome, and the elongated figures that feature in the latter's designs for three windows at Birmingham Cathedral (1887–97) refer back to the early Christian mosaics at Ravenna which so delighted him during his stay in Italy. Dense, brilliant and bold, this is Burne-Jones at his most complex. To view these windows is a kaleidoscopic, intense and somewhat mystical experience. There are touches of Byzantine and Symbolist influence, but what stays with one is the vibrancy, density, iridescence and saturation of colour reminiscent of Hollywood Technicolor at its best. The fiery angels and hopeful dead are enough to make any sinner repent.[60] These windows were outside the parameters of what clients had come to expect as 'Morris & Company', but Morris backed his friend's artistic judgment. An inconsolable Burne-Jones completed the designs only a few weeks after Morris's death in October 1896. Like the Kelmscott Press, they were one of the last ventures on which the old friends collaborated. This 'pictorial masterpiece of the Victorian age'[61] stands as a fitting memorial not only to these two men but also to the Firm that made it.

Morris & Company after Morris

After Morris's death his partners bought out his share of the business. His will made this easy to do and at first it seemed that little had changed. Morris had trained the staff to work in his ways and there were several big orders on the books. Dearle became artistic director, designing in a 'Morris' manner and reworking and rescaling existing designs – his role in the Firm, before and after Morris's death, is elaborated by Diane Waggoner (pp. 98–107) – and Jack continued to contribute designs. But there were differences, not least of which was the absence of Morris himself. May Morris contributed some designs but gave up supervision of the embroidery section, and Burne-Jones, who had kept an eye on stained glass production after Morris's death, died in 1898. By 1900, when Webb retired, there was no longer any direct connection between the Firm and any of the original partners. The high regard in which Morris & Company was held at that date can be judged by the commission to decorate part of the interior of the British Pavilion at the 1900 Exhibition in Paris, described as 'a bit of Old England on the banks of the Seine'.[62] Official respectability had been achieved in the 1860s; by 1900 the work stood for Englishness itself.

In 1905 the Firm was sold to Henry Marillier, a disciple of Morris who lived at Morris's former London home, Kelmscott House. He was a co-partner in a failing Arts and Crafts enterprise with William Benson, who began to supply the Firm with designs for furniture.[63] Marillier established a limited liability company, Morris & Company Decorators Ltd, the name of which sought to emphasize the interior design service offered. Unfortunately for such a Morris enthusiast, Marillier took over when Morrisian designs were becoming outmoded, and neither he nor Dearle had the inclination or artistic abilities to take it in new design directions. Marillier discovered that the company was not in as sound a financial shape as he had hoped. He was forced to introduce into the repertoire an increasing number of items similar to those sold by rival – and more commercially successful – interior design firms that catered to wealthy clients with conservative tastes. These were mainly in popular 'period' styles, or reproductions. At the same time the company continued to promote and sell what it called 'Morris Movement' products.

The company made much of its history, especially the association with William Morris. Marillier presented Morris as a poet, designer and founder of the 'Morris Movement', sanitizing his image by ignoring his socialism. He was by no means alone in this. The gentrification of Morris's ideas began during the last decade of his life, despite his constant and vocal protestations, and after his death it continued apace. Between 1905 and World War I 'Morris Movement' may not have been the most fashionable decorating choice but it retained a remarkable number of devotees. The Firm remained the main source of products based on designs by Morris, Burne-Jones, Webb and other 'heroes' of the Arts and Crafts movement, and of similar product lines in the 'Morris' style. Dearle's designs for textiles and wallpapers were derivative of, but different from, those of Morris; his general style, patterns and palette were more delicate but sufficiently close to please customers, who either assumed they were by Morris or did not care. It served the interests of the company for Dearle designs to pass as being by Morris, and Marillier appears to have allowed this knowingly.[64] Something similar happened in tapestry and stained glass, except that Dearle's reconfigurations and adaptations of Burne-Jones figures and Morris borders and backgrounds were much closer to the original cartoons that remained with the Firm. His own designs in these media drew heavily on Burne-Jones and Morris, and lay firmly within the tradition of the Firm as it was during the lifetimes of those two remarkable men. In 1911 the Firm celebrated the fiftieth anniversary of its foundation by publishing a history of what it called the 'Morris Movement' tradition, of which it was the living embodiment. By then, however, Morris & Company was a pale shadow of its former self.

At a time when Morris's writings, designs and commitment to handwork were inspiring designers and workshops all over the world to explore original paths within the parameters of Arts and Crafts ideals, Morris & Company's policy seems to have been to stick to old formulae wherever possible and, when in doubt, to ape rival firms. Dearle continued to work in a 'Morrisian' manner but spent a great deal of time skilfully reconfiguring and rescaling material from existing cartoons and patterns. Besides reproducing and pastiching old designs, the Firm adapted designs that had been successful in one medium for use in another. Wallpaper patterns were used for printed cottons, for example, and dark-ground fabric designs of the 1880s were reissued with pale backgrounds and no subsidiary colours. Multi-coloured patterns appeared in monochrome or greatly simplified, the better to accord with the then popular Georgian Revival ideals of lightness, simplicity, and elegance.[65] 'New' reproductions of historic textile patterns and furniture, 'reproductions' (items closely resembling but not directly copied from historic examples), the use of 'Morris' textiles to upholster a wide range of seating (some of which bore little stylistic resemblance to the materials that covered it), and a tapestry repair, restoration and maintenance service were all part of a pragmatic approach to business management that ensured a degree of profitability until World War I. One wonders what Morris

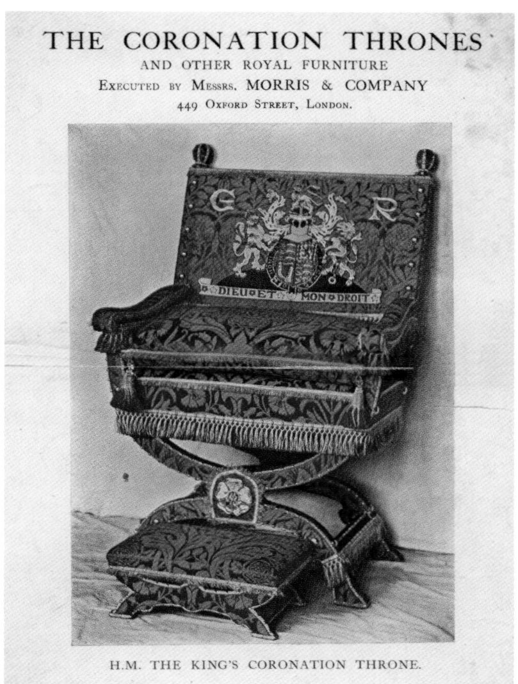
THE CORONATION THRONES
AND OTHER ROYAL FURNITURE
EXECUTED BY MESSRS. MORRIS & COMPANY
449 OXFORD STREET, LONDON.

H.M. THE KING'S CORONATION THRONE.

39 Morris & Company

'H. M. the King's Coronation Throne'

From the Morris & Company catalogue *The Coronation Thrones and Other Royal Furniture*, between 1911 and 1917

himself would have made of the changes. He would not have approved of transferring designs across very different media, and regarded reproductions and 'reproduction' furnishings as sterile and counter-productive to creativity. Commenting on the art of the past, his position was quite clear: 'Let us therefore study it wisely, be taught by it, kindled by it; all the while determining not to imitate or repeat it; to have either no art at all, or an art which we have made our own.'[66] It is not hard to imagine what he would have thought of the 1911 version of a seventeenth-century chair that served as coronation thrones for King George V and Queen Mary [39], to say nothing of the dull 'Chippendale', 'Hepplewhite' and 'Sheraton' copies and unimaginatively designed 'reproduction' furniture sold in the inter-war years.[67]

Dearle was left in charge when Marillier, together with many employees, joined the military during World War I. The furniture works survived by turning to propeller manufacture. Despite all that, and the closure of the tapestry section, along with a decline in stained glass sales, in 1917 the Firm moved to yet more fashionable premises, 17 George Street, off Hanover Square [40], in the hope of better things to come. Although World War I had seen the Firm almost go under, the memorials to the dead of that war helped it survive the slump of the immediate postwar years. Church furnishings sold relatively well and memorial tablets were offered in wood, stone and metal; but it was stained glass that saved the day, with orders from as far afield as Spain, Switzerland, the West Indies, Canada, Australia, New Zealand and South Africa.[68] While Marillier loved tapestry, the market for 'Morris' tapestry was limited. Production resumed in 1922, but the Eton College commission for four memorial tapestry panels was designed outside the Firm.[69] The reweaving of *The Passing of Venus* commissioned by George Booth, a rich American disciple of Morris who founded the Cranbrook educational centre in Bloomfield Hills, Michigan, used an existing design sketched by Burne-Jones before his death but completed by Dearle. Both Marillier and Booth suggested modifications and Booth was involved in discussions about the new, larger border.[70] Dearle's watercolour sketch

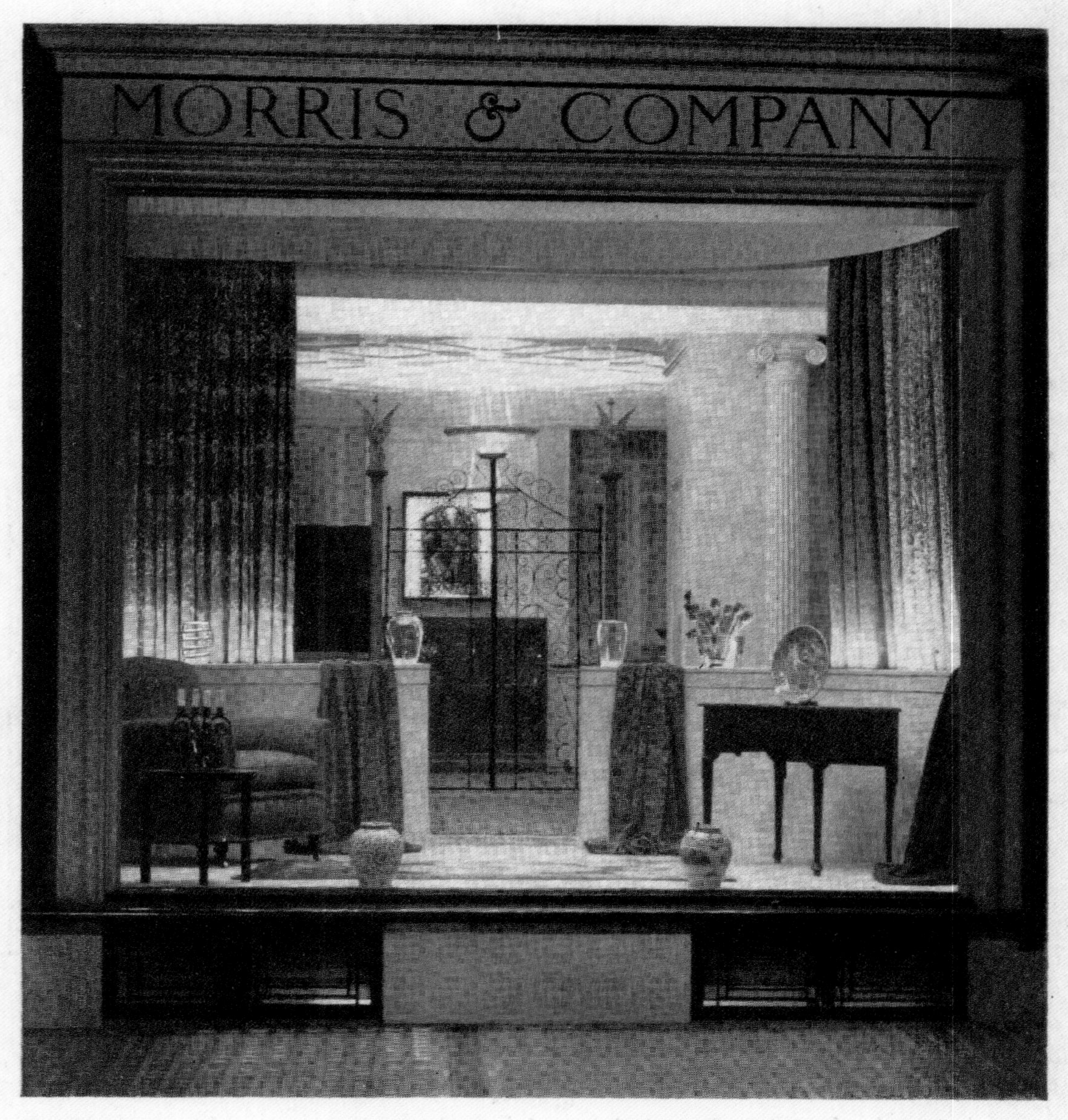

A FLOOD-LIT VIEW
OF THE NEW WINDOW
at
MORRIS and COMPANY
ART-WORKERS LTD.
17, ST. GEORGE STREET, HANOVER SQUARE, LONDON, W.1
Telephones : Mayfair 1664, 1665. Lift to all floors.

(now in The Huntington William Morris Collection) for Booth's 1925 order of two large tapestries for Christ Church, Bloomfield Hills, on themes from the Old and New Testaments, shows a continued reliance on Burne-Jones and Morris. The commission kept the tapestry works open and the attendant publicity attracted other clients.

Antiques were included in an attempt to match the services of other high-end interior decorating firms, but they were hugely outnumbered by 'Morris' items, reproductions, and hackneyed re-productions of 'old' (often eighteenth-century) designs. The continued use of 'Morris' fabrics to upholster furniture unrelated to the 'Morris Movement' indicates that there was money to be made in customizing Georgian Revival and other pieces with fabrics designed in the last thirty years of the nineteenth century. The reproduction floral chintzes and the plain carpets and wallpapers sold in the 1920s and 1930s also contributed to a popular 'period' look that fused 'tradition' and 'modernity'.[71] In 1925, in another attempt to drum up business, the name of the Firm again changed, this time to Morris & Company Art-Workers Ltd. The name raises the possibility that Marillier was trying to refocus on the types of goods associated with the heyday of the Firm, and on the stained glass that had done so well in the previous seven years. It is difficult to know if 'Art-Workers' would have been read as somewhat old-fashioned in 1925 or whether – and the inclusion of 'modern' studio pottery figures and glass supports this – it was another attempt to present the Firm as more 'modern' and 'arty' than it was. In any event, little seemed to change. In the 1930s, the economic downturn led to further attempts by Morris & Company, together with countless others, to update its image. This can be seen in the modernity of the showroom [40]. There was no longer any visual link between the cover image of the Firm's catalogues and 'Morris'. But this, like the showroom, was a 'front': inside the catalogue the displays were as dull as most of the products must have appeared to an inter-war customer. Neither the cover nor the inclusion inside of the odd 'modern' item for sale should blind one to the fact that the Firm continued to rely on 'heritage' pieces, on the one hand, and 'period' reproductions on the other. This mix, epitomized by the juxtaposition of the 'famous Morris "Acanthus" cotton damask' with a modern-style oak bookcase in the manner of Gordon Russell[72] appealed to the blending of traditionalism and modernity then popular in many parts of Europe and the United States. This eclecticism is seen in an elegant armchair that expressed Regency and Vienna Secession design traditions in a modern manner, as well as in a boring neo-Georgian bookcase and telephone table. The latter items probably would have made William Morris's blood boil; the lifeless reproduction of a seventeenth-century chair prominently featured in the catalogue certainly would have.

40 Morris & Company
Shop front
From an untitled Morris & Company catalogue, between 1925 and 1940

Dearle's death in 1932 and Marillier's stress-related breakdown in 1935 marked the beginning of the end. In 1940, when a second world war commandeered men and materials, the company that had once attracted attention all over the world, and still sold a selection of items designed by the man whose name it bore until the end, closed its doors. Just over a decade later, William Morris's designs and ideas began to be 'rediscovered' and so began the revival of interest in Morris and the Firm that continues today.

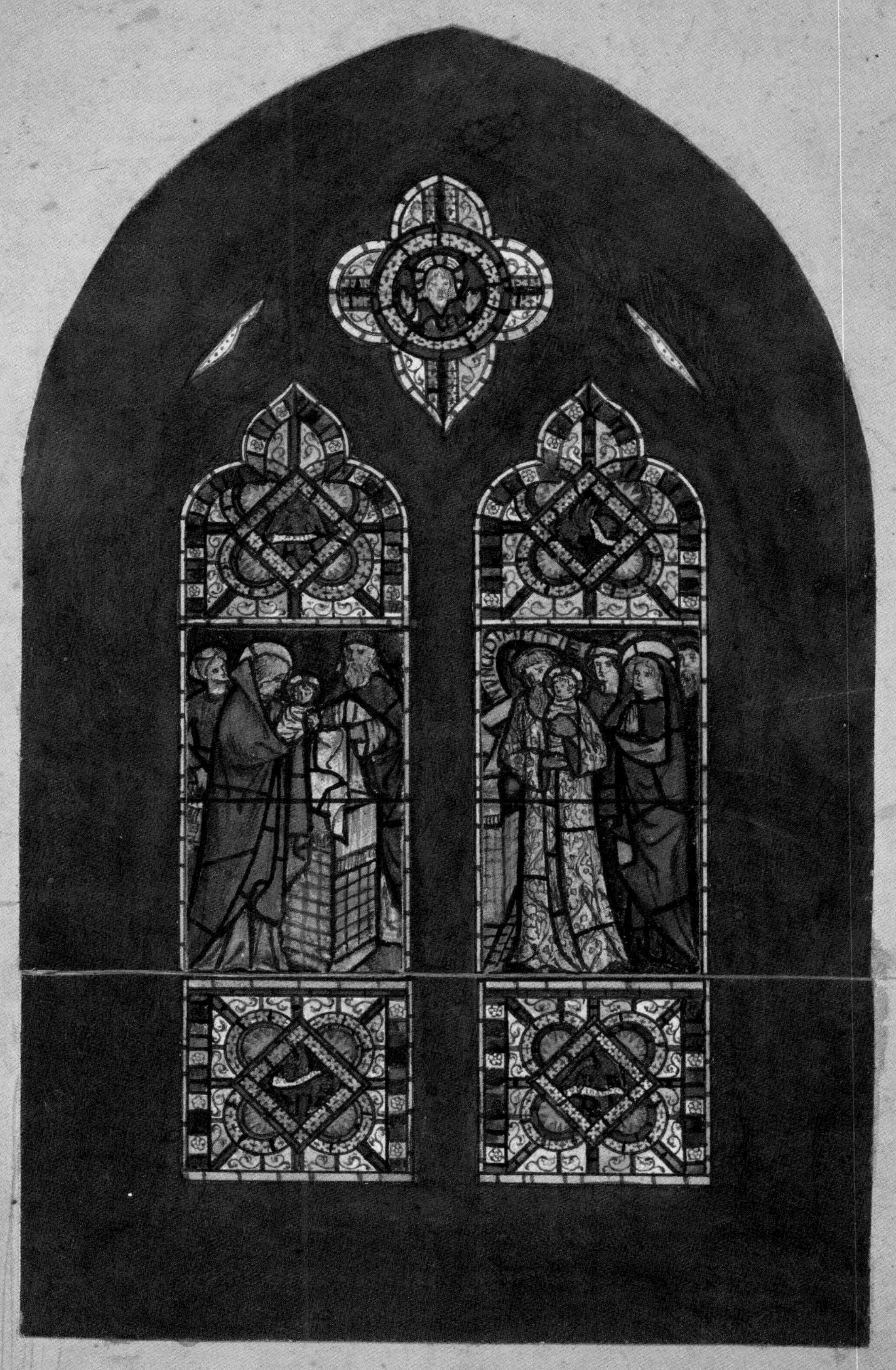
1" scale
Design for Stained Glass for E. window of Aisl
Tachbrooke Ch:
Morris, Marshall, Faulkner & Co 8 Red Lion

STAINED GLASS & CHURCH DECORATION

DIANE WAGGONER

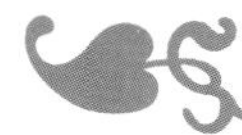

When Morris, Marshall, Faulkner & Company began designing and producing stained glass in the 1860s they found a sympathetic environment and a flourishing market for the craft. The growth of the British population, as well as the Gothic Revival and the Anglican High Church movement, led to an explosion of church building and restoration between the 1840s and 1870s. These factors also sparked a renewed interest in church decoration, particularly stained glass, which had received little attention since the medieval period. Demand rose, reaching a peak around 1870, and then gradually declined to the 1930s.[1] The number of windows the Firm designed throughout its life mirrors this trend. Hand in hand with the increase in commissions went an interest in the early techniques of stained glass production. Most of what had been produced since the medieval period consisted of clear glass painted with enamel. By the 1850s, the architect A. W. N. Pugin had revived interest in medieval-style coloured glass, and the antiquarian Charles Winston had rediscovered medieval techniques to produce 'pot-metal' glass, which was coloured throughout rather than just on the surface. In the mid-nineteenth century stained glass firms employed this thick, coloured glass in a medieval-inspired style, and the Firm was no exception.

From the Firm's inception, Morris took control of production and aimed to use the rich, subtle tones characteristic of medieval stained glass. 'The qualities needed in the design', he wrote, 'are beauty and character of outline; exquisite, clear, precise drawing of incident, such especially as the folds of drapery. ... Whatever key of colour may be chosen, the colour should always be clear, bright, and emphatic.'[2] His greatest strength was as a colourist. George Wardle, the firm's second manager (brother of Thomas Wardle, the dyer), recalled that 'Of course all the quality of what was called "Morris glass" was due to the interpretation Morris gave to the designs he received & to the practical use of colour, which in his hands gave results no other glass painters could imitate, though ... the same raw materials were at the disposal of all of them.'[3] The Firm did have competition from several other British firms, however, such as the prosperous James Powell & Sons (founded 1834) or Clayton & Bell (founded 1855), who tended to use even brighter, primary colours compared to the deeper, tonal colours employed by Morris.

Many of the earliest stained glass commissions are recorded in the Firm's Minute Book (1862–74), and the later commissions in the 'Catalogue of Designs used for Windows Executed' (1876–1916) and its continuation

41 William Morris for Morris, Marshall, Faulkner & Company

The Baptism of Christ and Presentation in the Temple, sketch design for the east window of an aisle at St Chad's, Bishop's Tachbrook, Warwickshire, 1863

Watercolour and ink, $13\frac{3}{8}$ x $9\frac{7}{8}$ (34 x 25.1)

42 William Morris for Morris, Marshall, Faulkner & Company

St Mary Magdalene, cartoon for a window at All Saints, Langton Green, Kent, *c.* 1862

Wash, graphite, and ink, 48 x 17¼ (121.9 x 43.8)

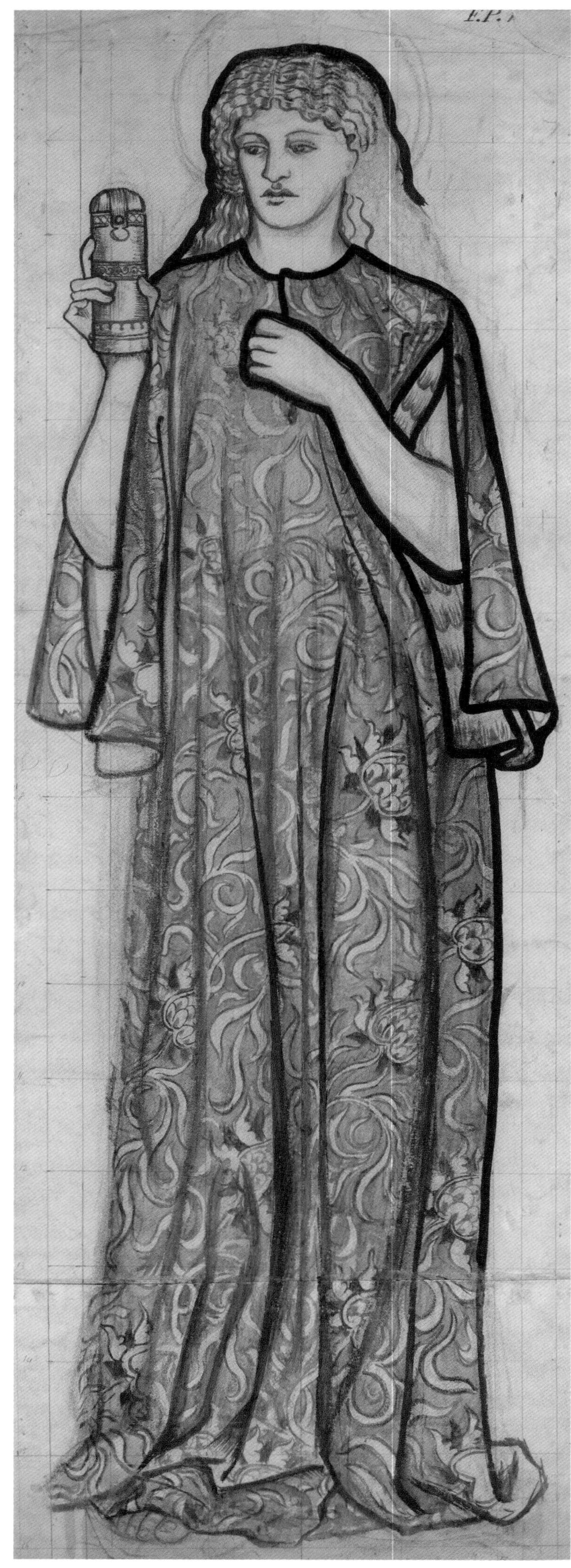

(1916–40), all in The Huntington's collection. Over one thousand of the Firm's watercolour designs are also preserved at The Huntington. Some of these drawings are by the original members of the Firm but the majority were executed by workmen in the Firm's studio. The Minute Book makes clear that the earliest designs were apportioned out among the partners – Brown, Rossetti, Burne-Jones, Webb, Morris, and even Marshall. George Campfield, an experienced glass painter, was hired as the foreman as early as 1861 and remained with the Firm throughout Morris's lifetime. Morris never manufactured his own glass: coloured glass was supplied by Powell & Sons, who had collaborated with Winston in his experiments and who produced high-quality pot-metal glass.[4] To begin, the Firm set up a kiln in the basement of 8 Red Lion Square for firing glass for the windows, and their first commissions came largely from the members' circle of acquaintances, which included the Gothic Revival architects George Edmund Street (with whom Morris had trained), George Gilbert Scott and George Frederick Bodley. (The Firm also designed a few secular windows for domestic settings: see p. 58.)

One of Morris's earliest designs for stained glass is the 1863 single-light window of St Mary Magdalene for the Gothic Revival church of All Saints, Langton Green, Kent, which had recently been built by Scott [42]. Morris worked with the figure only at this early stage in his career; later he re-used his figures, and produced new designs only for the patterned backgrounds. For this commission, the saint has the facial features and thick, wavy hair of Morris's wife, Jane [19], whom he had married in 1859, and she may well have served as his

Overleaf
43 Designed by William Morris, Edward Burne-Jones, Dante Gabriel Rossetti, Ford Madox Brown and Philip Webb for Morris, Marshall, Faulkner & Company

Christ with saints and prophets, first sketch design for the east window of St Peter's, Bradford, Yorkshire, *c.* 1864

Watercolour and ink, 14⅞ x 10¼ (37.8 x 26)

Overleaf
44 Designed by William Morris, Edward Burne-Jones, Dante Gabriel Rossetti, Ford Madox Brown and Philip Webb for Morris, Marshall, Faulkner & Company

Christ with saints and prophets, second sketch design for the east window of St Peter's, Bradford, Yorkshire, *c.* 1864

Watercolour and ink, 14⅞ x 9⅛ (37.8 x 23.2)

model. Jane had modelled for Morris's only extant painting, *La Belle Iseult* (1858, Tate Britain, London), and she also had sat for Rossetti (and would continue to do so in later years). The Mary Magdalene figure type and facial features were often to appear in Morris's work from these years, as in a series of hanging embroideries that he designed for Red House, each depicting a legendary woman in a patterned dress. In Morris's cartoon of Mary Magdalene his interest in textiles and in pattern is already evident in the flowing folds of the drapery as they fall over the figure. In the window itself, the saint appears against a ruby-red, mosaic-like background with a Gothic architectural canopy above. This was a medieval motif that appeared in a number of commissions for Scott and was favoured by Philip Webb, who was responsible for much of the patternwork of the Firm's stained glass in the 1860s.

Another early commission designed by Morris in the same year was for two windows depicting the Baptism of Christ and the Presentation in the Temple at St Chad's, Bishop's Tachbrook, Warwickshire, a medieval church with Victorian additions. The Minute Book entry indicates that the watercolour illustrated [41] is by Morris himself: 'Small drawings for E window of aisle of Tachbrooke Ch: assigned to Morris for 15/- each and the corresponding cartoons for 2£ 5/-.'[5] Morris's design gives equal weight to the decorative panels above and below the main narrative scheme and to the tracery lights. The geometric patterns (changed slightly in the window itself), jewel tones, and small crowded figure composition echo medieval designs. The patterns and arrangement were probably the work of Webb.

Many of the Firm's earliest multiple-light windows were collaborative efforts, with the different members designing the various figures and Morris and Webb supplying the pattern-work and overall composition. One of the Firm's first large-scale commissions was for the east window of the medieval parish church (now cathedral) in Bradford, Yorkshire. Morris, Burne-Jones, Brown, Webb and Rossetti all provided either figures or background details for the subject, Christ with saints and prophets. This ambitious composition contained fourteen main lights and fifty-four lights in the tracery above. The Minute Book documents the distribution of the figures to each member of the Firm. The Huntington's collection contains two overall designs for this window as well as a number of the figure studies that Morris drew upon or worked up while preparing the seven saints and prophets and twelve angels he designed [43, 44, 46]. Webb was responsible for the quarries (the small-scale squares or diamonds ornamented with plant or geometric motifs and repeated as the background for figures or narrative scenes) and borders. The first design [43] on a dark background is the more completed drawing, with all the figures, border designs, and tracery panels fully coloured. The second and final version [44] is inscribed 'Corrected for Bradford' and only partially colours in the decorative borders and the tracery panels. The figures, however, are fully coloured and have all been altered from the earlier simpler version, becoming more complex with layers of multi-coloured drapery. The quarries have diagonal bands containing the names of the saints and prophets as well as Morris's favourite floral motif of a clump of flowers (as in one of his earliest designs, the embroidered curtain for Red House

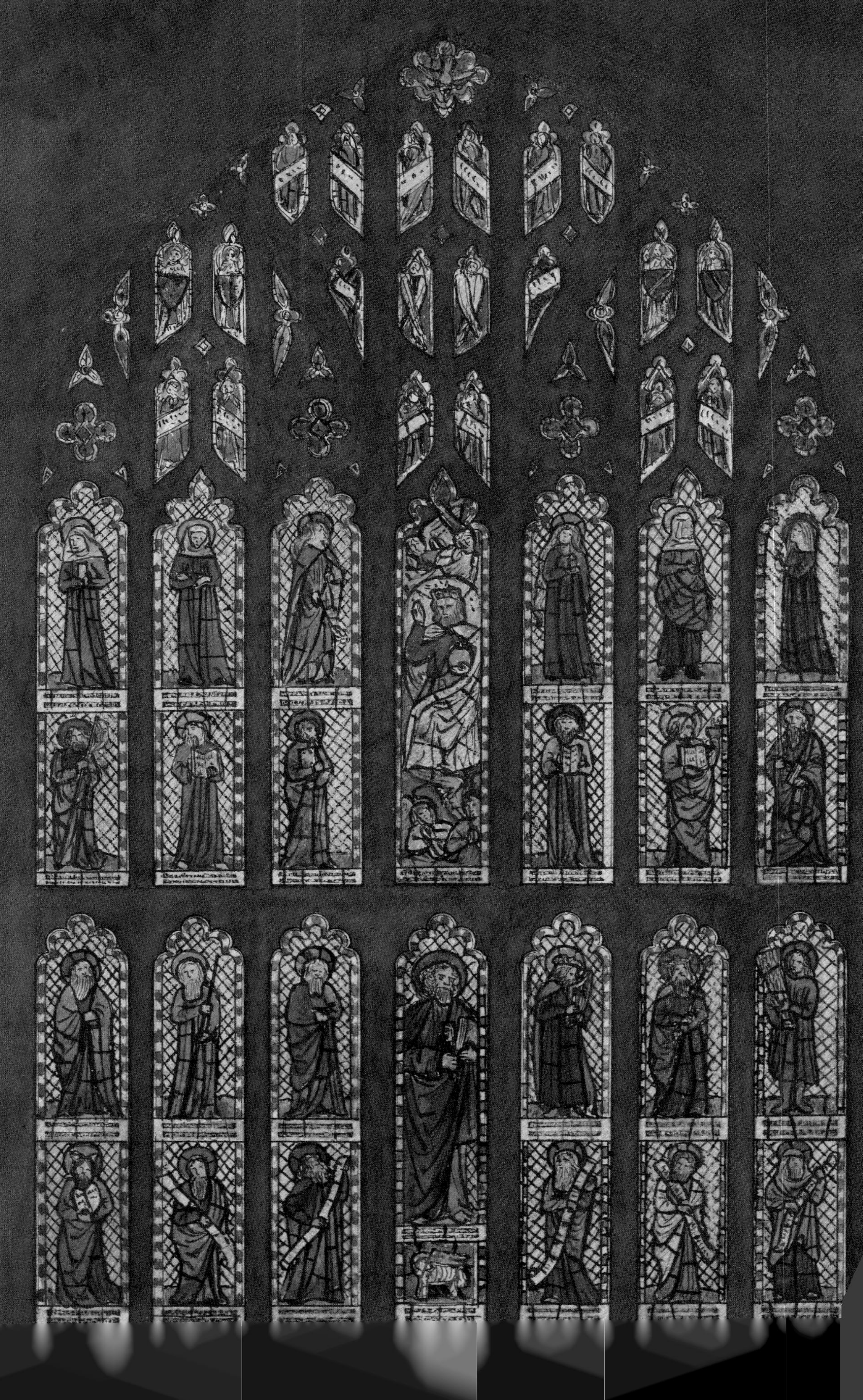

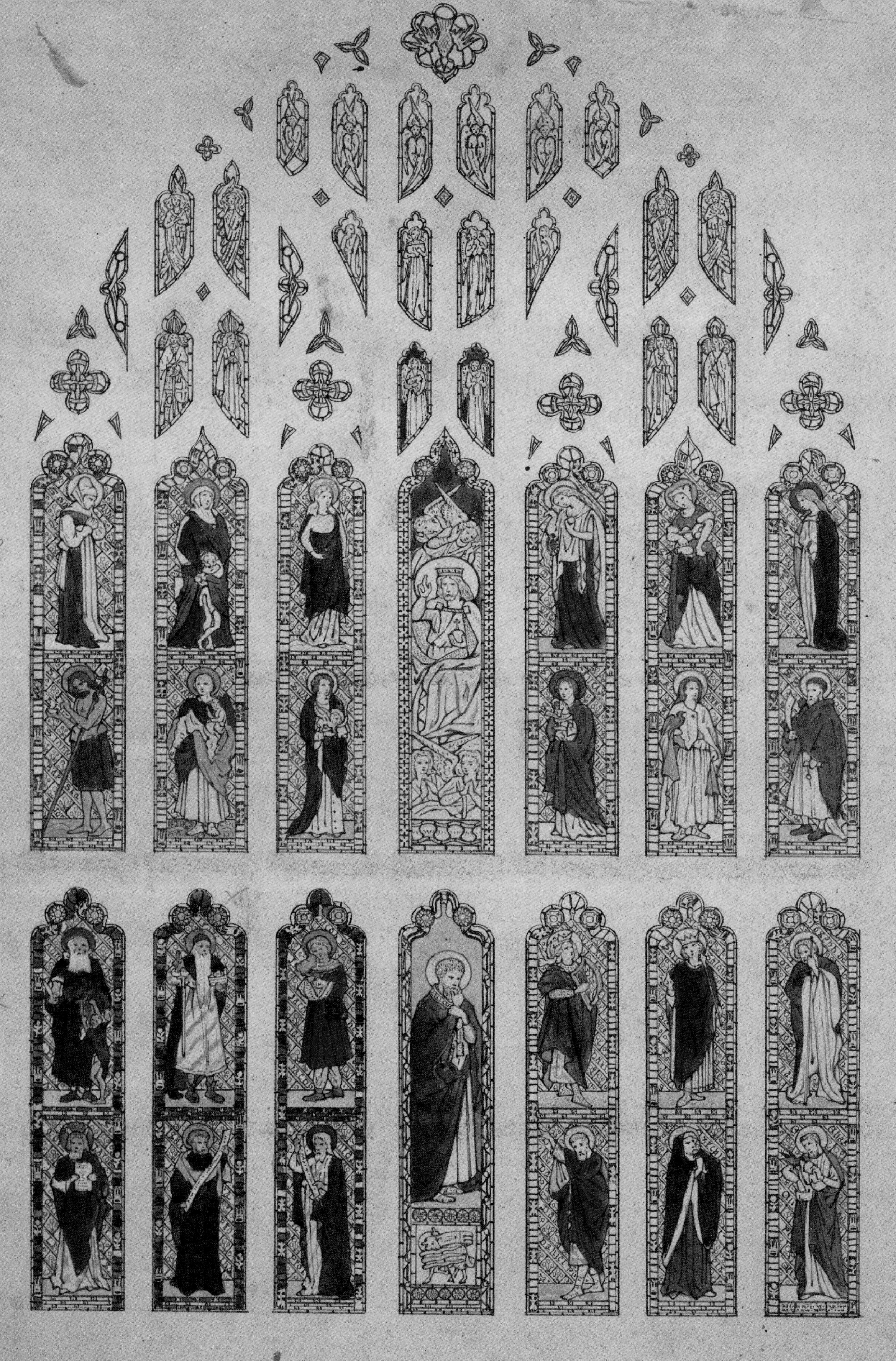

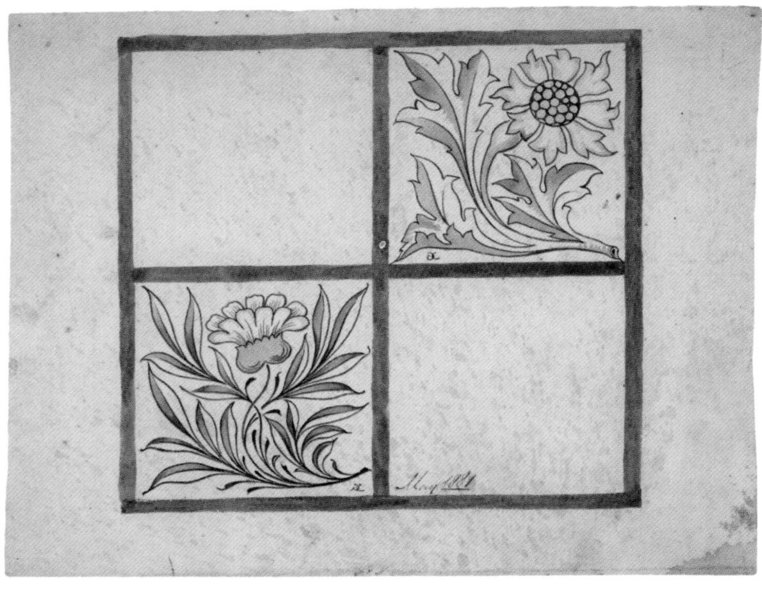

45 George Campfield for Morris & Company

Design for stained glass quarries, 1881

Watercolour and ink, 8⅝ x 11¼ (21.9 x 28.6)

46 William Morris for Morris, Marshall, Faulkner & Company

Mary of Bethany, figure drawing used in the Bradford commission, *c.* 1862

Graphite and wash, 22¼ x 14⅛ (56.5 x 35.9)

In the overall design (ill. 44) Mary appears top right.

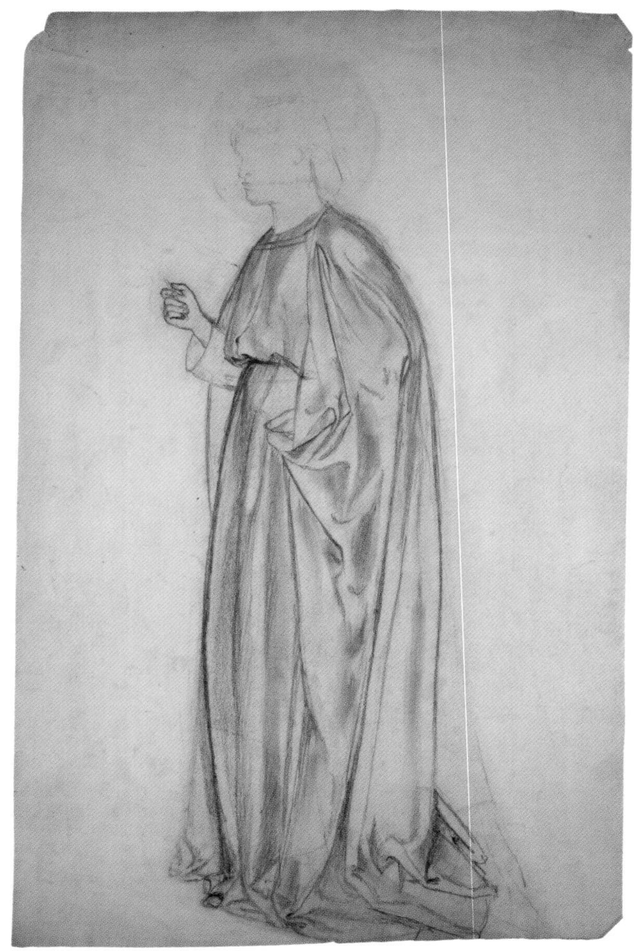

from the early 1860s [20]). Webb's borders, too, have blue added to the red and clear alternating rectangles of glass. The interplay of clear quarries with coloured glass in bold, geometric patterns was typical of Webb's work and provided the Firm's earliest recognizable style.

Quarries were produced by painting on clear glass with silver stain, which when fired would turn various shades of yellow and amber. They were a feature of backgrounds in medieval glass, and they also appear in nineteenth-century glass by other companies. For the Firm, Webb and Morris designed the earliest, but later other members of the stained glass workshop also produced designs. While several in The Huntington's collection are anonymous, one drawing bears the initials of George Campfield, and shows the influence of Morris's floral patterns in the delicate, curling leaves [45].[6]

The window designed by Burne-Jones and Webb in 1867 for St Wilfrid's Church, Haywards Heath, Sussex [47] shows the Firm continuing to work in the same style throughout the 1860s. Burne-Jones provided the figures, while Webb designed the layout and patternwork. Like the Bradford window, this one employs sets of colourful figures against clear floral quarries, outlined by Webb's characteristic geometric jewel-tone borders. Webb exploited the horizontal lines of the leading by dividing the design of the window into sections, alternating single figures, quarry sections and smaller-scale narrative panels depicting the Adoration of the Magi, the Nativity and the Adoration of the Shepherds. St Wilfrid's was a newly built Victorian Gothic church, designed by Bodley, whose preference for the placement of the figure against clear, palely ornamented quarries is evident here.[7]

47 Designed by Edward Burne-Jones and Philip Webb for Morris, Marshall, Faulkner & Company

Mary Virgin, Christ on the Cross, St John, Adoration of the Magi, Nativity, Adoration of the Shepherds, Angel of the Annunciation, Dove descending and Virgin Annunciate, sketch design for the east window of St Wilfrid's, Haywards Heath, Sussex, 1867

Watercolour and ink, 12¼ x 6 (31.1 x 15.2)

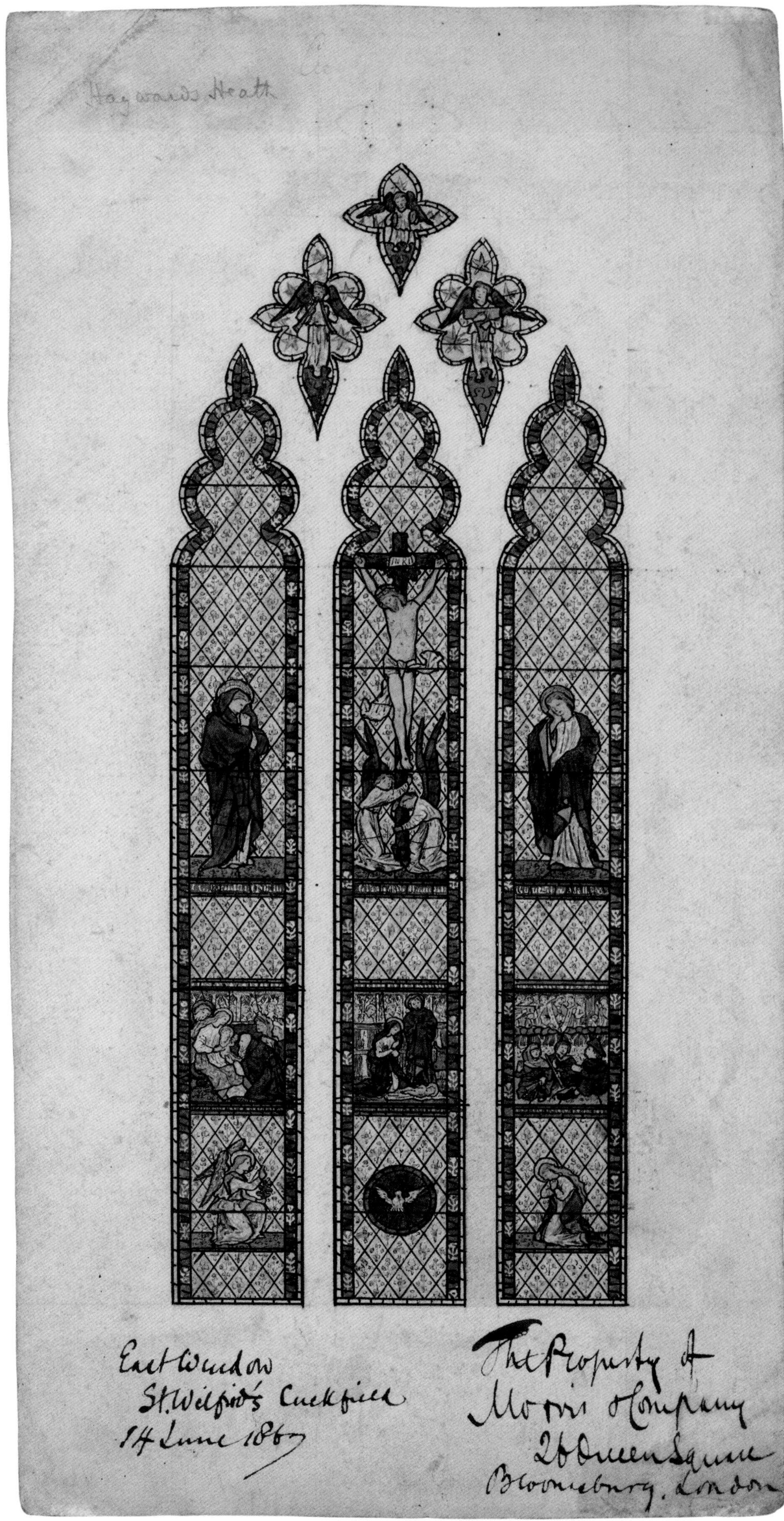

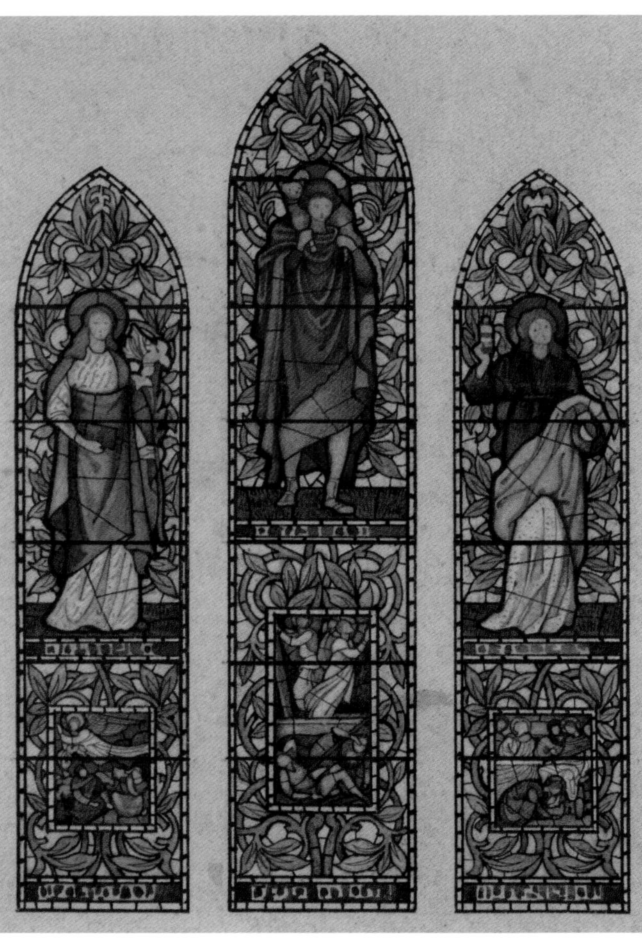

48 Designed by William Morris and Edward Burne-Jones for Morris & Company

Mary Virgin, the Good Shepherd and St Mary Magdalene, sketch design for the east window of Whitelands Training College Chapel, Chelsea, London (later reinstalled at West Hill, Putney, London), *c.* 1886

Watercolour and ink, full sheet 12 x 9 (30.5 x 22.9)

49 Designed by Edward Burne-Jones and J. H. Dearle for Morris & Company

Mary Virgin, Christ on the Cross, St John and angels, sketch design for the east window of St Mary the Virgin, Acocks Green, Birmingham, Warwickshire, *c.* 1895

Watercolour and ink, full sheet 13⅞ x 10 (35.2 x 25.4)

By 1875, after the reorganization of the Firm as Morris & Company, Burne-Jones had become its chief figure designer with Morris providing the colour and background details.[8] While early Morris, Marshall, Faulkner & Company windows had been notable for their geometric simplicity and medievalism, now they departed from medieval precedent. The Firm's distinctive middle-period style combined Burne-Jones's dynamic figure compositions and Morris's skill in pattern and colour, often using foliate backgrounds that echoed his wallpaper and textile designs. Morris eventually delegated many of the backgrounds to the workmen in the glass-painter's studio, but he chose the colours and reviewed the final window before sending it to the client. Wardle recalled how difficult this was at Queen Square: 'Mr. Morris showed how quick was his perception and how tenacious the memory. In passing all the parts of a large window one by one before the light, he never lost sight of the general tone of the colour or of the relation of this part & that to each other.'[9] When the Firm moved to Merton Abbey, the glass-painting workshop was spacious enough for each window to be more fully assembled in front of the light for Morris to observe it. Although many commissions for the Firm had been for medieval churches, like Bradford Cathedral, in 1877 Morris's involvement with the Society for the Protection of Ancient Buildings led him to make the bold decision that the Firm would no longer undertake work to restore or replace windows in historic buildings. From this time on, Morris & Company windows would not be designed for any medieval churches.

One commission for a modern building was for the chapel at Whitelands Training College in Chelsea, London, in 1886. Burne-Jones and Morris's design depicts three figures against a foliage background [48]. The Virgin Mary, by Burne-Jones, is in fact the same figure that had been first designed for Bradford [44], and the Mary Magdalene and Good Shepherd (replaced with Salvator Mundi in the window itself), by Morris and Burne-Jones respectively, had also both been created for other commissions. The figures are set above rectangular narrative panels in individual lights against green scrolling foliage on a white background, a colour scheme that departs from the primary colours of the Firm's earlier stained glass. Whitelands Training College, a school for women teachers, was associated with John Ruskin, whose ideas on art had so influenced Morris and his friends in the 1850s. Ruskin made the initial contact for the commission with Burne-Jones, writing: 'You will greatly help and exalt and comfort many good girls' hearts by accepting this petition of theirs, only please, for my sake, the lights mustn't be all brown and grisaille, but as opalescent as glass can be made.'[10] Burne-Jones replied to Ruskin's concern:

> on my bended knees, so to speak, have I besought him [Morris] to try experiments of glass, and make his own little bits, just as you say, the dark got by depths of

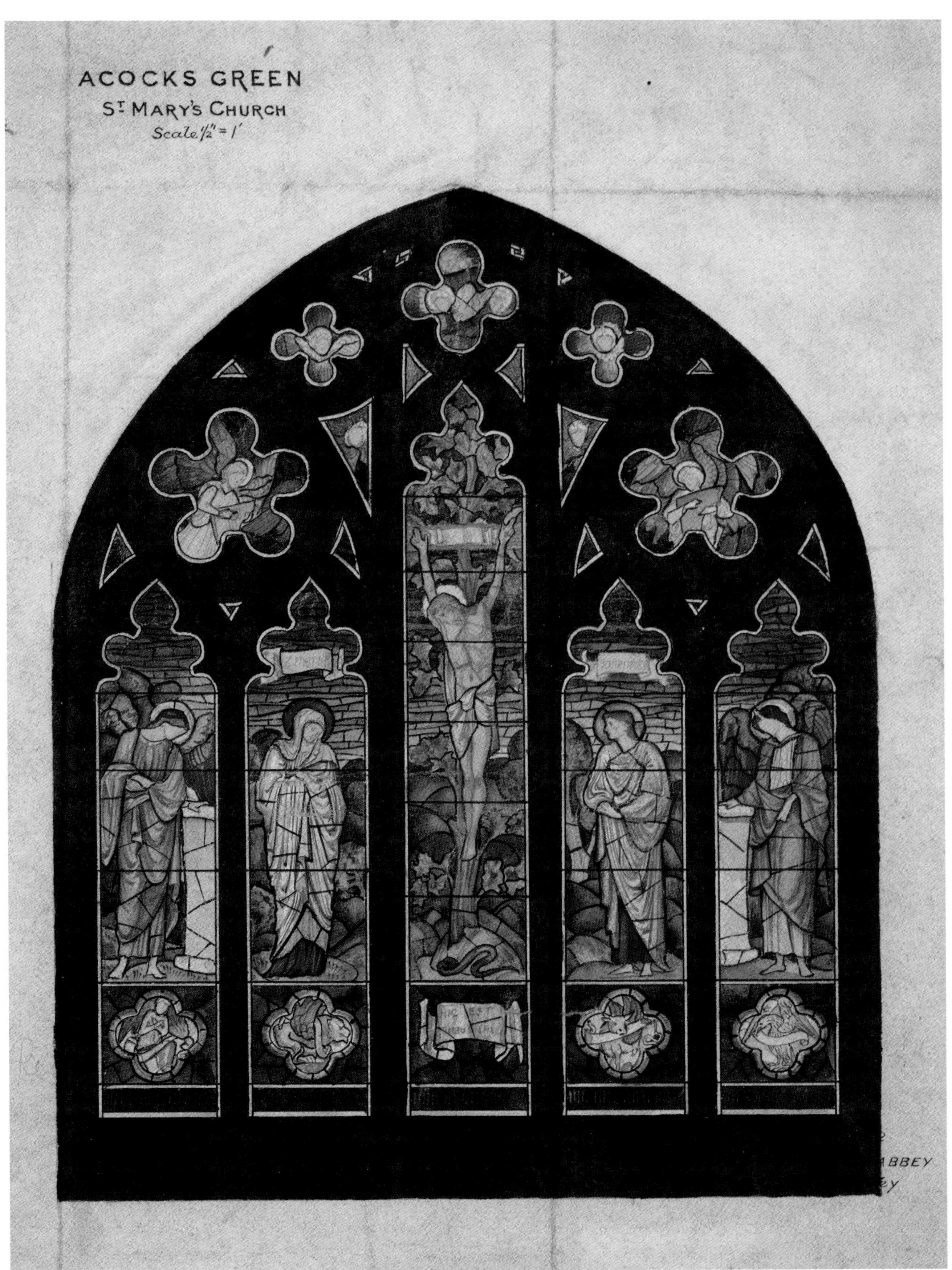
ACOCKS GREEN
ST MARY'S CHURCH
Scale ½" = 1'

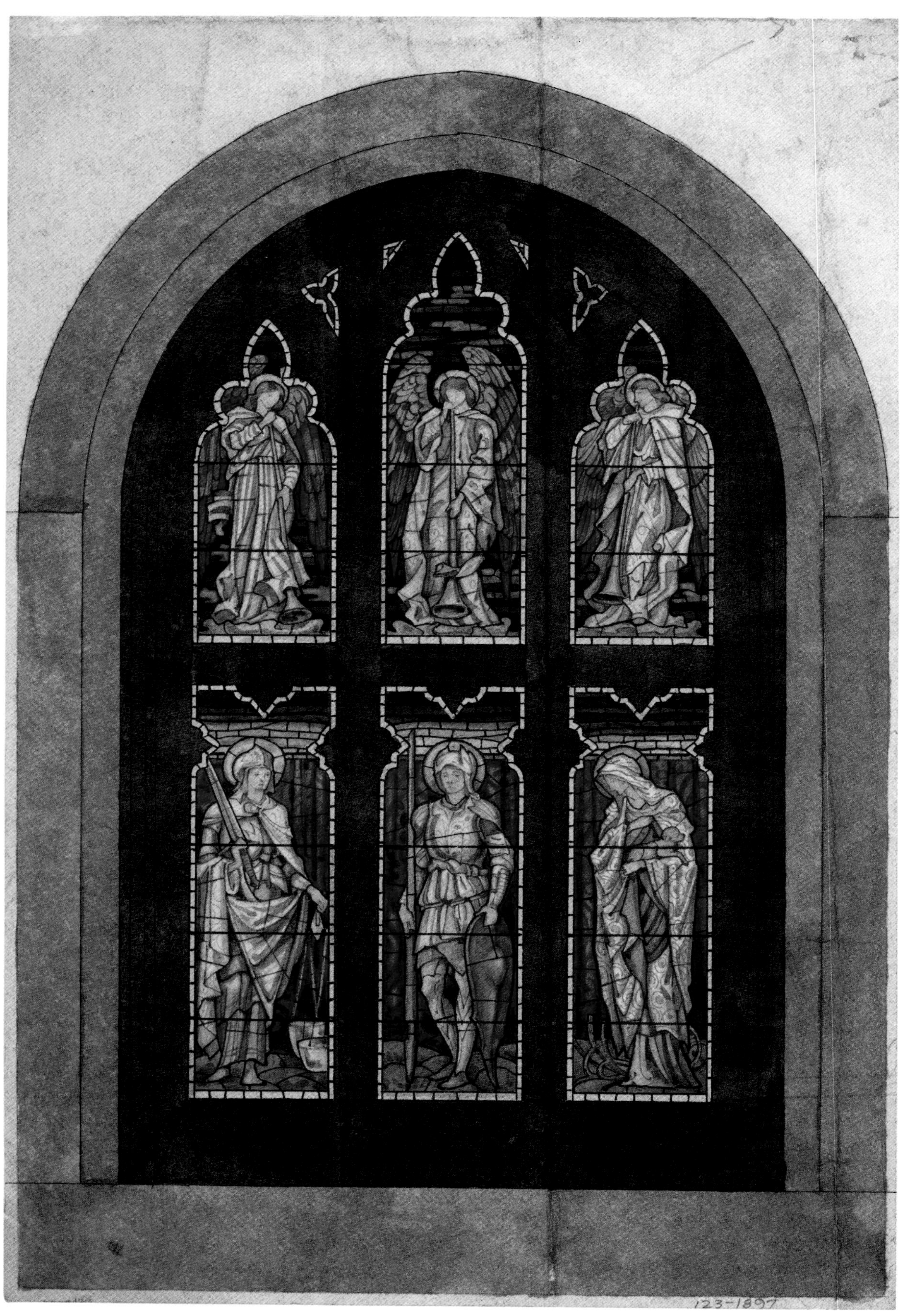
123-1897

50 Designed by Edward Burne-Jones and probably J. H. Dearle for Morris & Company

Justice, Courage, Humility, and angels, sketch design for the east window of St Mary the Virgin, Godmanchester, Huntingdonshire, *c.* 1897

Watercolour and ink, 9¼ x 6⅛ (23.5 x 15.6)

> itself – on bended knees with piteous words, and he won't. He gives many reasons against it, admirable as rhetorick. ... And I believe sometimes depth is got by doubling the glass, but I know that he often bewails his fate and dreams that in heaven glass will be much thicker; and I think so too.[11]

But Morris himself reassured Ruskin that

> all the glass is very thick: and that in some of the pot-metals, notably the blues the difference between one part of a sheet [and] another is very great. This variety is very useful to us in getting a jewel-like quality which is the chief charm of painted glass – When we *can* get it. You will understand that we rely almost entirely for our colour on the *actual colour of the glass*; and the more the design will enable us to break up the pieces, and the more mosaic-like it is, the better we like it.[12]

Ruskin was satisfied with Morris's promise that the Firm would produce windows that would, as Ruskin termed it, 'glow and glitter'.[13] They must have met with approval since the Firm continued to execute windows of female saints for the chapel over the next ten years.

Although the Firm's stained glass appeared in various styles throughout its history, the late windows, from the 1880s and 1890s, lost the geometric medievalism of the early decades and achieved brilliant depths of colour and dynamic, fluid compositions. Two commissions, an 1895 window for St Mary's, Acocks Green, Birmingham, Warwickshire [49] and an 1897 window for St Mary the Virgin at Godmanchester, Huntingdonshire [50], show the mastery of the medium achieved in the late style developed by Morris and Burne-Jones. Since the second of these two commissions occurred after Morris's death, it also shows the ability of the Firm's glass-painters and of J. H. Dearle, Morris's successor as artistic director, to continue to produce stained glass influenced by Morris's sense of colour even as they re-used and adapted Burne-Jones's figures. Dearle had begun designing backgrounds in the 1880s and would become the Firm's primary glass designer in the twentieth century. In the Acocks Green window, the figures stand in a continuous landscape across the five lights, with two angels and St Mary and St John positioned below Christ on the cross. The colour is balanced in masses – the red and white tracery panels, the variegated blue sky, the brown and green landscape, the red and white of the drapery of the figures, and the blue decorative panels below. Likewise, in the bottom tier of the Godmanchester window, the cream-coloured drapery of the figures stands out against the multi-hued solid backgrounds of blue sky, crimson drapery and green grass in a Renaissance-influenced composition. In the top tier, the leading is employed to create geometric patterns in the azure and light blue sky and to delineate the pink and red feathers of the angels' wings and set off the light ambers and creams of the angels' drapery. These windows glow and glitter with radiant, mosaic-like colour. Stained glass had been the Firm's first successful offering and, despite the changes in taste and style that occurred in the twentieth century, would remain a mainstay until its dissolution in 1940.

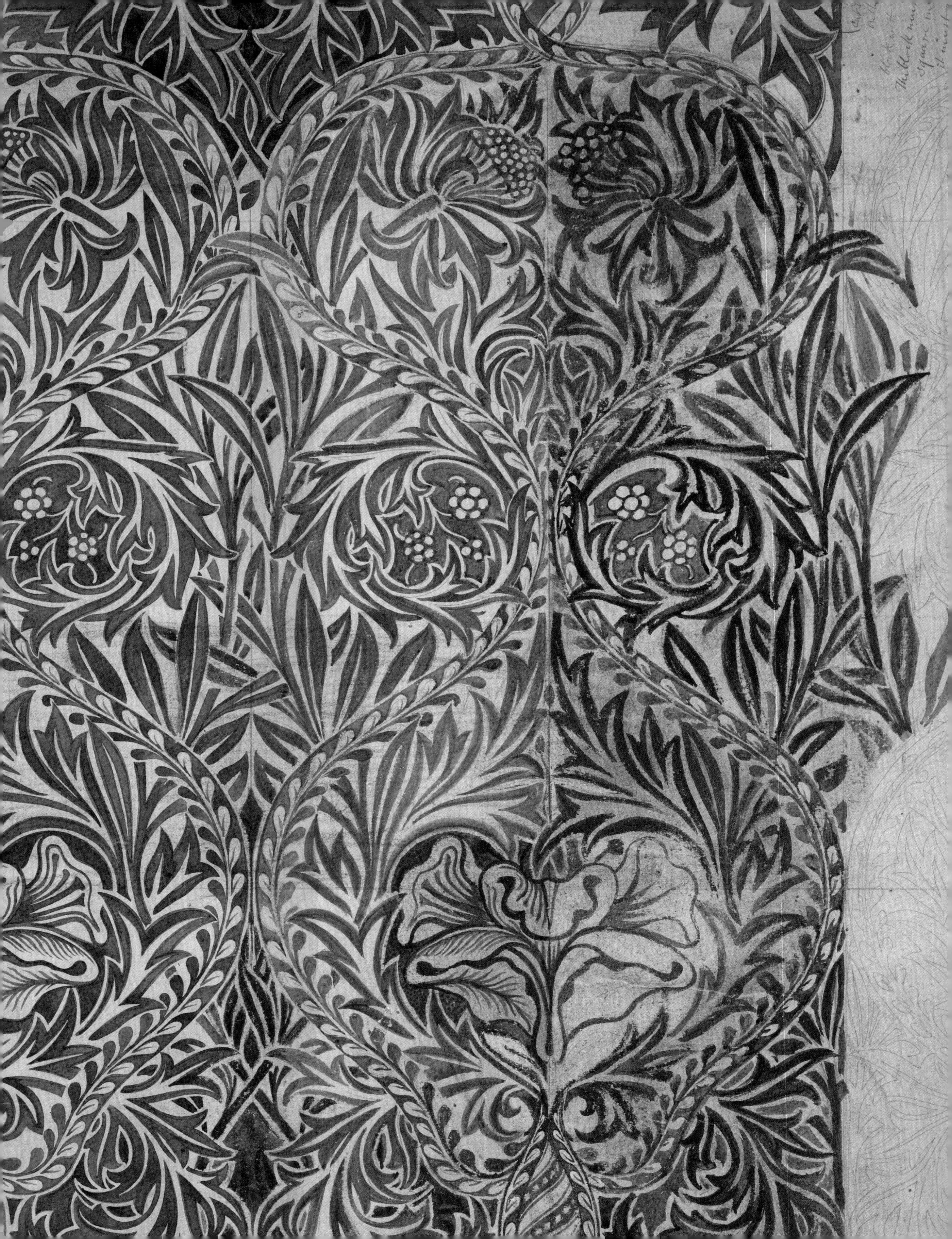

THE DECORATION *of* HOUSES

DIANE WAGGONER

In 1861 the fledgling Morris, Marshall, Faulkner & Company had announced its grand ambitions to provide a full range of decorative work for the interior, whether church or home. The Firm would be able 'to undertake any species of decoration, mural or otherwise, from pictures, properly so-called, down to the consideration of the smallest work susceptible of art beauty'.[1] Morris endeavoured to realize this goal and worked hard to build a successful business that could offer a full range of material to furnish the home. As stained glass orders slowly began to wane and the Firm reorganized under Morris's control in 1875, Morris flourished as a pattern designer. He learned how to produce domestic goods that satisfied him in terms of beauty and quality, first at Red Lion Square, then at Queen Square, and finally from 1881 at Merton Abbey. By 1883 he was able to claim that 'Almost all the designs we use for surface decoration, wallpapers, textiles, and the like, I design myself. I have had to learn the theory and to some extent the practice of weaving, dyeing and textile printing: all of which I must admit has given me and still gives me a great deal of enjoyment.'[2] In the late 1880s, however, Morris became increasingly involved in political activities and, although he did not relinquish control over the Firm's manufacturing, he eventually delegated most of the pattern designing to his assistant, John Henry Dearle.

Along with stained glass, one of the earliest media that Morris and his partners tackled was decorative tiles. The tile-painting was done by Morris himself, Charles Faulkner and the women of Morris's circle, in addition to the workmen employed by the Firm. Painted in enamels on tin-glazed earthenware blanks supplied by a Dutch manufacturer, the tiles were fired in the kiln used for stained glass in the basement of Red Lion Square and later at Queen Square. In 1862, Burne-Jones's account book with the Firm records a narrative tile scheme illustrating the story of Cinderella, for which he was paid £7.10*s*. The Firm produced three narrative tile-panels, *Beauty and the Beast*, *Sleeping Beauty* and *Cinderella*, for the recently built home of the painter Myles Birket Foster. The panel now at The Huntington [52] is the second, variant version of the Cinderella story, produced for an unknown client, and was probably painted by Charles Faulkner's sister Lucy. It was designed as an overmantel, to ornament what Morris called the 'chief object in the room', the fireplace.[3] The frame is original, decorated with daisies to match the daisy borders around each narrative scene.

51 William Morris for Morris & Company

Design for *Iris* printed cotton, *c.* 1876 (detail)

Watercolour and graphite, full sheet 26⅛ x 16¾ (66.4 x 42.5)

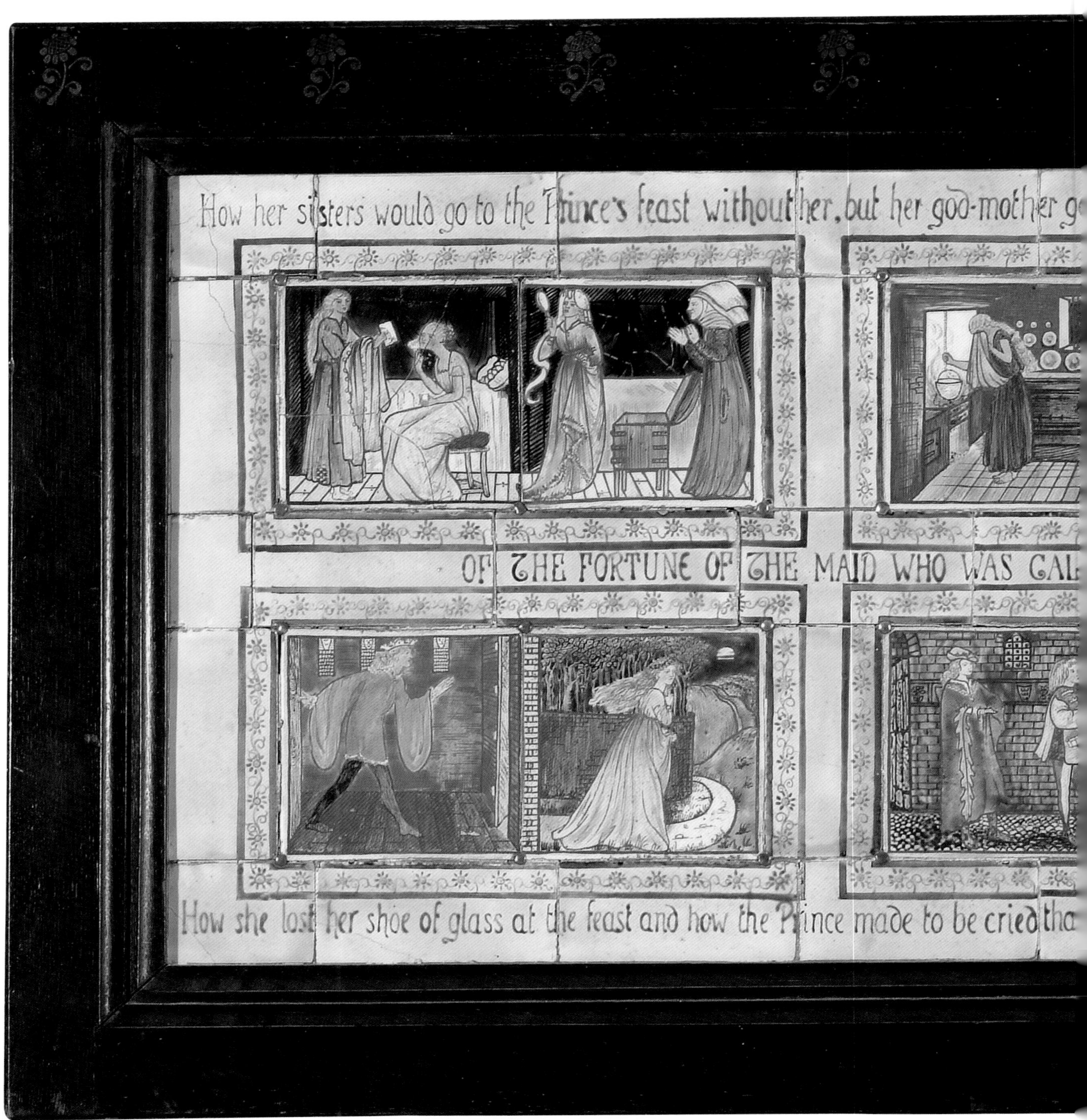
How her sisters would go to the Prince's feast without her, but her god-mother g
OF THE FORTUNE OF THE MAID WHO WAS CAL
How she lost her shoe of glass at the feast and how the Prince made to be cried tha

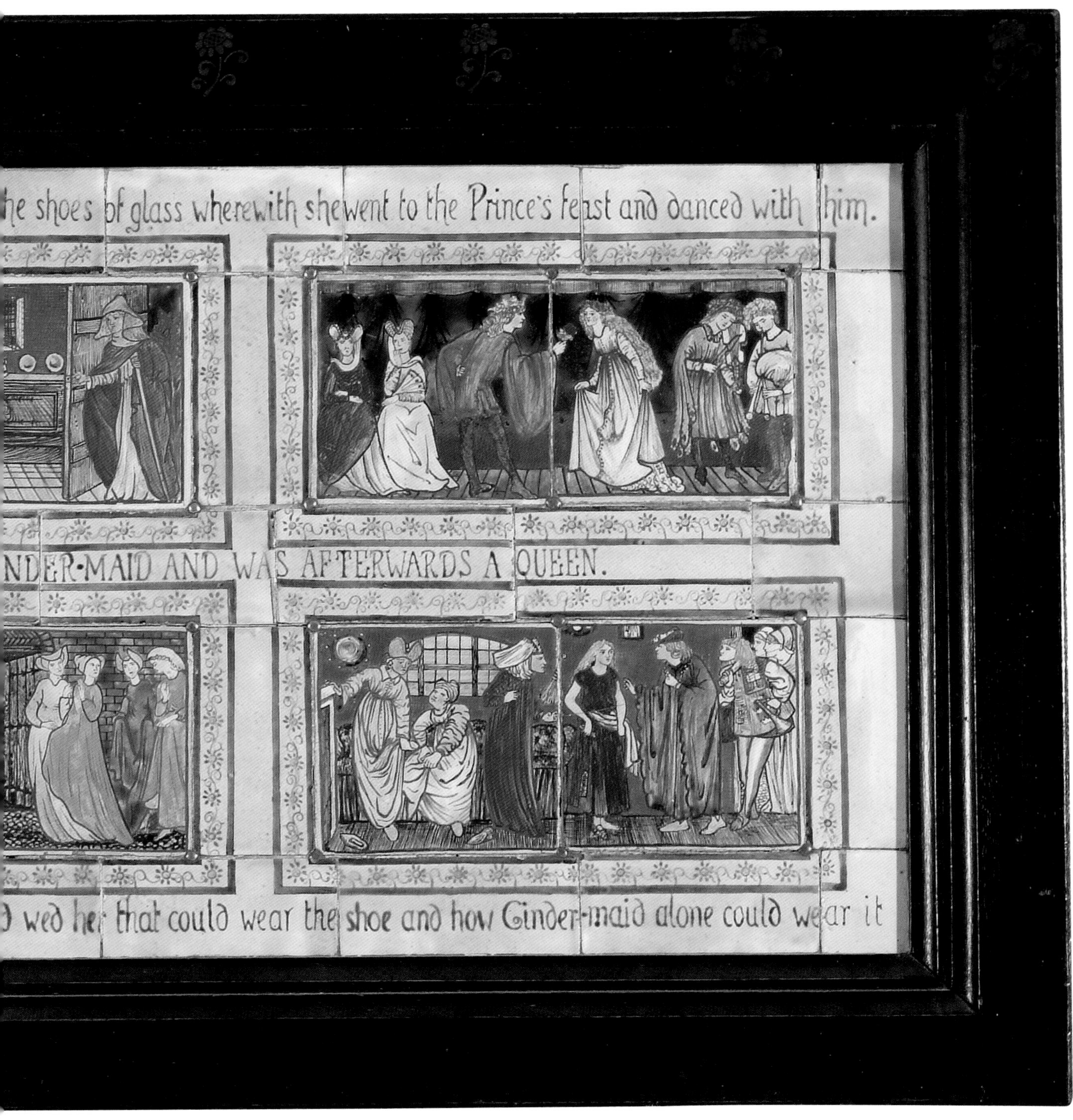

52 Designed by Edward Burne-Jones and probably painted by Lucy Faulkner for Morris, Marshall, Faulkner & Company

Cinderella tile panel, 1862–65

Overglaze polychrome decoration on tin-glazed Dutch earthenware blanks in ebonized oak frame, $28\frac{1}{2}$ x $55\frac{3}{4}$ x $2\frac{3}{8}$ (71.8 x 141.6 x 6)

53 William Morris
for Morris, Marshall,
Faulkner & Company

Design for embroidery,
1865–70

Graphite and ink,
14¼ x 9¼ (36.2 x 23.5)

The quaint simplicity of the tiles was characteristic of the Firm's early decorative ceramics. Morris & Company continued to produce tiles at Queen Square but by the 1880s Morris's friend William De Morgan was supplying them. De Morgan, whose designs were inspired by Middle Eastern decorative patterns, had founded his own tile works in 1869 [22].[4]

Embroidery was also an early endeavour, and it was one of the first crafts that Morris himself mastered. Before the Firm was founded Morris taught himself how to embroider, even picking apart medieval examples to learn how the stitching was done. His drawing for an unspecified embroidery of leaves with a sunflower [53], which probably dates from between 1865 and 1870 when the Firm had moved to Queen Square, is inscribed 'Lines for the direction / of the stitches'. He has shaded in some of the leaves to show how the stitches should be applied: familiar with the visual and tactile qualities of embroidery from his own hardwon experience, Morris knew that the direction of the stitches could enhance the beauty of the design. His correspondence with the accomplished embroiderer Catherine Holiday, which forms part of The Huntington's Morris collection, demonstrates his similar regard for the quality and colour of the wool and silk yarns used for embroidery.

'Whatever you have in your rooms think first of the walls, for they are that which makes your house and home', advocated Morris in an 1877 lecture.[5] After a few of the Firm's early wallpapers and textiles had been printed in the 1870s, Morris began in earnest to design repeating patterns for use as wall decoration, curtains and upholstery. He often drew upon native British plants and flowers and his patterns ranged in colour and scale from quiet to bold and brilliant, but his designs were always suited to the medium for which they were intended, whether laid flat on the wall or hung in folds. Morris's wallpapers were produced by traditional hand-printing with woodblocks [29], for which he always used an outside company. Until the Firm moved to Merton Abbey, Morris also worked with other firms to colour embroidery yarns and to produce woven and printed textiles to his exacting standards. He eschewed the new technique of using engraved rollers to print textiles, which was widely adopted in commercial manufacturing by the mid-nineteenth century, because he believed the quality of the colour suffered in comparison with the traditional technique of block-printing.

Morris also became disenchanted with the chemical dyes that had come into use in the first half of the century and in the 1870s he was preoccupied with rediscovering and reviving the art of dyeing with natural dyestuffs. In 1875 he started a collaboration with Thomas Wardle, the owner of a hand-dyeing and printing works in Leek, Staffordshire (and brother of George Wardle, the Firm's second manager). Morris began designing for printed cottons, or chintzes, from around 1876; *Iris* [51] was one of fourteen patterns that Wardle printed for Morris & Company. By this time, Morris was studying historic textiles at the South Kensington Museum, and he modelled this design in part on a German printed linen supposedly from the fifteenth century.[6] The pattern also shows the influence of contemporary Indian textiles, imported to Britain in large amounts in the latter half of the nineteenth century. In his drawing Morris coloured the *Iris*

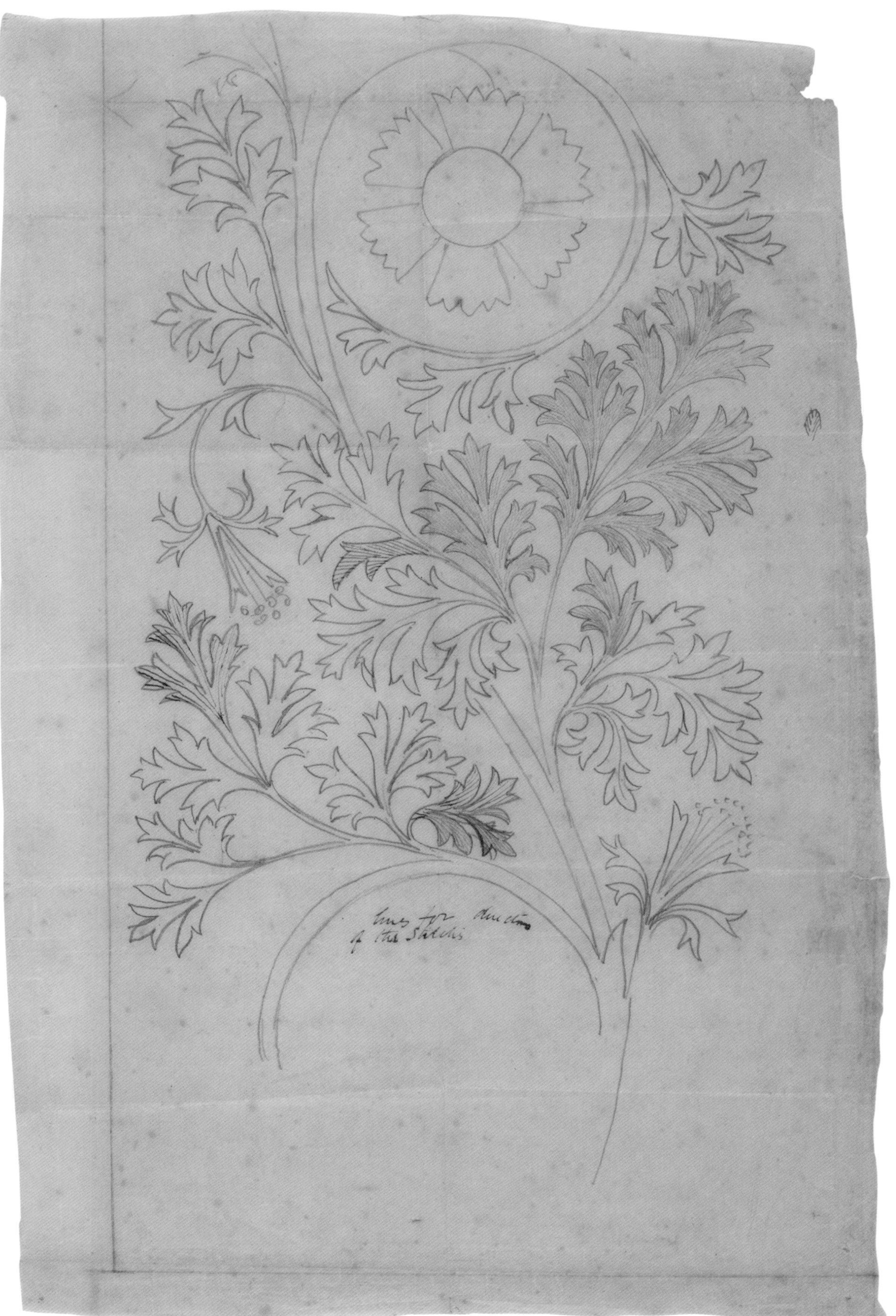
lines for direction
of the stitches

design in three different shades of brown, but the textile was printed in two colourways, a uniform madder red and also an olive. In a letter to Thomas Wardle, Morris, always attuned to the subtleties of colour, criticized a sample of the fabric printed in red as weak in colouring and added, 'I may say generally that this design wants rich colour & a lightish ground, good contrast in fact, to be successful.'[7]

With the Firm's move to Merton Abbey in 1881, Morris was able to assume full control of production by establishing his own dyeworks and printing facilities with the knowledge he had gained from working with Thomas Wardle. George Wardle saw Merton Abbey as the realization of Morris's potential as a colourist:

> The peacock blues, rusty reds and olive greens of that period [the 1870s] were not by any means Mr. Morris's ideal, but the best he could get done. As soon as he was able to set up his own dyehouse he turned at once to the frank full hues of the permanent dyestuffs – indigo blue, madder red, the yellow of weld etc. etc., & with these he produced the beautiful Hammersmith carpets and the Merton tapestry & chintzes.[8]

Snakeshead [54], a cotton in dusky blue, rusty red, pale yellow and white, is an example of a surface-printed textile first produced by Thomas Wardle in the 1870s; while *Lodden* [55], shown here in a colourway of light blue, pink, red, and green, was printed at Merton Abbey, using indigo-discharge and surface printing.

Morris prided himself on the colours that the Firm achieved from natural dyes in contrast to the new chemical dyes, 'the doom of cheap and nasty' as he called it, that produced 'hideous colours, crude, livid, and cheap'.[9] The Merton Abbey dye book records the recipes for printed textiles produced there from 1882, demonstrating Morris's passion for and success at reviving the use of vegetable dyes [56]. One of the Firm's signature offerings

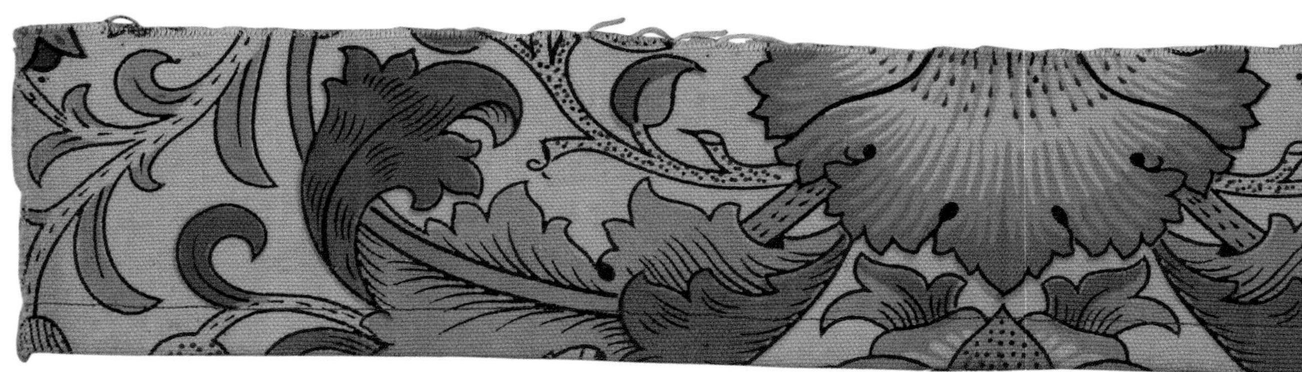

54 Designed by William Morris for Morris & Company

Snakeshead printed cotton, first issued 1876

Block-printed cotton, printed by Thomas Wardle, Leek, Staffordshire, 11⅜ x 38⅜ (28.9 x 97.5)

at Merton Abbey was fabric coloured by the traditional indigo-discharge method, which produced a rich blue and which Morris took great pains to revive [35, 55, 128]. Organized according to dye colour, the book, probably written by one of the workmen in the dyehouse, begins with red, from madder, progresses to yellows and buffs from weld, and then to indigo-discharge blues, and ends with mixed colours. Many of the recipes, accompanied by a sample of the fabric, show the intense amount of labour and time necessary to produce the fabrics. As Morris wrote in 1883, 'We are not getting on quite as fast we should with the printing; is very tough work getting everything in due order, the cloths seem to want so much doing to them before they can be printed & then so much doing to them after they are printed.'[10] The pages shown here are the dye recipes for *Blue and Yellow Kennet* and *Green Lea*. The *Green Lea* page also includes a swatch of medium-blue dyed with indigo. The pattern began with the fabric dyed this solid colour. The areas that required green were treated with a mordant. At the same time, the areas that did not require blue or green colour were bleached out and a mordant applied where yellow was required. The fabric was then re-dyed in yellow to turn the blue to green and to colour the mordant-treated bleached areas yellow. The page also includes the alternate method of steam-printing the yellow on the surface rather than dyeing it, but the writer notes that dyeing 'softens the whole and gives a warm effect ... and is thought best'. Morris always placed quality over efficiency.

In addition to printed textiles, Morris turned his energies to woven textiles. A number of outside firms produced these to his designs, and continued to do so even after the Firm set up hand-powered Jacquard looms, which used a series of punched cards to raise and lower the warp threads, at Queen Square and later Merton Abbey [36]. Dearle eventually began designing woven textiles as well: his working drawing for *Helena*, *c.* 1890 [57], is

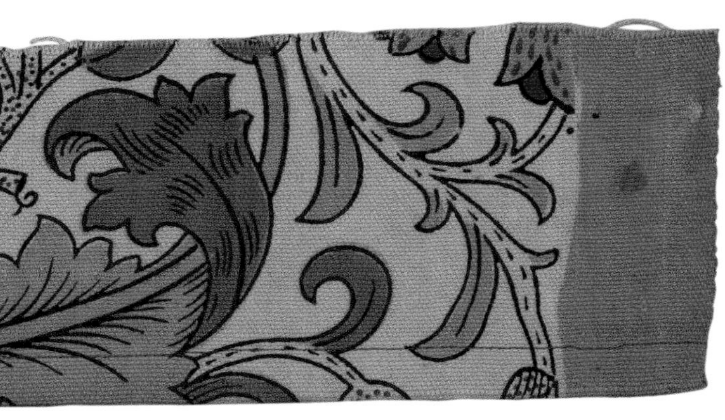

55 Designed by William Morris for Morris & Company

Sample of *Lodden* printed cotton, first issued 1884

Indigo-discharged and block-printed cotton, printed at Merton Abbey, full piece 3 x 19 (7.6 x 48.3).

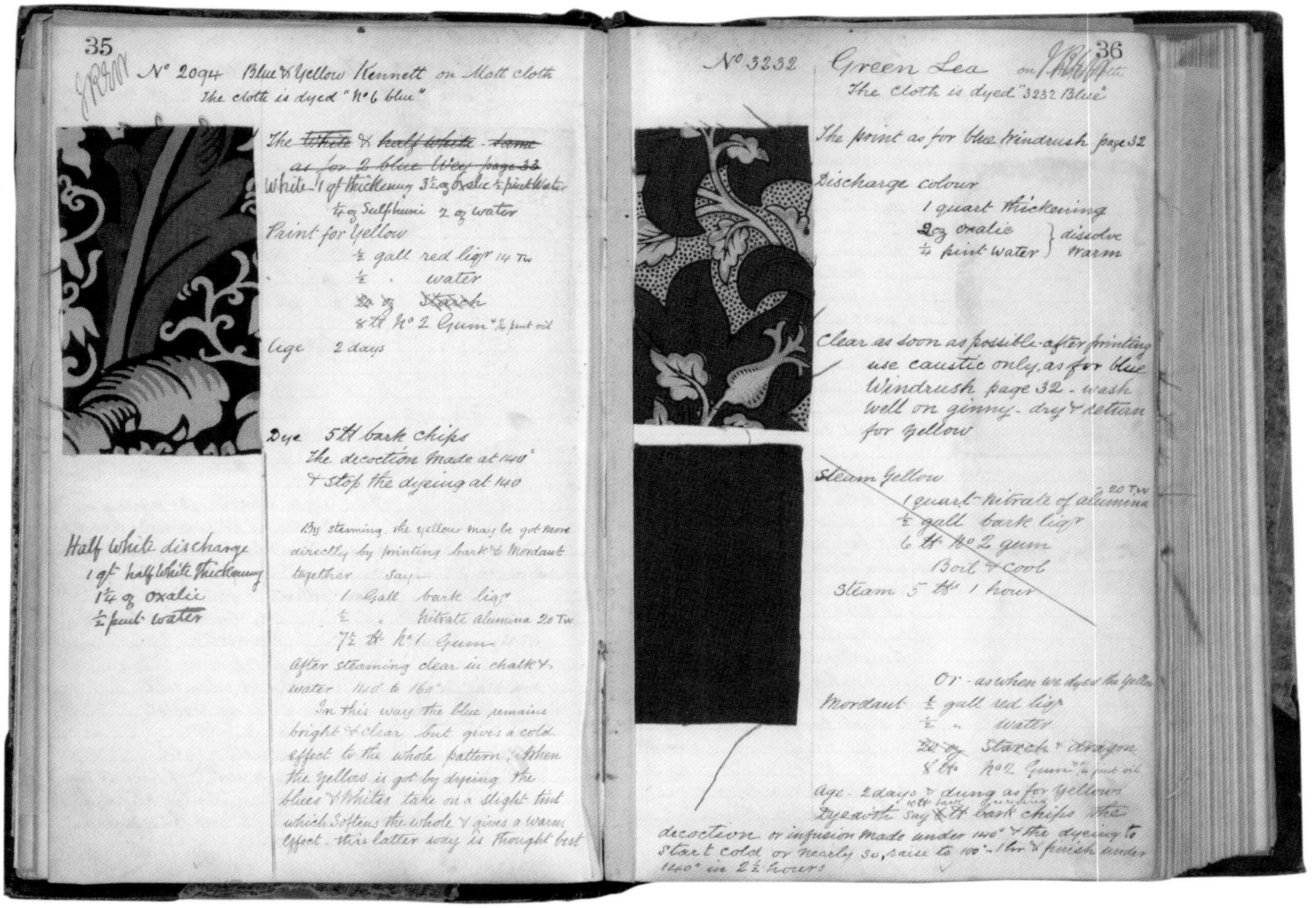

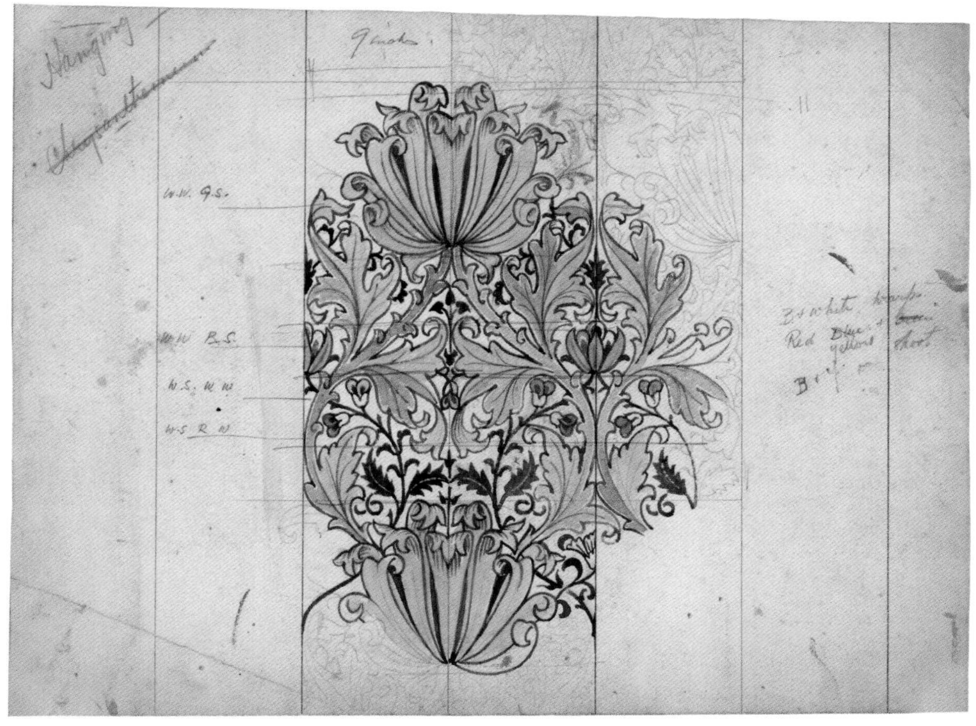

56 Morris & Company

Merton Abbey book of dye recipes for printed textiles, starting in 1882

Ink and printed fabrics glued to paper

This page shows the recipes for *Blue and Yellow Kennet* (first issued 1883; the name is misspelt here) and *Green Lea* (first issued 1885).

57 J. H. Dearle for Morris & Company

Design for *Helena* woven silk and wool double cloth, *c.* 1890

Watercolour, ink and graphite, $11\frac{1}{4} \times 14\frac{1}{2}$ (28.6 x 36.8)

58 Designed by William Morris for Morris & Company

Little Tree hand-knotted carpet, *c.* 1890

Wool pile with cotton warp, manufactured at Merton Abbey, 110½ x 50 (280.7 x 127)

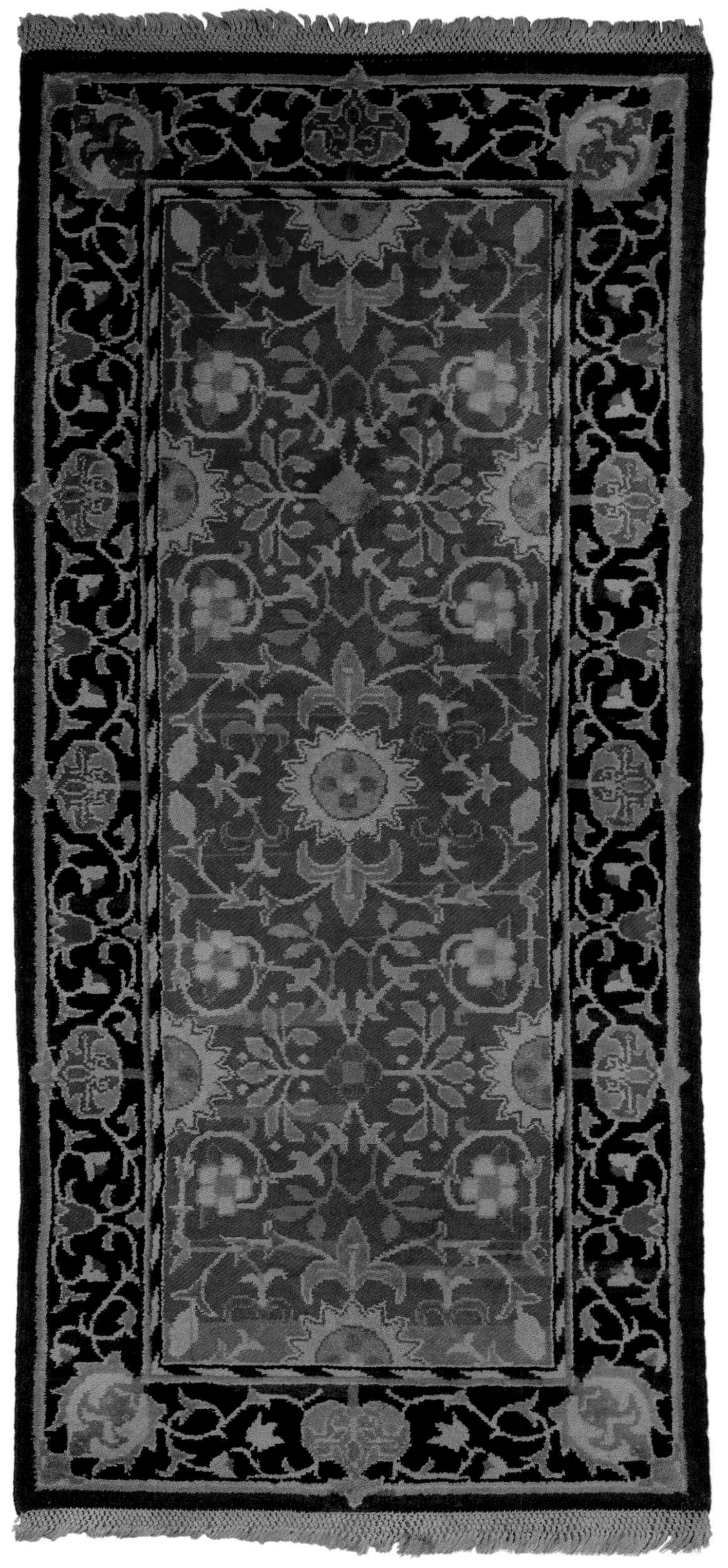

one of his earliest designs for the Firm. The pattern of stylized pale pink chrysanthemums stacked vertically among spreading light green foliage and blue flowers, based on historic textile designs, was produced as a silk and wool double cloth. It was woven by a Scottish firm – not by hand but on a steam-powered Jacquard loom, as were all the Firm's double cloths.[11]

Morris & Company also began offering carpets designed by Morris in the mid-1870s. At first created for a variety of machine-weaving processes, these were contracted to outside firms to manufacture. From 1879, the Firm was able to produce its own handwoven carpets, called 'Hammersmith' because Morris set up looms at Kelmscott House, his home in Hammersmith, before the move to Merton Abbey. George Wardle described Morris's practice: 'In designing for carpets everything of course depended upon him. He would first make a small drawing to a scale of, say, one-eighth of the full size, which he would colour carefully.'[12] One of Morris's earliest Hammersmith carpets was *Little Tree* [58]. The predominant colouring of deep blue and red was Morris's favourite combination for carpets. The decorative motifs, showing the influence of Middle Eastern carpets, are geometric and stylized, as suited to the hand-knotting technique implemented by the Firm.

By the 1870s Morris & Company was receiving commissions for major interior decoration schemes for the London homes and country houses of the wealthy (although catering to the rich did not always sit well with Morris as he became increasingly committed to political activities and socialism). The last of these schemes before Morris's death was for Stanmore Hall, Middlesex, the

59 J. H. Dearle for Morris & Company

Design for painted decoration for Stanmore Hall, Middlesex, *c.* 1888

Watercolour and graphite, full sheet 14 x 17 (35.6 x 43.2)

60 J. H. Dearle for Morris & Company

Design for *Greenery* tapestry, *c.* 1892

Graphite and ink, 20 x 26⅝ (50.8 x 67.6)

country home of William Knox D'Arcy, a mining engineer. At this time, Morris, immersed in politics, delegated dealings with clients to Dearle. From 1888 to 1896 the Firm provided carpets and textiles for the Stanmore commission from old designs, and Dearle produced new ones specifically for the project, including painted decoration for the walls and ceilings. A detailed drawing of coiling green vines, pink roses, yellow tulips, blue daisies and large acanthus leaves [59] is the design for the west side of the hall, covering the area between the wood panelling and the high ceiling. Dearle's drawing shows him working on a smaller scale than the more generous style of Morris, seen for example in the *Iris* design [51], though when executed to full size it was forceful.[13] Stanmore Hall was one of the most lavish schemes undertaken by the Firm [25]; it contrasted with Morris's own taste for a simple interior punctuated with colour and pattern.

In the 1880s, Morris was also able to realize his dream of weaving tapestries as ambitious as those produced in the medieval period. As with the other crafts that the Firm produced, Morris first taught himself how to execute it. He wove his own tapestry, *Cabbage and Vine*, on a loom constructed in his bedroom at Kelmscott House in 1879. Setting up a loom at Queen Square, Morris then taught the young Dearle, who had recently started with the Firm. As with stained glass, Burne-Jones was commissioned to design most of the figures. At first the decorative backgrounds were conceived by Morris, but eventually Dearle took over as their chief designer. The most ambitious tapestries woven by the Firm were those in the *Holy Grail* series designed by Burne-Jones, Morris and Dearle for the dining room of Stanmore Hall [25]. The *Greenery* tapestry [60] was designed by Dearle for Clouds, the Hon. Percy Wyndham's country home, of which Philip Webb was the architect. The tapestry was, in Morris's words, 'a piece done which was made specially for the place it is to occupy'.[14] Dearle's drawing shows pear, orange, and apple trees, each with a banner nestled in its branches. Below, he filled in only one side with greenery and animals. In the lower margin is a lone fox, directly copied from the fox designed by Webb for an earlier Firm tapestry, *The Forest.* In the final version, a somewhat differently posed fox would be placed between the left and middle trees. The tapestry was woven in 1892 and hung in the hall of Clouds, along with an early Flemish tapestry.

In his lecture 'The Beauty of Life' Morris described the contents of his ideal room, in which

> the wall itself must be ornamented with some beautiful and restful pattern. ... This simplicity you may make as costly as you please or can, ... you may hang your walls with tapestry instead of whitewash or paper; or you may cover them with mosaic, or have them frescoed by a great painter: all this is not luxury, if it be done for beauty's sake, and not for show.[15]

The 'beautiful and restful patterns' that Morris produced found favour with the middle and upper classes and they were widely used in fashionable interiors in London and country houses.[16] By offering a full range of goods for the home, the Firm was able to provide designs for an integrated interior, combining and blending their patterned fabrics and carpets into a coherent whole.

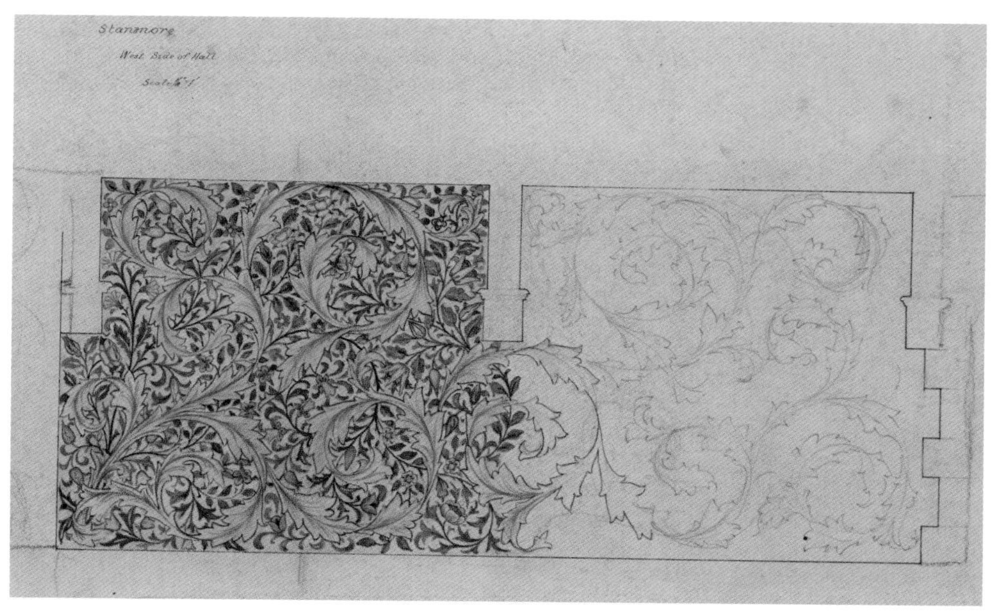
Stanmore
West Side of Hall

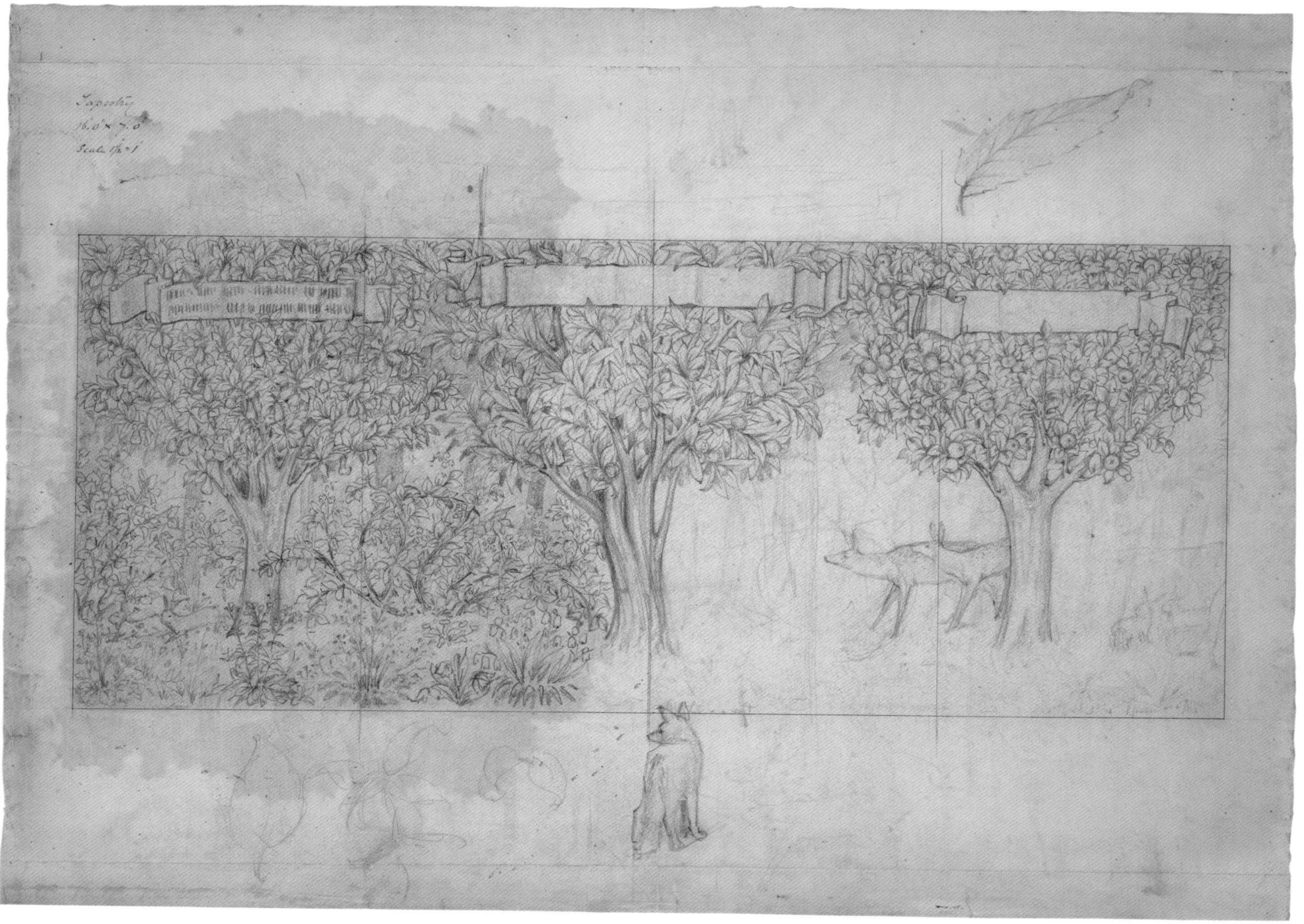

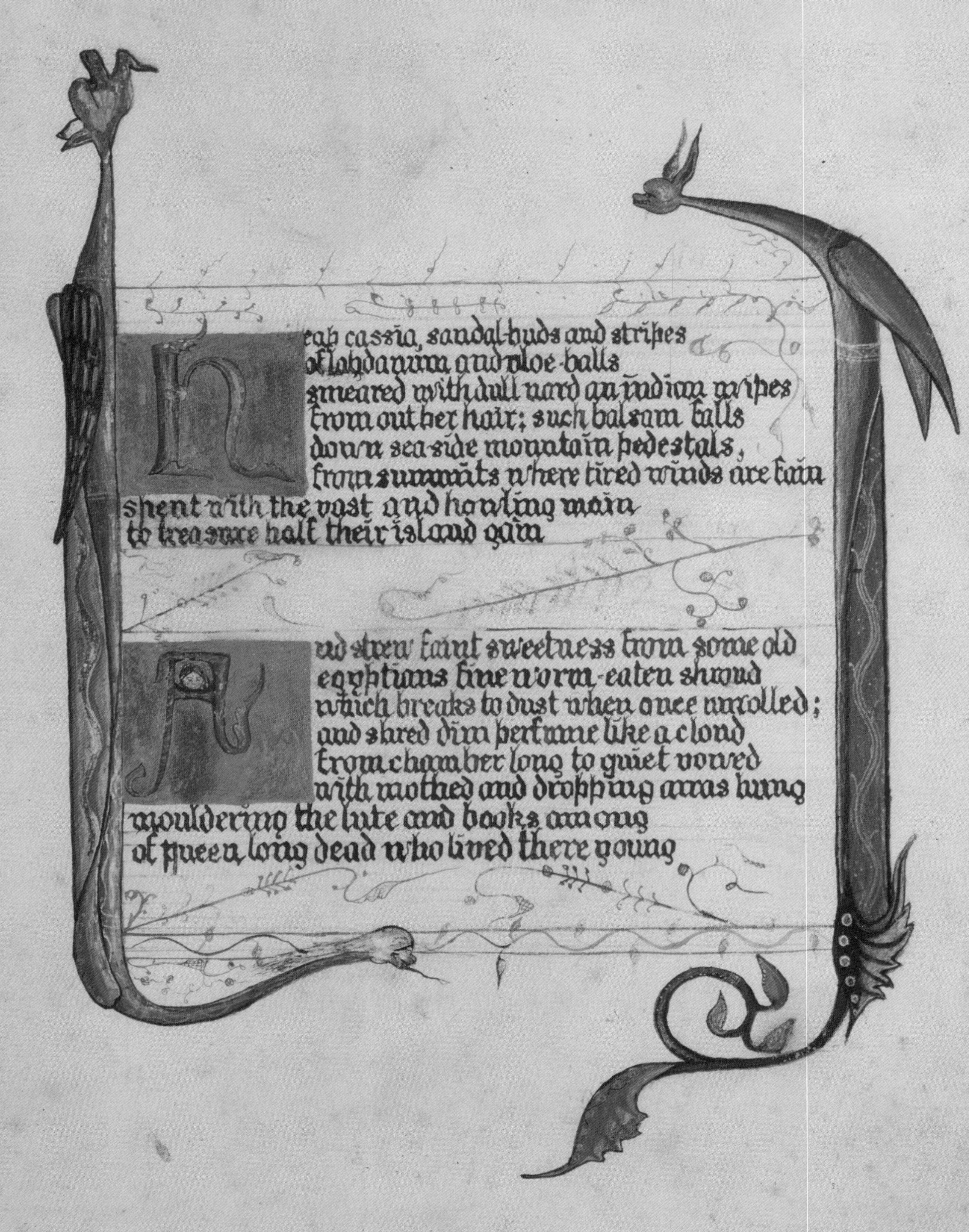
heap cassia, sandal-buds and stripes
of labdanum, and aloe-balls
smeared with dull nard an indian wipes
from out her hair; such balsam falls
down sea-side mountain pedestals,
from summits where tired winds are fain
spent with the vast and howling main
to treasure half their island gain
and strew faint sweetness from some old
egyptians fine worm-eaten shroud
which breaks to dust when once unrolled;
and shred dim perfume like a cloud
from chamber long to quiet vowed
with mothed and dropping arras hung
mouldering the lute and books among
of queen long dead who lived there young

THE ART *of* THE BOOK

DIANE WAGGONER

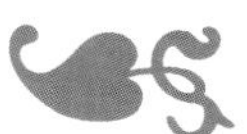

As a poet and writer, Morris was passionate about books. He recalled that as a boy he was 'a greedy reader of every book I could come across'.[1] The first volume that he is known to have owned was a small 1844 edition of the works of Horace, in which he drew on the flyleaf the figure of a peg-legged man holding a placard with the humorous inscription, 'W. Morris / His Horace' [62]. Morris's voracious reading ranged widely over his lifetime, from the ancient to the contemporary, encompassing classical mythology, medieval literature, Icelandic sagas, craft manuals, history, political writings, as well as novels, poetry and prose, such as the works of Scott, Keats, Dickens, Carlyle, Ruskin, Tennyson and the Brownings. A lifelong bibliophile, he amassed a collection

61 William Morris

Two verses from Robert Browning's *Paracelsus*, 1856–57

Ink, bodycolour and gilt, full sheet
6⅞ x 6 (17.5 x 15.2)

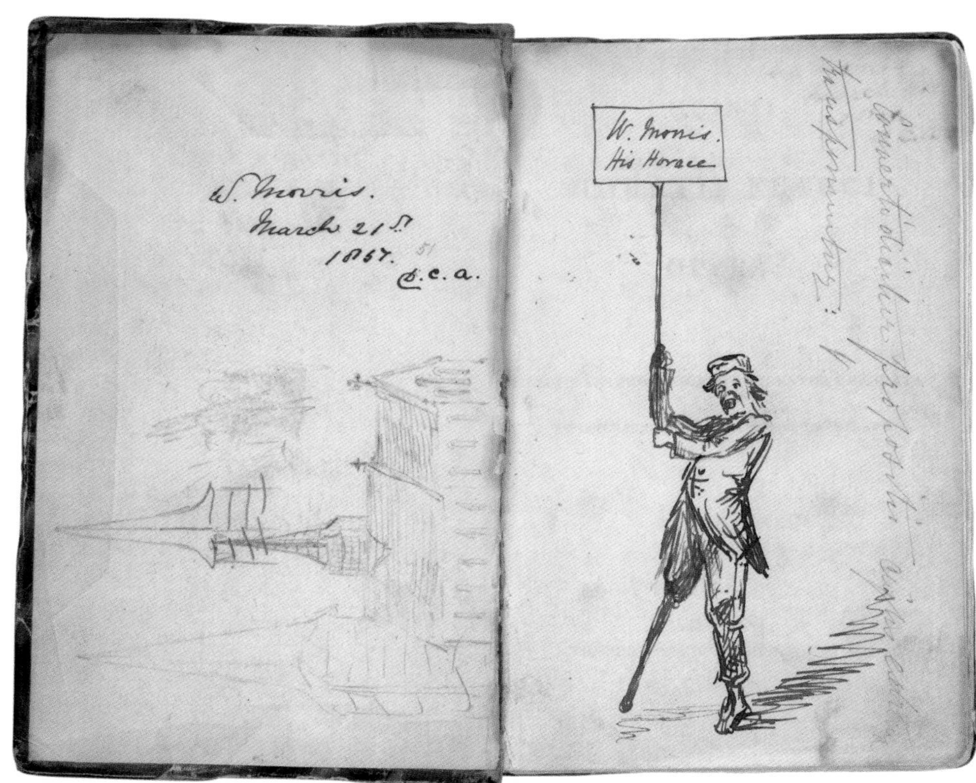

62 William Morris

Sketches at the beginning of his copy of *Quinti Horatii Flacci Opera* (London: Whittaker & Co., 1844)

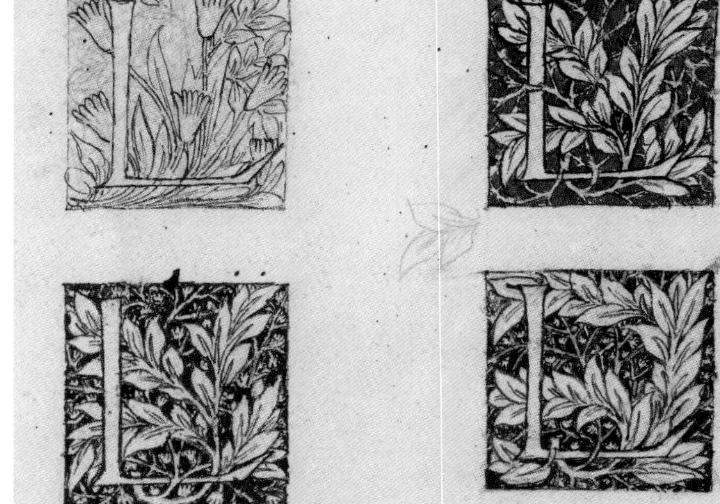

63 William Morris

Page from 'Acontius and Cydippe', in volume 4 of the bound printer's copy of the manuscript of *The Earthly Paradise*, *c.* 1869

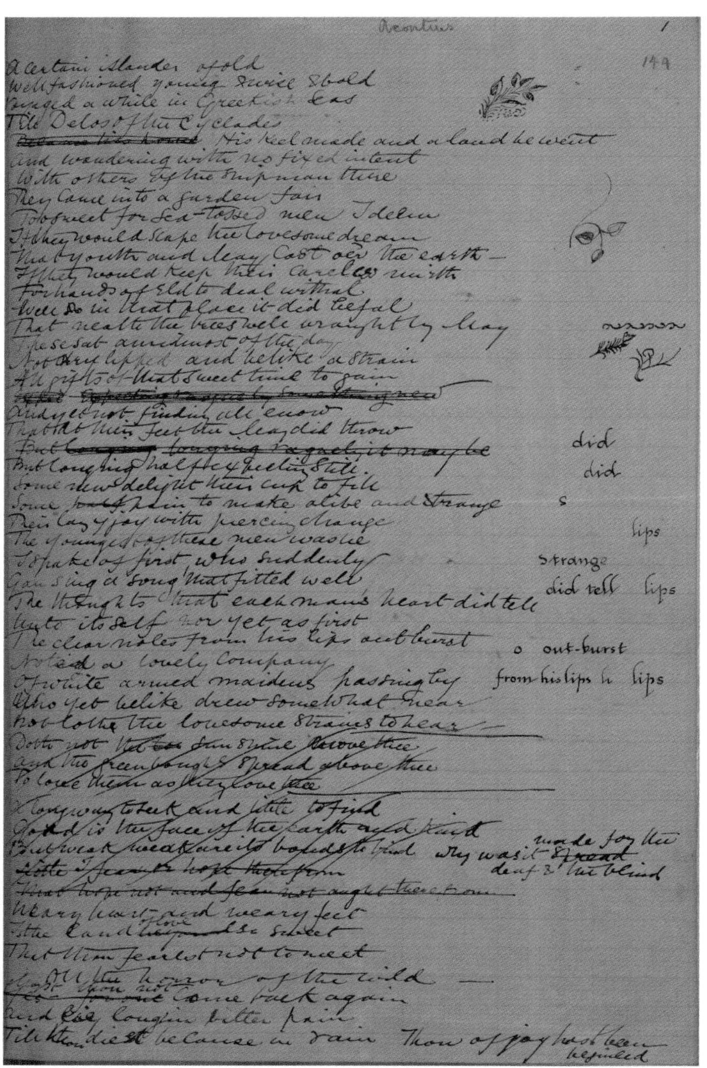

of rare books and manuscripts, including many superb examples of illuminated manuscripts, incunabula and early printing. In the 1890s, his home at Kelmscott House would be described as containing 'shelves and shelves of bulky old volumes, arranged not as if they were part and parcel of a "show-library," but as if they were in daily, hourly use'.[2] In the last decade of his life, Morris added the profession of book printer to his already tremendous number of accomplishments. He founded the Kelmscott Press to print books 'with the hope of producing some which would have a definite claim to beauty'.[3] Established in premises a few doors away from Kelmscott House, the Press would issue forty-two books before Morris's death. All aspects were conceived by Morris, from the typography and ornamented initials and borders to the page layout, format, and bindings, and all the printing was done in a hand-press on handmade paper. The books included Morris's writings, works by his friends and contemporaries, English classics, and Old English and medieval texts that he loved.[4]

In his twenties, Morris had briefly experimented with manuscript illumination.[5] He had studied medieval examples at the Bodleian Library during his Oxford days and then at the British Museum in London. An early attempt from the mid-1850s, one of only a few known examples of Morris's illuminated work from this period, is a single page of verse from Robert Browning's poem *Paracelsus* [61]. Morris had admired Browning's poetry from his youth, and the two became friends in the 1850s. The page is written in a shaky, crowded Gothic script, and the text is bordered with two strange, elongated shapes with bird wings and grotesque heads, each spiking irregularly out

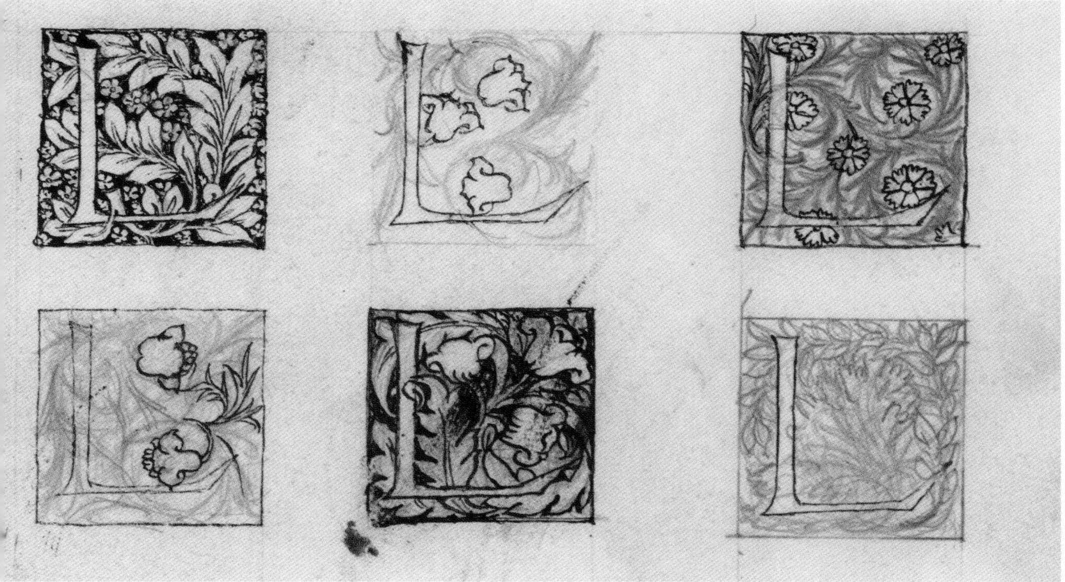

64 William Morris

Designs for the initial L, for a proposed edition of *Love is Enough*, 1871

Graphite and ink, full sheet 10 x 14 (25.4 x 35.6)

like the border ornamentation in a thirteenth- or fourteenth-century manuscript. The two initial capitals are set in blocks of gold paint and the rest of the empty space is ornamented with red and blue filaments sprouting curling leaves and buds. Rossetti felt that 'in all illumination and work of that kind he [Morris] is quite unrivalled by anything modern that I know – Ruskin says, better than anything ancient'.[6] In the early 1870s Morris mastered calligraphy and manuscript illumination in earnest, and, in his spare time away from business, worked on a number of calligraphic manuscripts of his translations of Icelandic sagas and other texts.

Morris achieved greatest fame in his lifetime as the writer of *The Earthly Paradise*, a long cycle of twenty-four narrative poems in the tradition of Chaucer, which included stories from classical mythology and from medieval, Norse and Icelandic tales. Written over a period of five years, it was completed in 1869. Since this was the decade which also saw the launching of the Firm, the range of Morris's activities in these years is prodigious. Several manuscript versions of these poems survive, but The Huntington houses the complete printer's copy in seven volumes, described by May Morris as 'those seven great folio volumes of *The Earthly Paradise*'.[7] Morris's corrections – and corrections to corrections – cover page after page of the blue paper. In many cases, pieces of notepaper have been interleaved to add new text. The page illustrated here [63] is from 'Acontius and Cydippe', and shows Morris's doodles of decorative leaves and experimentation with calligraphy. In the right margin, he has copied out a few words from the poem in a flattened italic script with experimental diagonal hair-strokes, which would reappear in some of his calligraphic manuscripts.

Morris never lost sight of the visual image even in his literary work. While working on *The Earthly Paradise*, he collaborated with Burne-Jones to achieve an ambitious combination of word and image for a proposed edition of the poem. This vast undertaking would never be realized, but Burne-Jones completed over one hundred drawings, most illustrating one of the poems in the cycle *Cupid and Psyche*. The project moved far enough along that around half of these drawings were transferred to woodblocks, mostly cut by Morris himself. Another uncompleted project was for his poem *Love is Enough*, published after *The Earthly Paradise* in 1872. Morris planned an ornamented and illustrated edition and produced a number of experimental designs for it, including ten variations for the decorated initial 'L' [64]. These designs have more in common with the designs Morris was producing for wallpapers and textiles at the same time, such as *Larkspur* (*c.* 1872), *Jasmine* (*c.* 1872) [30] or *Marigold* (1875), and are very different from the kind of interlacing ornament he would produce twenty years later for the Kelmscott Press books. In the ten designs, Morris tries different ways of filling in the block capital square with foliage and flowers, alternately employing leaves or tulip- and daisy-like flowers. A few of these designs already show the layering effect of dominant leaves over a smaller, more intricate pattern that Morris developed in his repeating patterns in the 1870s.

After his triumph with *The Earthly Paradise*, Morris turned to translating Icelandic sagas and writing lectures on art and socialism, more poetry, and, beginning in 1888,

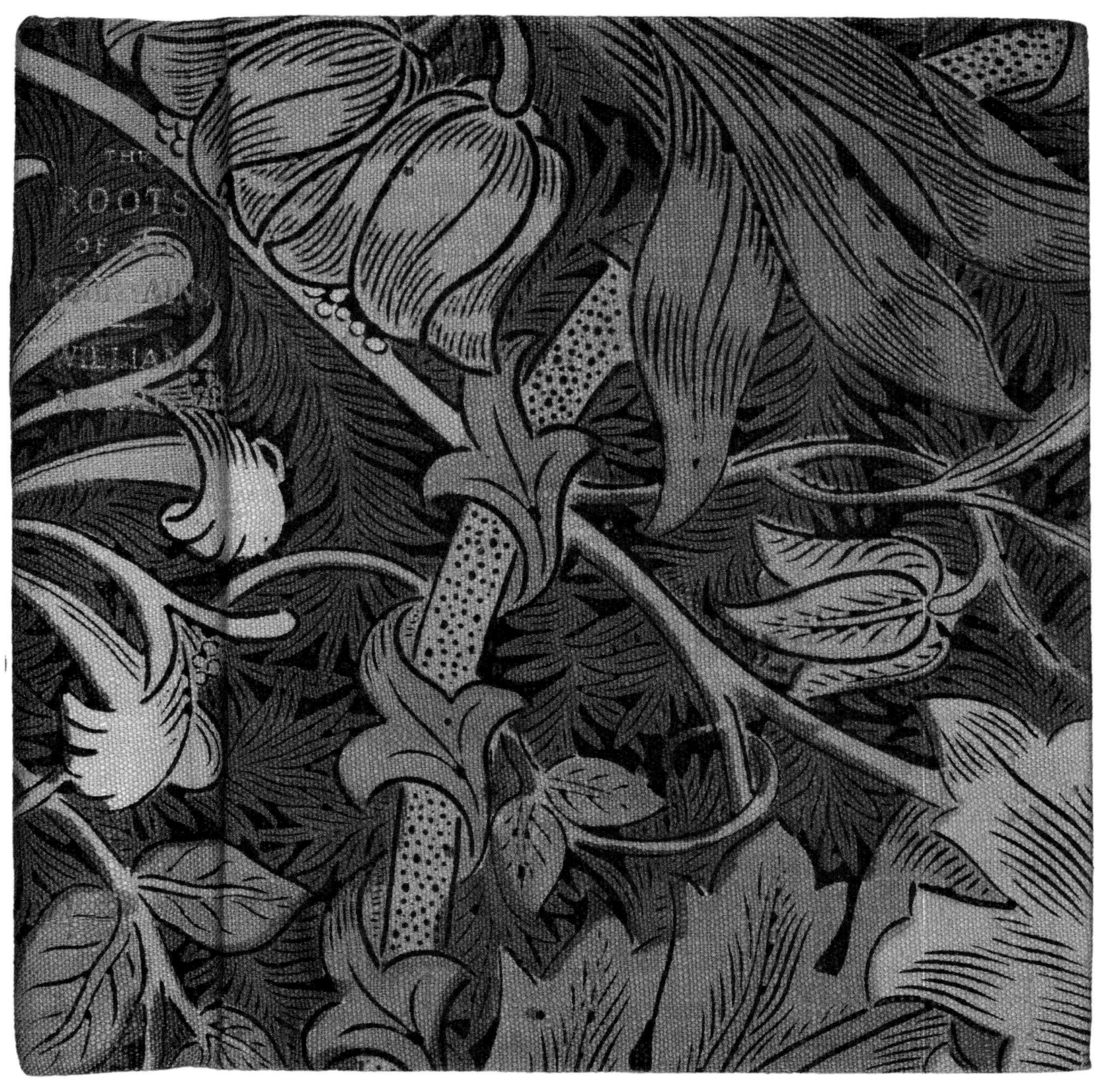

65 William Morris

The Roots of the Mountains (London: Chiswick Press, 1890), bound in *Honeysuckle* printed cotton

prose romances. Before establishing his own printing press, he became involved in the design of a number of the romances with the Chiswick Press. One was the Icelandic-inspired *The Roots of the Mountains.* Two hundred and fifty copies were bound in two of the Firm's chintzes, one of which was *Honeysuckle* [65]. Morris had written to his daughter Jenny that 'we are thinking of binding the Large paper in our own chintzes – that would be amusing wouldn't it?' And to his wife Jane he wrote, 'I have had a dummy book bound up in our chintz. It looks so nice and such fun: the gold letters on the back look very well on the linen cloth.'[8] The copy now in The Huntington collection

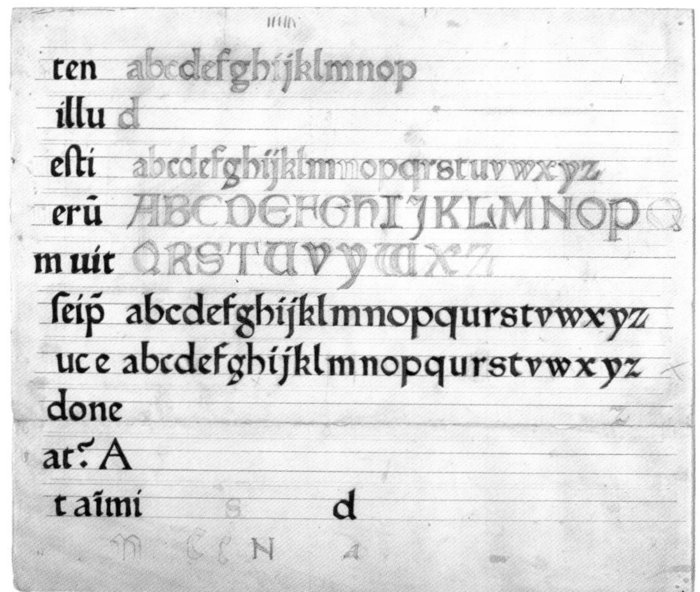

66 William Morris for the Kelmscott Press

Preliminary designs for the Troy typeface, 1891

Graphite and ink, 14 x 15½ (35.6 x 39.4)

is inscribed by Morris to his mother and mentioned in a letter to her: 'I am going this afternoon to tell my publishers to send you a copy of my new book, which I hope you will like, with my best love.'[9] Morris was thrilled with the experimental cloth binding and the design of *The Roots of the Mountains*. It was exhibited at the 1890 Arts and Crafts Exhibition, and he wrote: 'I am so pleased with my book – typography, binding, and must I say it, literary matter – that I am any day to be seen huggling it up, and am become a spectacle to Gods and men because of it.'[10] The text was set in Basel Roman type (based on an early sixteenth-century typeface), had wide margins, and side-notes rather than headers. Its design was innovative and strikingly different from the ordinary run of Victorian books.

In the event, however, Morris was dissatisfied with the abilities of the contemporary publishing world, calling printers 'the conceited numskulls [*sic*] of today' in comparison with those in the fifteenth and sixteenth centuries.[11] Shortly thereafter, in 1891, he founded the Kelmscott Press with the help and advice of his friend, the engraver Emery Walker. Morris was still involved in the day-to-day operations of the Firm and still visited the works at Merton Abbey, but he had relinquished most of the design-work and supervision to Dearle, and much of the business arrangements to Frank and Robert Smith, who had become his official partners. He was thus able to turn his energies to designing his ideal book. After his experience with publishing *The Roots of the Mountains* and other writings, Morris wanted to return to the quality he perceived in early modern printing. These qualities included strong, black type on the page, in contrast to the widely spaced and lightly inked type printed with narrow margins typical of nineteenth-century typesetting. He also believed that facing pages should be designed as a unit rather than individually. Morris designed three different typefaces for the Kelmscott Press [96]: the roman Golden and the gothic Troy and Chaucer (a smaller version of the Troy). In his preliminary designs for the Troy type in 1891 he experimented with a number of different forms [66]. On the left he has copied letters from a fifteenth-century printed book, enlarged by photographic means in order to study their details. The name 'Troy' came from the first book printed at the Press in this type, *The Recuyell of the Historyes of Troye*, written by Raoul Lefevre and translated and first published by William Caxton in 1474. Another book published in Troy type was Caxton's translation of *The History of Reynard the Foxe*. The final versions have headings in red ink, but Morris apparently considered printing the entire title-page, with his intricate, scrolling foliate border and large-scale lettering, in red [67] rather than the black that was finally used. Although some of the Kelmscott Press books included red initials, Morris never printed a title-page or even a large initial in red, making this proof a unique experiment.

The Kelmscott Press produced two editions of Morris's 1890 prose romance, *The Story of the Glittering Plain*. The second version appeared set in the Troy and Chaucer types with illustrations by Walter Crane. As he did with all the Kelmscott books, Morris designed the title-page lettering and decoration [68]. His drawings are built up in graphite, ink and Chinese white, the combination of the white over the dark ink creating the blueish hues that give a depth not possible in the printed version.

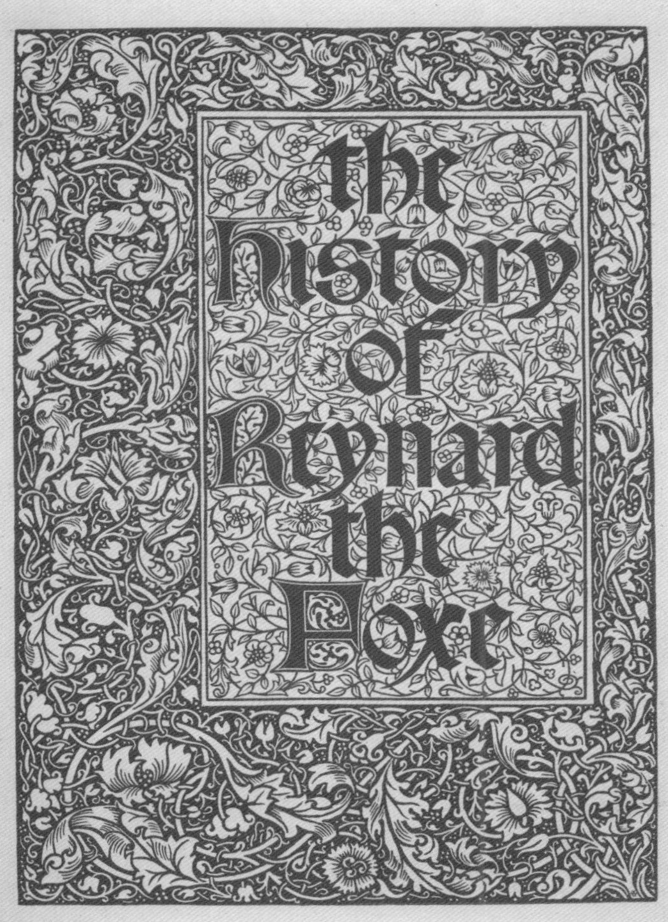

67 Designed by William Morris for the Kelmscott Press

Proof for the title-page of *The History of Reynard the Foxe*, 1893

Red ink, full sheet 16¼ x 1¼ (41.3 x 27.3).

68 William Morris for the Kelmscott Press

Design for the title-page of *The Story of the Glittering Plain*, 1894

Graphite, ink and Chinese white, 14 x 10 (35.6 x 25.4)

The architect W. R. Lethaby, observing Morris at work, explained:

> He would have two saucers, one of Indian ink, the other of Chinese white. Then, making the slightest indications of the main stems of the patterns he had in mind, with pencil, he would begin at once his finished final ornaments by covering a length of ground with one brush and painting the pattern with the other. If a part did not satisfy him, the other brush covered it up again, and again he set to put in his finished ornament. ... The actual drawing with the brush was an agreeable sensation to him; the forms were led along and bent over and rounded at the edges with definite pleasure; they were *stroked* into place, as it were, with a sensation like that of smoothing a cat. ... It was to express this sensuous pleasure that he used to say that all good designing was felt in the stomach.[12]

In the margins, Morris's pencil scribblings and trial brushstrokes are visible [68]. While the lighter background pattern to the title text echoes Morris's wallpaper and textile patterns in its swirling flowers and leaves, the outer border and the capital letters combine elements of intricate medieval interlace with Morrisian flowers and leaves. As Morris himself described it, 'All the designs are my own, but I have been guided in my designs by those in old books.'[13]

One of Morris's most ambitious projects for the Press was the edition of a favourite work, Froissart's *Chronicles*, a compilation of the historical deeds of the early kings and queens of England and France. 'No book that I could do would give me half the pleasure I am getting from the *Froissart*. I am simply revelling in it. It's such a noble and glorious work, and every page as it leaves the press delights me more than I can say.'[14] Morris died before the book was completed, but he produced many designs for the decoration of the margins. The Press produced a number of proofs of the text set in the Chaucer type, and The Huntington has four of these with Morris's pencil sketches of heraldic shields and border ornament. When asked what guided him in the ornamentation of his pages, Morris replied, 'The subject, of course. In my *Froissart*, for instance, on which I am now very busy, I have made special designs, floriated ones, but having the coats of arms of all the nobles mentioned in the History.'[15] At the bottom of this proof page chronicling the beheading of the earl of Lancaster [69], Morris placed a shield below the text and sketched interlacing foliage in the empty space around it. The capital 'Y' in the left column is an unusual shape, echoing in print the irregularity of thirteenth- and fourteenth-century manuscripts. It is a reminder of the *Paracelsus* illumination [61], done by Morris so many years before.

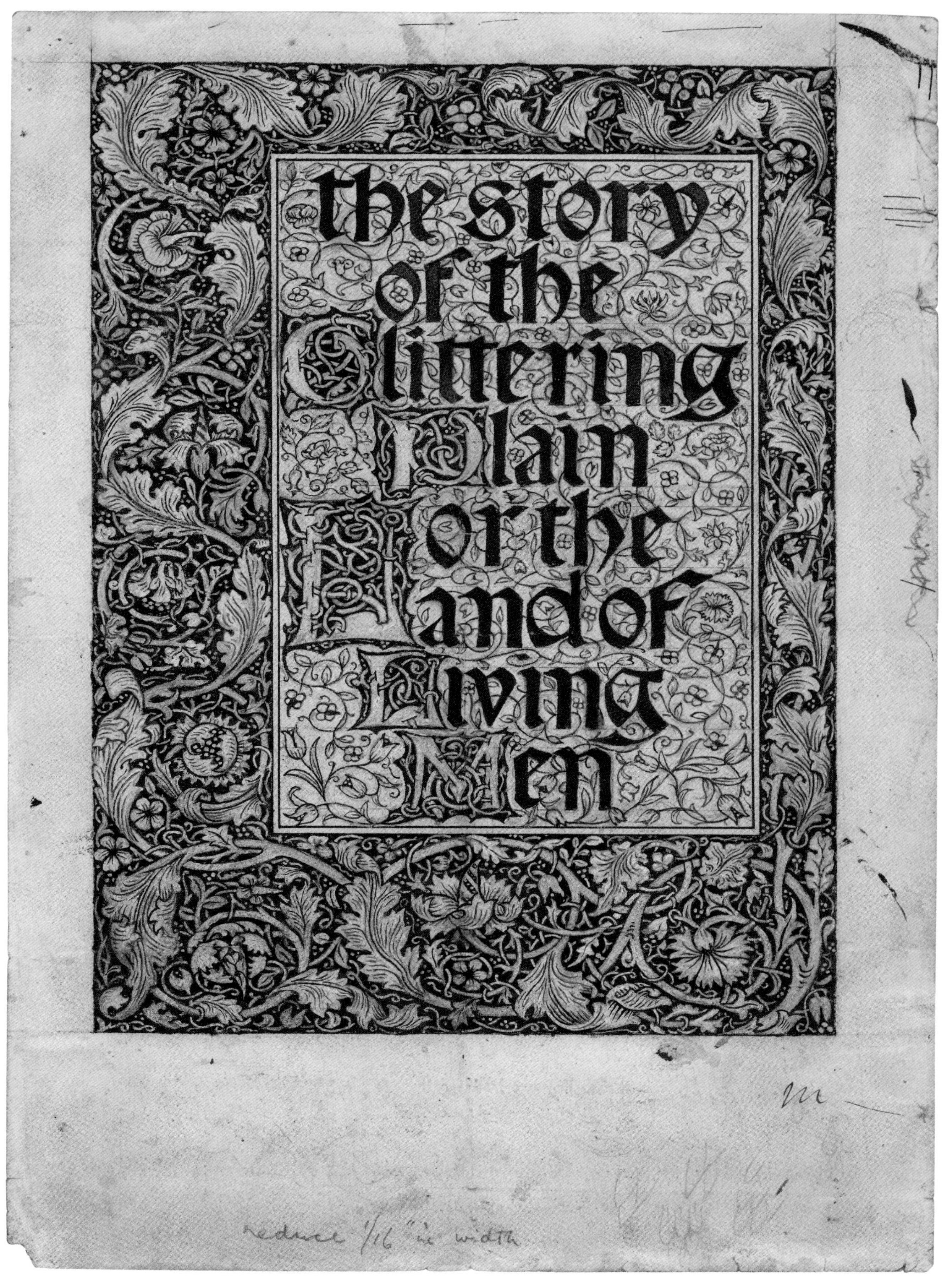
the story
of the
Glittering
Plain
or the
Land of
Living
Men
reduce 1/16" in width

Of the erle Thomas of Lancastre, and twenty-two other of the great lordis and knyghtis of Inglande that were beheeddyd. Cap. VI.

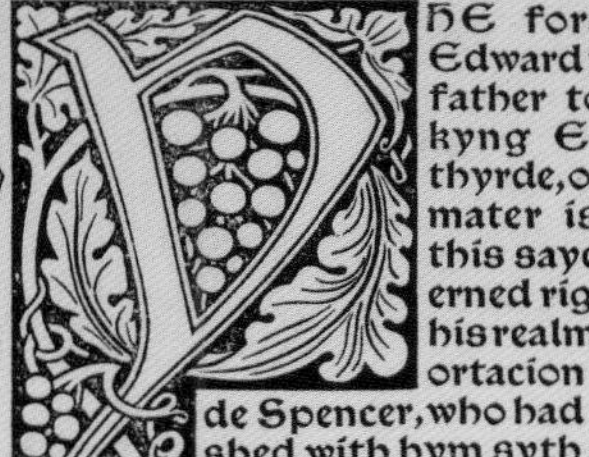

PHE forsaid kyng Edward the second, father to the noble kyng Edward the thyrde, on whom our mater is founded, this sayd kyng gouerned right diversly his realme by the exortacion of sir Hewe de Spencer, who had been norisshed with hym syth the begynnyng of his yongth; the whiche sir Hewe had so enticed the kyng that his father and he were the greattest maisters in all the realme, and by enuy thought to surmount all other barons of Ingland, wherby after the great discomfeture that the Scottes at Sterlyng, great murmoryng therin arose Inglande bitwene the noble barons and the kyng's counsell, & namely, ageynst sir Hewe Spencer. They put on hym that by his counsell they were discomfeted, & that he was fauorable to the kyng of Scottes. And on this poynt the barons had diuers tymes communication together, to be aduised what they myght do; wherof Thomas erle of Lancastre, who was uncle to the kyng, was chief. And anon whan sir Hew Spencer had espied this, he purueyed for remedy, for he was so great with the kyng, and so nere hym, that he was more beloued with the kyng than all the worlds after.

SO on a day he came to the kyng and said: "Syr, certain lordes of your realme have made aliaunce together agaynst you, & without ye take hede therto by tymes, they purpose to put you out of your realme". And so by his malicious meanes he caused that the kyng made all the sayd lordes to be taken, & theyr heedis to be striked of without delay, and without knowlege or answere to any cause. Fyrst of all sir Thomas erle of Lancastre, who was a noble and a wyse holy knyght, and hath done syth many fayre myracles in Pomfret, where he was beheedded, for the whiche dede the sayd sir Hewe Spencer achyued great hate in all the realme, and specially of the quene, & of the erle of Kent, brother to the kyng. And whan he parceyued the dysplea-sure of the quene, by his subtile wytte he set great discorde bitwene the kyng and the quene, so that the kyng wold not se the quene, nor come in her company; the whiche discord endured a long space. Than it was shewed to the quene secretly, & to the erle of Kent, that withoute they toke good hede to themselfe, they were lykely to be distroyed; for sir Hewe Spencer was about to purchase moch trouble to theym. Than the quene secretly dyd puruey to go in to Fraunce, & toke her way as on pylgrymage to saynt Thomas of Canterbury, and so to Wynchelsey; and in the nyght went into a shyp that was redy for her, and her yong sonne Edward with her, & the erle of Kent and sir Roger Mortymer; and in a nother ship they had put all theyr purueyaunce, and had wynde at wyll, and the next mornyng they arryued in the hauyn of Bolayn.

Howe the quene of Ingland went and complayned her to the kyng of Fraunce, her brother, of syr Hewe Spencer. Cap VII.

THAN quene Isabell was arryued at Bolayn, and her sonne with her, and the erle of Kent, the capytayns & abbot of the towne came agaynst her, and ioyously receued her & her company into the abbey, and ther she aboode two dayes: than she departed, and rode so long by her journeys, that she arraued at Paris. Than kyng Charles her brother, who was enfourmed of her comyng, sent to meet her dyuers of the greattest lordes of his realme, as the lorde syr Robert de Artoys, the lorde of Coucy, the lorde of Roye & dyuers other, who honorably dyd receue her, & brought her in to the cite of Paris to the kyng her brother. And whan the kyng sawe his suster, whom he had nat sene long before, as she shuld haue entred into his chambre, he mette her, and toke her in his armes, and kyst her, and sayd: Ye be welcome, feyre suster, with my feyre nephewe your sonne; and toke them by the handis, and led them forth.

THE quene, who had no great ioy at her harte, but that she was so nere to the kyng her brother, she wold haue kneled downe two or three tymes at the feet of the kyng, but the kyng would nat suffre her, but held her styl by the right hande, demaunding right swetely of her astate & besynesse. And she answered him ryght sagely, and lamentably recounted to hym all the felonyes & iniuries done to her by syr Hewe Spencer, and requyred hym of his ayde & comfort. Whan the noble kyng Charles of Fraunce had harde his suster's lamentation, who wepyngly had shewed hym all her nede and besynesse, he sayd to her: "Fayre suster, appease your selfe, for

4

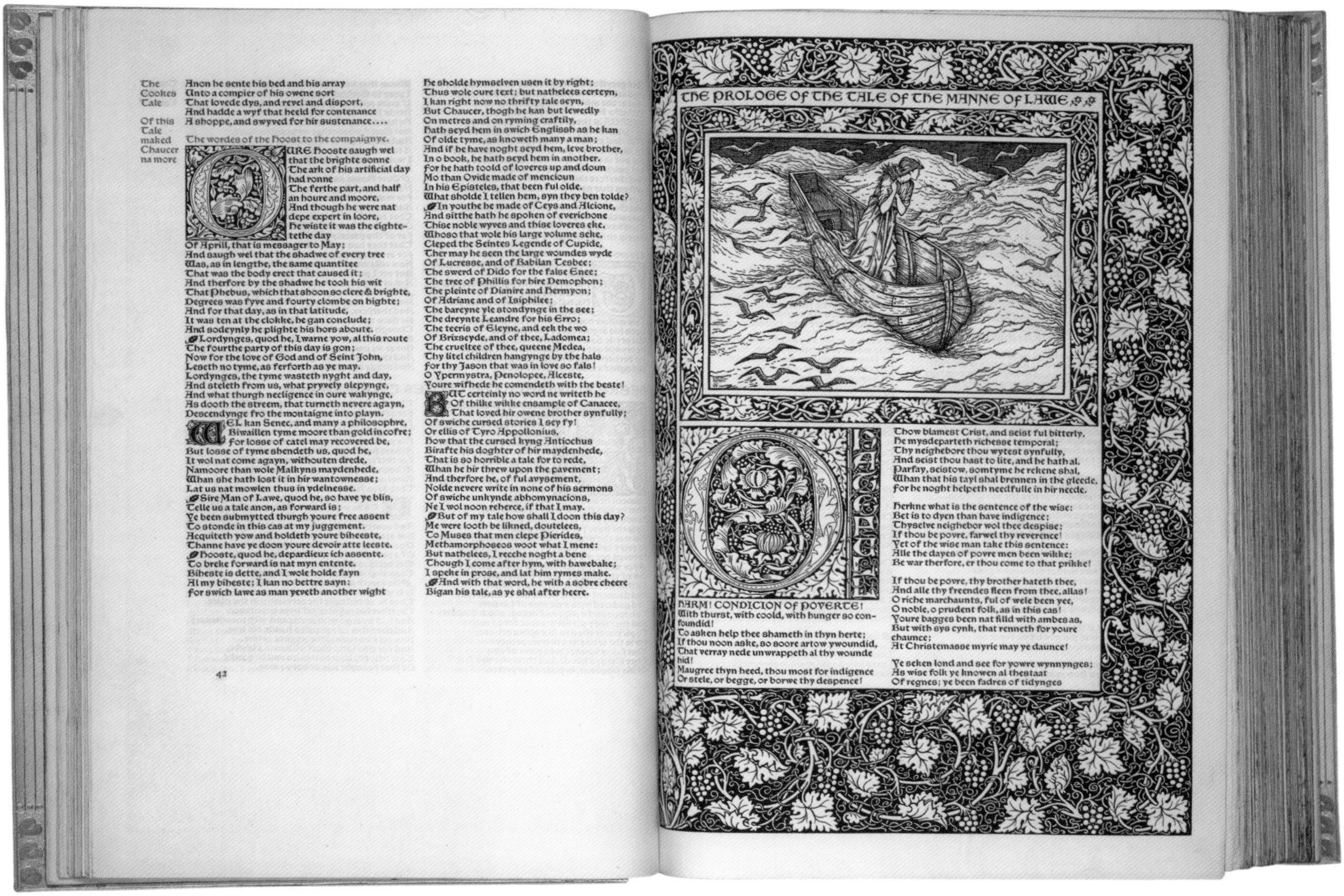

70 Designed by William Morris with illustrations by Edward Burne-Jones

The Works of Geoffrey Chaucer, showing the Prologue to the 'Tale of the Manne of Lawe' from *The Canterbury Tales* (Hammersmith: The Kelmscott Press, 1896)

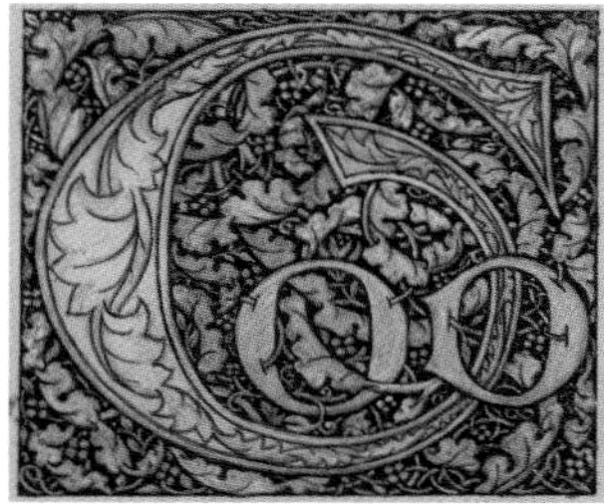

71 William Morris for the Kelmscott Press

Design for the initial word 'God' in *The House of Fame*, for *The Works of Geoffrey Chaucer*, 1895

Ink and Chinese white, 5½ x 7⅝ (14 x 10.2)

69 William Morris for the Kelmscott Press

Proof for Froissart's *Chronicles*, with sketched decoration in the lower margin, *c.* 1895

Ink and graphite, 16½ x 11¼ (41.9 x 28.6)

The Kelmscott Press edition of *The Works of Geoffrey Chaucer* was the most ambitious and ornamented of all its books [70]. A final collaboration between Burne-Jones and Morris, it too looked back to their youthful enthusiasm at Oxford for Chaucer and the medieval period. Burne-Jones produced over eighty wood-engraved illustrations that were integrated with the text, and Morris designed all of the borders, the full-page title-page, and twenty-six large initial words. This small drawing of the word 'God' [71] is one of these, executed in the same manner as the *Glittering Plain* border [68]. Interlacing vines and leaves, again reminiscent of early medieval manuscripts, surround the three letters. Burne-Jones wrote, 'when the book is done, if we live to finish it, it will be a little like a pocket cathedral – so full of design. & I think Morris the greatest master of ornament in the world.'[16] The Kelmscott Chaucer was issued by the Press in 1896, just before Morris's death, and it was the final, crowning achievement of his artistic life.

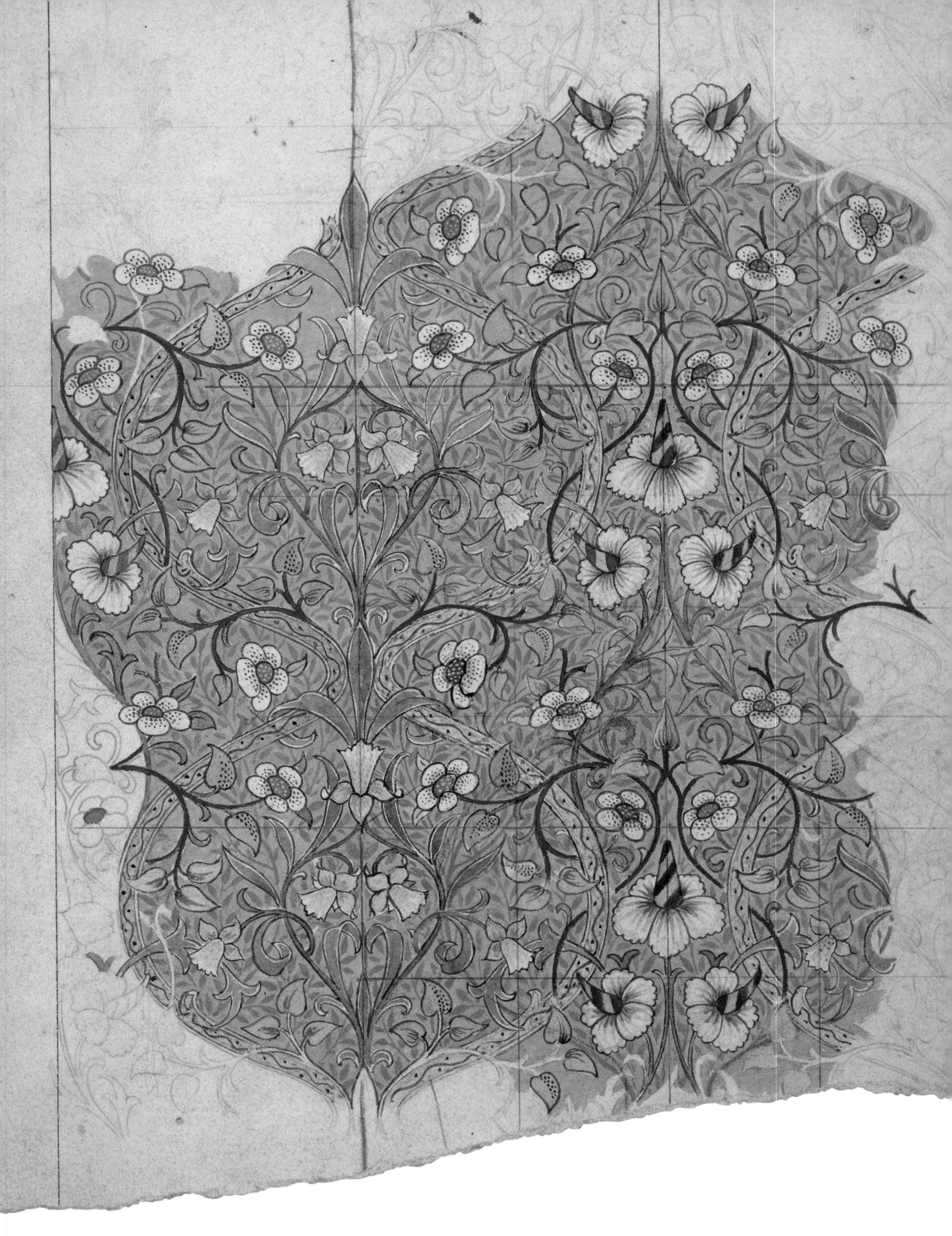

JOHN HENRY DEARLE

DIANE WAGGONER

John Henry Dearle (1860–1932) [73], described by the author and designer Lewis F. Day as 'a disciple of William Morris', was Morris's chosen artistic successor as the chief designer of Morris & Company. He skilfully carried on the Firm's work in the late 1880s and 1890s, first because Morris was becoming increasingly involved in political activities and book printing, and then in the years after Morris's death.[1] In 1905 Dearle described his inauspicious first meeting with Morris, which had taken place some thirty years earlier in 1878:

> During my first week I was sent to his room with a bottle of whisky, I think – bottle it was, for certain – and Mr. Morris said: 'Thank ye, thank ye; just wait a moment and post these letters for me.' I retired into the corner of the room near the door, and waited many moments; the letters were written and enclosed, and no further order given me; but sheet after sheet of foolscap was written and put aside, and it dawned upon me that he had forgotten me and his request, so that I ventured upon a slight timid sort of cough. Morris looked up and said: 'What the — do you want?' 'I thought you asked me to post some letters, sir?' 'No,' was his roaring reply; and, as speedily as possible I was on the other side of the door – the outside – and going downstairs; but before I had descended a dozen steps he was out after me with, 'Yes I did! Yes I did! I beg your pardon.' I must have seemed most alarmed; but from that moment to the last I never again came under his evident displeasure. I think I began to love him then; for I was mightily impressed with his manliness, and the seemingly amused way in which he observed the scare he had given me.[2]

72 J. H. Dearle for Morris & Company

Design for *Daffodil* wallpaper, *c.* 1903 (detail)

Watercolour and graphite, full sheet 12½ x 10⅝ (31.8 x 27)

73 J. H. Dearle at work on a cartoon for stained glass, early twentieth century

Photograph

This was the essential Morris that the young Dearle encountered, utterly absorbed in his work and gruff but kind to the scared young man, and it was the beginning of a close working relationship that would last for nearly thirty years. Dearle had joined Morris & Company as an assistant in the Oxford Street showroom. He soon

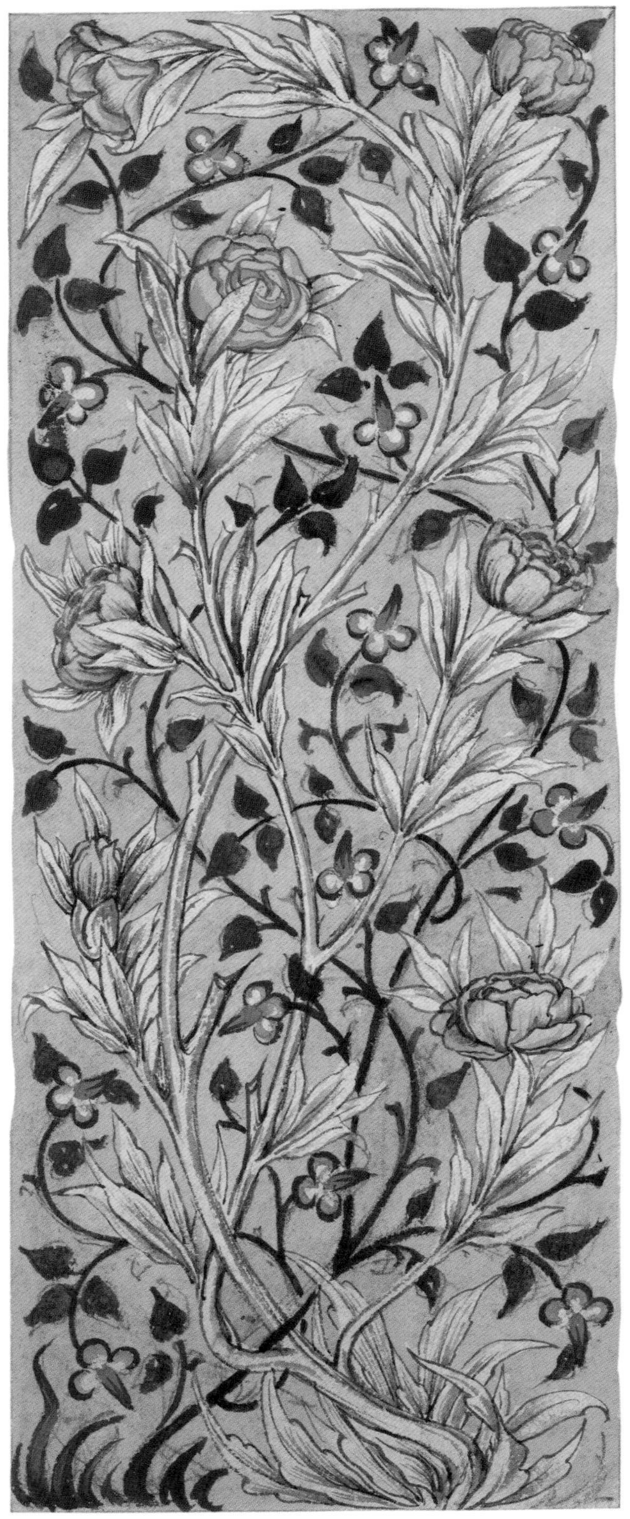

74 J. H. Dearle for Morris & Company

Design for *Peony* embroidery, *c.* 1885–90

Watercolour and ink, full sheet $12\frac{1}{2}$ x $13\frac{3}{8}$ (31.8 x 34)

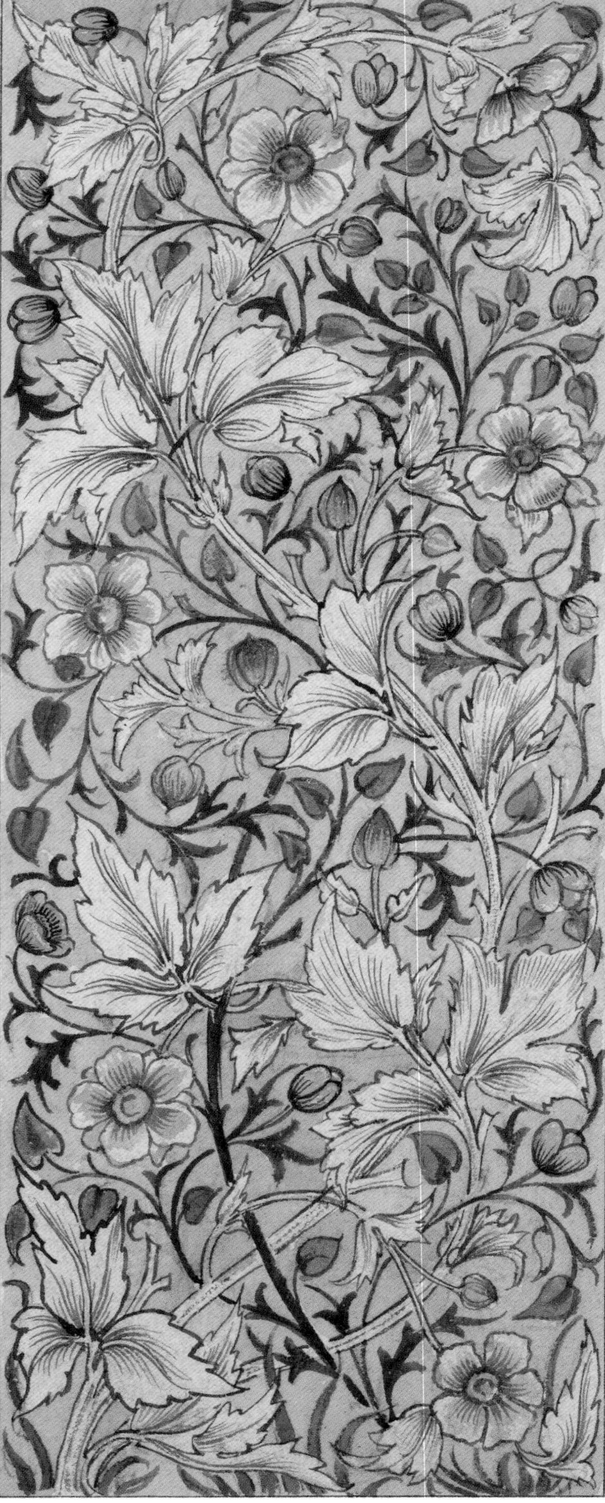

75 J. H. Dearle for Morris & Company

Design for *Anemone* embroidery, *c.* 1885–90

Watercolour and ink, full sheet $12\frac{1}{2}$ x $13\frac{3}{8}$ (31.8 x 34)

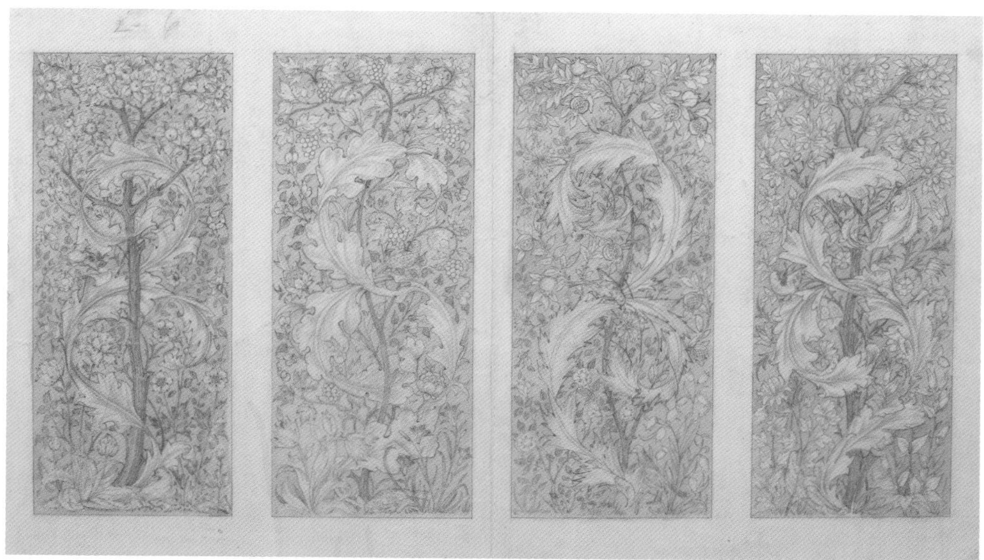

76 J. H. Dearle for Morris & Company

Design for *Apple Tree, Grapevine, Pomegranate,* and *Plum* embroidered panels, *c.* 1895

Graphite, 20 ⅝ x 30 ⅞ (52.4 x 78.4)

transferred to working in the Queen Square glass-painting studio in the morning and studying draughtsmanship and design in the afternoon.[3] The Huntington collection includes an example of a sketchbook by Dearle containing early drawings, which show him to be an accomplished draughtsman already at a young age.

When Morris first set up looms at Queen Square to explore tapestry weaving in 1879, he chose Dearle as his apprentice and taught him how to work the loom. Dearle completed the Firm's first figural tapestry in 1883 at Merton Abbey, *The Goose Girl*, designed by Walter Crane. George Wardle, the Firm's manager, later recalled that 'in putting Dearle to the work in the first instance Mr. Morris was influenced by the evident intelligence & brightness of the boy. Dearle was the teacher of all who followed him & is now I think the Director of the Merton Works.'[4] It is not evident whether Dearle had any outside training in draughtsmanship or pattern-designing, but he was clearly trained by Morris in all the crafts that the Firm produced.[5] In his lectures, Morris passionately lamented the division of labour in modern production, where the designer had no connection to the craftsman who produced the work, and he advocated again and again that the designer understand the material for which he designed, as he himself mastered the craft of every art he turned his hand to. As Day wrote, however, 'When [Morris] had once mastered an art or industry, he left it to others to pursue it.'[6]

It was not so much one art as his whole philosophy that Morris passed on to Dearle. The younger man began designing for wallpaper and textiles in the late 1880s and by the 1890s had emerged as the Firm's chief pattern designer, and had begun to supervise the Firm's design and production as well as serving as the principal adviser to the Firm's customers. Later, after Burne-Jones's death, he would become its primary stained glass designer and, at Morris's death, he became the Artistic Director. Dearle's initial pattern designs followed Morris's style, but as time passed, he developed his own aesthetic, drawing upon historic examples as Morris himself had done and also adapting his designs to suit changing tastes. The Huntington's collection of the only surviving letters from Morris to Dearle shows a friendly and sociable working relationship. Morris was to describe Dearle as both his pupil and, unofficially, his partner.[7]

When Morris's daughter May, an accomplished embroiderer [121], began to do a good deal of the designs and superintendence of the embroidery at the Firm in 1885, Morris himself ceased designing for the medium.[8] While May supplied many of the future embroidery designs, Dearle was responsible for the rest, such as this watercolour design for an embroidered screen panel [74, 75]. Dearle's delicately coloured drawing, almost like one of Morris's manuscript illuminations, has designs on both sides, one entitled *Peony* [74], the other *Anemone* [75]. *Peony* is inscribed by May Morris, commenting as head of the embroidery department: 'This is most likely to be most suited / as A is rather too like the / Anemone panel already worked. / MM'. Another beautiful example of Dearle's disciplined draughtsmanship is the design for four embroidered panels to be used as either wall hangings or a screen [76]. These drawings, each of one particular plant motif spreading upward, are typical of the embroidery designs by both Dearle and May. Each panel with the central motif of a branching tree – apple, grape vine,

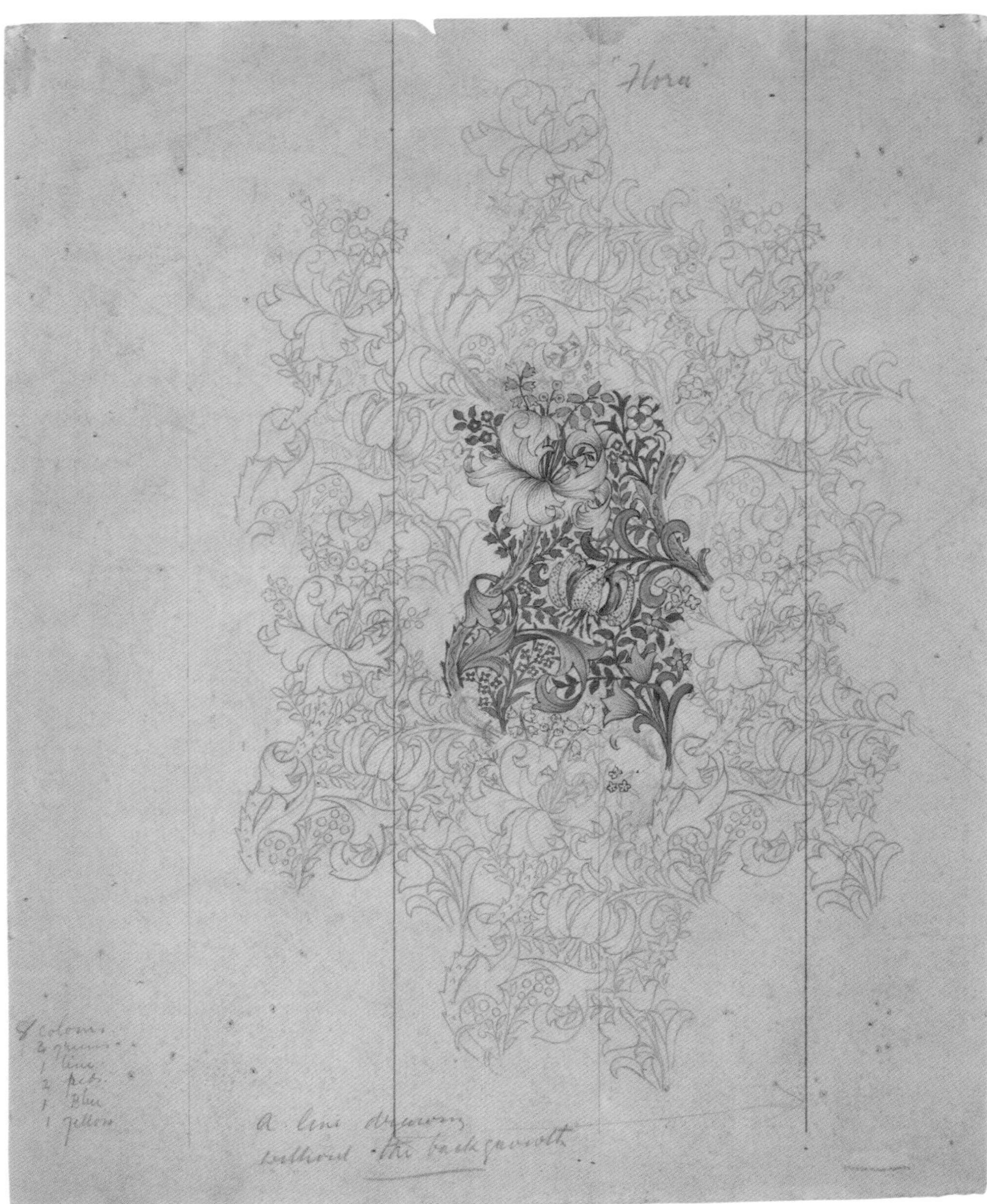

77 J. H. Dearle for Morris & Company

Design for *Golden Lily* wallpaper, *c.* 1897

Watercolour and graphite, 13½ x 10¾ (34.3 x 27.3)

pomegranate and plum – intertwined with swirling acanthus leaves shows Morris's influence, but the format is not one that Morris himself often used in his embroidery designs.[9] Dearle's embroideries were still being advertised in the firm's early twentieth-century catalogue, *Embroidery Work.*

While Morris continued to design wallpaper in the 1880s and the 1890s, and to visit Merton Abbey ('among the patterns and business') to supervise the work, Dearle eventually took over the designing of new paper-hangings.[10] His intricate skill is evident in his design for the 1897 wallpaper *Golden Lily* [77] (originally titled *Flora*, as inscribed in the upper right). He has drawn the repeating design in graphite six times around the centre, and, following standard practice, coloured only the central repeat, to indicate to the block-cutter how the eight colours were to be distributed on separate woodblocks. Dearle lists at the lower left the colours to be used. This pattern, of pale blue, pink and green intertwining tulips, lilies, and leaves, exhibits one of the two underlying structures employed by Morris in his own repeating schemes: the 'net', as he called it, in which vines curve vertically throughout, alternately separating and converging to create an ogee shape. (The other pattern, the 'branch', is based on parallel diagonal lines.) A departure can be seen in Dearle's design for the wallpaper *Seaweed* (first issued

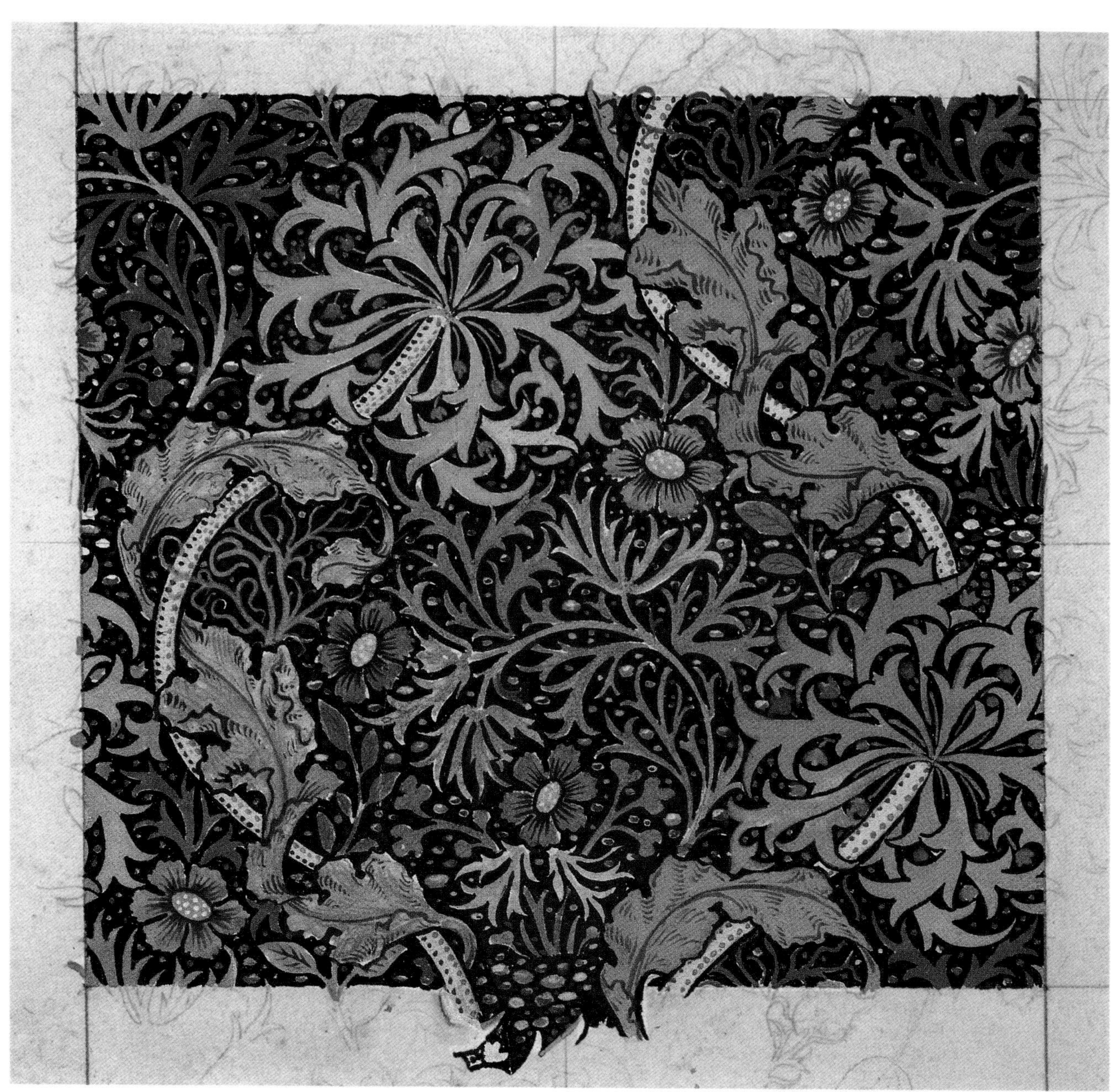

78 J. H. Dearle for Morris & Company

Design for *Seaweed* wallpaper, *c.* 1901

Watercolour and ink, $6\frac{1}{4}$ x $8\frac{1}{2}$ (15.9 x 21.6)

in 1901) [78]. It is the only Morris & Company pattern employing ocean plant motifs; but even here the fully coloured design, in vibrant blues, carries on Morris's distinctive style in the layering of coloured bubbles, seaweed, and blue flowers underneath the familiar acanthus scrolls twining around ogee-shaped kelp fronds.

Dearle also took over as principal designer of the Firm's carpets in the late 1880s. The design illustrated [79] was probably intended for the handlooms at Merton Abbey. As usual, only one of the quarter-repeats is shown coloured. Dearle has written above his drawing: 'Ground of centre blue as McCulloch with / light blue tracery running over as / McC. Other colours as McC. / leaving

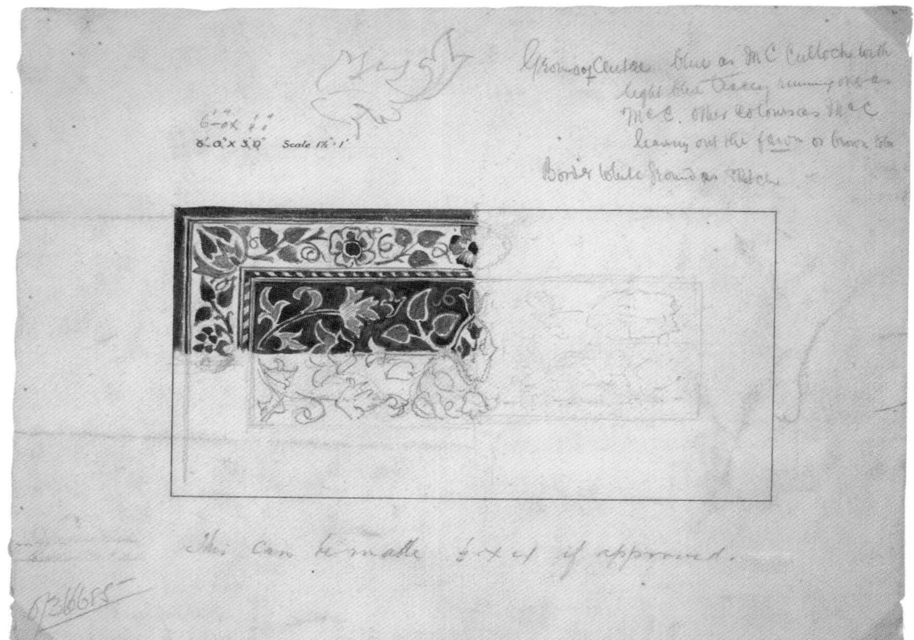

79 J. H. Dearle for Morris & Company

Design for Hammersmith hand-knotted carpet, 1898–1902

Watercolour and graphite, 10 x 13⅜ (25.4 x 34)

out the *fawn* or brown colour / Border white ground as sketch.' These notes seem to indicate proposed changes to the design, perhaps following consultation with the client. The centre ground of blue with light blue tracery refers to that seen in the *McCulloch* carpet, produced for that client, which became Dearle's most popular large-scale carpet design.[11] It indicates that an underlying tracery pattern would be added in the final product to create a rich, layered effect similar to the Firm's wallpaper and textile patterns.

In addition to the handwoven Hammersmith carpets, the Firm also designed several types of machine-woven carpets, which were then manufactured by other firms. One of these was the Wiltshire-based Wilton Royal Carpet Factory, which had begun producing Wilton pile (named after the factory itself) and Brussels carpets designed by Morris in the mid-1870s. This design by Dearle for a Wilton carpet [80] employs Persian motifs, which appear in much of his later work, inspired by his knowledge of historic textiles.[12] It is simplified and geometric in its forms, and thus more suited to machine-weaving.

As fashions changed, with taste in the later Victorian and Edwardian years demanding lighter colours, Dearle re-coloured many of Morris's wallpaper and textile patterns to boost sales. The colour palette of his own designs also became lighter, as in the wallpaper design *Daffodil* (*c.* 1903) [72] and the design for a printed cotton, *Rosebud* (*c.* 1905) [81]. *Daffodil* still exhibits a characteristic Morris structure: a leaf pattern beneath the dominant design of spiky, striped flowers and daffodils curling around abstract ogee lines. Dearle's vivid, light blue ground and pale pink and yellow flowers, however, are a departure from Morris's richer, intense colours. In the *Rosebud* drawing, Dearle has quickly sketched the basic ogee-shaped scheme of the pattern before filling in one repeat with precision. The delicate complexity of foliate rows curving around each other is derived from Turkish textile patterns and was a new direction in pattern-designing for Dearle.

Dearle also became the Firm's chief stained glass designer after the death of Burne-Jones in 1898. He had already been supplying ornamental backgrounds, taking Morris's place, for several years before this. For many subsequent stained glass commissions, Dearle continued to adapt Burne-Jones's compositions. The archive was stored in what one artist described as the 'office and drawing and designing room', which 'contained the large portfolio of all designs for stained glass windows made by Madox Brown, Burne-Jones and others'.[13] Dearle would therefore have had easy access to earlier works by the Firm as he assembled ideas for a new commission, but he also created original designs. One major commission was the west window, installed in 1902, for the Victorian Gothic chapel at Rugby School [83]. In addition to the sketch of the whole window, The Huntington collection also includes a number of cartoons of individual figures [82]. Dearle's overall design, consisting of seven large lights and forty-one smaller lights in the tracery head, is an ambitious multi-figure scene that travels effortlessly across the lights. It depicts Christ in Glory, surrounded by angels and other figures, linked in the landscape of Paradise by the winding River of Life. The leading patterns show the strong mosaic style of the Firm's later years. Dearle's manipulation of the jewel-tone colours of the glass

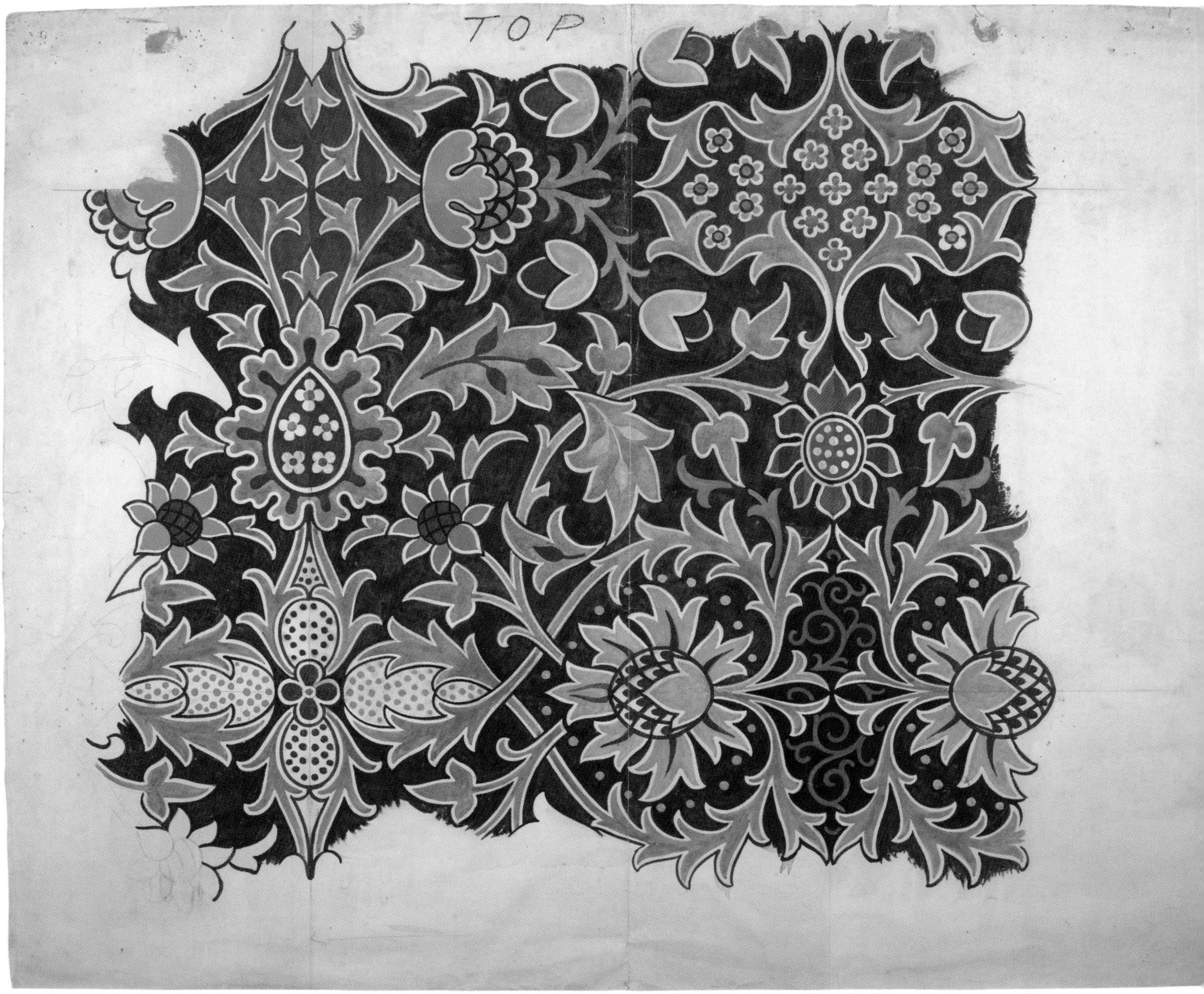

80 J. H. Dearle for Morris & Company

Design for Wilton machine-woven carpet, *c.* 1900

Watercolour and graphite, 26 3/8 x 32 5/8 (67 x 82.9)

81 J. H. Dearle for Morris & Company

Design for *Rosebud* printed cotton, *c.* 1905 (detail)

Watercolour and graphite, full sheet 13 1/2 x 8 3/4 (34.3 x 22.2)

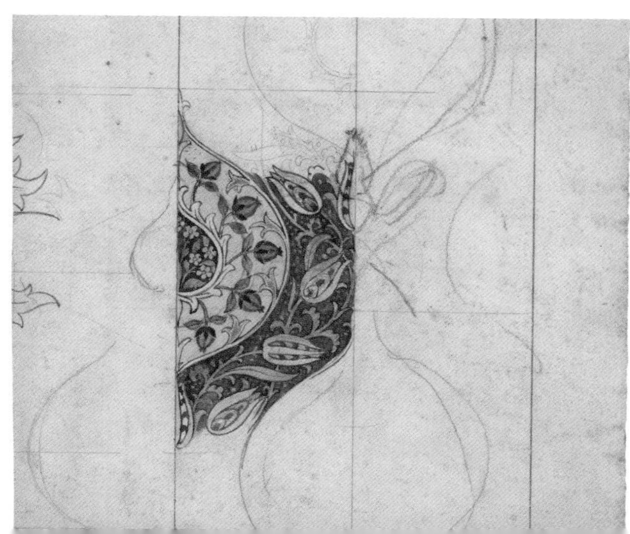

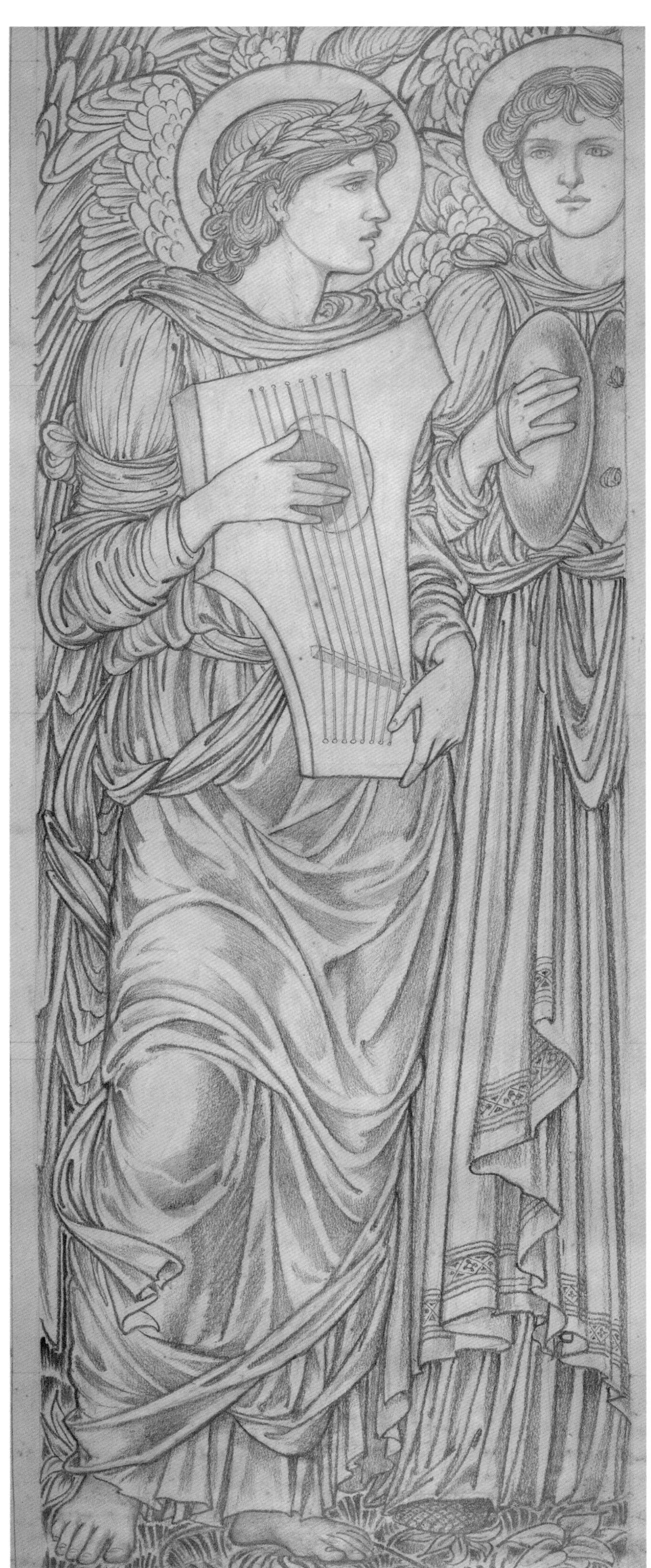

83 J. H. Dearle for Morris & Company

Christ in Glory in Paradise, sketch design for the west window of Rugby School Chapel, Rugby, Warwickshire, *c.* 1902

Watercolour and ink, 24⅞ x 17⅞ (63.2 x 45.4)

The drawing has a note attached detailing the subject of the window.

82 J. H. Dearle for Morris & Company

Angels, cartoon for the west window of Rugby School Chapel, Rugby, Warwickshire, *c.* 1902 (detail)

Graphite, full sheet 262⅝ x 24 (667 x 61)

balances blue, green and red in the bottom half of the window with, above, the creams and reds of Christ and the angels, and at the top glimpses of mosaic-patterned blue sky. Although the design is his own, it is clear that Dearle had absorbed the lessons of Burne-Jones and Morris.

In 1877, shortly before meeting Dearle, Morris had written of the qualities he was looking for in a craftsman:

> 1. General feeling for art, especially for its decorative side. 2. He must be a good colourist. 3. He must be able to draw well; i.e. he must be able to draw the human figure, especially hands and feet. 4. Of course he must know how to use the stitch of the work. ... I have no idea where to lay my hands on such a man, and therefore I feel that whatever I do I must do chiefly with my own hands.[14]

These were the qualities he found and nurtured in Dearle, and even though Dearle was always to be in Morris's shadow, his own handiwork as a craftsman-designer paid a handsome if often underestimated tribute to Morris's ideals and lifework.

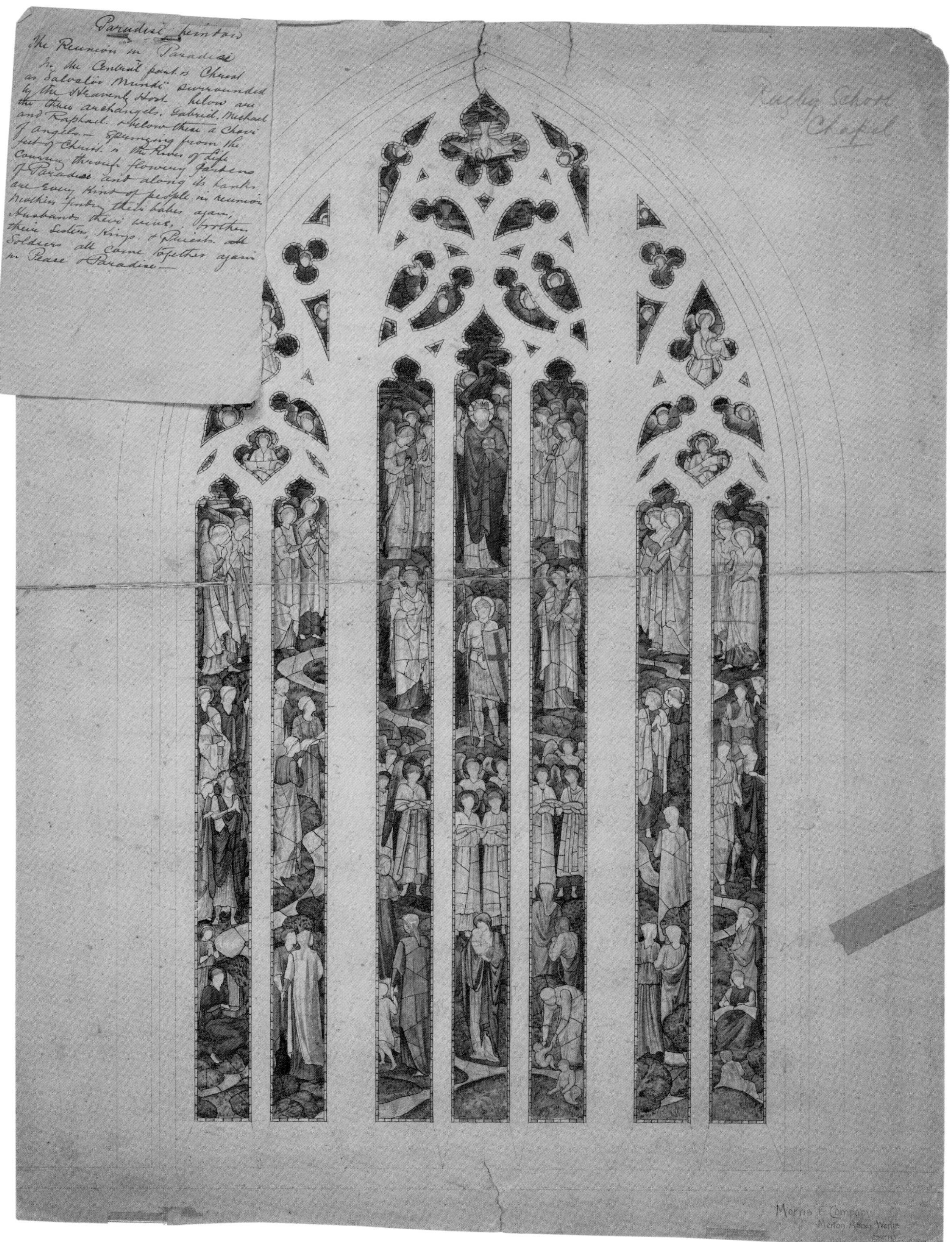
The Reunion in Paradise
In the Central part is Christ
as Salvator Mundi surrounded
by the Heavenly Host. below are
the three archangels. Gabriel. Michael
and Raphael. & below these a Choir
of angels.— Springing from the
feet of Christ. is the River of Life
coursing through flowery gardens
of Paradise and along its banks
are every kind of people. in reunion
Mothers finding their babes again;
Husbands their wives. brothers
their sisters, Kings. & Priests.
Soldiers all come together again
in Peace & Paradise—
Rugby School
Chapel
Morris & Company
Merton Abbey Works
Surrey

THE THINGS THAT MIGHT BE:

I DO NOT HOPE TO BE GREAT AT ALL IN ANYTHING, BUT PERHAPS I MIGHT REASONABLY HOPE TO BE HAPPY IN MY WORK, AND SOMETIMES WHEN I AM IDLE AND DOING NOTHING, PLEASANT VISIONS GO PAST ME OF THE THINGS THAT MIGHT BE.

William Morris, letter to his mother, 1855

BRITISH DESIGN *after* MORRIS

GILLIAN NAYLOR

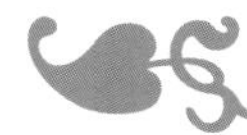

Morris wrote the words quoted opposite when he was twenty-one and meant to be studying theology at Oxford;[1] he had made some friends, written stories and poetry, and had read a great deal. He had travelled in England, Northern France and Belgium visiting cathedrals and churches, and he was now trying to justify his decision to become an architect. The discipline would be good for him, he told his mother. He would be working apprenticeship hours and learning a new trade; he would not be wasting time or family money; and he might even enjoy himself. As far as Morris was concerned, these were practical considerations to placate his mother. On a more personal level he was obviously following his own obsessions, teaching himself, and being taught, how to re-invent the past through making as well as observation.

No one could have anticipated 'the things that might be' in these visions of the 1850s. When Morris and his colleagues began to design stained glass, embroidery, wallpapers and furniture in the 1860s, they contributed to a renaissance in British craftsmanship and to a redefinition of the design profession, 'a force that impinged decisively on the world of practice'.[2] Morris was to become a symbol for new ideals of domesticity as well as for the politicizing of design. His philosophy and achievements still remain the focus of a wide range of studies, and William Morris scholarship and research has survived undiminished into the twenty-first century.[3]

Morris, along with John Ruskin, is generally considered the founder of the Arts and Crafts movement. This was a movement in design in the late nineteenth and early twentieth centuries that resisted industrialization and the rise of machine production. Its adherents condemned the division of labour brought about by commercial industry, in which the craftsman had no relationship to design and in which production was divided into a series of separate tasks performed by different workers. Seeking to re-integrate life and work, Arts and Crafts ideology was linked with British socialist thought. It also sought to break down the traditional barriers between the fine arts and the decorative arts.

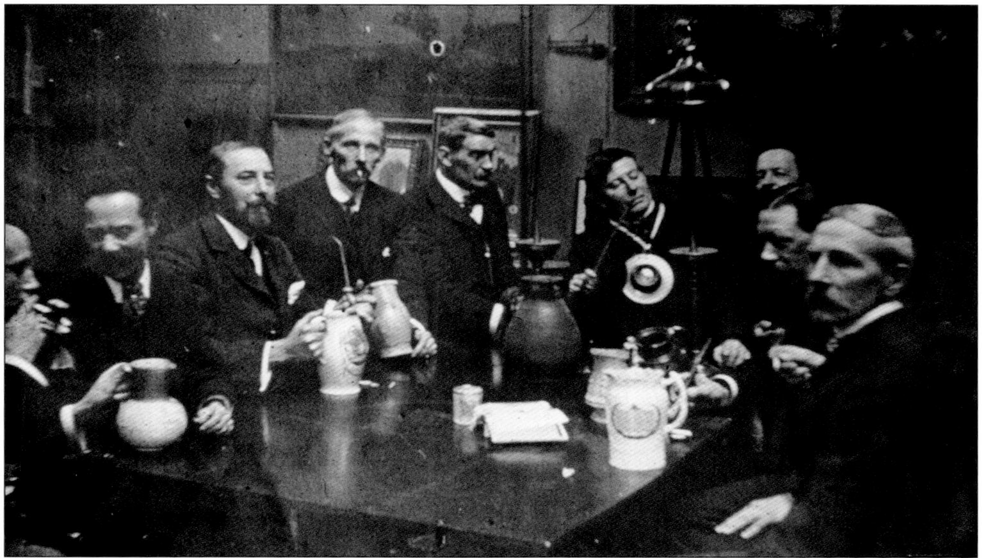

84 Members of the Art Workers Guild, *c.* 1903–9

Photograph
Courtesy of the Art Workers Guild

From left to right, the members are Archibald Macgregor, painter; Frank Marriott, painter; S. Melton Fisher, painter; unknown; William Strang, painter and etcher; George Frampton, sculptor; unknown; W. Harrison Townsend, architect; Frank Troup, architect.

In the late nineteenth century, Morris's ideals and philosophies inspired such practitioners of the Arts and Crafts as the Century Guild, a collective of designers founded in 1882 by A. H. Mackmurdo whose aim was to raise the status of the designer and to improve the quality of the decorative arts. Another group was the Art Workers Guild [84], established in 1884 as an exclusive society of architects and designers formed as an alternative to the Royal Academy of Arts, whose aim was also to elevate the status of the decorative arts. One of the most important organizations for the promotion of the decorative arts was the Arts and Crafts Exhibition Society, with which Morris himself was involved, founded in 1888 to provide a forum for the display of progressive design work. The name, devised by the book designer and binder T. J. Cobden-Sanderson, subsequently became attached to the movement as a whole. Designer C. R. Ashbee took Morris's ideals a step further when he moved his Guild of Handicraft, originally founded in London in 1888, to Chipping Campden in the Cotswolds in 1902, where it was organized on democratic principles and sought to return to a simpler life and earlier principles of hand craftsmanship [85].

This essay will concentrate on some British reactions to Morris, in terms of how designers viewed Morris's work and ideas and how they took inspiration from him, specifically in the design and production of stained and domestic glass, textiles, and typography. Transformed by the Morris example, the nature of professionalism in design and decoration was radically redefined. The role and status of the designer changed during this period, design becoming a suitable profession for the middle and upper-middle classes. The Arts and Crafts ideology of truth to materials and fitness for purpose came to dominate teaching in British design schools in the 1880s and 1890s [86]. In 1896, a month after Morris's death, a new institution, the Central School of Arts and Crafts, was established in London, and W. R. Lethaby, a follower of Morris, who had helped to launch the Art Workers Guild, was appointed its first principal. The Central School would play an important

85 Guild of Handicraft cabinet-makers at Chipping Campden, *c.* 1906

Photograph
Guild of Handicraft Trust

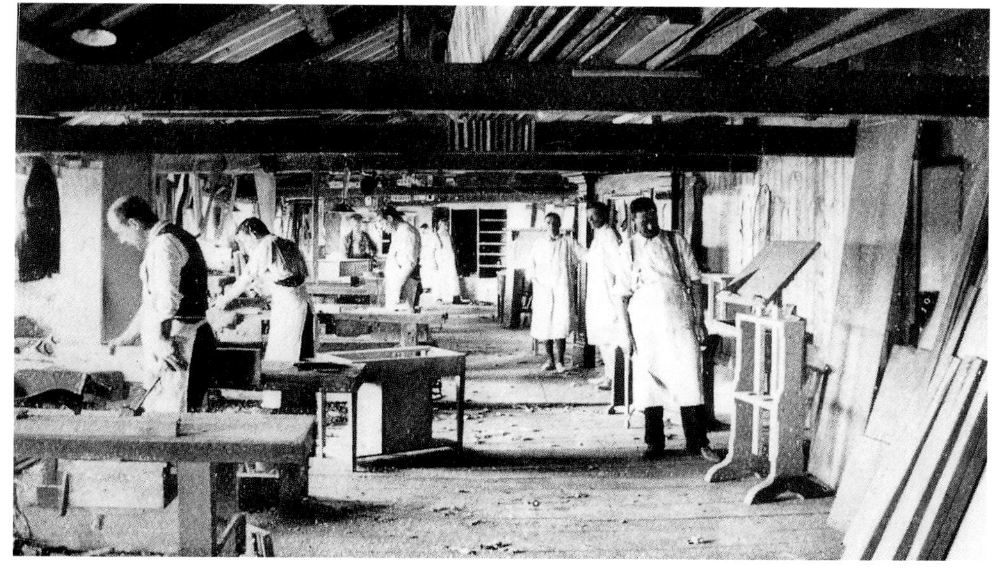

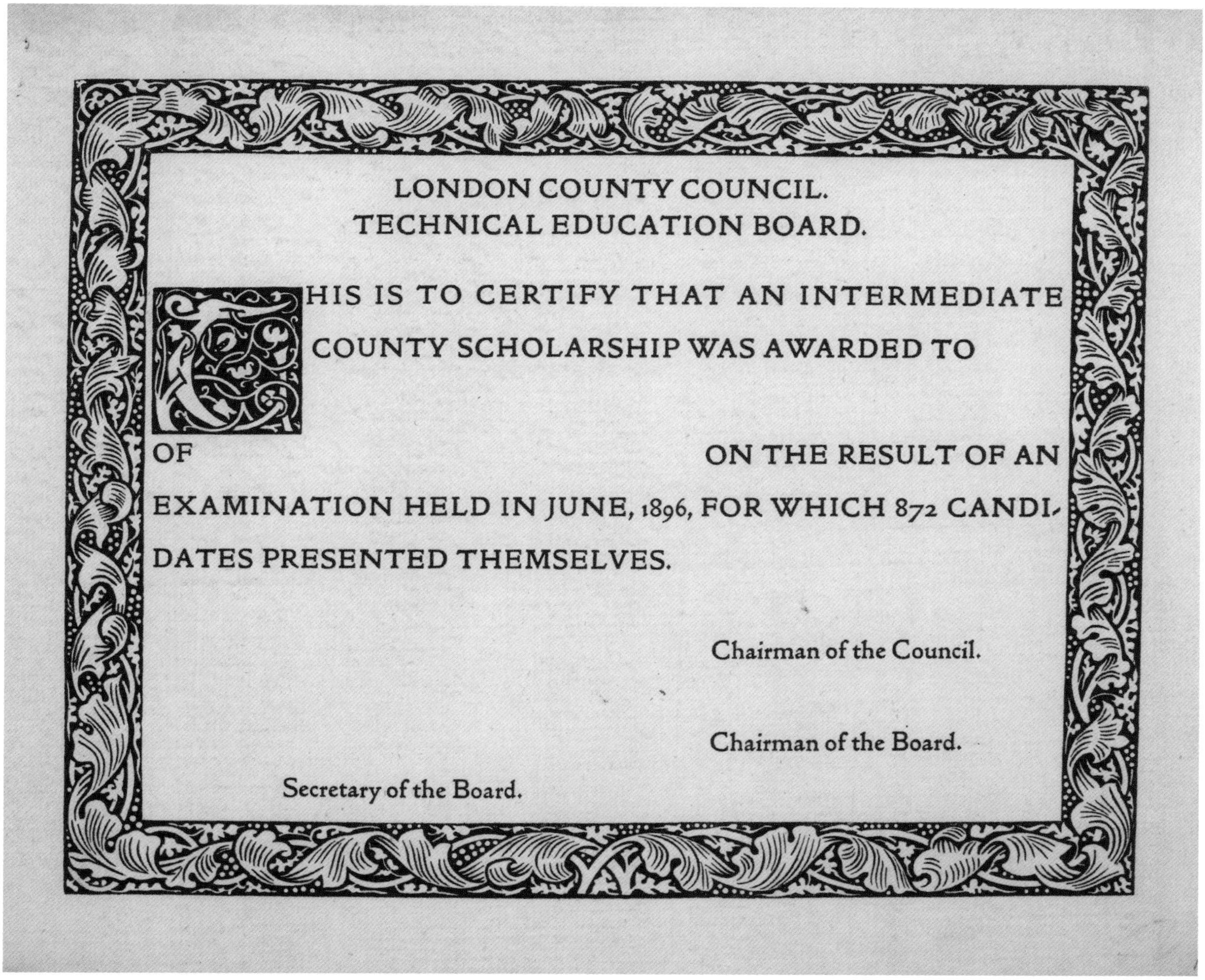

86 London County Council Technical Education Board Diploma, 1896

Printed by the Kelmscott Press,
$7\frac{3}{8}$ x $9\frac{1}{4}$ (18.7 x 23.5)

LONDON COUNTY COUNCIL.
TECHNICAL EDUCATION BOARD.

THIS IS TO CERTIFY THAT AN INTERMEDIATE COUNTY SCHOLARSHIP WAS AWARDED TO

OF ON THE RESULT OF AN EXAMINATION HELD IN JUNE, 1896, FOR WHICH 872 CANDIDATES PRESENTED THEMSELVES.

Chairman of the Council.

Chairman of the Board.

Secretary of the Board.

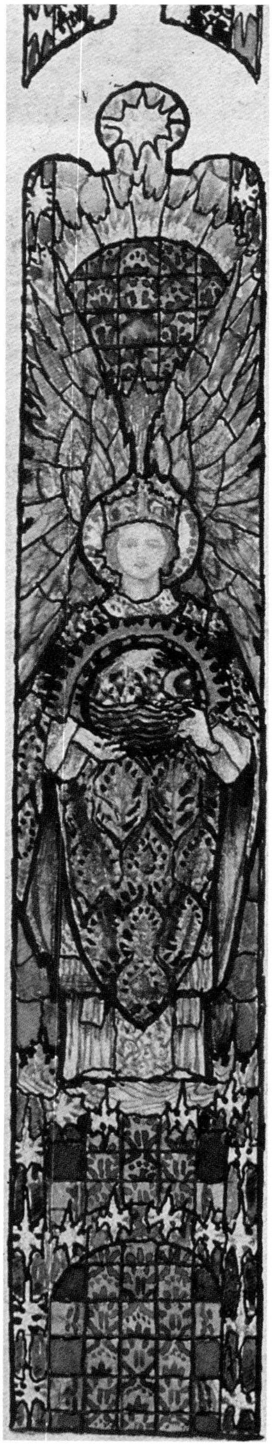

role in raising the status of the designer. The designer set standards for creativity as well as style, becoming as important as – or perhaps more important than – the fine artist.

Stained Glass and Table Glassware

Morris & Company stained glass was always produced as a collaborative effort. In the early years, one or more of the partners would make sketch designs for a window and then full-scale cartoons. Morris and Webb came up with the layout and decorative backgrounds. The cartoons would then be given to the glass painters in the studio, who would translate the design on paper into glass. Morris would supervise the choice of colour and make final approval of the window. In the later years, when Burne-Jones became the chief figure designer, he would provide cartoons for new commissions [9–11] or the glass painters would adapt earlier figure designs into cartoons. Morris or Dearle or one of the glass painters would provide the decorative details. Then the painters would be in charge of translating the overall design into glass, with Morris again giving final approval. In an influential article in the 1887 issue of *The Hobby Horse*, a magazine published by A. H. Mackmurdo, B. J. Aldam Heaton, of the stained glass firm of Heaton, Butler & Bayne, articulated objections to this practice of Morris & Company. Drawing designs for glass on paper – 'even by such an accomplished designer as Mr. Burne-Jones' – and then having a copyist transfer the designs to glass was unacceptable. 'What would a man think, having given an order for a picture to an eminent artist, when he discovered that the eminent artist had only drawn it in chalk on paper, and then handed it to his "young man" to copy it in colours on canvas! Yet this is done universally in stained glass.'[4] The design and production of stained glass was, in fact, one area where some of Morris's successors rejected the Firm's example. This was in part because so many Arts and Crafts designers, following Ruskin's teaching, rejected the division of labour.

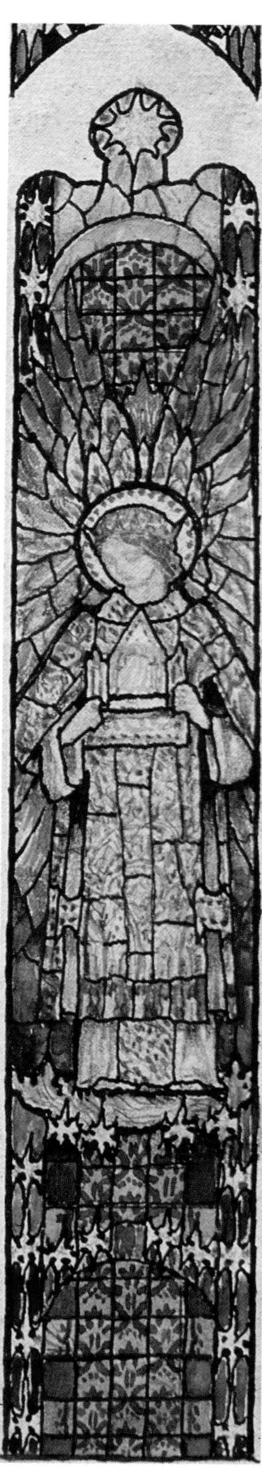

87 Christopher Whitworth Whall

Princedoms and Thrones, panels from a sketch design for a two-light clearstorey window at Holy Trinity, Sloane Street, London, 1911/12

Watercolour, ink and graphite, full sheet 13 x 5¾ (33 x 14.6)

William Morris Gallery, London

From the 1890s, the new generation of men and women who decided to specialize in stained glass – a training then available in art colleges oriented towards Arts and Crafts – would break with this tradition and attempt to integrate the design and production processes. Christopher Whall, an innovator in the production of stained glass [87], taught at the Central School of Arts and Crafts from 1896 and at the Royal College of Art from 1901. Initially a painter, he set out to learn the craft because he was dissatisfied with the way firms made up his work.[5] After reading Aldam Heaton's *Hobby Horse* article, Whall set up a studio in 1887 and trained his own pupils as well as students at the art colleges. His book, *Stained Glass Work*, was published in the 'Artistic Crafts' series edited by Lethaby in 1905 and is a persuasive piece of work, with its evocations of nature and colour – 'rich, deep, satisfying colour' – and its exhortations to students: 'all you people in art schools – do you really appreciate what you have got?'[6] Whall, like Heaton, rejected the division of labour and regretted its presence in Morris & Company. Although he believed Burne-Jones and Morris to be 'men of high genius, dauntless courage and energy', they did not, in his opinion, practice stained glass as a craft. Burne-Jones 'made beautiful drawings ... but they were not ideal as working drawings for a craft', and both 'allowed design and execution to be separated'.[7] By insisting on the unity of design and execution Whall isolated craft from any form of serial production, and in this case established the craftsperson as an artist.

Commissions for stained glass ensured Morris & Company's survival for a period after the First World War, but many younger designers felt that the Firm had become fossilized. Edward Payne, the son of Henry Payne who had taught in the Birmingham Municipal School of Art and Design and worked in stained glass for the Bromsgrove Guild, had met and admired Christopher Whall. Payne went on to study stained glass at the Royal College of Art and in 1929 went to work at Merton Abbey, with the Firm about to enter its last decade. He recalled that among the complex of buildings there the stained glass rooms were 'badly lit' and on the ground floor 'easels and boards occupied the centre ... on which were pinned the full sized photographically enlarged cartoons by

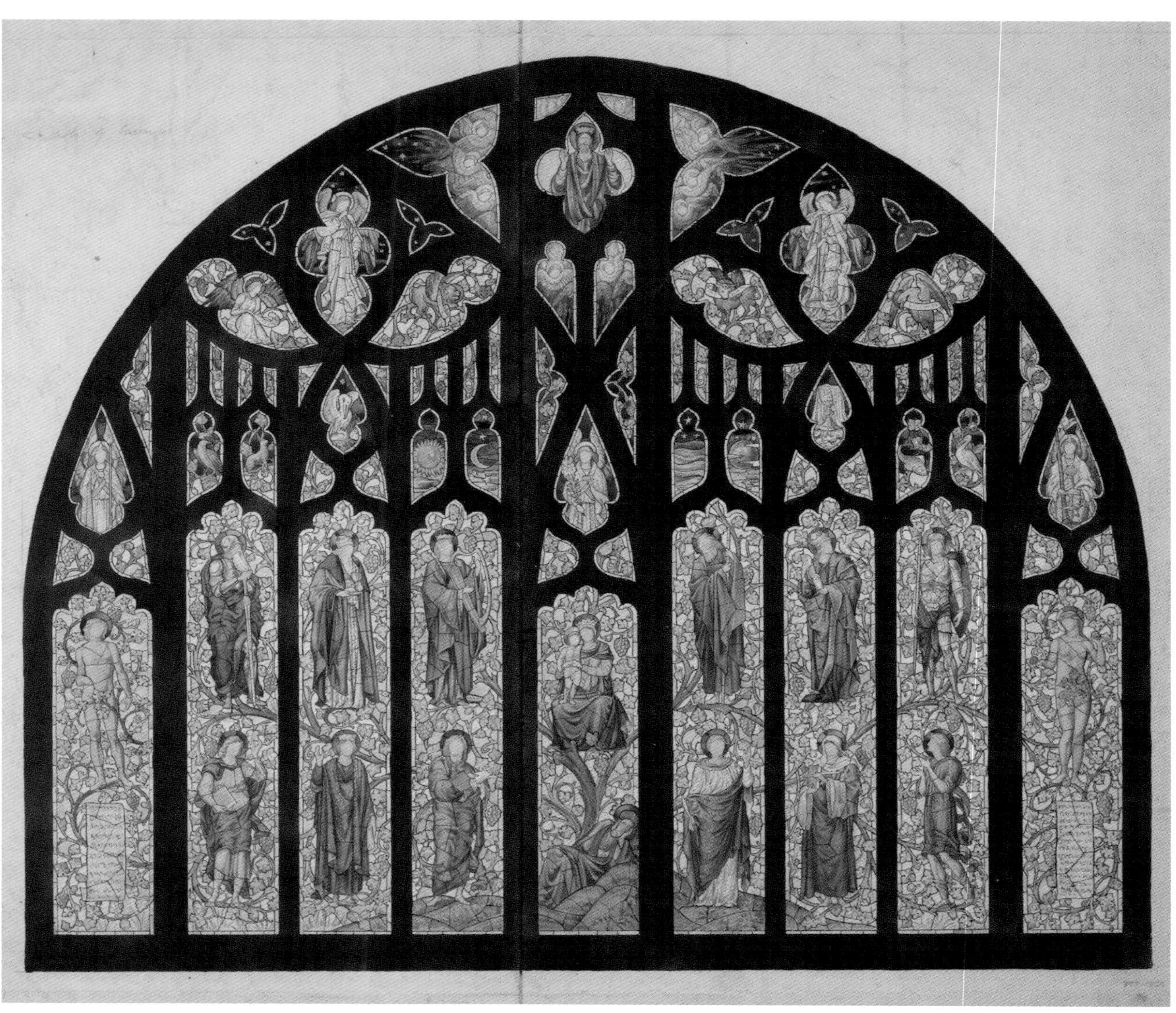

88 J. H. Dearle, with figures adapted from designs by William Morris and Edward Burne-Jones, for Morris & Company

Tree of Jesse, sketch design for the east window of All Saints, Compton, Leek, Staffordshire, *c.* 1923

Watercolour and ink, 22¼ x 23⅜ in. (56.5 x 59.4)

Burne-Jones'. When orders came in, the figures were adapted and adjusted as appropriate, and 'it was the strength of the Burne-Jones designs which kept the vitality – or what was left of the Morris vitality – in the glass windows produced at Merton. There may have been scope for original design, but the framework was too massive and full of Morris tastes to allow for a breakthrough' [88]. Payne felt that 'the Bauhaus and everything was going on, and here was this place where shadowy figures were creeping about in the gloom, waiting for orders from head office, who were transmitting orders from a dwindling number of clients as the taste of the time changed'.[8]

In spite of Edward Payne's frustration at Merton Abbey, there was a renaissance in the whole approach to stained glass in the inter-war period in Britain. This was focused on Chelsea and Fulham, where Whall's pupil Mary Lowndes and her partner Alfred Drury set up the Glass House to work with other artists in stained glass. In Dublin, Harry Clarke and Wilhelmina Geddes (trained at the Dublin Metropolitan Art School by Alfred Child, a student of Whall) established stained glass as an individual and individualist's art, drawing on Continental and Expressionist sources rather than Burne-Jones's visions of angels [89].

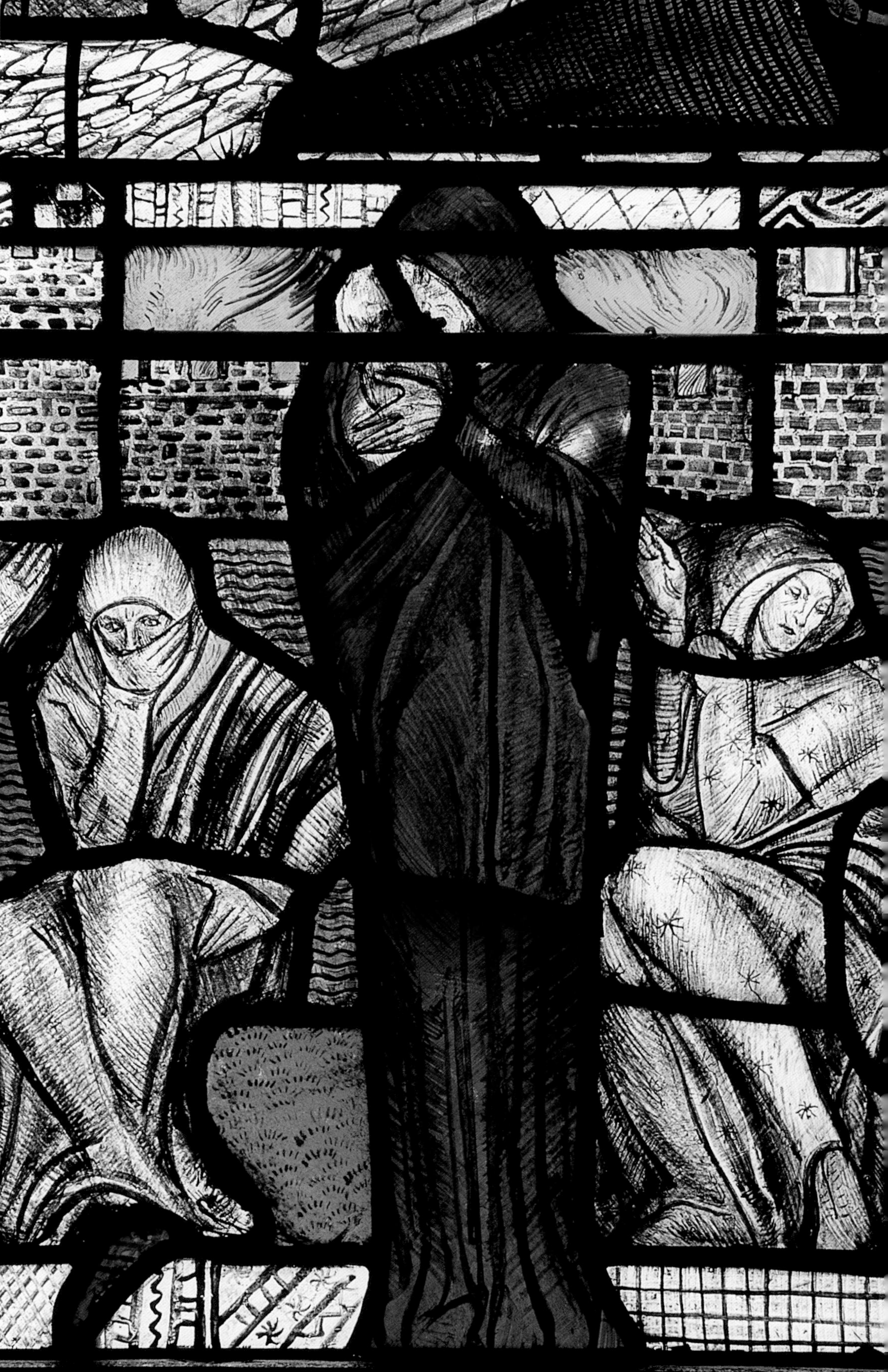

89 Wilhelmina Geddes

Women mourners, detail of the east window of St Bartholomew's, Ottawa, Canada, 1919

Photograph by Peter Cormack

This window, made in the 'Tower of Glass' workshop in Dublin, was exhibited at the Fulham Glass House before being shipped to Canada. Geddes's only window in North America, it was much admired by Charles J. Connick.

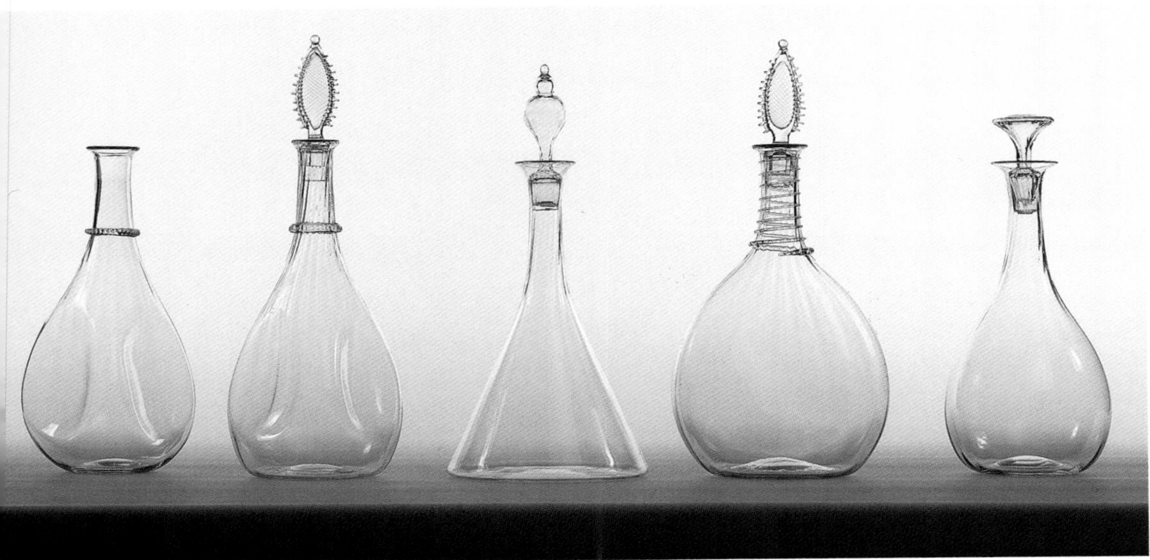

90 Harry Powell for Whitefriars Glass

Standard decanters, 1880s

Richard Dennis Publications

But if Morris & Company stained glass eventually came to seem outdated to progressive designers, the table glassware associated with the Firm was more radical. Philip Webb had designed drinking and wine glasses for Morris and his first home, Red House, in the early 1860s. These glasses were made by James Powell & Sons, owners of the Whitefriars Glassworks since 1834. They had begun their long collaboration with the Firm in its early years by supplying coloured glass for windows, and had exhibited glass at the International Exhibition in London in 1862 as had Morris, Marshall, Faulkner & Company. The simplicity of Webb's designs – the reliance on subtleties of form rather than cutting – acknowledged Ruskin's conviction that all cut glass was barbarous.

Several British firms began to produce similar ranges, especially towards the end of the century, and Harry Powell, who joined the family firm in 1873 and who became manager of Whitefriars in 1875, and chief designer in the 1880s, continued to work in the Webb tradition. Powell designed glass that was exhibited in Britain, Europe and the United States, and the clarity of its aesthetic demonstrated both Arts and Crafts and Modernist ideals [90]. The *Art Journal* in 1889 claimed that Powell's glass was achieving 'a beautiful quality which may be accounted of quite modern origin, whilst it wants nothing of the essential beauty of the ancient prototype'[9] – the ancient prototype, in this case, being old Venetian glass. Modernity in Britain in the 1880s and 1890s was generally attributed to contemporary designs that acknowledged a past, a very Morrisian sentiment and one which persisted, since Powell's continued to produce these glasses until the 1930s.

Textiles

William Morris did not entirely reject commercial methods of textile production when he set up his own works at Merton Abbey. Neither did he reject commercial methods for their sale and distribution. By the turn of the century, Morris & Company had become part of an expanding and complex network of designers, manufacturers, specialist shops and department stores who were providing ranges of textiles for domestic and fashion use. The customers – the affluent middle classes – now had an increasingly important role to play in stimulating design *and* consumption, since the judicious use of textiles could signal the celebration of the House Beautiful, so frequently mentioned by the art press. Potential consumers could also learn about domestic taste in a growing range of books and magazines. *The Studio*, for example, was launched in 1893 and covered Arts and Crafts exhibitions as well as Arts and Crafts developments. The textile designs available at the turn of the century were, like Morris's, for the most part related to nature, showing a taste for flora and fauna and natural form. What Morris had described as the 'meaningless stripes and spots and other tormentings of the simple twill of the web, which are so common in the woven ornament of the eighteenth century',[10] were no longer in demand. Neo-classical abstractions were replaced by vibrant pattern-making, in the work of both specialist designers and textile manufacturers. Department stores such as Liberty & Co., originally founded on the Eastern trade, were dedicated to the House Beautiful [91]. Liberty bought their textiles from designers as well as manufacturers, and even set up a store in Paris in 1890, pioneering Britain's prestige in the centre of fashion. Thomas Wardle (who had collaborated with Morris in the 1870s and produced printed cottons for Morris & Company), G. P. & J. Baker, Alexander Morton (who had also made woven fabrics for Morris & Company), and Warner & Sons all produced textiles for Liberty, and free-lance designers included the architect C. F. A. Voysey [92], the Silver Studio, Lindsay P. Butterfield and George C. Haité. By the turn of the century art colleges, many of them staffed by Art Workers Guild

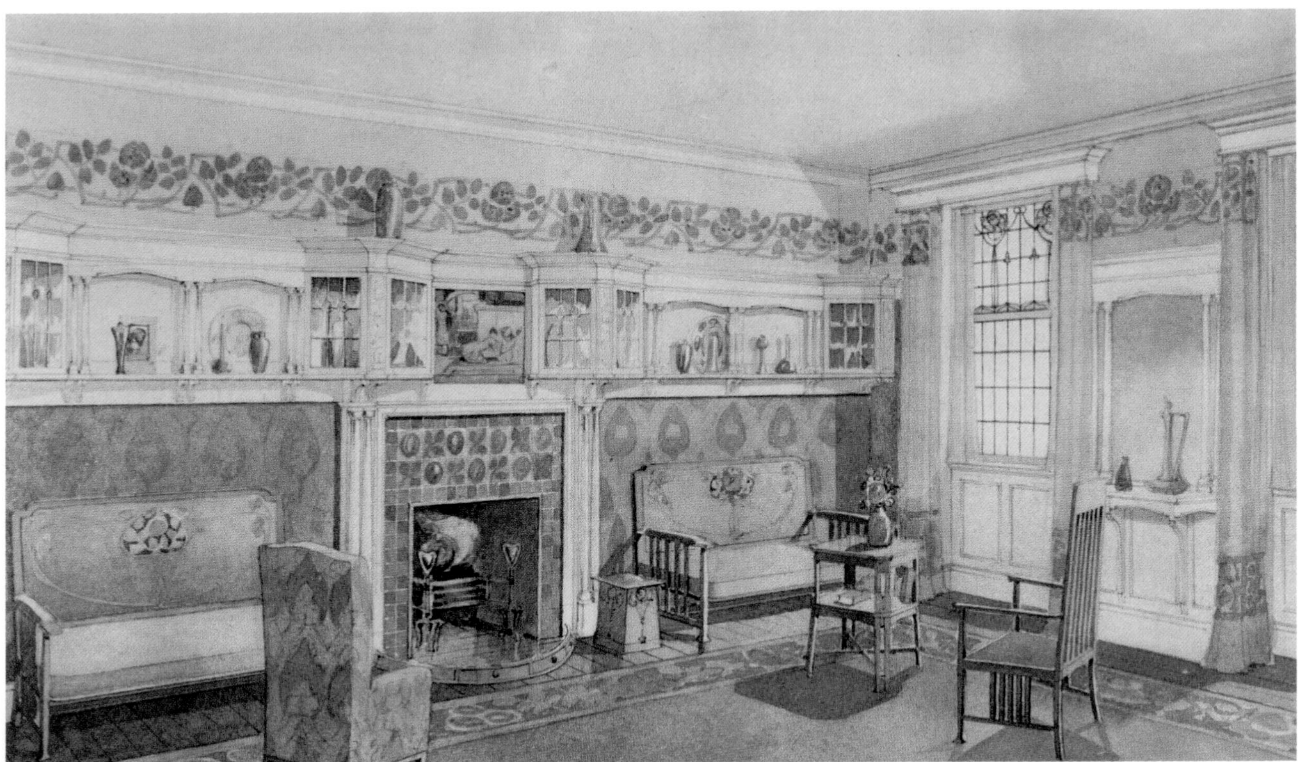

91 Liberty & Co.
Design for a drawing room
From *The Studio Yearbook of Decorative Art* (London: Studio Ltd, 1906)

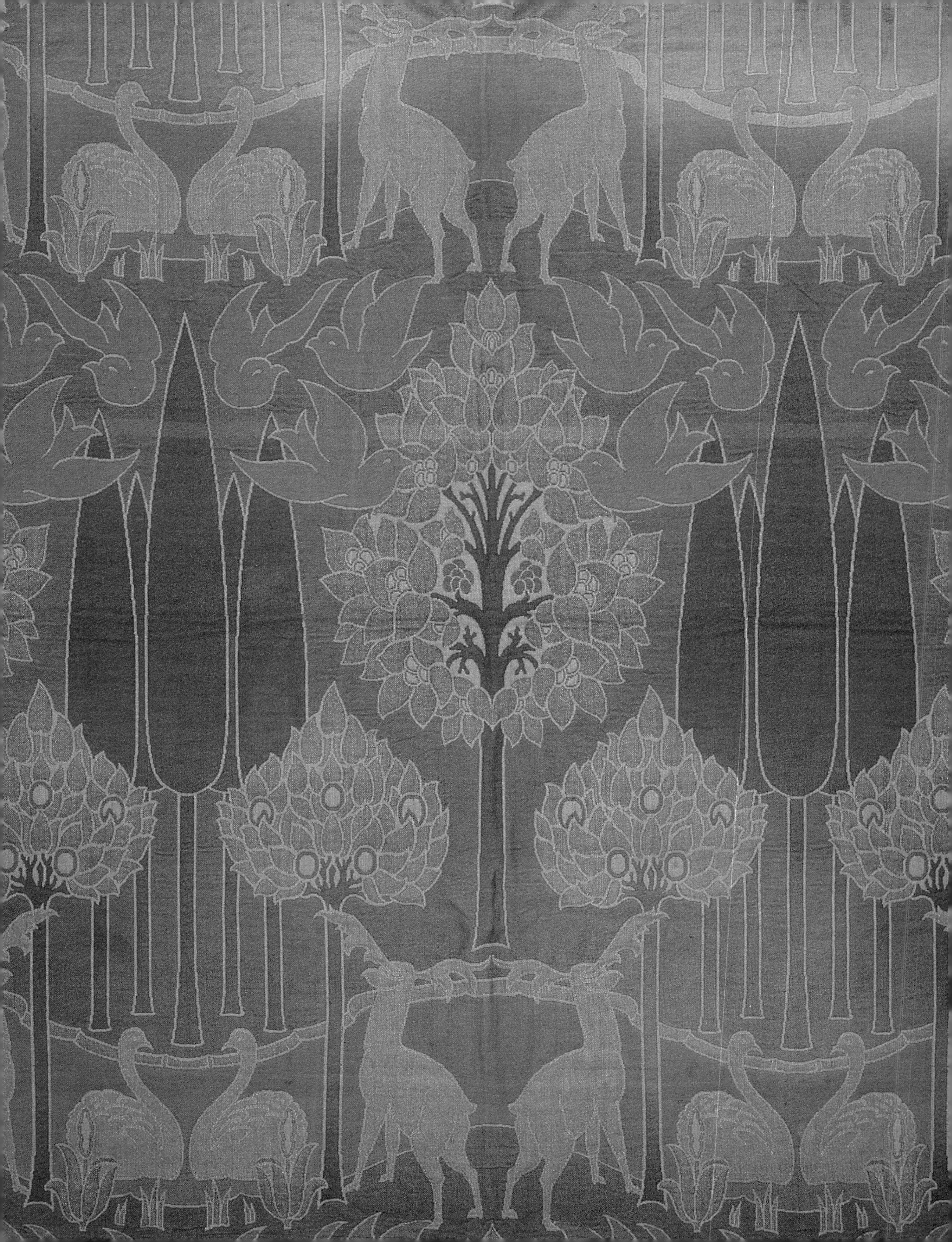

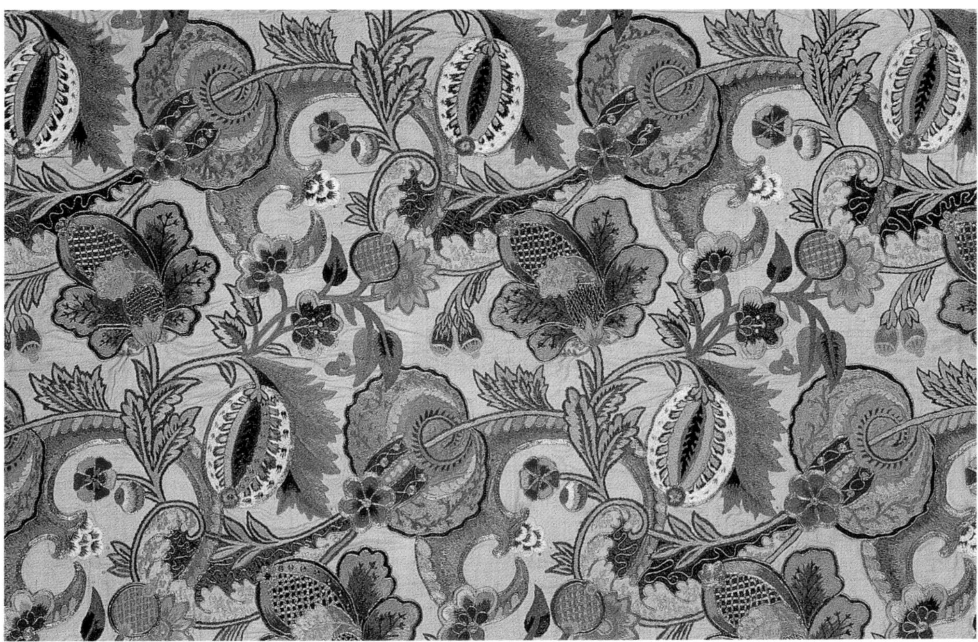

93 Frances Mary Templeton

Leek Embroidery Society panel, 1892 (detail)

Embroidered in wools, silks, gold thread and silver sequins on a cream tusser silk ground printed with the design by Thomas Wardle, Leek, Staffordshire, full piece 31 x 31 (78.8 x 78.8)

Victoria & Albert Museum Picture Library, London

members, were turning out more trained designers to work either free-lance or within industry.

At this same period embroidery, as practised by Morris and May Morris and many of the Firm's founders and friends in the early days, had become a major art. The Royal School of Art Needlework had been set up in 1872, its aim to improve the standard of commercial embroidery and provide 'suitable employment for educated women'.[11] Many of the 'educated women' worked on commissions by men, but the School also offered teacher-training courses so that embroidery could be taught as a domestic skill. The Leek Embroidery Society was founded in 1879 or 1880 by Elizabeth Wardle, the wife of Thomas Wardle [93]. Morris & Company's silks and yarns were used to produce William Morris's designs, church embroidery and other commissions. Encouraged in art colleges, embroidery became an inventive and creative skill. One centre was Glasgow, where Ann Macbeth and Jessie Newbery, the wife of Francis Newbery, the principal of the Glasgow School of Art, taught Margaret and Frances Macdonald and their colleagues to use embroidery as art [94]. When she retired from the Glasgow School of Art in the 1920s Ann Macbeth went to live in the Lake District, where she painted and produced tapestry. The Lake District, where Ruskin had had a home since the 1870s and where he was to spend his final years, had been supporting local industries since the 1880s. In 1883 Albert Fleming, a devotee of Ruskin, had set up the Langdale Linen Industry, to produce hand-woven linen; the Keswick School of Industrial Arts was also founded in 1883. Annie Garnett, who grew up in Cumberland during the hand-craft revival there, and who also knew Ruskin, set up The Spinnery, a textile workshop, in 1891. From the 1880s to the First World War, followers of Ruskin sponsored and created a craft revival that they felt was specific to the locality. It was focused on local skills and based, as far as possible, on traditional craft industries. The cottagers – spinners, weavers, embroiderers and carvers – were paid for their work and the School of Industrial Arts (privately run, and independent from the South Kensington Schools of Design) taught local skills.[12]

92 C. F. A. Voysey for Liberty & Co.

Woven fabric, originally designed as a wallpaper frieze, 1897 (detail)

Jacquard-woven wool double cloth, manufactured by Alexander Morton & Co., Darvel, Scotland, complete width 63 ½ (161.3)

Victoria & Albert Museum Picture Library, London

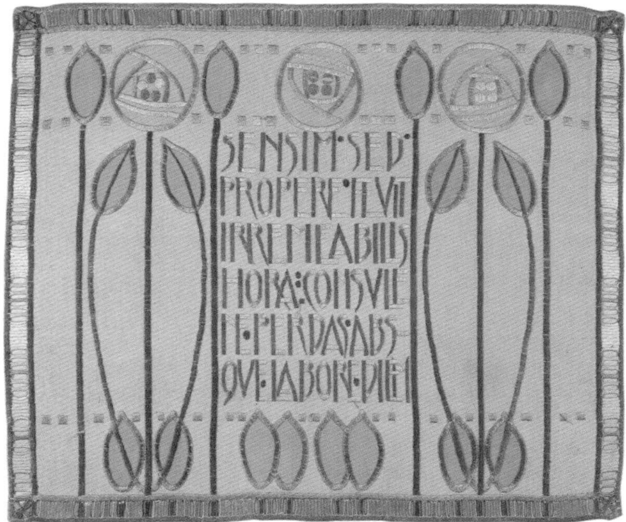

94 Jessie Newbery

Cushion, *c.* 1900

Linen appliqué embroidered in silks with edges of needleweaving, 22¾ x 25½ (57.8 x 64.8)

Victoria & Albert Museum Picture Library, London

95 Dorothy Larcher

Small Feather, 1930s (detail)

Hand block-printed and indigo-discharged linen, complete width 28 (71.1)

Victoria & Albert Museum Picture Library, London

Attempts to protect and sustain cottage industries and to prevent a migration to the city were also evident in rural Scotland and Wales, and these initiatives were complemented by the policies of the Home Arts and Industries Association, an organization that was set up in 1884. The Home Arts were dedicated to teaching and sponsoring 'spinning and knitting, sewing and tailoring, carpentry and cabinet making, basket work and boat-building'.[13] These philanthropic organizations were generally sponsored by the local aristocracy and run by the wives of the wealthy; their aim was to provide the rural working classes (especially the women) with the vernacular skills of their locality and ensure the survival of traditional and affordable crafts. Their exhibitions (in London and in local venues) were well attended, and they encouraged home craft movements that were popular in the 1920s and 1930s (when domestic science, another skill that could be learned and practised by the housewife, was also developing). Such endeavours, like the segregation of craft and industry, tended to categorize the crafts. Home Arts and Industries and similar projects focused on traditional and home-based skills; they supported regional crafts, and many of them came to be associated with the Tudor Revival, the stamped leather stools, the lace doilies and the ubiquitous metal bowls of the suburban home.

By the 1920s and 1930s, however, craft, especially textile craft, had established its own avant garde which, while it accepted Morris's ideals, nevertheless transformed his practice. Textile designers like Ethel Mairet, Dorothy Larcher [95], Phyllis Barron and Enid Marx were experimenting with vegetable dyes, and with hand-weaving and block-printing techniques, in order to produce work that was totally unlike that of the previous generation. They seemed to be contributing to an international vernacular which was consciously and confidently designed, evoking the weaves and structures of Eastern European, Scandinavian and Italian folk art. Enid Marx went on to apply her ideas to industrial practice, while Ethel Mairet was working near C. R. Ashbee's Guild of Handicraft at Chipping Campden, and at Ditchling in Sussex, where Eric Gill had founded his Guild of St Joseph and St Dominic.[14]

While Gill was catholicizing Morris's philosophies, Ethel Mairet was re-orienting his skills. She rejected Morrisian picture making and pattern design in her weaving, creating abstract designs that could be related to Scandinavian folk textiles, and like the designers at the Weimar Bauhaus she considered her weaves as prototypes for industrial production.

Book Printing and Typography

Standards in book and type design as well as calligraphy preoccupied many collectors and practitioners in the latter half of the nineteenth century and Morris was much involved in these debates. He had collected early books and manuscripts and had produced his own work, experimenting with calligraphy. Before the Kelmscott Press was founded he had worked with the Chiswick Press on the design of three of his own books, *The House of the Wolfings* (1889), *The Roots of the Mountains* (1890) [65], and *The Story of Gunnlaug the Worm-Tongue* (1891), and he had also been involved with the publication of the socialist weekly, the *Commonweal*, in the 1880s: 'I was much among type', he told a reporter, 'when I was editor of the *Commonweal*.'[15] His most important associate in book printing was his neighbour in Hammersmith, Emery Walker, whose lecture, 'Letterpress Printing and Illustration', delivered to the Arts and Crafts Exhibition Society in 1888, determined Morris to design his own typefaces and to set up the Kelmscott Press [96]. It is worth quoting at length from Morris's account of his reasons for launching the Press, since it was to provide a basis for subsequent debates about the theory and practice of book design. 'I began printing books', he wrote in *Aims in Founding the Kelmscott Press*,

96 Kelmscott Press Circular, showing examples of Golden, Troy and Chaucer typefaces, 1897
8 x 5¾ (20.3 x 14.6)

> with the hope of producing some which would have a definite claim to beauty, while at the same time they should be easy to read and should not dazzle the eye, or trouble the intellect of the reader by eccentricity of form in the letters. I have always been a great admirer of the calligraphy of the Middle Ages, and of the earlier printing which took its place. As to the fifteenth century books, I had noticed that they were always beautiful by force of the mere typography, even without the added ornament, with which many of them are so lavishly supplied. And it was the essence of my undertaking to produce books which it would be a pleasure to look upon as pieces of printing and arrangement of type. Looking at my adventure from this point of view then, I found I had to consider chiefly the following things: the paper, the form of the type, the relative spacing of the letters, the words and the lines; and lastly the position of the printed matter on the page.[16]

These were to remain the foremost considerations of Modernist typographers until the 1960s.

The launch of the Kelmscott Press in 1891 was followed by the establishment of several private presses in England which emulated the Morris achievement if not the Kelmscott style. C. R. Ashbee's Essex House Press, founded in 1898, was the nearest in aim to Kelmscott, since Ashbee had bought Morris's two Albion presses when Kelmscott was closed and had set out, not entirely successfully, to work in the Morris tradition.The Ashendene Press [98], founded by C. H. St John Hornby in 1894, was

KELMSCOTT PRESS, UPPER MALL, HAMMERSMITH.

July 28th, 1897.

Note. This is the Golden type.
This is the Troy type.
This is the Chaucer type.

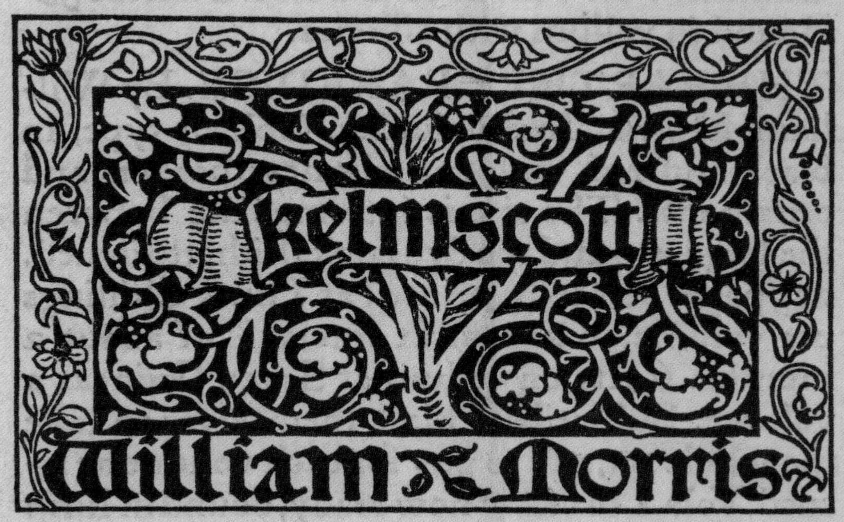

Secretary:
S. C. Cockerell, Kelmscott Press, Upper Mall, Hammersmith, London, W., to whom all letters should be addressed, or to

Morris & Company
449 Oxford Street
London W.

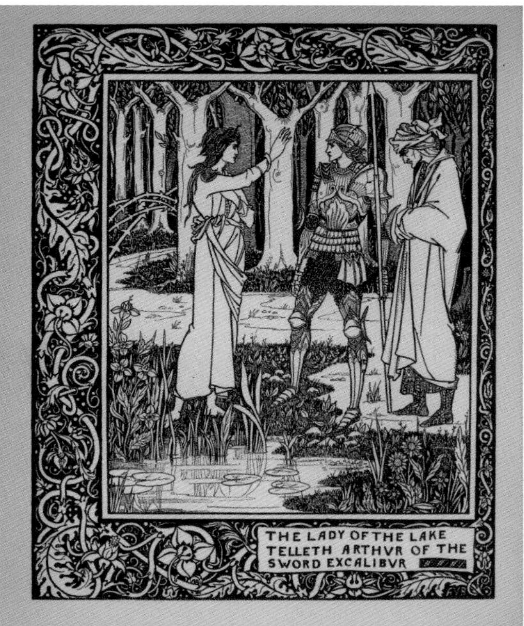

97 Aubrey Beardsley
'The Lady of the Lake telleth Arthur of the Sword Excalibur', illustration from Sir Thomas Malory, *Le Morte d'Arthur* (London: J. M. Dent & Company, 1893–94)

more restrained and several of those involved, including Sydney Cockerell and Emery Walker, as well as Edward Johnston and Graily Hewitt, were to contribute to the Modernist concern for balanced layout and legible typography in Britain in the 1920s and 1930s. Johnston and Hewitt also worked for the Doves Press [99], which was founded by T. J. Cobden-Sanderson and Emery Walker in 1900 to demonstrate 'the wholeness, symmetry, harmony, beauty without stress or strain, of the BOOK BEAUTIFUL'.[17] Lucien Pissarro came to London in 1890 'at the time when William Morris's "Arts and Crafts" movement was in full swing' in order to set up the Eragny Press.[18] Charles Ricketts and Charles Shannon, whom he visited 'at their studio in The Vale, Chelsea', helped Pissarro with the production of his first book. The Vale Press, which ran from 1896 to 1903, was influenced by Aubrey Beardsley and Art Nouveau. Beardsley had been rejected as an illustrator for the Kelmscott Press in 1892 and was bitterly opposed to William Morris and all his works. In 1897, responding to a proposal for a new magazine to be called *Peacock*, he wrote: 'On the art side I suggest that it should attack untiringly and unflinchingly the Burne-Jones and Morrisian medieval business, and set up a wholesome seventeenth- and eighteenth-century standard of what picture making should be.'[19] Beardsley's *Le Morte d'Arthur* [97], published by Dent in 1893–94, was a vengeful parody of the Morris manner.

98 *Tutte le opere di Dante Alighieri* (London: Ashendene Press, 1909)
The typeface is Subiaco.

Debates and developments reflected reactions both to Morris's medium and to his message, and by the turn of the century calligraphy, book design and typography were part of an energetic and eclectic profession. In 1905 the Central School of Arts and Crafts set up a department of book design and printing. The first instructor of printing was J. H. Mason, chief compositor at the Doves Press. Edward Johnston taught calligraphy (his book, *Writing & Illuminating, & Lettering*, was first published in 1906 and frequently reprinted throughout the 1920s and 1930s) and his students at the Central School included Graily Hewitt, Anna Simons, Noel Rooke and Eric Gill. Noel Rooke was appointed the teacher of book illustration at the Central School in 1905 and pioneered a revival in wood-engraving. The Central School's philosophies

QUI COMINCIA LA SECONDA CANTICA DELLA COMMEDIA DI DANTE ALIGHIERI, DETTA PURGATORIO. CANTO PRIMO.

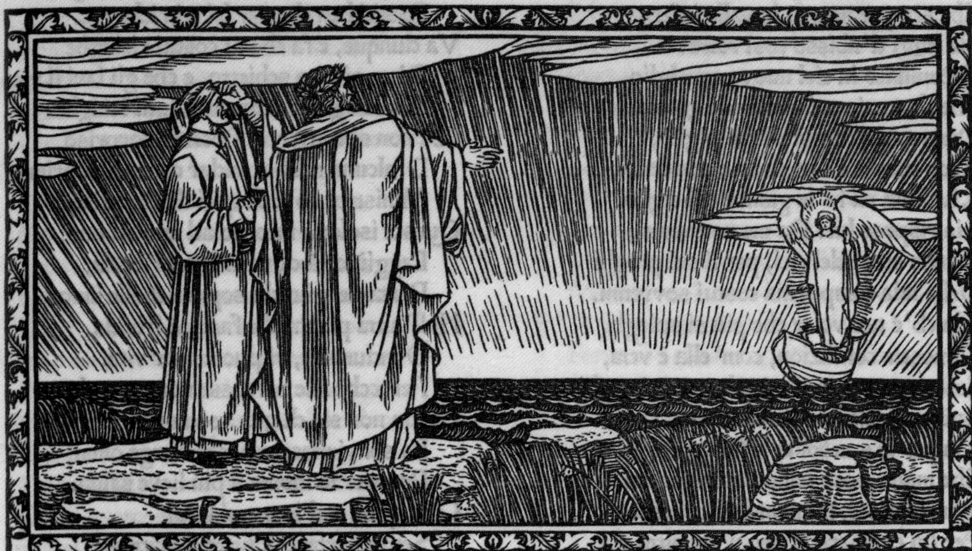

PER CORRER MIGLIOR ACQUA ALZA LE VELE
  Omai la navicella del mio ingegno,
  Che lascia retro a se mar sì crudele.
E canterò di quel secondo regno,
  Dove l'umano spirito si purga,
  E di salire al ciel diventa degno.
Ma qui la morta poesì risurga,
  O sante Muse, poichè vostro sono,
  E qui Calliopè alquanto surga,
Seguitando il mio canto con quel suono
  Di cui le Piche misere sentiro
  Lo colpo tal, che disperar perdono.
Dolce color d'oriental zaffiro,
  Che s'accoglieva nel sereno aspetto
  Dal mezzo puro infino al primo giro,
Agli occhi miei ricominciò diletto,
  Tosto ch'i' uscii fuor dell'aura morta,
  Che m'avea contristati gli occhi & il petto.
Lo bel pianeta che ad amar conforta
  Faceva tutto rider l'oriente,
  Velando i Pesci ch'erano in sua scorta.
Io mi volsi a man destra, e posi mente
  All'altro polo, e vidi quattro stelle
  Non viste mai fuor che alla prima gente.
Goder pareva il ciel di lor fiammelle.
  O settentrional vedovo sito,
  Poichè privato sei di mirar quelle!
Com'io dal loro sguardo fui partito,
  Un poco me volgendo all'altro polo,
  Là onde il carro già era sparito,
Vidi presso di me un veglio solo,
  Degno di tanta riverenza in vista,
  Che più non dee a padre alcun figliuolo.
Lunga la barba & di pel bianco mista
  Portava, e i suoi capegli simigliante,
  De' quai cadeva al petto doppia lista.
Li raggi delle quattro luci sante
  Fregiavan sì la sua faccia di lume,
  Ch'io 'l vedea come il sol fosse davante.
Chi siete voi, che contro al cieco fiume
  Fuggito avete la prigione eterna?
  Diss'ei, movendo quell'oneste piume.

IN THE BEGINNING GOD CREATED THE HEAVEN AND THE EARTH. ¶ AND THE EARTH WAS WITHOUT FORM, AND VOID; AND DARKNESS WAS UPON THE FACE OF THE DEEP, & THE SPIRIT OF GOD MOVED UPON THE FACE OF THE WATERS. ¶ And God said, Let there be light: & there was light. And God saw the light, that it was good: & God divided the light from the darkness. And God called the light Day, and the darkness he called Night. And the evening and the morning were the first day. ¶ And God said, Let there be a firmament in the midst of the waters, & let it divide the waters from the waters. And God made the firmament, and divided the waters which were under the firmament from the waters which were above the firmament: & it was so. And God called the firmament Heaven. And the evening & the morning were the second day. ¶ And God said, Let the waters under the heaven be gathered together unto one place, and let the dry land appear: and it was so. And God called the dry land Earth; and the gathering together of the waters called he Seas: and God saw that it was good. And God said, Let the earth bring forth grass, the herb yielding seed, and the fruit tree yielding fruit after his kind, whose seed is in itself, upon the earth: & it was so. And the earth brought forth grass, & herb yielding seed after his kind, & the tree yielding fruit, whose seed was in itself, after his kind: and God saw that it was good. And the evening & the morning were the third day. ¶ And God said, Let there be lights in the firmament of the heaven to divide the day from the night; and let them be for signs, and for seasons, and for days, & years: and let them be for lights in the firmament of the heaven to give light upon the earth: & it was so. And God made two great lights; the greater light to rule the day, and the lesser light to rule the night: he made the stars also. And God set them in the firmament of the heaven to give light upon the earth, and to rule over the day and over the night, & to divide the light from the darkness: and God saw that it was good. And the evening and the morning were the fourth day. ¶ And God said, Let the waters bring forth abundantly the moving creature that hath life, and fowl that may fly above the earth in the open firmament of heaven. And God created great whales, & every living creature that moveth, which the waters brought forth abundantly, after their kind, & every winged fowl after his kind: & God saw that it was good. And God blessed them, saying, Be fruitful, & multiply, and fill the waters in the seas, and let fowl multiply in the earth. And the evening & the morning were the fifth day. ¶ And God said, Let the earth bring forth the living creature after his kind, cattle, and creeping thing, and beast of the earth after his kind: and it was so. And God made the beast of the earth after his kind, and cattle after their kind, and every thing that creepeth upon the

27

99 *The English Bible* (London: The Doves Press, 1903–5)

The beginning of the Gospel according to St John, set in Doves typeface.

were shared by the Royal College of Art (RCA) in London: Lethaby had been appointed head of design at the RCA in 1901 and Johnston began to teach calligraphy there in the same year. In spite of his reluctance to abandon calligraphy for typography – according to his daughter he believed that the proper person to design type was the punch cutter – Johnston was commissioned to design the sans serif typeface for the London Underground in 1916, and Johnston's former student Eric Gill designed one of the most celebrated sans serif faces, Gill Sans, for the Monotype Corporation

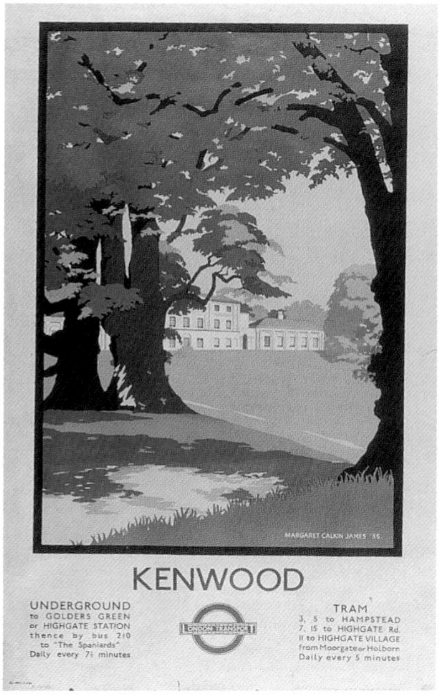

100 Margaret Calkin James

Kenwood, poster for the London Underground, 1935

40 x 25 (101.6 x 63.5)

London Transport Museum

in 1928. Commercial printing standards, therefore, were re-examined in the light of Kelmscott convictions and work that was designed, in Morris's words, to be 'a pleasure to look upon as pieces of printing and arrangement of type' set a standard throughout the 1920s and 1930s. As Carl P. Rollins, at that time Printer to Yale University, wrote in the 1940s, 'The new movement [in printing standards] got its greatest impetus from William Morris. ... If the work of the Kelmscott Press was in the nature of a *tour de force* so far as actually setting a new style is concerned, its influence turned the whole attention of printers into new and fecund channels.'[20]

The 'finest flowering' of Johnston-inspired calligraphy also flourished in the inter-war period. The italic hand was taught to designers and teachers and one of its most noted practitioners was Margaret Calkin James, who went to the Central School in 1914 where she was taught calligraphy by Graily Hewitt (who had been taught by Johnston). James also designed book covers for Jonathan Cape, posters for the London Underground [100], and pattern papers for the Curwen Press, as well as designs for fabrics and embroidery. 'If we could all begin at home and be satisfied with bare necessities, banishing from our lives all those things that not only are not made or fitted for a specific purpose, but that we could do without, we should then find the country would only produce things that mattered, that work could be done well, and the workers would be happy', she is reported as saying in 1921.[21] Happy workers and work done well – Morris's philosophy in a nutshell – had obviously inspired a generation of designers, makers and manufacturers.

In the 1920s and 1930s 'good' design was associated with social responsibility, and the Arts and Crafts values and aesthetic were, especially in establishment circles, now considered appropriate to design for industry. What constituted 'well done work', however, was to be challenged by the programmes of an avant garde who aimed to substitute formal and spatial geometries for the 'new traditionalism' of their contemporaries. Jan Tschichold, for example, promoting the 'New Typography' in *Circle* (1937),[22] described how both it and the 'New Traditionalism' in typography avoided

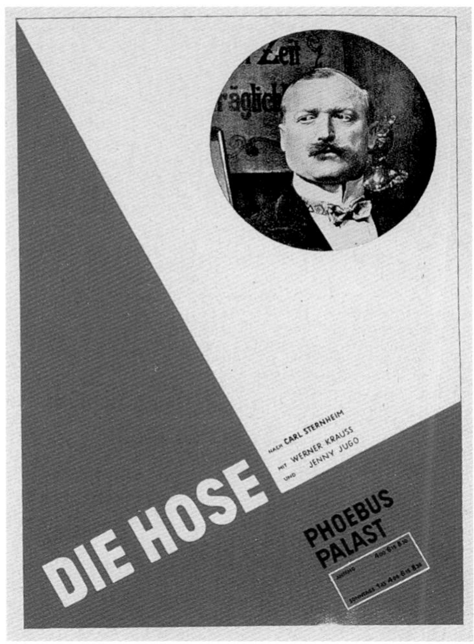

101 Jan Tschichold

Film poster for Phoebus Palast, 1927

From *Die Neue Typographie: ein Handbuch für zeitgemäss Schaffende* (Berlin: Bildungsverbandes der deutschen Buchdrucker, 1928)

ornament and paid attention to careful typesetting and good proportional structure. Nevertheless, the 'New Typography', according to Tschichold, triumphed over the traditional by ignoring the past; it sought contrasts rather than harmony in the manipulation of type; it stressed asymmetry rather than symmetry, and functionalism rather than pleasing appearance in the layout; and it preferred the use of photographs to woodcuts and drawings [101]. Tschichold's typography and page layout were totally different from those of William Morris. Similarly, avant garde textile designers in the 1920s and 1930s ignored the Morris aesthetic, and stained glass artists rejected Morris & Company methods of production. Yet if Morris's style no longer seemed relevant, his ideals and his social commitment persisted in the activities of this next generation of designers.

Morris in the Twentieth Century

In the decades following his death Morris's reputation went through many changes. At the beginning of the twentieth century, his philosophies and those of the Arts and Crafts movement were associated with the rise of national ideals of craftsmanship in several European countries – especially in Scandinavia and Germany – as well as with the craft revival in the United States. Art Nouveau's re-assessment of form and decoration was also attributed to Morrisian radicalism: in 1904, for example, Hermann Muthesius, who was to be the co-founder of the Deutscher Werkbund – a pioneer design reform association set up in Munich in 1907 in order to improve the design of mass-produced consumer goods and to campaign for craftsmen to work in industry – had written that William Morris 'laid the groundwork for the development which all branches of the new art movement experienced later'.[23]

The Design and Industries Association (DIA) was established in London in 1915 in order to promote the production of manufactured goods that would match the Morris ideal; its model was the Deutscher Werkbund. The DIA's spokesman in the early years was Lethaby, who wrote in 1915: 'What is needed at the present time is the

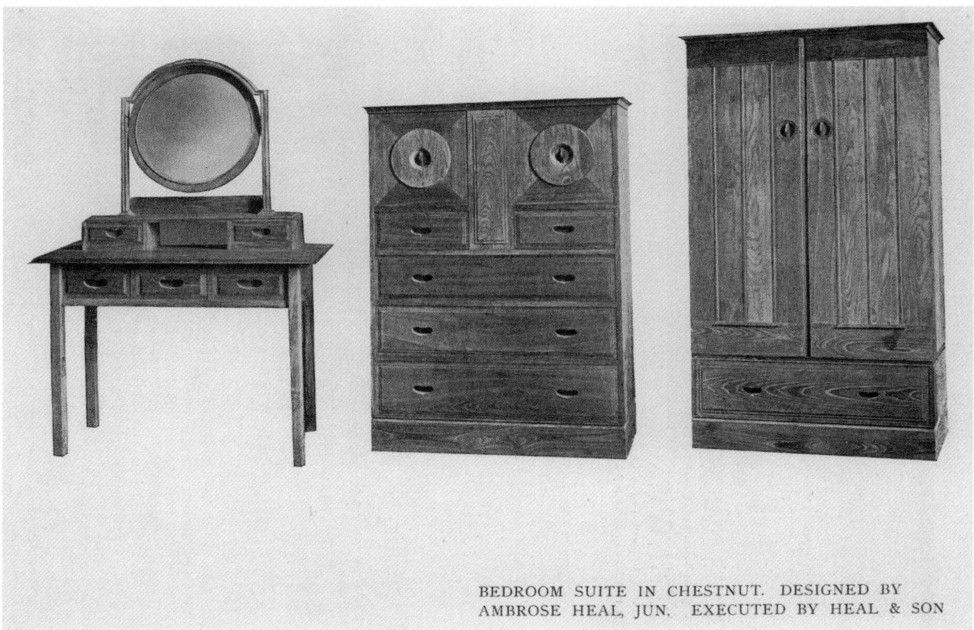

102 Ambrose Heal, Jr, for Heal & Son

Bedroom suite in chestnut

From *The Studio Yearbook of Decorative Art* (London: Studio Ltd, 1906)

gathering together of all the several interests concerned with industrial production into a closer association; an association of manufacturers, designers, distributors, economists and critics.'[24] The founder members of the DIA, which was never as large or as prestigious a body as the Deutscher Werkbund, were a close association of designers, craftsmen and manufacturers. Early DIA members had been associated with the Arts and Crafts movement. They included Harold Stabler, who had trained as a metalworker and woodcarver at the Ruskin-inspired Keswick School of Industrial Art and had exhibited with the Arts and Crafts Exhibition Society;[25] Ambrose Heal, a furniture designer and director of Heal's in London, who was to dedicate the store to the sale and promotion of well-designed consumer goods [102]; and Harry Peach, who had founded the Dryad company to produce wicker furniture.[26]

By the 1920s and 1930s the DIA was supported by makers and institutions who claimed Morris's social theories as their inspiration, but who felt that Morris's designs – the Morris style – no longer seemed relevant. In 1925, for example, the British selectors of the country's contribution to the Paris Art Deco exhibition were 'looking for a new movement in England to take the place of that of which William Morris became the typical representative'.[27] While Morris's social commitment was still acknowledged, his designs were considered outdated, and this interpretation persisted until the post-war period. As one design commentator of the 1930s and 1940s described it, 'Morris's ideas are much more important than his works. ... [he] produces beautiful but ineffectual masterpieces. His tapestries, books, tiles, carpets, illuminated manuscripts, and stained glass windows are museum pieces from birth'.[28]

Modernism rejected the Morris style, but re-established Morris the thinker as a pioneer designer for industry. The acknowledged promoter of this interpretation was Nikolaus Pevsner, whose *Pioneers of the Modern Movement*, first published in London in 1936, was given the subtitle *From William Morris to Walter Gropius* [103] and is still in print today.[29] This book had a positive impact on British post-war design

103 Circular for Nikolaus Pevsner, *Pioneers of the Modern Movement* (London: Faber & Faber, 1936)

theory: it established a historical context for the values of William Morris and the Arts and Crafts movement and it sustained the policies of the pre-war design establishment into the post-war period. Pevsner echoed Morris when he wrote, 'The question of design is a social question. It is an integral part of the social question of our time.'[30] Pevsner, a refugee from Nazi Germany, had come to England in 1935 with an awareness of the work of the Deutscher Werkbund and the Bauhaus, as well as familiarity with Hermann Muthesius's writings about England and the English house.[31] Pevsner believed that the historian should be committed to a social ideal and be aware of contemporary developments. 'In this century of ours', he wrote in *Academies of Art Past and Present*, '... the historian can no longer shut himself off from contemporary needs.'[32] In Pevsner's interpretation, Morris became a pioneer of Modernism because of his commitment to the social role of design. 'What business have we with art unless all can share it?' he had asked in 1883.[33] It was this question, according to Pevsner, that made Morris the true prophet of the twentieth century. 'We owe it to him', Pevsner wrote, 'that an ordinary man's dwelling house has once more become a worthy object of the architect's thought, and a chair, a wallpaper, or a vase a worthy object of the artist's imagination.'[34]

But by the 1940s and 1950s, Morris & Company belonged to the past, and the responses to William Morris's aesthetic dwindled as the taste of the time changed. It is significant, however, that Sanford and Helen Berger first acquired their original Morris material in 1968. This was the year of the student revolutions, which in Britain and Scandinavia had, through the activities of art and design colleges, questioned the nature of commitment in design. By 1968, in spite of this grass-roots questioning of an inherited design theory – Modernist as well as Arts and Crafts – a new wave of books on Morris was being published, and it signalled a new interest in William Morris's work and working processes.

This acceleration of primary research in the 1960s coincided with post-modernism, which challenged both the nature and processes of industry, as well as

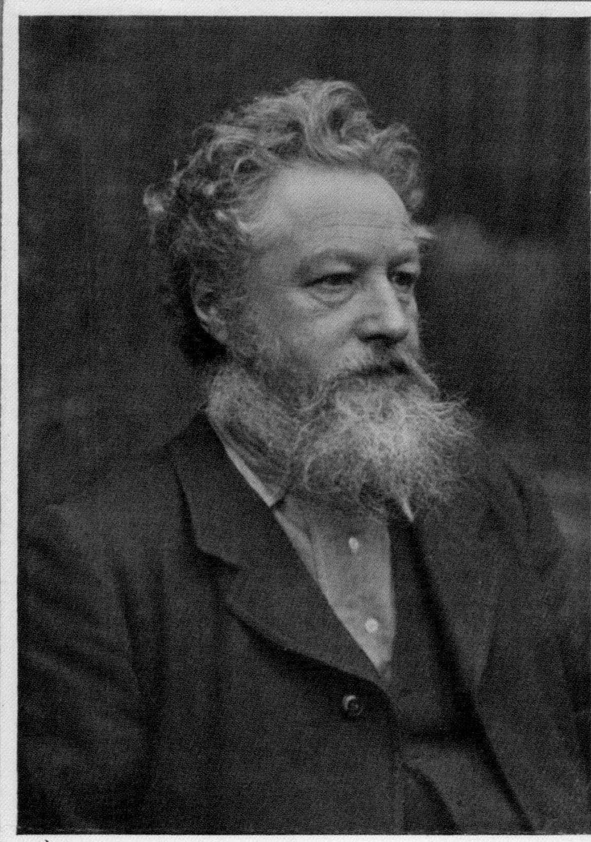

PIONEERS OF THE MODERN MOVEMENT

FROM

WILLIAM MORRIS

TO

WALTER GROPIUS

●

by

NIKOLAUS PEVSNER

With 80 illustrations 10s. 6d. net

●

FABER AND FABER

24 Russell Square London W.C.1

Doctor Pevsner, formerly lecturer on the history of art and architecture in the University of Göttingen, has been making for the past five years a special study of the origins of the modern movement in architecture and of modern art theories. The present book is the outcome of this study, and is the first definitive treatment of the subject.

Beginning with William Morris, Dr. Pevsner goes on to discuss the doctrines of such men as Ashbee, Loos, Wright, and van de Velde, until he reaches the German Werkbund and Walter Gropius. In the practical field of architecture and industrial art, he deals with many significant figures—Morris, Loos, van de Velde and Gropius are, of course, among them; other

[*Continued overleaf*]

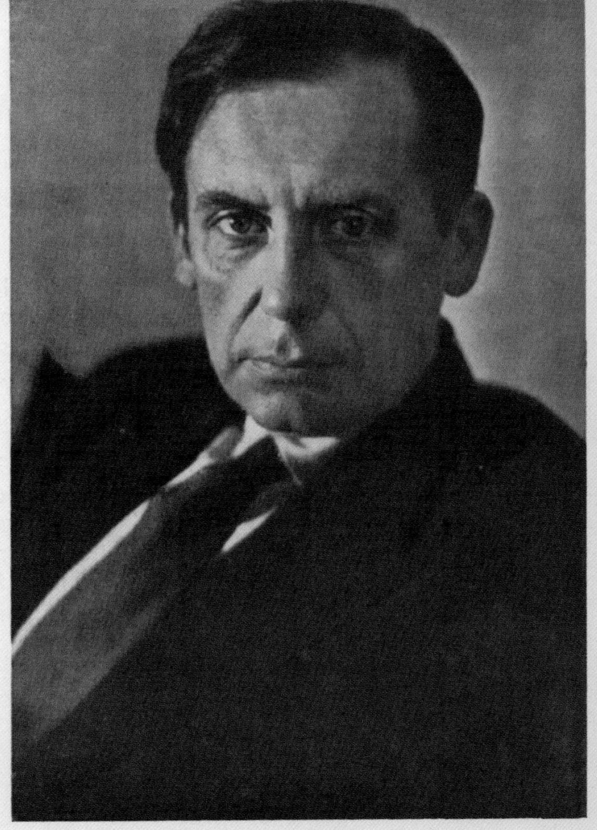

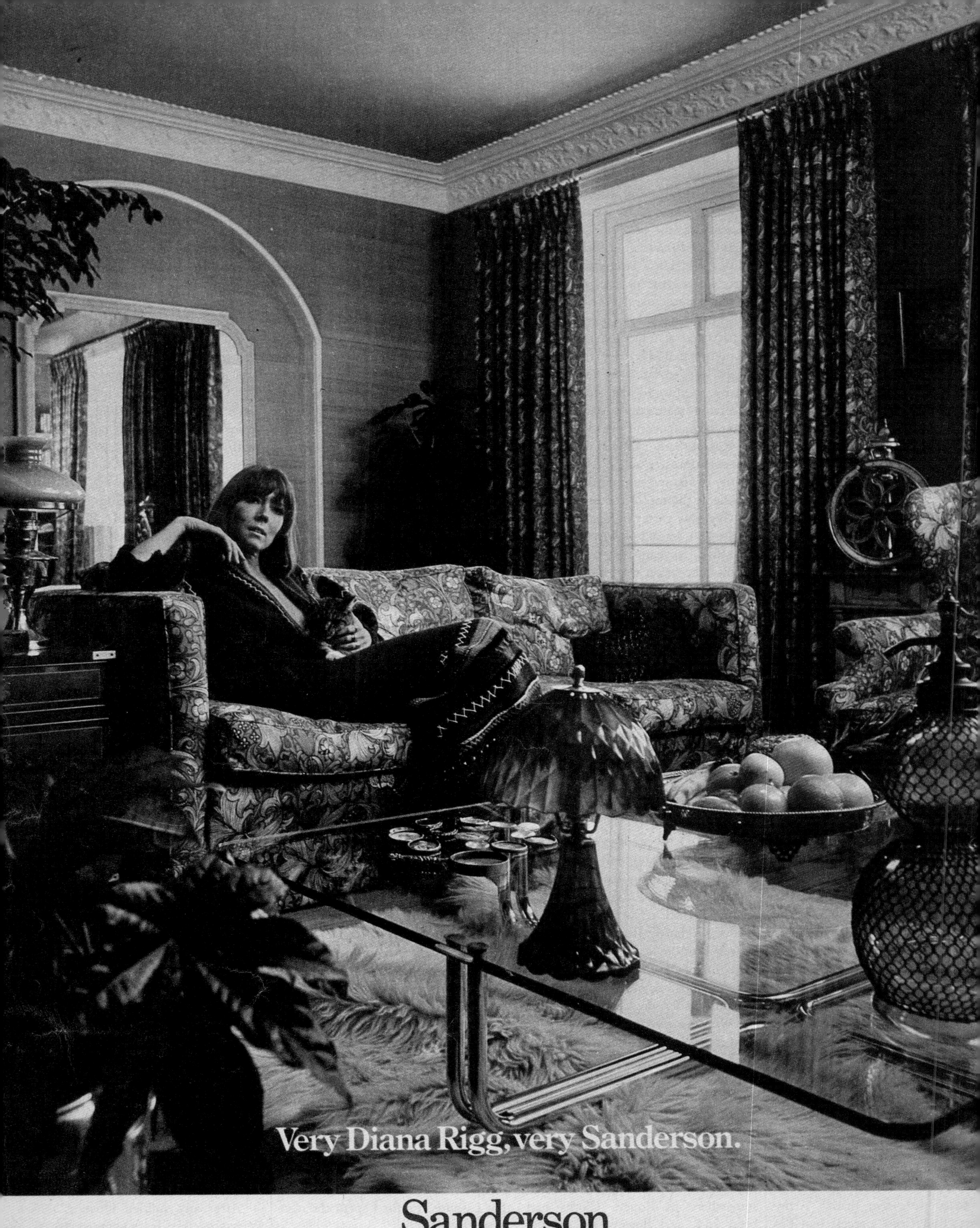

Wallcovering: YS326 Japanese shiki silk. Chair covers and curtains: ZE872/9 William Morris printed linen/cotton, Golden Lily design.

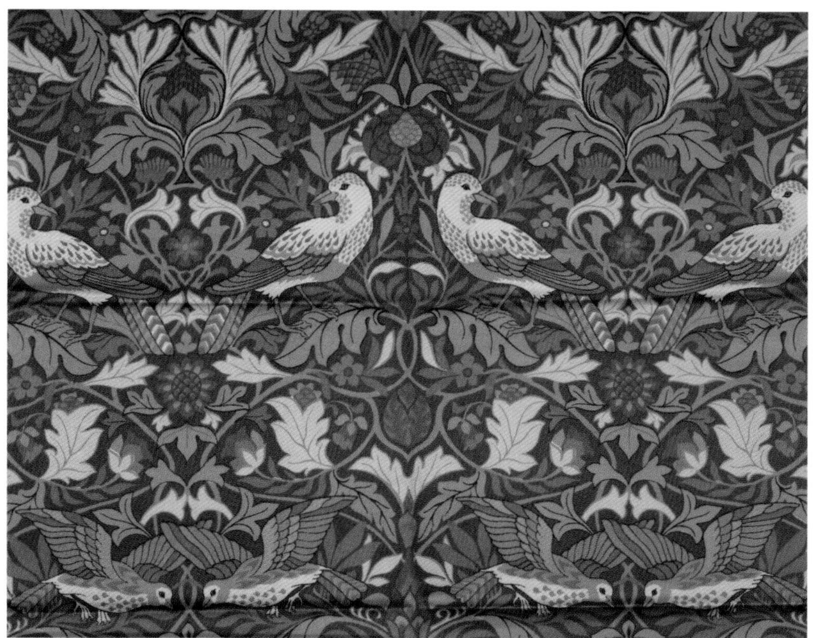

105 John Lewis Partnership

Bird printed fabric, 1970s

Probably printed by Stead McAlpin, full piece 36½ x 50 (92.7 x 127)

This is a recoloured, printed adaptation of Morris's design for the Jacquard-woven wool fabric shown in ill. 36.

assumptions about the role and the responsibility of the designer. And it also anticipated the Morris design revival of the later 1960s and early 1970s, when firms produced fabrics and wallpapers for suburban as well as stately homes (mostly altered and adjusted to fit in with modern manufacturing processes and fabric widths [105]). Peter Floud, who organized the exhibition 'Victorian and Edwardian Decorative Arts' at the Victoria & Albert Museum in London in 1952 (designed to celebrate the centenary of the Museum of Ornamental Art, established at Marlborough House in 1852), had written:

> There can be little doubt that at every stage in his development Morris's best papers demonstrate an instinctive mastery of the art of pattern designing hardly reached by the cleverest of his contemporaries, and bear a classic imprint quite lacking in papers which in their day must have seemed much more *avant-garde.* It is just this timeless quality which makes one confident that sooner or later some enterprising manufacturer will decide to put a selection of Morris's designs back on the market again.[35]

Floud did not live to see the retrofests of the 1970s, when dresses, shirts and trousers (male and female) were made from Morris fabrics, when plastic table cloths, cutting boards and tea-towels inundated our kitchens, when tea-cups and Morris-patterned mugs filled our museum shops, and wallpapers, curtains and upholstery distinguished our homes [104]. Morris the designer had obviously created an art for mass consumption. Morris the thinker could scarcely have anticipated it. But he still has his following as a designer, maker, and entrepreneur, as a writer, poet and traveller, as a romantic and a revolutionary. Morris, as he described it, had the 'power of making the past part of the present', and the growth of today's scholarship and interest indicates the continuing relevance of his ideas and his work.

104 Sanderson advertisement, 1970s

The actress Diana Rigg is seated on a sofa upholstered in recoloured *Golden Lily* printed fabric.

TWO SIDES OF THE RIVER:

**NO MORE ALONE MY LOVE THE LAMP SHOULD BURN,
WATCHING THE WEARY SPINDLE TWIST AND TURN.**

William Morris, *The Two Sides of the River*, 1868

MORRIS AND AMERICAN ARTS & CRAFTS

EDWARD R. BOSLEY

'William Morris does not love America . . . Morris has never been to America, and says he has no wish to go', complained William Clarke in the February 1891 number of *New England Magazine*. While this sentiment accurately reflected William Morris's feelings about America, which he would never visit, his disdain earned mostly love in return from the land beyond the Atlantic. By the late 1870s, many Americans whose opinions would shape the nation's aesthetic and cultural identity had vigorously embraced Morris and his message, and well beyond his lifetime Morris's views on art and labour held sway over American thought. That his beliefs informed American design and craft in a sweeping way is indisputable, even if those Americans who sang his anthem of reform did not always do so in perfect harmony. This essay seeks to characterize selected aspects of Morris's presence and influence in North America in the late nineteenth and early twentieth centuries, in a broad, philosophical context as well as by looking at examples of some of the stylistic interpretations that emerged from the studios of North American Arts and Crafts practitioners. Inescapably, Morris's influence left a deep and lasting legacy, one that would fill volumes to describe thoroughly, and Americans today continue to take inspiration from his example as surely as those who did more than a century ago.

During the second half of the nineteenth century, William Morris focused his considerable gifts on expressing and implementing a holistic philosophy of art as a way of life that drew from his own observations as well as from the inspiration that he absorbed from the works of John Ruskin, A.W. N. Pugin, Thomas Carlyle and others. In particular, Morris brought into the realm of the practical Ruskin's message of the moral importance of honest craftsmanship. He did so by designing and creating objects – and a market for them – that would enrich domestic, public and ecclesiastical environments, all the while celebrating the worth of the labour that brought the objects forth. According to Morris's interpretation of Ruskin, to effect a meaningful symbiosis between artistic creativity and craft labour would elevate the decorative or 'lesser arts' to the same plane as the fine arts. All the while, Morris believed, the human condition would be improved through the production of, and daily contact with, beautiful and useful objects. If society did not nurture this symbiosis, he was convinced, the Arts would ultimately exist only as a diversion for the élite. This may have seemed an especially relevant view to express when considered in the context of the living conditions of working-class families in British cities in the 1860s and 1870s, conditions made particularly infamous through the novels of Charles Dickens. In them, grim, overcrowded, and shoddily conceived urban housing was the backdrop for the decorative arts that were born of the Industrial Revolution. Morris, who remained an unapologetic socialist to the end of his life, preached that the world could be a more harmonious place, and the human condition generally improved, if craft and art operated symbiotically to permit objects of everyday utility to be imbued with beauty, which, he believed, would come naturally through the imprint or 'soul' of their makers. He further believed that humankind ought to view life as presenting a continuous opportunity for such artistic expression. The inherent optimism suggested by these beliefs, and his own rapacious appetite for work, inspired Morris and his circle of gifted friends to labour with impressive inventiveness, sensitivity and skill to prove their truth.

Ironically, Morris's message of reform, voiced in reaction to the ill effects of the Industrial Revolution, took root in America too where industry's hold over society was seen in a far less negative light than in Britain. The contagious competitiveness and optimism that prevailed during the intensive industrialization that followed the Civil War caused Americans increasingly to welcome industrial efficiency and progress, as well as the machine that made it possible. Morris found acceptance in the United States nonetheless, but primarily on aesthetic rather than political grounds. Americans paid attention to the Morris-inspired tastemakers of the day, whose opinions appeared in national magazines such as *The House Beautiful* and *Ladies Home Journal*, but most took from Morris only what they felt was relevant for life in America.

While Morris and his followers laboured to resurrect medieval traditions in pattern design, embroidery, tapestry making, stained glass manufacturing, typography, fine printing and other pursuits, America searched its own capacity to turn Morris's stylistic and craft-elevating message into viable models. America, of course, had its share of anti-modernists who remained in opposition to machine manufacturing, but in the centres of North American industry and culture, such as Philadelphia, Boston, Montreal, Toronto, New York and Chicago, proponents of mainstream design movements maintained a truce (albeit a sometimes uneasy one) with machine manufacturing. Nor did Morris himself hate the machine *per se*; he merely regretted industry's abuse of it, particularly in the relentless and repetitive production of mass-market goods that by their nature denied the imprint of a human maker. He believed that misuse of the machine would eventually kill Art and the Artist's (therefore humankind's) desire to create.

Indeed, among the anti-modern and anti-machine proponents in America can be found some of the most compelling stories of the Arts and Crafts movement. Rural craft communities, similar to C. R. Ashbee's Guild of Handicraft in the Cotswolds, emerged in the late nineteenth and early twentieth centuries, inspired by an Emer-

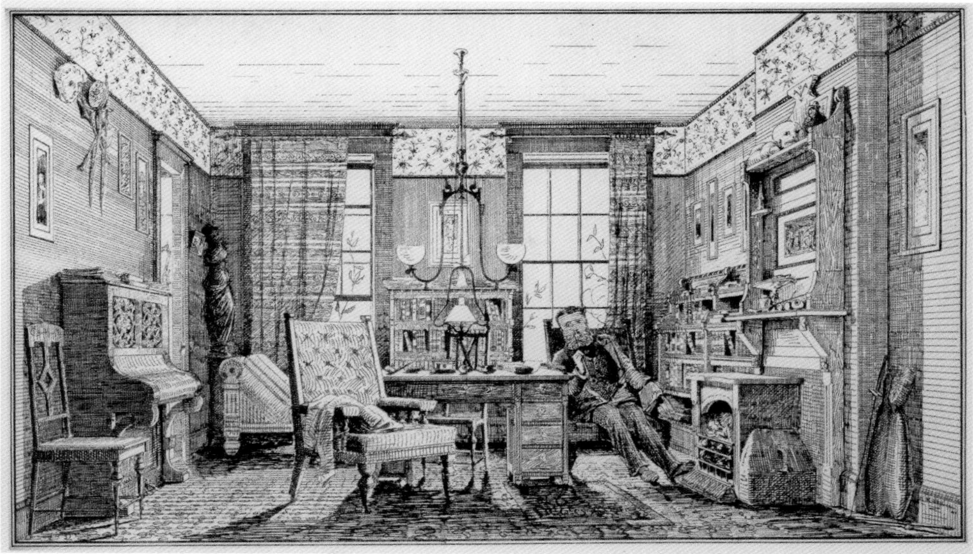

106 The Study, Harvard College

From Charles Wyllys Elliott, *The Book of American Interiors* (Boston: J. R. Osgood and Co., 1876)

Morris's *Daisy* wallpaper appears as a decorative frieze.

sonian respect for Nature in keeping with Morris's own views. Among them were cooperative communities such as the Shakers, who produced chairs with the stylistic sobriety of Morris & Company's most reductive furniture. The consciously utopian colonies of Byrdcliffe in rural Woodstock, in New York State, and Rose Valley in Pennsylvania, produced beautifully hand-crafted and carved furniture and other decorative arts that owe as much of a debt to Morris's socialism as to his aesthetic philosophy. At Chicago's Hull House, Jane Addams and Ellen Gates Starr were thinking of Morris when they taught the virtues of hand work to the urban poor,[1] and even as late as the 1920s and 1930s the Swedenborgian religious community of Bryn Athyn, north of Philadelphia, pursued a classic collaboration of art, craft and community spirit to design and construct a cathedral in the Gothic tradition of the trade guilds. Each of these groups reflected distinctly American cultural responses to the social and aesthetic message of William Morris.

But to understand the full reach of Morris's influence across America we must examine the presence of his own work in the United States, consider its effect on taste-makers and critics, and examine the popular (and sometimes vulgarized) manifestations of his philosophies. These would, by the early years of the twentieth century, become part of the very fabric of American culture.

Morris & Company Sets Sail

Although William Morris's poetry had found its way into the hands of the culturally adventurous in North America in the 1860s, the first offering of the actual goods of Morris & Company (then Morris, Marshall, Faulkner & Company) in America began in April 1871, when N. Willis Bumstead opened retail rooms in Boston that were decorated with Morris-designed rugs, stamped and unstamped velvets, curtain stuffs and laces, all for sale. Charles Eliot Norton, Harvard's president and a personal friend of John Ruskin, purchased Morris's goods [106], as did Norton's friend, the writer William Dean Howells. But overall the Firm's offerings did not spark wide popular success, probably due to lack of familiarity and a somewhat higher cost than that of domestic products. Broader exposure and acceptance came in Philadelphia at the Centennial International Exhibition of 1876 and, thanks to the intense media attention surrounding Oscar Wilde's American lecture tour of 1882, the ideals of Ruskin and Morris, upon which Wilde frequently expounded, became better known across the country. In his lecture 'The House Beautiful', Wilde's message included such Morris-like pronouncements as 'art must begin with the handicraftsman, and you must reinstate him into his rightful position, and thus make labour, which is always honorable, noble also'.[2] By the autumn of 1883, Morris & Company's range of home decorating goods – wallpaper, printed chintz, rugs, tapestries and embroideries – was represented in a large booth at Boston's Foreign Fair. Earlier that year, probably in preparation for orders they anticipated receiving at the Fair, they had appointed Elliot and Bulkley of New York to be their official American agents. By now Morris & Company had a foothold on American soil, if not yet a deep niche in the American mind.

In addition to Morris & Company's growing presence, important endorsements made Americans more receptive to both the products and philosophies of William Morris. One such endorsement came from the highly influential American architect of the era, Henry Hobson Richardson. With the completion in 1877 of his masterpiece, Trinity Church, in Boston's Back Bay, the thirty-nine-year-old Richardson's influence on subsequent American architectural design was nothing short of revolutionary. He was, in the words of his biographer, 'America's first "signature" architect and the first consciously to create an architectural language that respected history as a creative springboard for designing buildings that were nonetheless clearly distinct from their European origins'.[3] With the abundant use of natural materials – primarily unadorned stone and wood – Richardson successfully shifted America's self-image away from a strict reliance on European and classical precedents towards a more Emersonian (and Morrisian) identification with Nature. During Richardson's trip to

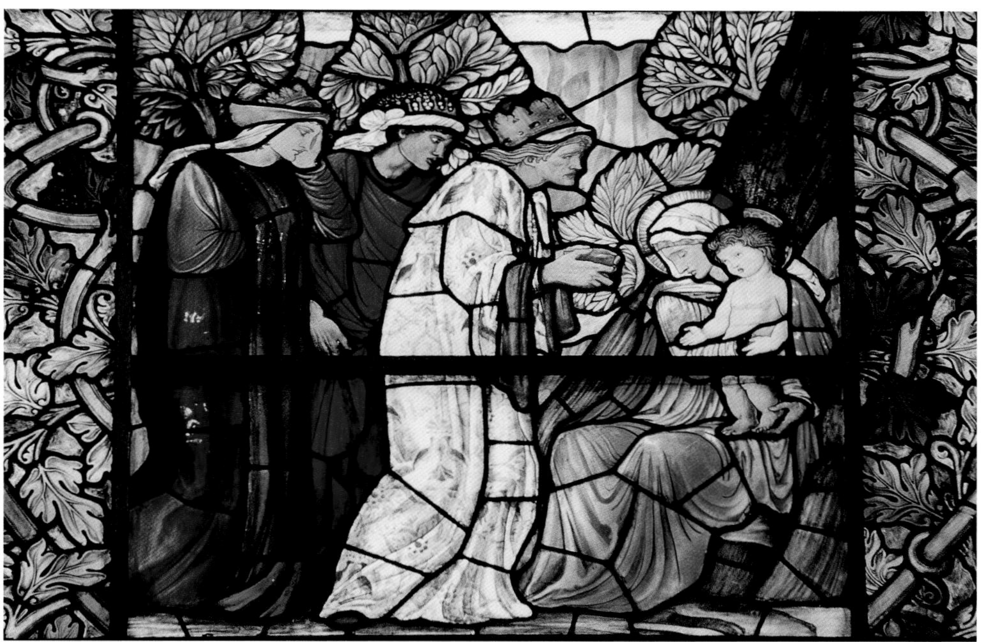

107 Designed by Edward Burne-Jones for Morris & Company

The Adoration of the Magi, stained glass in the north transept of Trinity Church, Copley Square, Boston, Massachusetts, 1880

Photograph by Jen Matson

Continental Europe and England in 1882 he visited William De Morgan, whose tiles [22] he found 'astonishing', and called on William Burges, whose architecture he revered. But perhaps most significantly he made a personal visit to artist and Morris & Company partner Edward Burne-Jones, and then to William Morris himself at his Hammersmith home and at the firm's Merton Abbey works in Surrey.[4] The American architect, just four years younger than his host, found much to admire in Morris's views on design and craftsmanship. Since Richardson relied on the goodwill of the wealthy he showed no particular interest in Morris's social philosophy, and the two men probably found common ground in aesthetic rather than political issues. After the visit Richardson wrote to his wife, 'I was more than pleased with Morris, his straightforward manner etc.'[5] Richardson acquired a copy of Morris's collected lectures, *Hopes and Fears for Art*, while he was in London, and his robust, craft-oriented architecture back home reflected Morris's assertion that architecture cannot 'exist alive and progressive by itself, but must cherish and be cherished by all the crafts whereby men make the things which they intend shall be beautiful, and shall last somewhat beyond the passing day'.[6] For his part, Morris also held Richardson in high regard, calling him, according to a colleague of Morris's, 'one of the few modern architects anywhere who have produced a distinctively original style'.[7]

Since Richardson's buildings reflected a medievalist's tendency towards robust and explicit craftsmanship, like that of Morris's own work in other disciplines, it is not surprising that Richardson would use Morris & Company designs in some of his clients' interiors. Within Trinity Church are two stained glass installations designed by Edward Burne-Jones and manufactured by Morris & Company. The first is a triple-light window in the north transept, with the Adoration of the Shepherds, the Adoration of the Magi [107] and the Flight into Egypt (1880) – adapted from similar windows at Castle Howard, Yorkshire. In the second window (1883), which is set into the east wall of Trinity's baptistery, the scene of David instructing Solomon is also a subject by Burne-Jones that was adapted from designs for other clients; it was re-used

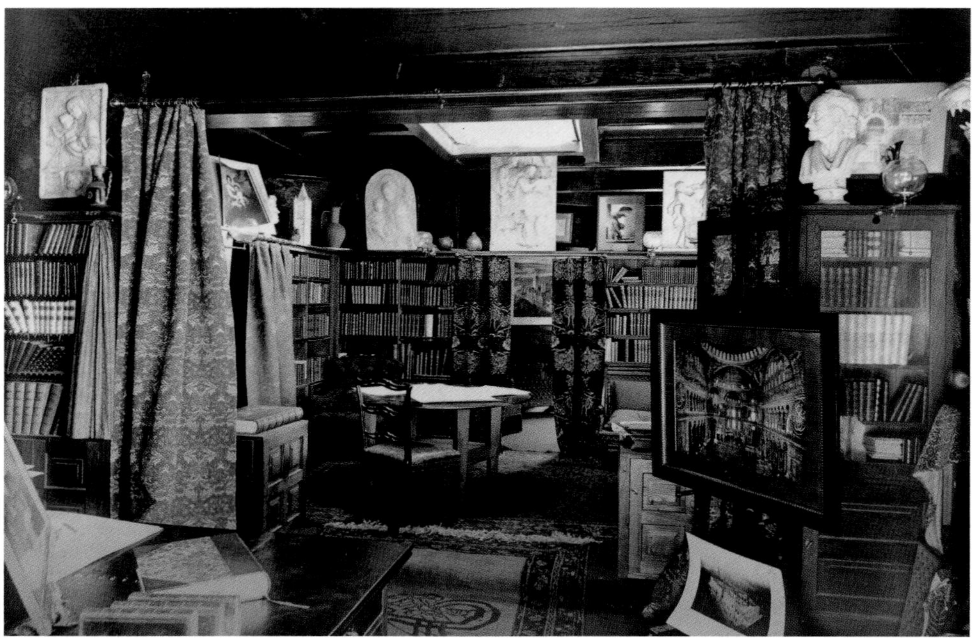

108 Studio library of H. H. Richardson, Brookline, Massachusetts, *c.* 1885

Photograph
Courtesy of the Society for the Preservation of New England Antiquities

again later [109]. In Richardson's work, however, Morris & Company furnishings were most assertive in his house for John and Frances Glessner in Chicago (1885–87). Within the Glessner interiors could be found Morris's *Poppy* and *Sunflower* wallpapers, *Rose and Thistle* printed chintz curtains, and *Bird and Vine* and *Peacock and Dragon* in woven wool. Significant also was Richardson's choice of Morris & Company textiles as portières for the library of his own Brookline, Massachusetts, studio where the many colleagues he regularly entertained could see them [108].

Nor was Richardson now alone among Americans in using Morris & Company products. Ogden Codman, the fashionable Boston decorator who had transformed numerous Back Bay interiors into elegant salons, corresponded directly with Morris in 1883 to coordinate the design and execution of stained glass, rugs, woven textiles and other decorative arts for Vinland, the Newport, Rhode Island, 'cottage' designed for tobacco heiress Catherine Lorillard Wolfe. Boston architects Peabody & Stearns designed the neo-Romanesque house, while Morris, Burne-Jones and Walter Crane created selected designs for the interiors. The decorative theme of Vinland was inspired by Longfellow's poem *The Skeleton in Armor* that recounts the romantic Norse legend of Leif Eriksson's ninth-century American landfall. Longfellow was enchanted by Newport's local mythology, which held that a ruined stone tower near the harbour had originally been built by the early Norse explorers. While this is now discredited by scholars, the myth was nonetheless sufficient grounds for Miss Wolfe to proceed with the connection she and her designer sought to make between her domestic present and the romanticized past; and, given his early extensive studies of Nordic mythology, one can see the attraction of this commission for Morris. For Vinland, Morris and Burne-Jones proposed a monumental composition (now dismantled) of two rows of three stained glass lights and a row of three smaller panels to illuminate the stairway with jewel-like coloured light. In the three central lights the Norse gods Odin, Thor and Frey were each shown seated in front of a castle. The lower lights depicted the Vinland explorers Thorfinn Karlsefne, Gudridr and Leif the

109 Adapted from the design by Edward Burne-Jones for Morris & Company used at Trinity Church, Boston

David instructing Solomon for the building of the Temple, sketch design for a window at the Convent of the Salesian Sisters of St John Bosco, Friar Park, Henley-on-Thames, Oxfordshire, *c.* 1922

Watercolour and ink, full sheet $9\frac{7}{8}$ x $6\frac{1}{2}$ (25.1 x 16.5)

This is an adaptation of the design originally made for Trinity Church, Boston, in 1883, itself adapted from earlier designs.

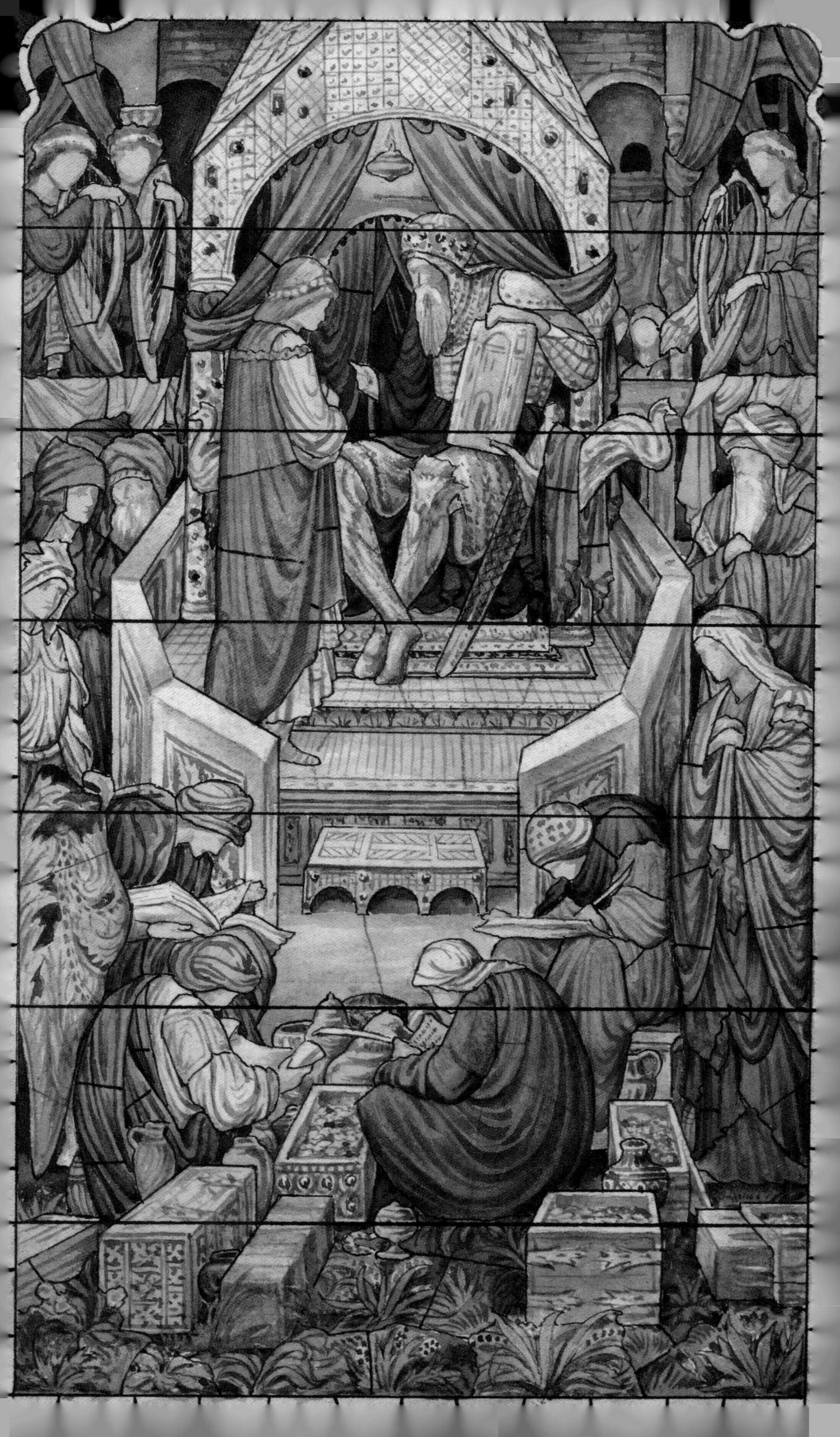

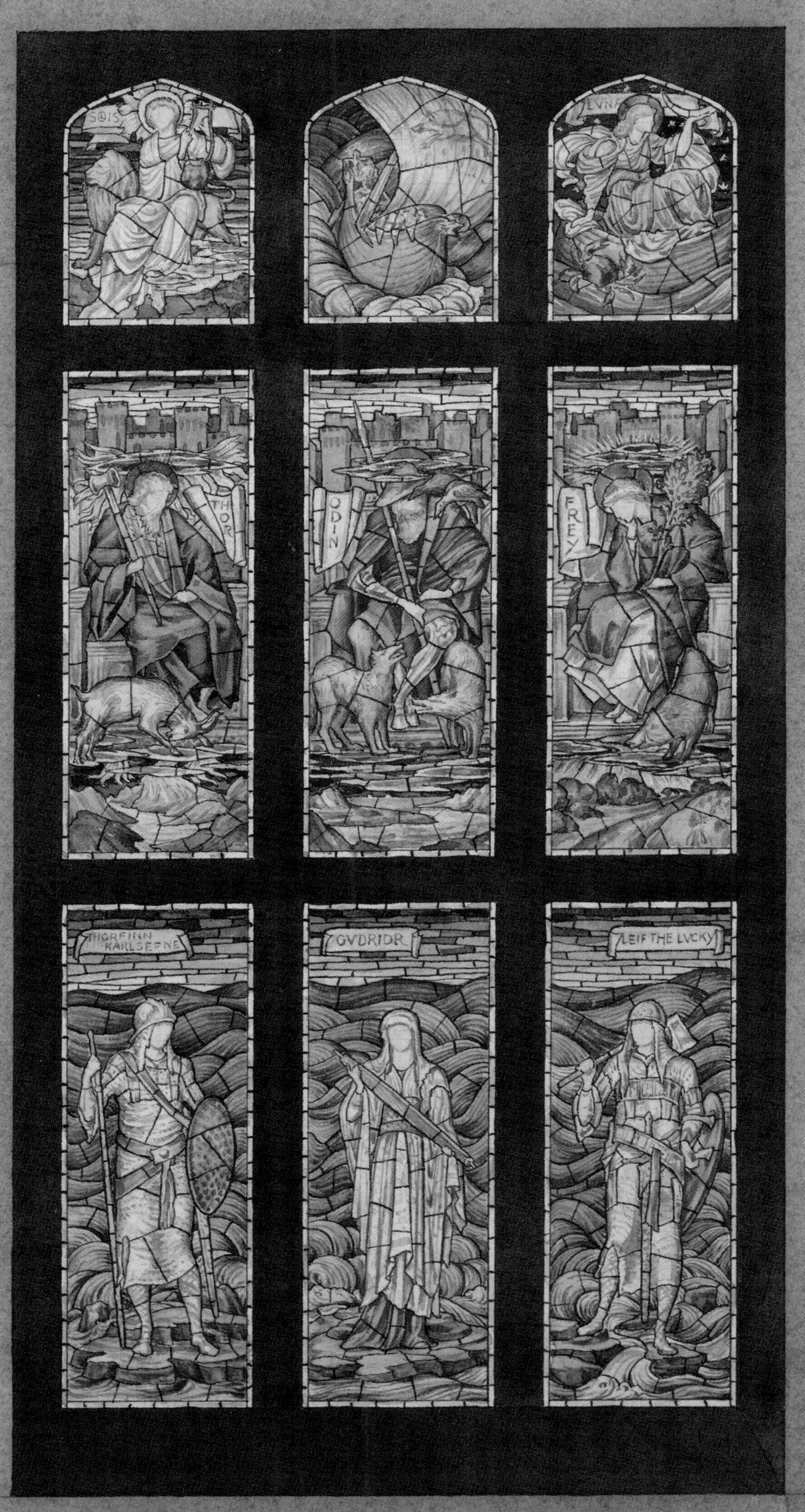

SCALE 3/4" = 1'

RETURN TO MORRIS & Co.
MERTON ABBEY
Surrey

Lucky, figures chosen by Morris. A Morris & Company sketch for a similar scheme at Folkestone, Kent (*c.* 1913) shows the seated gods and the explorers standing on rocky pedestals amid swirling waves of sea green and blue below a darkening sky of tessellated glass [110]. At the top, a Viking ship under full sail occupies the centre panel. The flanking panels in the sketch depict Solis and Luna, but the Vinland panels were designed with scrolls of Scandinavian runic verse, 'with the passages', wrote Morris to his client, 'about undying fame'.[8] Longfellow's poem provided, it seems, the ideal blend of medieval myth, drama and romantic spirit to inspire Morris and Burne-Jones to collaborate for an eager American patron. It was not, however, enough to lure Morris to America. He would conduct all of the business of the commission from London. In a letter to Miss Wolfe regarding the Vinland windows he declined her invitation to visit Newport, saying 'I fear I am not likely to get so long a holiday as would carry me to America for a long while – longer than I can look forward to.'[9] Morris had spoken out so often and so bluntly against capitalists and the political forces that inhibited change that for practical purposes he had banned himself from visiting a place that he believed suffered from both. It is tempting, nonetheless, to wonder where he might have gone, to whom he might have paid a call, and what he might have thought of the whole experience if he had allowed himself a visit to America.

110 Adapted from the design by Edward Burne-Jones for Morris & Company made for Vinland, Rhode Island

Sketch design for a window, probably for J. A. Roberts, 6 Earls Avenue, Folkestone, Kent, *c.* 1913

Watercolour and ink, 12¾ x 7⅞ (32.4 x 20)

In the upper row are Solis (the Sun), a Viking ship, and Luna (the Moon); in the centre, the gods Thor, Odin and Frey; at the bottom, the explorers Thorfinn Karlsefne, Gudridr and Leif the Lucky.

If They Could, They Did

From 1896, the year of Morris's death, the American Arts and Crafts movement began to assert an institutional identity. Hundreds of Arts and Crafts societies were established from coast to coast, nearly all of which not only claimed Morris as their inspirational high priest but modelled themselves after the Arts and Crafts Exhibition Society, founded by Morris and others in 1888. Societies in Minneapolis (founded in 1896), Boston (1897), Chicago (1897), and hundreds of other communities across North America became recognized centres for design reform and sometimes even political activism. The Industrial Art League, founded in Chicago in 1899, took Morris's own words for its motto: 'One day we shall win back art again to our daily labor; win back art, that is to say, the pleasure of life, to the people.' The members of the Arts and Crafts Society of Canada, begun in 1903, similarly acknowledged their debt to Morris. One of its founding members, Mabel Adamson, spent several months during 1902 and 1903 working at C. R. Ashbee's Guild of Handicraft in Chipping Campden.[10] Ashbee unabashedly (and not entirely unfairly) styled himself 'the direct successor of William Morris'.[11]

Direct and symbolic references to Morris are numerous, especially with American Arts and Crafts societies that were establishing their identities and associations. 'If I Can' was the personal motto that Morris had adapted from Van Eyck's 'Als ich kanne', the result of a journey he had made to the Low Countries in 1856. This became 'Si Je Puis' when used on the tiles he installed at Red House about four years later. The motto was adapted by Gustav Stickley to 'Als Ik Kan' for his United Crafts furniture enterprise based in Eastwood, New York, explaining that it was 'an incentive to the craftsman who seeks to advance the cause of art allied to labor'. In California, the motto evolved a step further to the collective and positivist 'We Can' for the Arroyo Guild of Fellow Craftsmen, founded in 1909 along the banks of the Arroyo

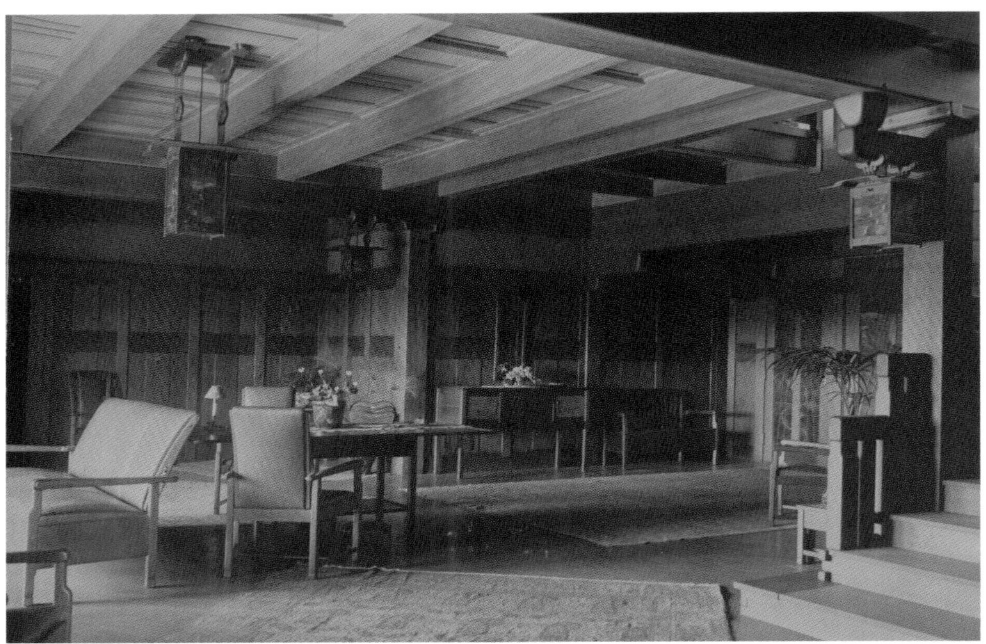

Seco, a picturesque, nearly dry river bed which ran from the San Gabriel Mountains near Pasadena towards Los Angeles. The Arroyo Guild published the *Arroyo Craftsman* which, in its single issue, had interspersed throughout the magazine the Morris aphorism, 'Art is the expression of a man's joy in his work.' George Wharton James, the magazine's editor and a former associate editor for Stickley's *Craftsman* magazine, acknowledged inspiration from Stickley and called him 'the American William Morris'. Despite the short life of the Arroyo Guild of Fellow Craftsmen (its building burned in 1910), its members persisted independently as important contributors to the Southern California art and craft communities for decades. In Northern California it was Charles Keeler and the Hillside Club in Berkeley that brought Morrisian ideals into practice. The club, founded in 1898, exerted gentle pressure on an entire neighbourhood to build and decorate with nature as its guiding principle, going so far as to recommend specific treatments – 'broad slabs of redwood treated only with a wax dressing' – for interiors. Keeler published his manifesto of taste, *The Simple Home*, in 1904, successfully spawning a generation of woodsy cottages for the community surrounding the University of California.

111 Designed by Greene & Greene

Entry hall of the Robert R. Blacker house, Pasadena, California, 1907–9

Photograph by Leroy Hulbert

The adjustable-back armchair and sofa are visible at the left.

Concurrent with the founding of the first North American Arts and Crafts societies in the mid-1890s was a proliferation of books and magazine articles discussing practical matters of home decoration. Foremost in magazine circulation were *The House Beautiful*, edited by Herbert S. Stone, and *Ladies Home Journal*, edited by Edward Bock. The October 1898 number of *The House Beautiful* featured 'Practical Application of Decorative Art: Hints from Many Sources', which quoted William Morris at length. The published advice was apparently meant as simultaneously practical and piquant, such as this admonition from Morris regarding colour: 'do not fall into the trap of the dingy, bilious-looking green, a colour to which I have a special hatred because I have been supposed to have brought it somewhat into vogue'.[12] When *The Craftsman* began publishing in October 1901 [112], however, it quickly earned the *de facto* position as the popular voice of the American Arts and Crafts

112 *The Craftsman*, October 1901 (Eastwood, New York: United Crafts)

This, the first issue of the magazine, was dedicated to William Morris.

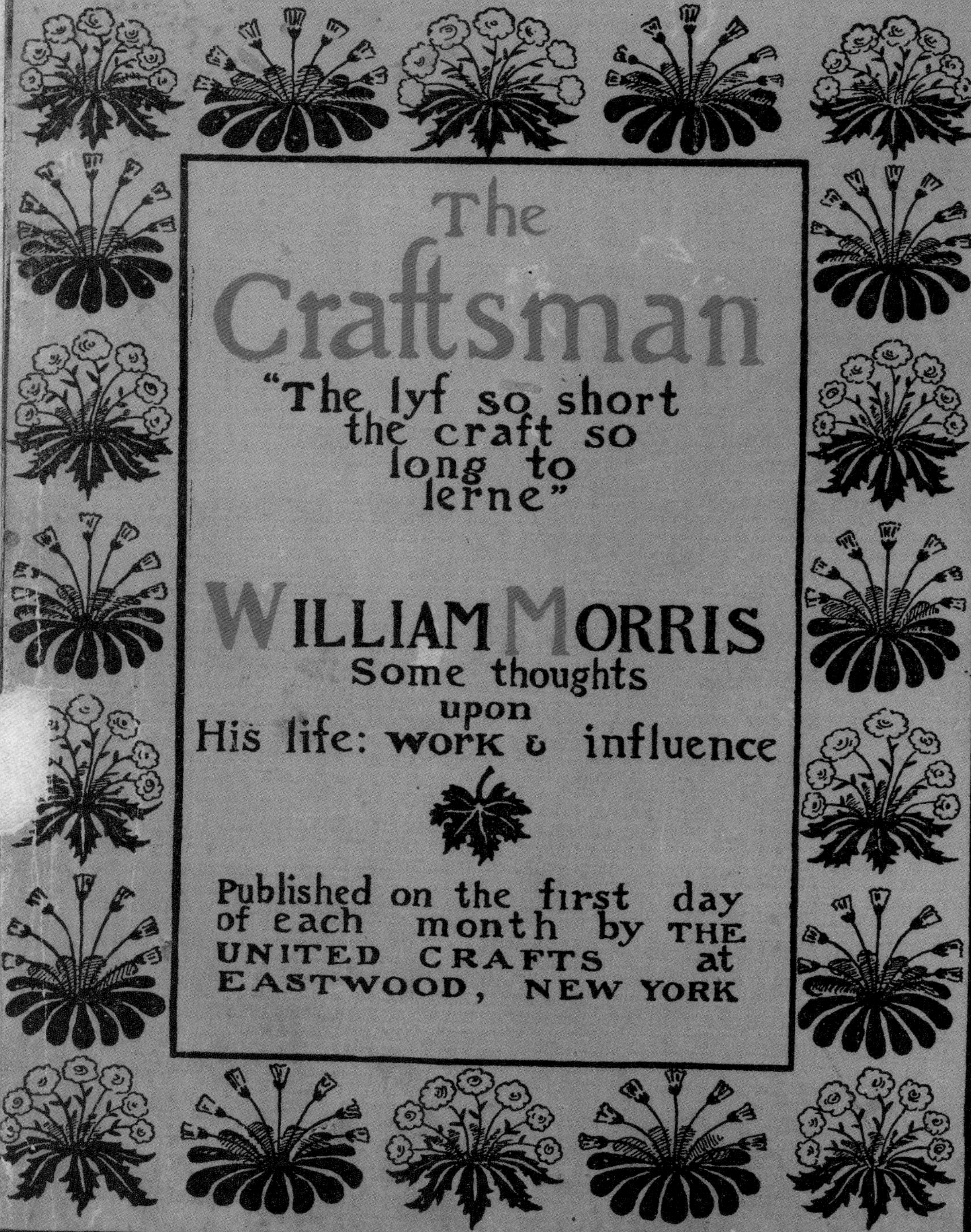
VOL. I
October, MDCCCCI
NO. 1
The Craftsman
"The lyf so short the craft so long to lerne"
WILLIAM MORRIS
Some thoughts upon His life: work & influence
Published on the first day of each month by THE UNITED CRAFTS at EASTWOOD, NEW YORK
Price 20 cents the copy
Copyright, 1901, by Gustave Stickley

movement. At the same time, it promoted United Crafts, Gustav Stickley's commercial furniture-making venture. The first issue of *The Craftsman* was devoted to the legacy of William Morris and sought to characterize United Crafts as the legitimate offspring of Morris & Company. It explained that

> the new association is a guild of cabinet makers, metal, and leather workers, which has been recently formed for the production of household furnishings. The Guild has had but one parallel in modern times, and this is found in the firm organized in London, in 1860, by the great decorator and socialist, William Morris. ... The United Crafts endeavor to promote and extend the principles established by Morris, in both the artistic and the socialistic sense.

Calling Morris a 'household word throughout America',[13] *The Craftsman* also claimed that it was 'needless to trace the development of the Firm at length; since the results of its work may be measured by any one who has the means to compare the household art of England and America, as it stands to-day, with the ugliness and barrenness of the upper- and middle-class homes of those countries, forty years ago'.[14] To cement the association with Morris, the fifth number (February 1902) included an article that described in detail a visit to the Morris & Company retail shop at its 449 Oxford Street location in the busy heart of London. While *The Craftsman* later fell silent on socialism, Stickley nonetheless maintained a lively devotion to Morris and his call for a close relationship between design and craft. Not surprisingly, one of Stickley's most successful pieces of furniture was his massive, adjustable, reclining armchair, known as the 'Morris chair', which was copied in one way or another by nearly every American furniture manufacturer. Stickley continued to disseminate Morris's philosophy of art and labour through *The Craftsman* until it ceased publication in 1916.

113 Designed by John La Farge

Detail of the Resurrection, stained glass in Trinity Church, Copley Square, Boston, Massachusetts, 1876

Photograph by Jen Matson

Morris's influence touched even the rarified world of the architects Greene & Greene in Pasadena, California, whose Japanese-inspired 'bungalows' were favoured by the wealthy and powerful and by the artistically inclined who could afford them. Charles Sumner Greene, chief designer for the fraternal firm, wrote to one of his clients, James A. Culbertson, on 7 October 1902: 'The suggestions enclosed in your letter for the living room pleased me very much, as I am in thorough sympathy with the Wm. Morris movement, in fact the whole inside of the house is influenced by it in design. I think the Durrie rugs very good indeed and I have in mind a color that will harmonize well with them and the wood if it is stained brown or olive.'[15] Charles Greene had recently married Alice Gordon White, an Englishwoman, and it was only a year after returning from their honeymoon in England, Scotland and the Continent that Charles wrote this letter to James Culbertson. One of the honeymooners' visits was to the Victoria & Albert Museum, where they would have seen the fashionable Green Dining Room designed by Morris, Marshall, Faulkner & Company [23]. The Greenes did not design furniture for Mr Culbertson, but Stickley's United Craft pieces were selected to evoke the Morris 'movement' about which Greene had written to his client. Soon, however, Greene & Greene would start to design furniture – and in particular a version of the Morris chair – for client Robert R. Blacker in the highly refined, wood-craft manner that became known as their signature style [111].

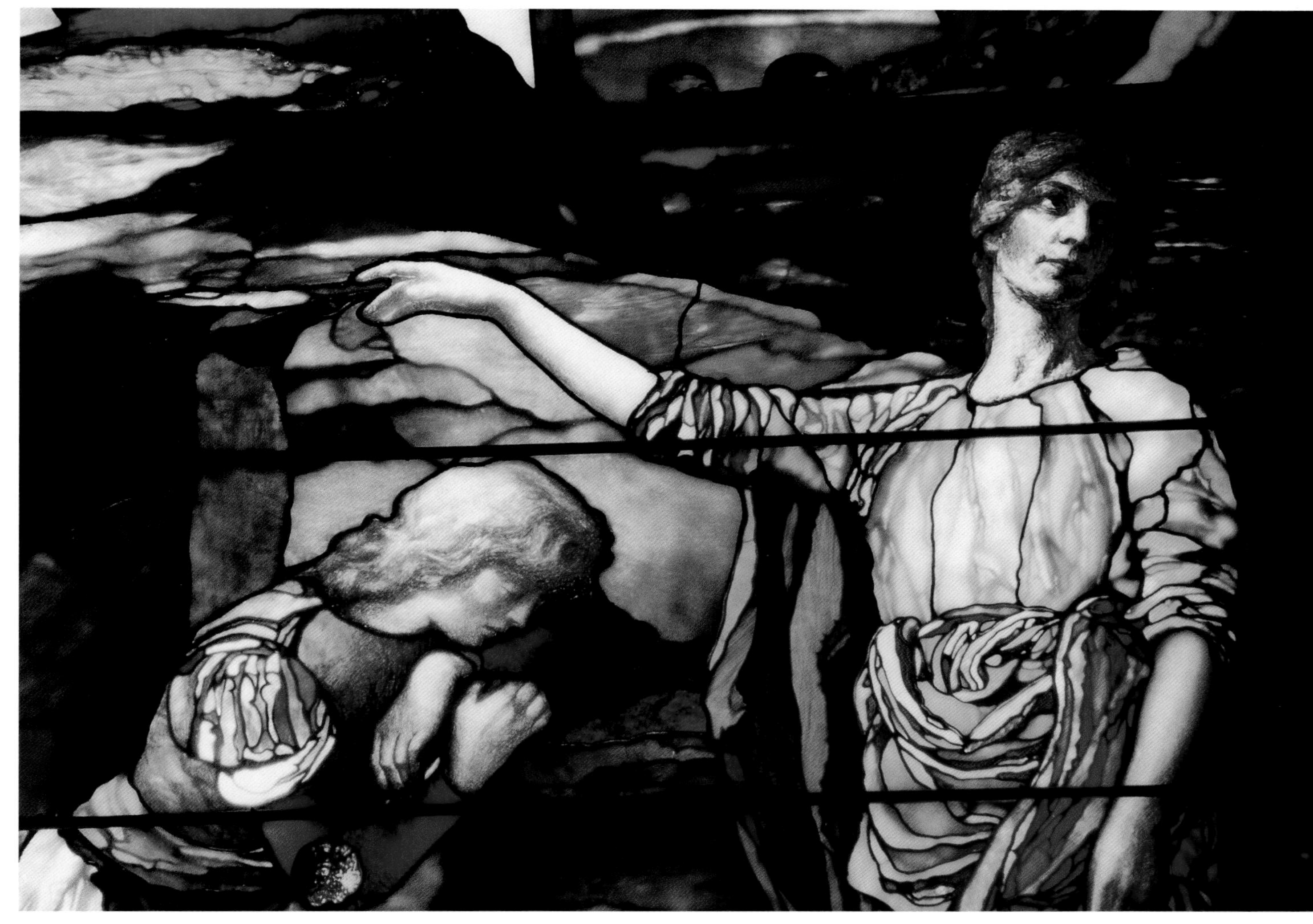

Benediction in Light: American Stained Glass and the Debt to Morris

Since stained glass comprised an important part of Morris & Company's output, its influence accordingly came to bear on American stained glass. Louis Comfort Tiffany and John La Farge both claimed influence from Morris, as well as from the Pre-Raphaelites Dante Gabriel Rossetti and Ford Madox Brown. Tiffany apparently corresponded with Morris[16] but he and La Farge would diverge from Morris's preference for recreating the jewel-like colour and clarity of medieval glass. La Farge instead developed a new style of glass (reportedly after seeing light pass through an inexpensive tooth-powder bottle) and his invention became known as American opalescent art glass. Tiffany simultaneously worked on a similar type of glass and perfected the iridescence for which it became famous. Each used his own glass to dramatic effect, La Farge's stained glass in Trinity Church, for example, a foil to the medieval style of the Morris & Company windows there [113, 107]. There was a steady appreciation in America for the traditional stained and painted pot-metal glass that was favoured by Morris & Company as well as for the opalescent glass that La Farge and Tiffany promoted, so it was not uncommon to see both kinds used in the same setting. At the Boston Foreign Fair of 1883, Morris & Company glass was characterized in detail in a circular printed by the Firm to educate the American public:

> These, then, are the first conditions of good glass painting as we perceive them – well-balanced and shapely figures, pure and simple drawing, and a minimum of light and shade. There is [a] reason for this last. Shading is a dulling of the glass; it is therefore inconsistent with the use of a material which was chosen for its brightness. After these we ask for beautiful colour. There may be more of it, or less; but it is only rational and becoming that the light we stain should not be changed to dirt or ugliness. Colour, pure and sweet, is the least you should ask for in a painted window.[17]

The Boston-based architectural firm of Cram, Goodhue & Ferguson, in particular, ennobled its Gothic Revival churches with windows modelled on the English medieval precedent as revived by Morris & Company. Ralph Adams Cram, who believed William Morris to be 'the most wholly great man', took charge of stained glass production for the firm's ecclesiastical work, in hopes of challenging the national preference for opalescent glass, which he called 'decadent and old-fashioned'. Cram won adherents along the way. From 1891 to 1896 his glass craftsman of choice was Otto Heinigke of New York and, from 1896 until 1910, Harry E. Goodhue, the brother of Cram's partner Bertram Grosvenor Goodhue, also made windows for the firm's churches. In 1902 Harry Goodhue's window for the firm's Emmanuel Church in Newport, Rhode Island, was the first church window of American origin to be made entirely of hand-blown glass.[18] In 1910 Cram engaged Charles J. Connick, who became one of the dominant manufacturers of stained glass in Boston in the early to mid-twentieth century. In preparation for the design of windows for one of his churches [114], Cram urged Connick to study the stained glass designs of Edward Burne-Jones.

114 Designed by Charles J. Connick for Charles J. Connick Associates

St Agatha, detail of stained glass in the south aisle of All Saints, Ashmont, Massachusetts, 1924

Photograph by Peter Cormack

Connick's conversion away from a tacit acceptance of American opalescent glass, however, was also inspired by the English glassmaker Christopher Whall, who associated professionally and socially with leading figures of the English Arts and Crafts movement, including Morris, by way of London's Arts and Crafts Exhibition Society and the Art Workers Guild. During his career, Whall made windows for many of the leading English Arts and Crafts architects, including J. D. Sedding [87], W. R. Lethaby, E. S. Prior and C. R. Ashbee. Whall employed 'slab' glass, which had been developed by Prior using the classic Arts and Crafts approach of respecting the unique characteristics of the material in determining its method of use. Prior's 'Early English' glass was blown into a flat mould and cut into slabs that were naturally thicker at the centre than at the edges. This produced windows with the translucent, jewel-like effect that Whall sought, and which in turn inspired and instructed Connick.[19] Charles Connick knew of Whall's work from Boston's Church of the Advent, Brimmer Street, where he was present at the unpacking of Whall's windows prior to installation. At first he and his friends scoffed at the dull-looking lights in the crate, thinking that the church had been sent inferior goods, but when the windows were placed and the light flooded through, Connick was dumbstruck by their tran-

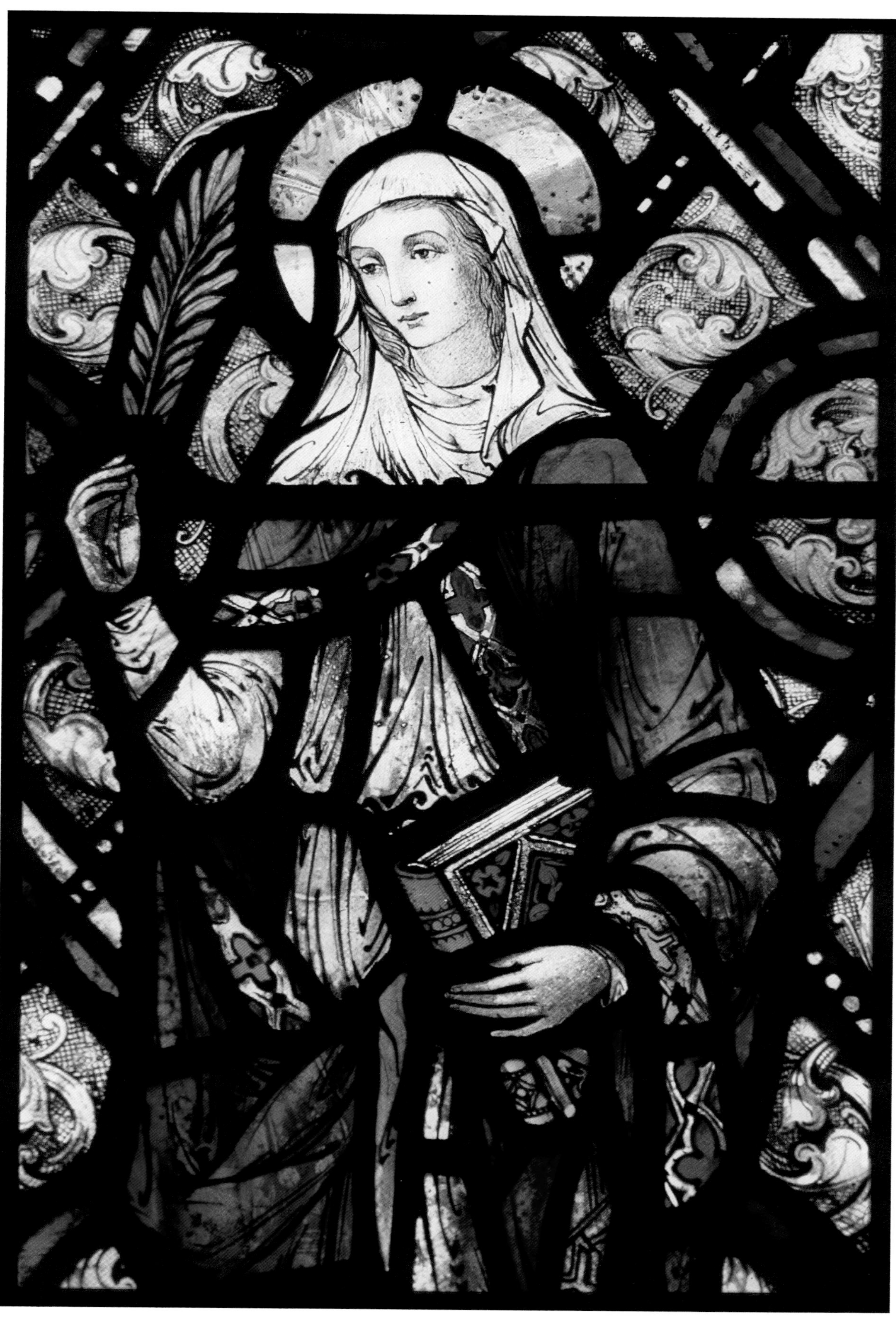

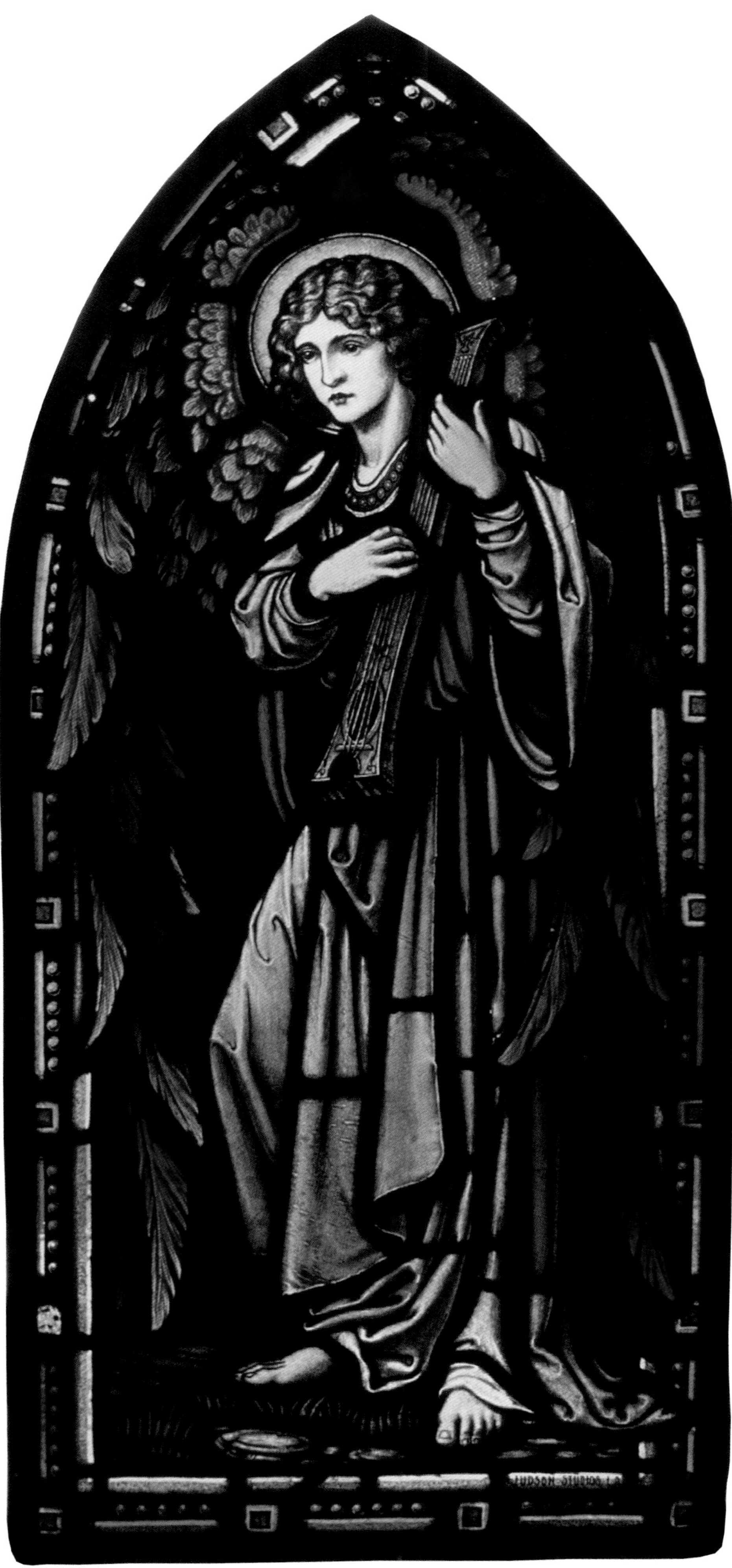

115 Judson Studios

Angel, stained glass in All Saints, Pasadena, California, *c.* 1925

Photograph by Edward R. Bosley

scendent beauty and he regretted his jibes.[20] Connick's windows for Cram's All Saints Church, Ashmont [114], are a particularly worthy example of the Morrisian legacy, via Whall, of glassiness and transparency.

Morris's influence on American stained glass was not limited to the Atlantic seaboard. In California after the turn of the century Walter Horace Judson and the craftsmen at the Judson Studios followed in the footsteps of Morris to create and promote 'antique', pot-metal glass. Walter H. Judson, son of the noted artist and educator William Lees Judson, dedicated his life to stained glass, which he believed demanded the ideal balance of artistic creativity and technical craftsmanship. Judson embraced Morris's philosophy of uniting art and craft, although he did not share Morris's politics and referred to him only as 'that student of Ruskin'.[21] Like Cram, Judson sided with Morris in his love of traditional medieval glass and he avoided the opalescent art-glass style of window made popular by La Farge and Tiffany. Walter's son, Horace, later recalled that his father's dislike was strong: 'He was probably the first artist on the Pacific Coast to realize and utilize the beauty of antique glass ... and his struggle to wean the public away from the sloppy sentimentalism of pictorial opalescents was a long and bitter one.'[22] Judson's premier designer was Frederick Wilson, who had come from New York in the early 1920s where he had been Tiffany's master figure draughtsman. Wilson was competent to design in opalescent glass but rejected it soon after coming to Judson Studios when he found in Walter H. Judson such a strong advocate for the Morris-inspired medieval style. Wilson remained with Judson, becoming chief designer, and was ultimately one of the Studios' longest-serving employees. Among the Judson Studios designs that evoke a debt to Morris & Company is one for All Saints Episcopal Church in Pasadena [115]. A small window in the medieval style, its composition, colour, attention to drapery detail, and quality of glass pay homage to the Firm, and the face of the angel playing a lyre is Pre-Raphaelite sweetness itself. Judson Studios, now in its fifth generation of family management, continues to evoke the memory of Morris in designs for contemporary commissions. A 1995 window for the wedding chapel of the Imperial Hotel, Osaka, whose theme is Ideal Love, illustrates the figures of King Arthur, Queen Guinevere and the Twelve Knights of the Round Table, all in classic Burne-Jones style.

Common Thread: American Art Textiles and Morris

While stained glass commissions in England and abroad provided a solid stream of revenue for Morris & Company, it was embroidery and other textile arts that captured Morris's personal affection and gave him the greatest satisfaction in the design and production process. Embroideries sold by the firm were chiefly of Morris's own design, though Burne-Jones, Philip Webb, John Henry Dearle and Morris's daughter May provided designs as well. As with his re-discovery of forgotten methods of producing stained glass, Morris's contribution to a complete reassessment of embroidery as 'art needlework' in the medieval tradition was nothing less than revolutionary. He was particularly drawn to developing new methods of dyeing silk to produce colours and shadings that more closely reflected the subtleties of nature. Catherine Holiday, one of his favourite needlework students and embroiderers, commented on the Firm's range of colours: 'The amethyst had flushings of red;

and his [Morris's] gold (one special sort), when spread out in the large, rich hanks, looked like a sunset sky.'[23] Morris wrote in *Some Hints on Pattern-designing* (1881) that needle-workers should consider their skill as 'gardening with silk and gold thread'.[24] Eventually the Firm's dyeing methods, promotion of artistic stitching and use of fine materials caused a perceptible shift of public interest away from the typical embroidery of the first half of the nineteenth century, goods commonly called 'Berlin wool-works' whose garishly bright threads, predictable 'counted-stitch' technique, and tired subject matter (often depictions of Old Master paintings) had begun to repel even mainstream artistic sensibilities.

One of the more influential and long-lasting catalysts of this shift was the establishment in London in 1872 of the Royal School of Art Needlework, which sought to employ educated women to improve the quality of commercially available art needlework. Morris, Burne-Jones, Walter Crane and others provided designs for the students to work from, and the school won awards at the 1876 Centennial International Exhibition in Philadelphia and at the Paris Exposition of 1878. Soon after, regional needlework societies, many modelled directly on the Royal School of Art Needlework, began to appear in England and America. The common basis of such societies, consciously or not, came in the form of received wisdom from William Morris: that careful study of great examples of medieval textiles would lead to meaningful and beautiful contemporary needlework.

One woman who was particularly inspired by the Royal School of Art Needlework's spectacular exhibition booth at the Philadelphia exposition – an elaborately designed construction of embroidered silk walls and portals [116] – was Candace Wheeler. A significant force behind the development of American art textiles and home decoration in the late nineteenth and early twentieth centuries, Wheeler credited her early professional interest in textile design to the Philadelphia Exhibition and the Royal School.[25] In 1877, one year after the Exhibition, Wheeler helped to organize the Society of Decorative Arts in New York, which had as its aim 'to encourage profitable industries among women who possess artistic talent, and to furnish a standard of excellence and a market for their work'.[26] Wheeler's intent was to raise needlework from 'craft' to 'Art', but while the Society was a commercial enterprise it was also philanthropic. Wheeler planned to associate with other societies around the United States, to create a network of affiliated groups of ladies of education and aesthetic talent whose circumstances compelled them to work outside the home. The Society would act as a studio and clearing-house for the design, execution and sale of decorative arts of all sorts, but with particular emphasis on textiles. Proceeds would benefit the makers themselves. While Wheeler gave credit directly to the Royal School of Art Needlework as her model, her true interest was in creating a uniquely American paradigm. She recruited some of the most socially prominent women in New York to attract the support and prestige necessary to succeed in the venture, and she persuaded some of her well-known and well-connected artist friends to act as jurors to select the goods that would be sold in the Society's retail showroom. Jurors would also be asked to contribute designs to be executed by members. In this way the relationship between the jury and the organization closely resembled William Morris and Walter Crane's relationship to the Royal School of Art Needlework, to which

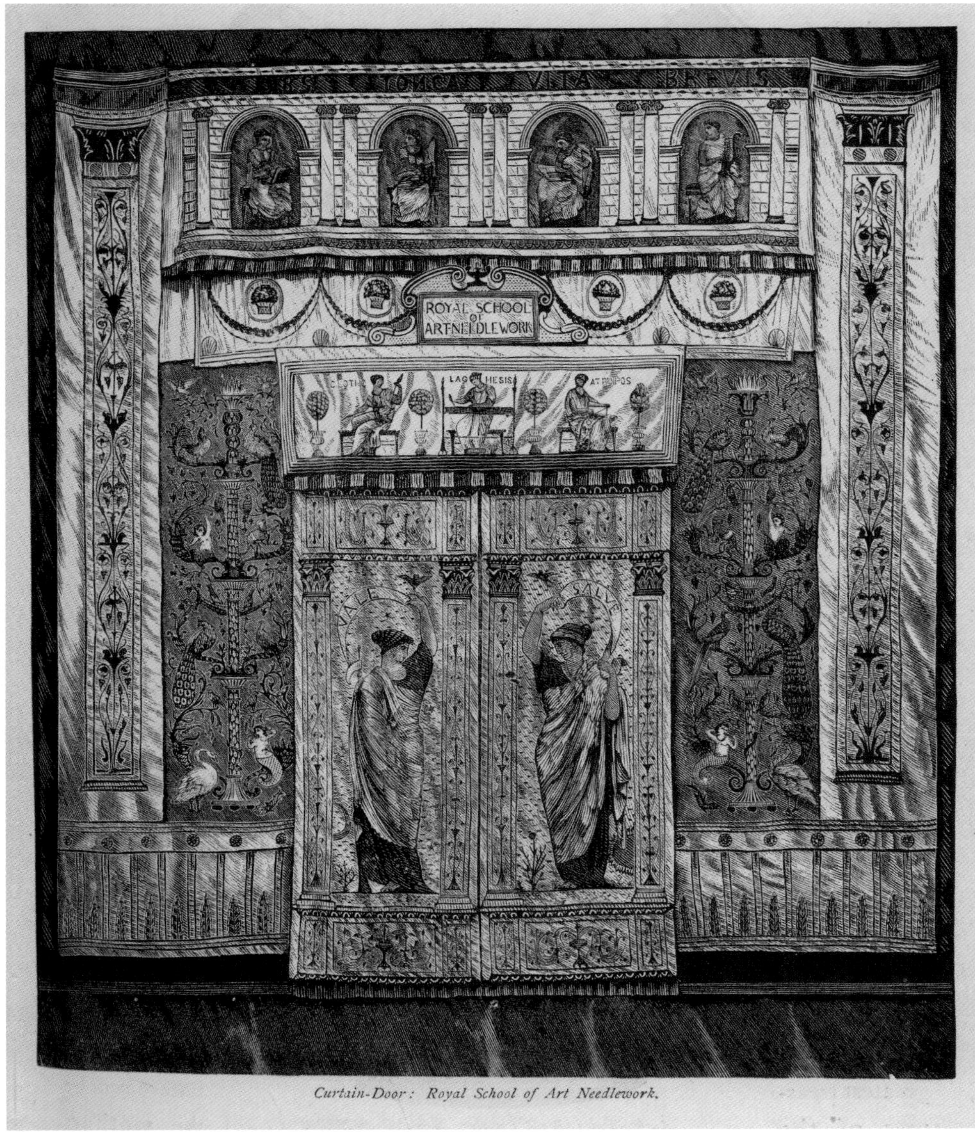

Curtain-Door: Royal School of Art Needlework.

116 Royal School of Art Needlework

'Curtain-door' for the School's booth at the Centennial Exhibition, Philadelphia, 1876

From Walter Smith, *The Masterpieces of the Centennial International Exhibition* (Philadelphia: Gebbie and Barrie, 1876)

each contributed designs. The Society's Committee on Design, as it was known, included Louis Comfort Tiffany who was about to establish his own decorating firm, Samuel Colman, a prominent New York painter and designer, and Lockwood de Forest, a painter, designer and connoisseur of exotic furnishings and decorative arts. Each would soon be associated with Wheeler professionally. Wheeler's younger daughter Dora was also involved, both with needlework and in the administration of the Society, acting as its secretary. She was soon recognized as a talented designer and innovative needle-worker in her own right, especially for her 'needlewoven' tapestries which were distinguished by stitching designs into, rather than on top of, the base fabric.

Ultimately, the high-art aspirations of the trustees of the Society of Decorative Arts did not mesh well with Candace Wheeler's deeply felt philanthropic impulse to raise the station of educated ladies in distressed financial circumstances. Accordingly, she founded another, more inclusive organization called the New York Exchange for Women's Work (known as the Woman's Exchange) in 1878. While Wheeler could certainly appreciate the clear distinction between the Woman's Exchange and the Society of Decorative Arts, some of the latter's board members felt it to be a competitive group, and by the following year Wheeler had left the Society. The Woman's Exchange, like the Ladies' Depository founded in Philadelphia in 1833, sought to benefit women who had to support themselves. Unlike the Society of Decorative Arts, however, the salesroom would accept any goods made by women to be sold, regardless of artistic excellence. In this respect, Wheeler's encouragement of productive craft paralleled William Morris's devotion to the social and economic ideal of art as the expression of joy in work.

In addition to her philanthropic objective, Wheeler's artistic aim was to encourage American design for America. But the legacy of England lingered nonetheless. In 1879, Wheeler, under a pseudonym, designed a pair of portières entitled *Consider the Lillies* [sic] *of the Field* [117], which won a $50 prize from the *Art Interchange*, the weekly magazine affiliated with the Society of Decorative Arts. Wheeler, who was now busy establishing the Woman's Exchange, was nevertheless still one of the magazine's supervisors. She even acted as a juror for the competition that awarded her the prize.[27] *Consider the Lillies of the Field* evokes the splendour of nature in its flowers and grasses, and Gothic lettering of words from the gospel of Matthew provides the kind of religious overlay that often accompanied home decoration that aspired to moral instruction. Like Morris, Wheeler believed that a beautiful home environment could shape character, and the broader English and American Arts and Crafts movements are notable for the explicit moral messages they often conveyed in mantel carvings, tiles and textiles. The crewelwork and conventionalized treatment of Wheeler's lilies may have been inspired by portières that came to America from the Royal School of Art Needlework the previous year.[28] It is worth wondering if Wheeler, in essentially awarding herself the prize, was sending the gospel message (Matthew 6:28, 29) to Society's board members: 'Consider the lilies of the field, how they grow; they toil not, neither do they spin; And yet I say unto you, Solomon in all his glory was not arrayed like one of these.' Wheeler may well have wondered why the board members, in all their glory, could not accept the more inclusive Woman's Exchange – her lilies of the field – as a complement to the fully juried work of the Society.

Between 1879 and 1883, Wheeler entered an official business association with Louis Comfort Tiffany in two sequential ventures, Tiffany & Wheeler and Louis C. Tiffany & Company, Associated Artists. Knowing Candace Wheeler's talent and energy from serving with her in the Society of Decorative Arts, Tiffany recruited her to carry out the embroidery side of his interior decorating venture, which he had begun in 1878. Wheeler's activity in pattern design also included printed cottons, silk damasks and wallpaper, all of which provided additional opportunity for her to study Morris & Company precedents. A discharge-printed denim design of swimming carp, one of the first from Associated Artists, was clearly inspired by Japanese precedents, but the method and philosophy behind it – that of an inexpensive way of creating a beautiful pattern on fabric – could just as easily have come from Morris & Company designs such as *Lea*, which translated well to the indigo-discharge technique [128]. In this technique, denim's blue colour is selectively removed by pressing bleach onto the fabric with a pattern design block.

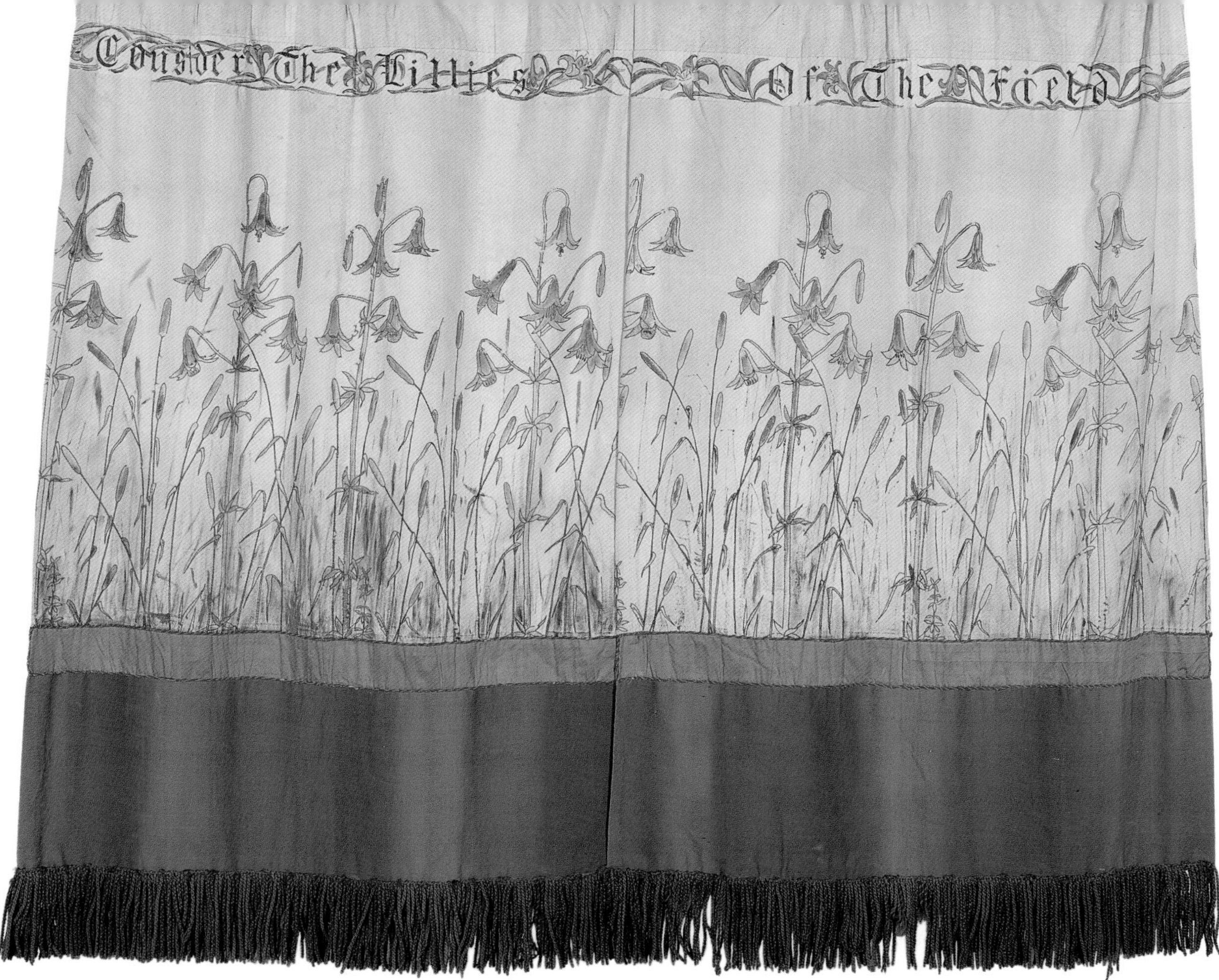

117 Candace Wheeler

Consider the Lillies of the Field portières, 1879

Cotton embroidered in wools and painted, wool borders, 74¼ x 44½ (188.6 x 113); 73 x 45½ (185.4 x 115.6)

The Mark Twain House, Hartford, Connecticut, Gift of Mrs. Francis B. Thurber III, 1972

Associated Artists also produced prints on plain woven cotton. In these they expressed three-dimensionality through the use of varying shades of colour, or adjacencies of colour, much as in Morris's textiles and wallpapers such as *Scroll* (1871), *Willow* (1874), and *Apple* (1877) [119]. Stylistically, Wheeler often looked to Japanese models, but the objective of creating depth in patterns is likely to have been adapted from Morris & Company examples. When the New York wallpaper manufacturing firm of Warren, Fuller & Lange advertised the results of an international competition for wallpaper design held in 1881, Candace Wheeler, her daughter Dora, and two of Wheeler's students garnered the $2,000 in cash prizes. In their designs, the sophisticated use of animals and plants had the unmistakable imprint of Morris & Company's influence, particularly in Dora Wheeler's winning entry. Her design, called *Peony* [120], uses leaves in an overall field pattern, with the blooms themselves occurring in an almost imperceptible repeat. Among the Morris documents in The Huntington Morris collection is a watercolour design for a border that was never produced, also called *Peony* [118], whose similarity goes beyond the mere presence of the flower to the manner in which it is conventionalized. Wheeler's *Bees and Honeycomb* design, which earned her the $1,000 first prize, was produced as a wallpaper for Warren, Fuller & Lange in 1882. The bees swarm freely in a seeming random fashion, but the overall structure and generously spaced repeat recall Morris & Company designs such as *Scroll* (1871) or *Fruit* (1866).

118 Probably J. H. Dearle for Morris & Company

Design for *Peony* wallpaper border, *c.* 1910 (detail)

Watercolour and graphite, full sheet 13½ x 21½ (34.3 x 54.6)

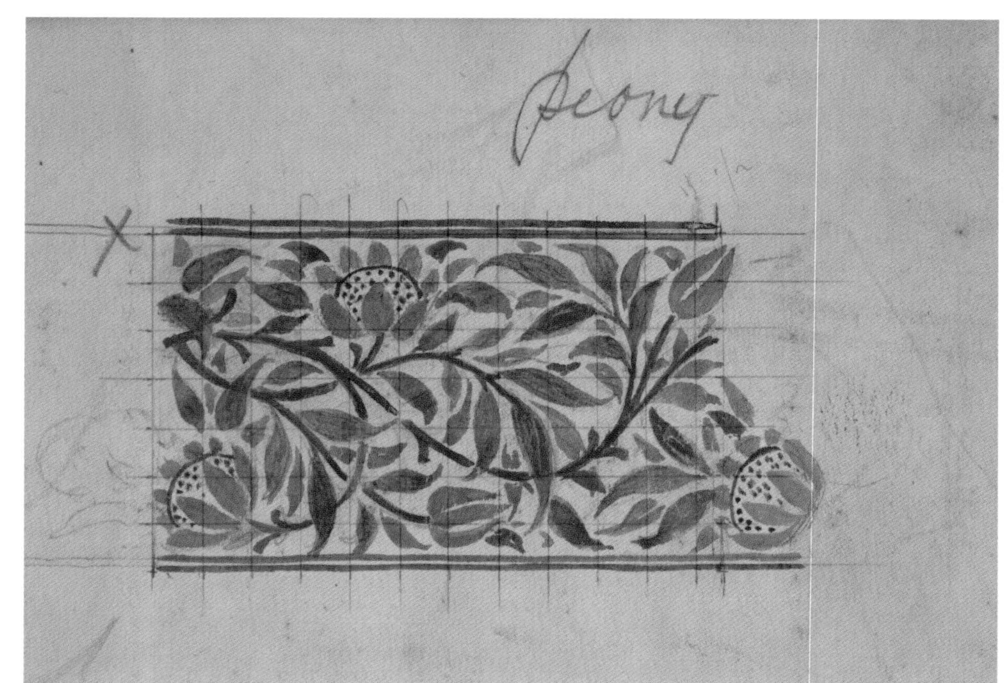

119 Designed by William Morris for Morris & Company

Apple wallpaper, first issued 1877 (detail)

Block-printed in distemper colours, printed by Jeffrey & Company, London, full piece 31½ x 21 (80 x 53.3)

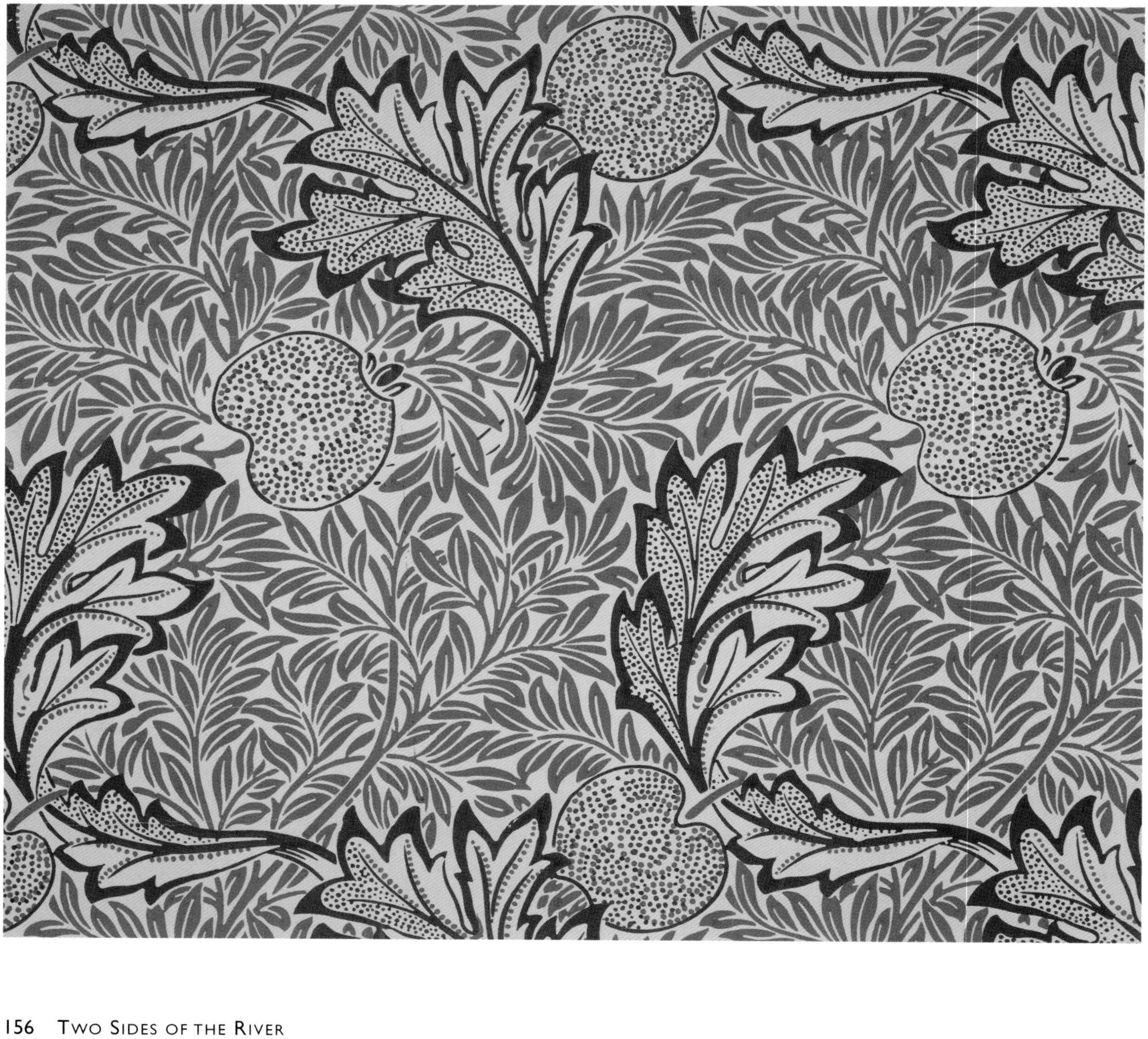

120 Dora Wheeler

Design for *Peony* wallpaper, *c.* 1880

From Clarence Cook, *What Shall We Do With Our Walls?* (New York: Warren, Fuller & Lange, 1884)

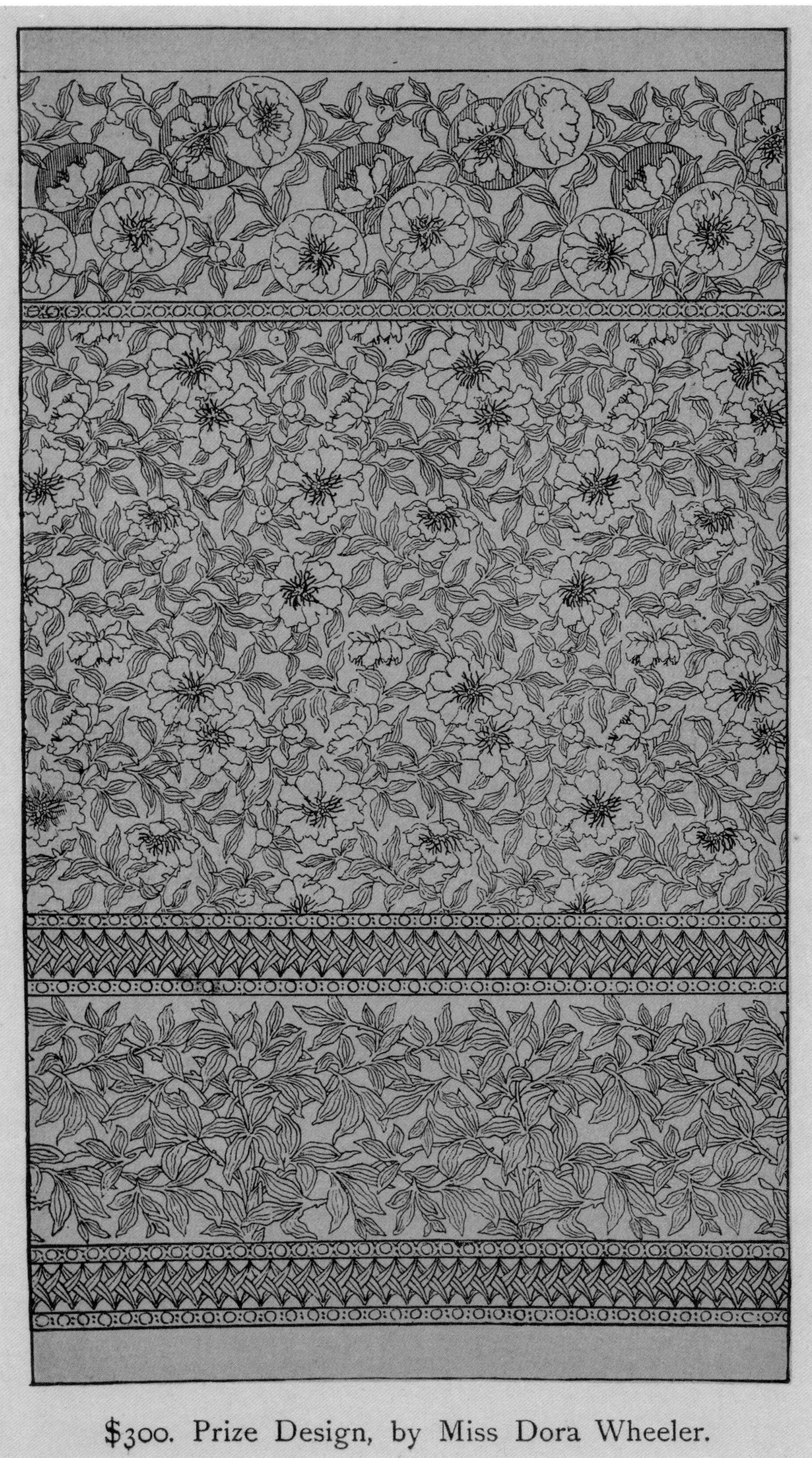

Candace Wheeler's acknowledged debt to Morris provides a direct link with American pattern design, textiles and embroidery. Morris's daughter May, however, made the link to America personal. May had studied needlework and historical examples at the South Kensington School of Design before joining the Embroidery Department in her father's firm in 1883 and becoming its head in 1885. In 1892 May was commissioned to create a set of four portières in a design called *Fruit Garden* [121], featuring dense foliage that reflects the classic pattern language of Morris but is fresh in its treatment of the fruit bursting with seed, the sinuous vines and the carpeting of naturalistic flowers and leaves. Medieval-inspired lettering – selected lines from Morris's poem *The Flowering Orchard* – is stitched across the top of each panel. Commissioned by Mrs J. Munro Longyear for her home in Marquette, Michigan, May Morris worked the panels herself on a silk damask ground with floss silk stitching, which she loved as 'quite the foremost of embroidery silks'. Similar portières were ordered by other clients, either as kits or to be executed by Morris & Company needle-workers. May Morris did not share her father's disquiet about America and Americans and ultimately brought her interpretation of the Morris & Company philosophy on textiles directly to the United States through a series of North American appearances in 1909–10. In a letter to Morris's Hammersmith neighbour, the printer Emery Walker, she exclaimed, 'You'll be surprised to hear I am enjoying New York. . . . I ought to be bored but I'm not.' Of Chicago she said, 'Fancy having pleasant experiences in so unromantic and violent a corner of this country.'[29] May Morris's visually compelling *Fruit Garden* portières, commissioned as they were by an American client, are emblematic of America's coming of age in the appreciation of art needlework.

Further proof was the collaboration of Margaret Whiting and Ellen Miller to establish the Society of Blue and White Needlework in Deerfield, Massachusetts, in 1896, whose aim was to preserve the rapidly vanishing legacy of seventeenth- and eighteenth-century Colonial American embroideries. Whiting said of the venture, 'Rub Oriental art through the Puritan sieve and how odd is the result; how charming

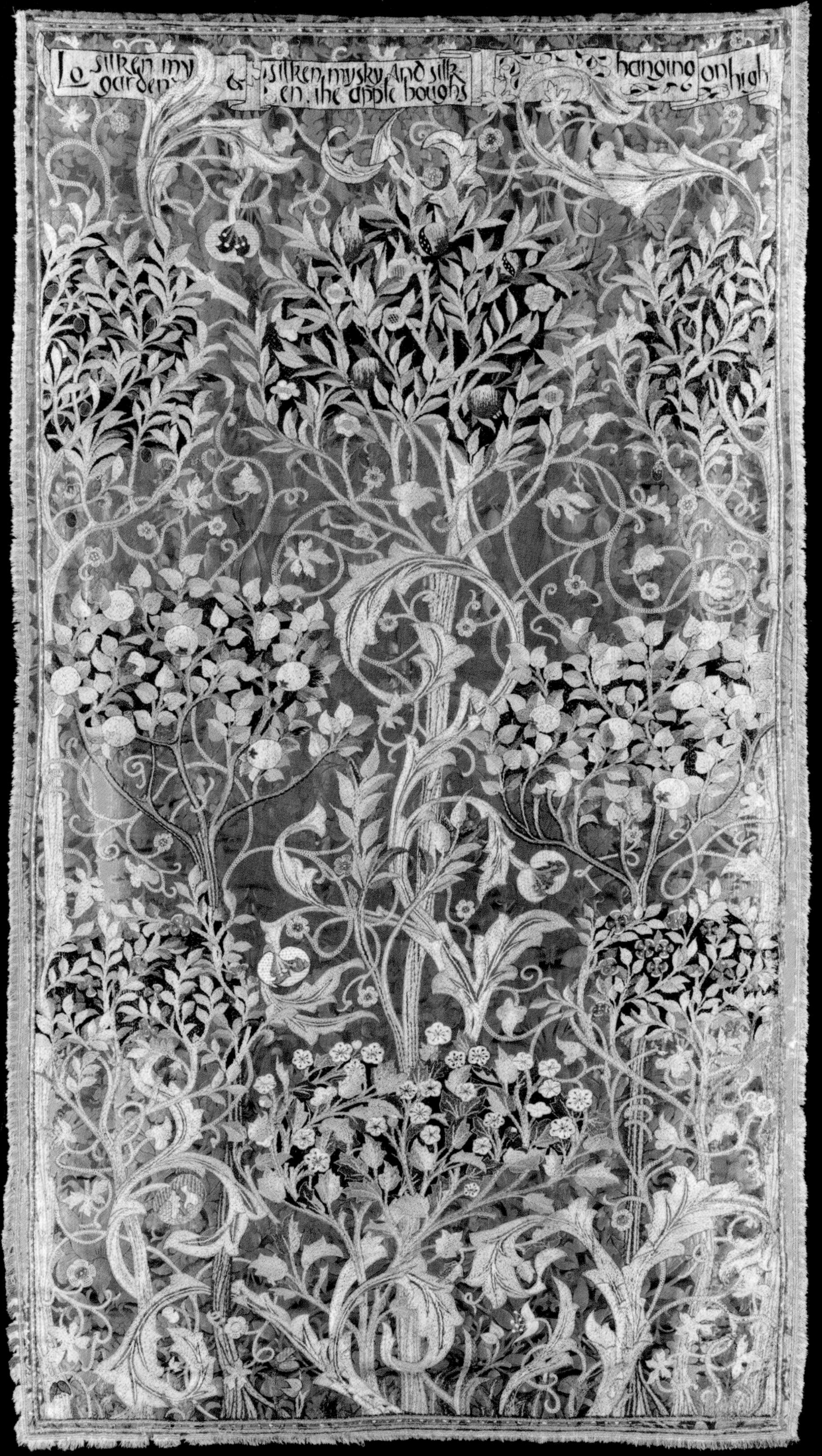

121 May Morris for Morris & Company

Fruit Garden portière (one of four), 1892–93

Silk damask designed by William Morris, with silk embroidery, silk fringe and cotton lining, 102 x 54 (259.1 x 137.2)

© 2003 Museum of Fine Arts, Boston, in memory of J. S. and Sayde Z. Gordon from Myron K. and Natalie G. Stone

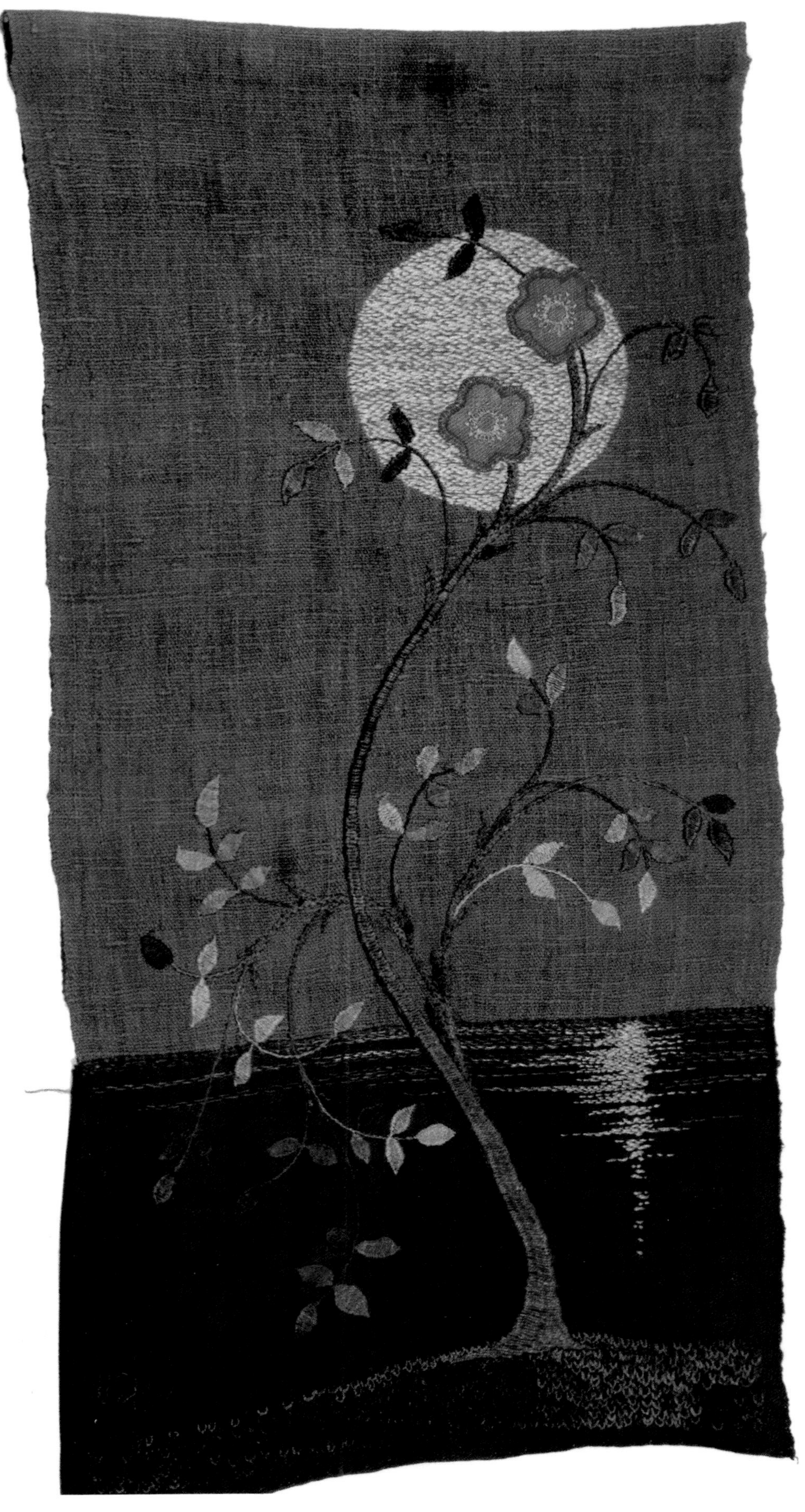

122 Deerfield Society of Blue and White Needlework

Two Red Roses Across the Moon, c. 1919

Appliqué and embroidery on linen, 31½ x 14½ (80 x 36.8)

Pocumtuck Valley Memorial Association, Memorial Hall Museum, Deerfield, Massachusetts

and how individual.' Whiting and Miller believed that 'it might be possible to adapt Ruskin's theory to the Deerfield effort and establish a village industry which should be at once unique and in entire sympathy with its environment'.[30] According to Deerfield historian Suzanne Flynt, Whiting not only envisioned a Ruskinian community but also promoted a Morrisian one. Morris's novel, *A Dream of John Ball*, was circulated for all of the Deerfield stitchers to read.[31] Deerfield needlework reflects the Puritan sobriety to which Whiting refers, particularly in its uncluttered compositions [122]. Compared to the dense richness of a William or May Morris embroidery, Deerfield work communicates Yankee practicality and the shunning of luxury. It is rather a reflection of the restored importance of hand needlecraft in America and, while this was in part prompted by the improving status of embroidery as a result of the focused attention on the work of Morris & Company, the Deerfield community did not attempt to bring English design principles to bear on its own artistic productions. It should be noted, however, that American art needlework's association with the Arts and Crafts movement, through Candace Wheeler's diligent efforts, prefigured by twenty years most other manifestations of the Arts and Crafts movement in America. The textile arts, in effect, paved the road on which the other wagons of William Morris's influence rode.

The Kelmscott Press and American Printing

Perhaps the most profound legacy that William Morris left to America was the revolution spawned in typography and printing by the appearance of the Kelmscott Press books. Printing in America, while it had sometimes shown isolated artistic aspirations, had been driven until the late 1800s primarily by economics, not aesthetics. Since the 1850s, there had been a growing, albeit specialized, demand for finely printed books, proof of which was the increasing establishment of collectors' clubs across the country. The most prestigious of these, the Grolier Club of New York, was founded in 1884 with the expressed purpose of encouraging the 'study and promotion of the arts pertaining to the production of books'.[32] In 1888 Emery Walker presented a lecture entitled 'Printing' for the first exhibition of the Arts & Crafts Exhibition Society in London. Spurred by Walker's passion, and troubled by his own abortive attempts to get publishers to design and print his writings the way he believed they should be, William Morris took up printing himself. He established the Kelmscott Press in 1891 at the age of fifty-seven. Morris oversaw every stage of making a book, from the choice of subject matter (often his own writing) to typography (he designed three typefaces, Golden, Troy, and Chaucer), to paper and ink selection, format and page layout, press work and binding [66–71, 96]. He treated each phase as an artistic pursuit and the whole process as a symbiotic collaboration of crafts. Kelmscott books were praised by the American press for their artistic qualities, but from the beginning critics also expressed heated opinions regarding their cost, legibility and appropriateness to the average reader. Such criticism did not deter other printers and publishers, however, from emulating Morris.

The first publisher to bring the Kelmscott style of printing to America was Roberts Brothers of Boston, who published a facsimile edition of *The Story of the Glittering Plain* (Kelmscott's first publication) in October 1891. *The Nation* was criti-

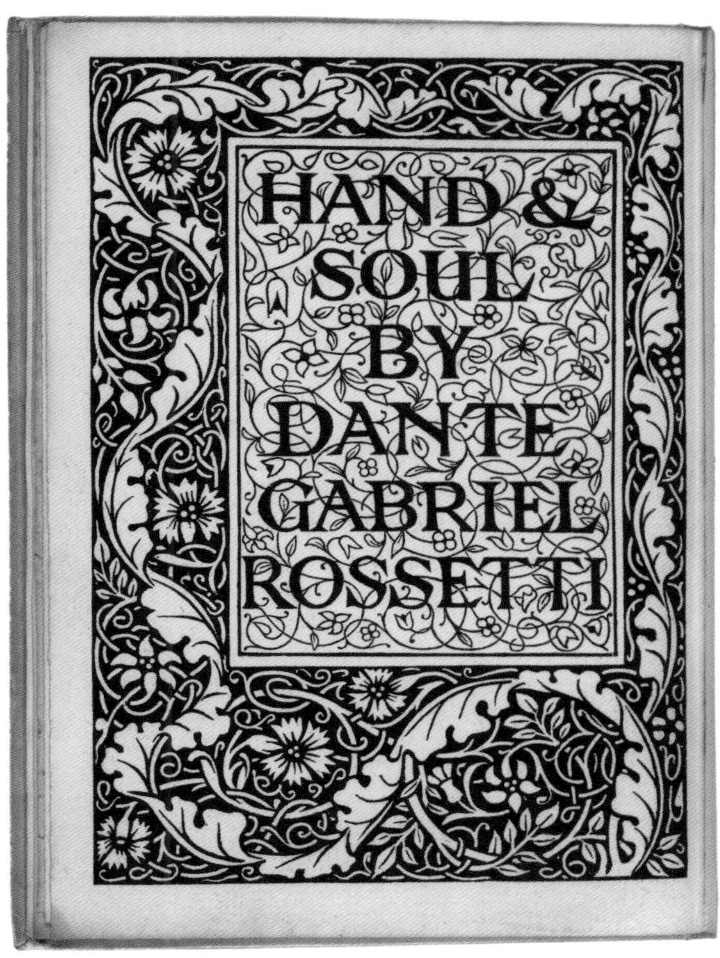

123 Designed by William Morris

Hand and Soul, by Dante Gabriel Rossetti (Hammersmith: The Kelmscott Press, 1895)

Printed for distribution by Messrs Way & Williams of Chicago

cal: 'In default of any other *raison d'être*, we imagine that this artistic combination of imitation vellum, parchment, and antique lettering may be intended to take a place with other bric à brac on a drawing room table.'[33] Some writers were more positive, however, and Chicago's *Inland Printer* became typical of early detractors who later warmed and became supportive, calling it 'a credit to English craftsmanship, [which] assuredly stands at the head of all specimens of book typography hitherto produced'.[34] Regarding cost, however, Morris had no doubt become accustomed to the sort of critique published in the *Engraver and Printer* (March 1896): 'his books, owing to their great cost, are not for the people. They are for the rich few only.'[35] In 1895, Morris agreed to print an edition of Dante Gabriel Rossetti's *Hand and Soul* to be distributed in America by Way & Williams [123]. It was the only Kelmscott Press book printed for the American market and then only because W. Irving Way, the bibliophile-turned-publisher, had made a pilgrimage to the Kelmscott Press to discuss the joint venture with Morris himself.

Meanwhile, an eager American printing trade had been swift to attempt various interpretations, if not outright imitations, of the Kelmscott style. Ralph Adams Cram and Bertram Goodhue, partners in the noted architectural firm that defined American Gothic church architecture in the early twentieth century, designed and published the first American periodical to pay homage to the Kelmscott style. *The Knight Errant*, a short-lived 'quarter-yearly review of the liberal arts', ran for four numbers from April 1892 to January 1893 [124]. Its medieval cover design drawn by Goodhue,

124 *The Knight Errant being a Magazine of Appreciation* (Boston: printed for the proprietors at the Elzevir Press, 1892)

The first number, with illustration by Bertram Grosvenor Goodhue.

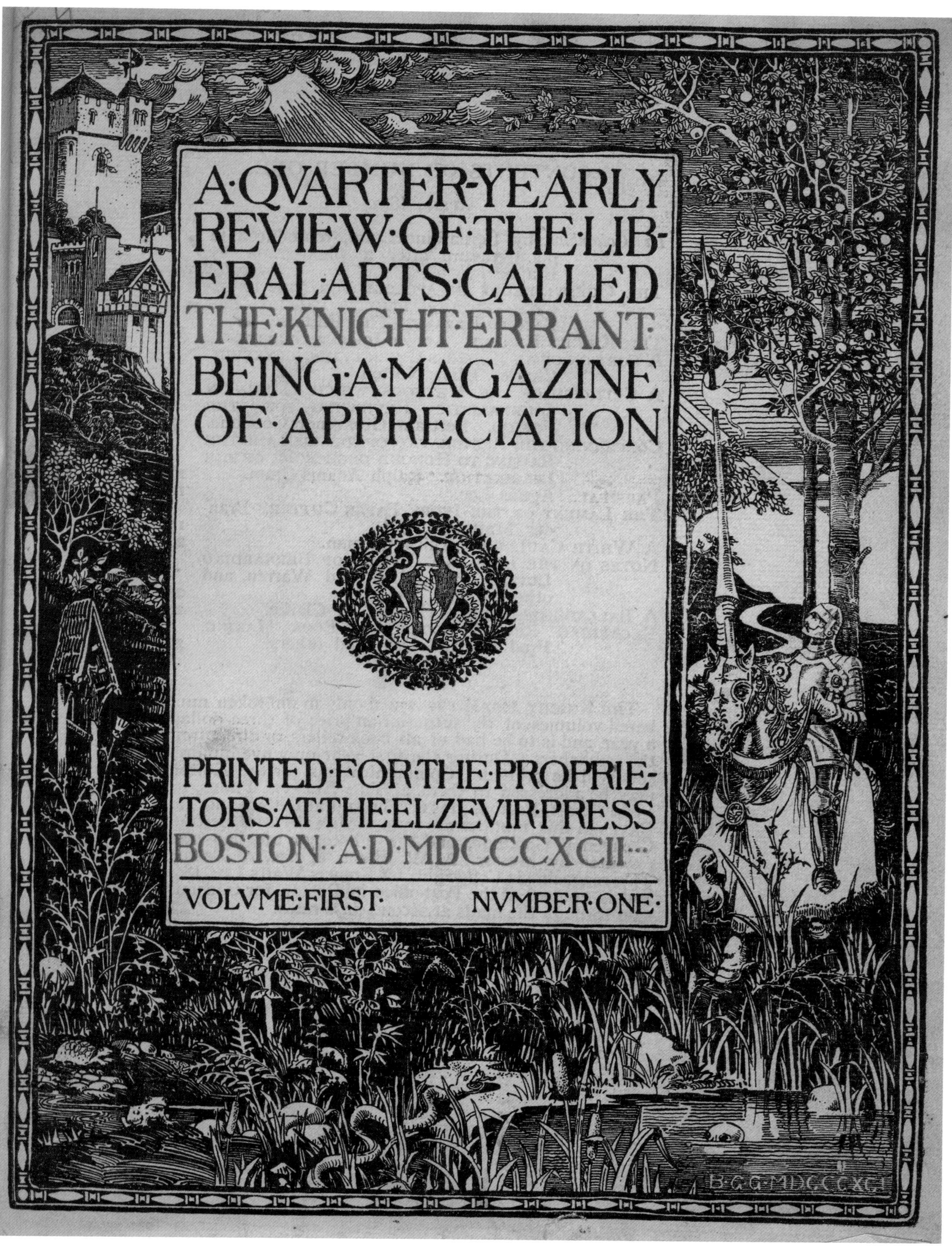
A·QVARTER·YEARLY
REVIEW·OF·THE·LIB-
ERAL·ARTS·CALLED
THE·KNIGHT·ERRANT·
BEING·A·MAGAZINE
OF·APPRECIATION
PRINTED·FOR·THE·PROPRIE-
TORS·AT·THE·ELZEVIR·PRESS
BOSTON·A·D·MDCCCXCII
VOLVME·FIRST· NVMBER·ONE·
B.G.G. MDCCCXCI

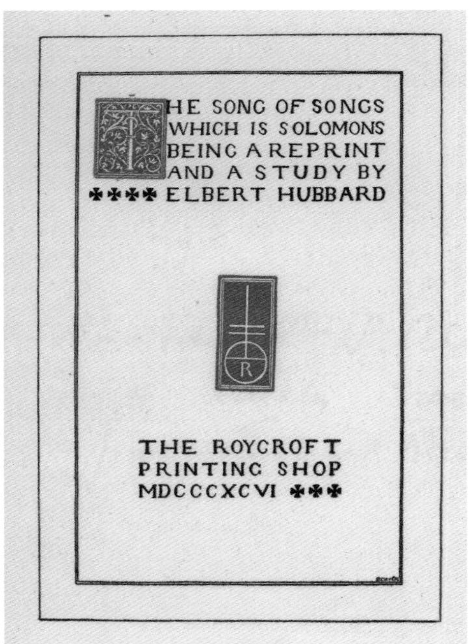

125 Designed by Elbert Hubbard

The Song of Songs Which is Solomon's (East Aurora, N.Y.: The Roycroft Printing Shop, 1896)

Courtesy of André Chaves

combined with a heavy typeface, robust paper and wide-margined page layout, was strongly reminiscent of the Kelmscott Press style and echoed a similar periodical, *The Hobby Horse*, published by A. H. Mackmurdo and the Century Guild in London. Goodhue also designed Kelmscott-style titlepages for Copeland & Day, an Arts and Crafts publisher in Boston, from 1893 to 1899. Publishers and printers across the country would capitalize on the growing popularity (and value to collectors) of Kelmscott Press books. Thomas B. Mosher of Portland, Maine, was one of the most enthusiastic publishers to adapt popular styles, including Kelmscott, but because of his tendency to borrow designs and overlook royalty payments to the authors of the books that he published he was known more or less affectionately as the 'literary pirate' of Portland.

Similarly, Elbert Hubbard, whose Roycroft Printing Shop began its operations in 1895 in East Aurora, New York, had no qualms about adapting the style, though sometimes only crudely. The January 1896 printing of *The Song of Songs Which is Solomon's*, ten months before the appearance of Morris's *Works of Geoffrey Chaucer*, showed Hubbard's early and prescient grasp of the importance of the Kelmscott Press to the world of book collecting. The *Song of Songs* featured Morrisian borders and initials; but the poor registration of the black and red on the title-page [125], for example, betray Hubbard's willingness merely to suggest, rather than adhere to, the high standards of Kelmscott printing. Hubbard's most adept designer in the Morrisian style was Samuel Warner, whose title-page designed in 1900 for *Maud* by Alfred, Lord Tennyson showed a more sophisticated understanding of Morris's principles of design. Similarly, Jerome O'Connor's title-page design for the Roycroft's *Dreams* by Olive Schreiner (1901) is also a competent interpretation. Later, Dard Hunter would contribute spectacularly to the Hubbard legacy in all aspects of book design and printing.

Joseph M. Bowles, publisher of the Indianapolis-based magazine *Modern Art*, first saw Kelmscott books in 1892 and showed them to his friend Bruce Rogers, who

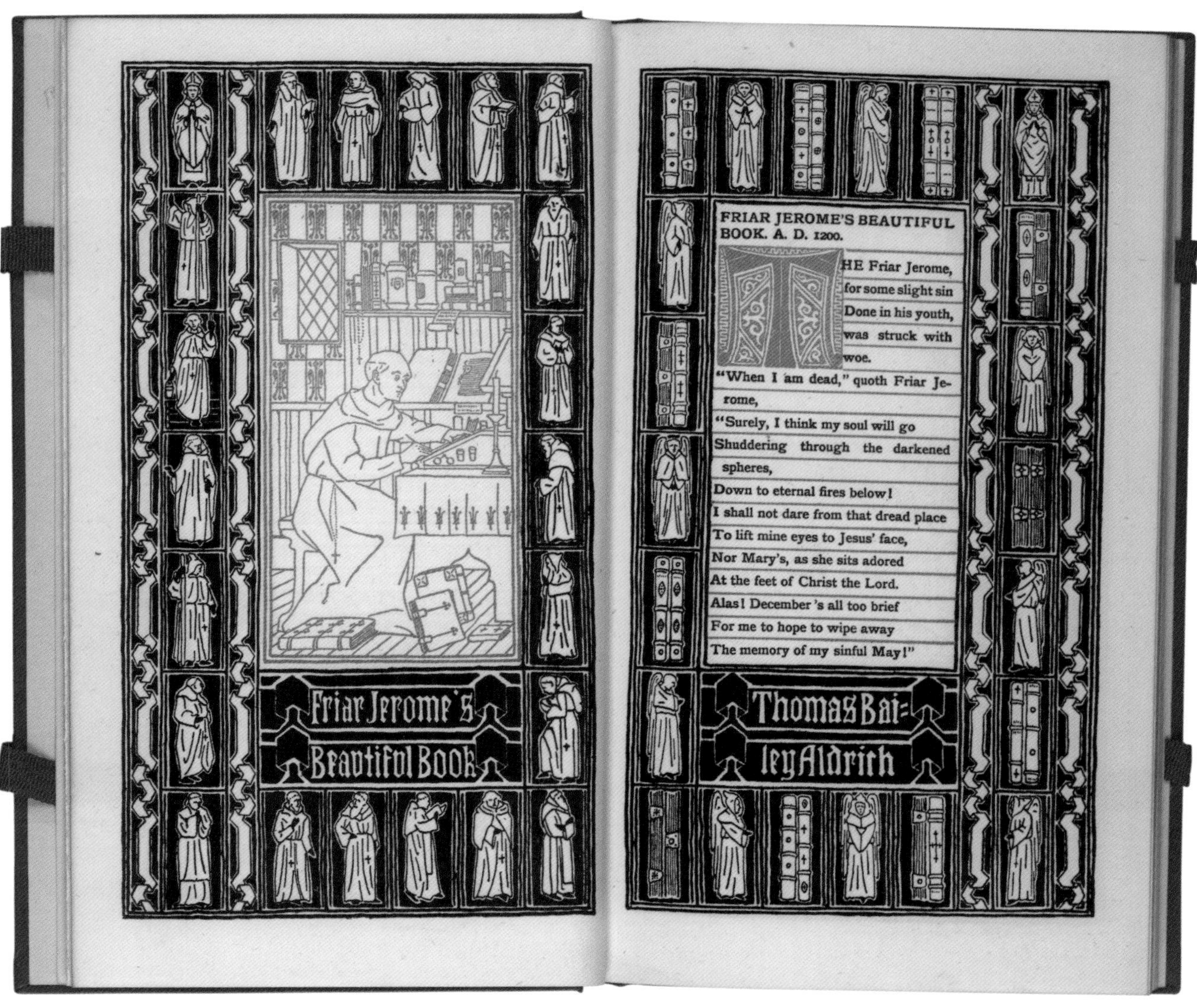

126 Designed by Bruce Rogers

Friar Jerome's Beautiful Book, by Thomas Bailey Aldrich (Boston: Houghton, Mifflin & Company, 1896)

became one of America's most respected book designers. Kelmscott volumes were an epiphany for him, inspiring his early designs for L. Prang, Thomas B. Mosher, Stone and Kimball, Way & Williams, and Houghton, Mifflin & Company's Riverside Press, for whom he worked for sixteen years. One such design was for *Friar Jerome's Beautiful Book* by Thomas Bailey Aldrich, published by Houghton, Mifflin & Company in 1896 [126]. *Friar Jerome* is not an imitation of a Kelmscott design but instead pays a compliment to the underlying principles of Kelmscott work as articulated by William Morris and Emery Walker: colour (very black type with red accents), page layout (margins ascending in size from bottom and fore margin to top and back), and decoration which, in the case of *Jerome*, is architectural, the page treated more like the reredos of a Gothic cathedral than a two-dimensional plane.

Another Boston printer of the same period, Daniel Berkeley Updike, showed even greater zeal regarding Morris and Walker's principles of printing. Updike had worked at Houghton, Mifflin from 1891 to 1893, during which time he designed *On the Dedications of American Churches*, his first book, which was praised by one critic as

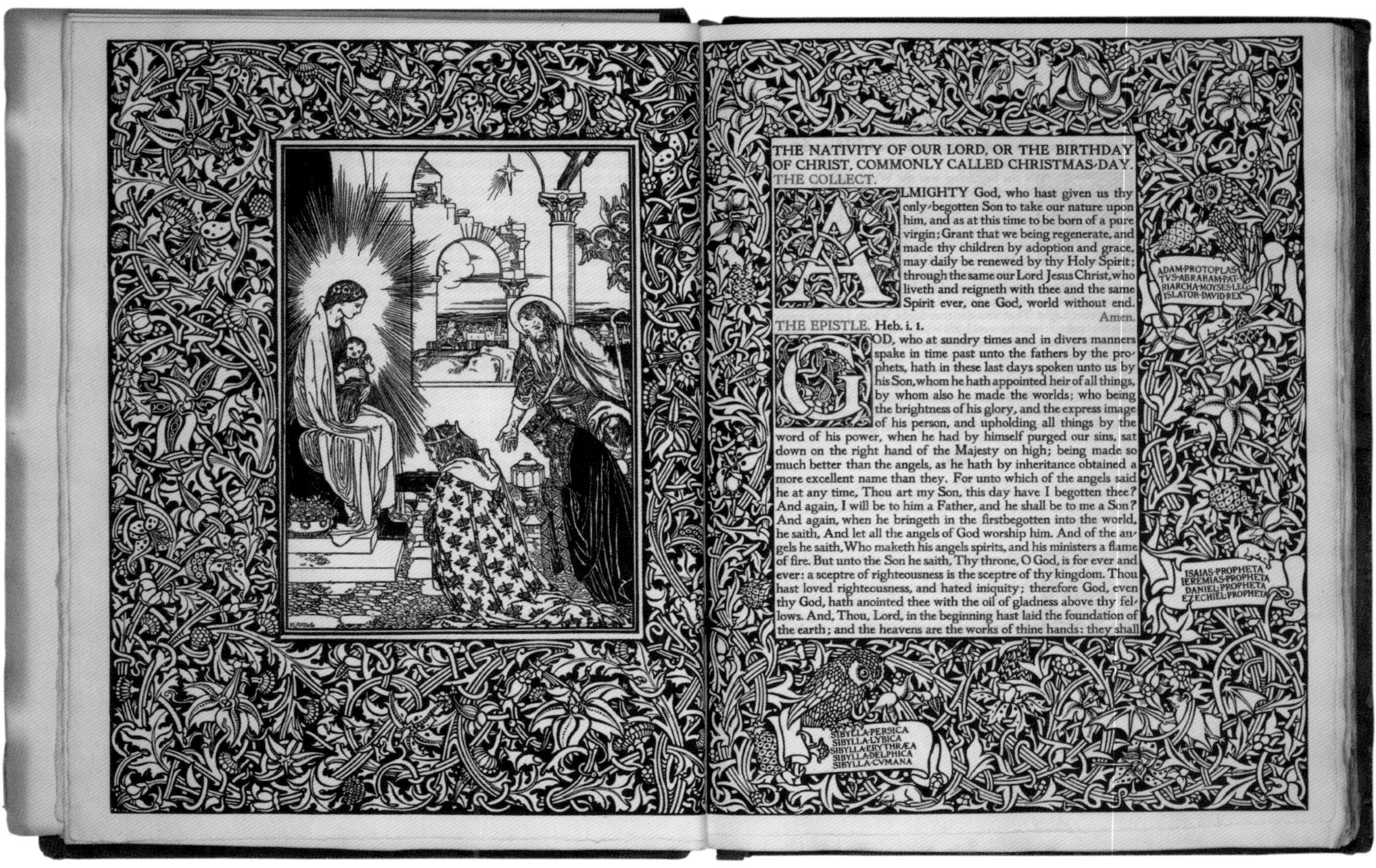

THE NATIVITY OF OUR LORD, OR THE BIRTHDAY OF CHRIST, COMMONLY CALLED CHRISTMAS-DAY.

THE COLLECT.

ALMIGHTY God, who hast given us thy only-begotten Son to take our nature upon him, and as at this time to be born of a pure virgin; Grant that we being regenerate, and made thy children by adoption and grace, may daily be renewed by thy Holy Spirit; through the same our Lord Jesus Christ, who liveth and reigneth with thee and the same Spirit ever, one God, world without end. Amen.

THE EPISTLE. Heb. i. 1.

GOD, who at sundry times and in divers manners spake in time past unto the fathers by the prophets, hath in these last days spoken unto us by his Son, whom he hath appointed heir of all things, by whom also he made the worlds; who being the brightness of his glory, and the express image of his person, and upholding all things by the word of his power, when he had by himself purged our sins, sat down on the right hand of the Majesty on high; being made so much better than the angels, as he hath by inheritance obtained a more excellent name than they. For unto which of the angels said he at any time, Thou art my Son, this day have I begotten thee? And again, I will be to him a Father, and he shall be to me a Son? And again, when he bringeth in the firstbegotten into the world, he saith, And let all the angels of God worship him. And of the angels he saith, Who maketh his angels spirits, and his ministers a flame of fire. But unto the Son he saith, Thy throne, O God, is for ever and ever: a sceptre of righteousness is the sceptre of thy kingdom. Thou hast loved righteousness, and hated iniquity; therefore God, even thy God, hath anointed thee with the oil of gladness above thy fellows. And, Thou, Lord, in the beginning hast laid the foundation of the earth; and the heavens are the works of thine hands: they shall

127 *The Altar Book: containing the Order for the Celebration of the Holy Eucharist according to the Use of the American Church* (Boston: D. B. Updike, The Merrymount Press, 1896)

Bertram Grosvenor Goodhue designed the Merrymount type and the borders and initials, while Robert Anning Bell provided the illustrations.

'probably the first product of the modern renaissance of printing in this country'.[36] While he later converted to a more austere, Renaissance style, Updike's early years interpreting the Kelmscott style for America were successful and influential. He became one of the most revered figures in twentieth-century typography, producing more than eight hundred books and sixteen thousand pieces of 'job' printing at his Merrymount Press. His best-known work of this period is *The Altar Book*, published in 1896 for the use of the Episcopal Church in America [127]. For it, Updike commissioned illustrations from Robert Anning Bell of Liverpool, and employed Bertram Goodhue's custom typeface, Merrymount, as well as his Kelmscott-style initials and borders. In 1895, the *Inland Printer* praised a circular Updike had issued, 'which . . . is printed in a type and manner highly complimentary to himself and Mr. William Morris and the Kelmscott Press. It is a treat to look upon.'[37] While Updike later regretted *The Altar Book*, possibly for its too-close references to the Kelmscott Chaucer [70], his dedication to creating the volume was noteworthy and important to America's development in book design and fine printing. Three years in the making (1893–96), *The Altar Book* reflects an American interpretation of the work that was progressing simultaneously on the Kelmscott Chaucer, Morris's magnum opus, which appeared shortly before Morris's death. As in the Chaucer, Updike's dense title-pages are heavily decorated with foliage-rich borders that depict vines, fruit and flowers. Regular text pages, again reflecting Morris's style, are left free of borders, with decorations limited to occasional initials, and red ink used for running titles and instructions to the liturgical celebrant. Initials, usually decorated with vines and other foliage, are sometimes augmented with robed figures, either kneeling or standing, and occasional Latin text. The Christmas service opening pages [127] have fanciful borders that surpass any whimsy of Kelmscott books, with depictions of bats, owls, and even moles.

In 1900, Updike printed a small volume entitled *The Prince Who Did Not Exist*, with text by Edward Perry Warren and illustrations by Arthur J. Gaskin. Its subject matter would have naturally suggested a Kelmscott-like design, but its simplicity testified to Updike's maturing interpretation of principles over style. The 1903 printing of *In the Dawn of the World, Being Twenty-five Pictures Illustrative of a Portion of the Book of Genesis* by Edward Burne-Jones, shows Updike's reverence for Morris through content, page layout, quality of paper, simplicity of presentation and exactness of presswork. His affection for Morris, Emery Walker and the Kelmscott legacy was evident in his books, and also personally in his press rooms in Boston, where he had framed and hung a specimen page from the Kelmscott Chaucer, a portrait of Emery Walker, and one of William Morris.[38]

Towards the end of his life, William Morris felt that his quest to elevate the 'Lesser Arts' and his goal of bringing them to people at all levels of society had not succeeded. He sadly recognized that his work could only be purchased by the élite. This troubled him even more than it would have troubled Ruskin, who believed that great art should be neither too plentiful nor too cheap. Morris was a creative artist of tremendous generosity and integrity, however, and he persevered in the hope that his toil would nonetheless make a difference to humankind. More so now than ever we know that it did, to every corner of society and in myriad ways. In the America that he disliked his aims were achieved perhaps better than anywhere, and we can be confident that the man who lived as if he were living the lives of ten will likely, on some level, continue to make the difference that he hoped to.

NOTES 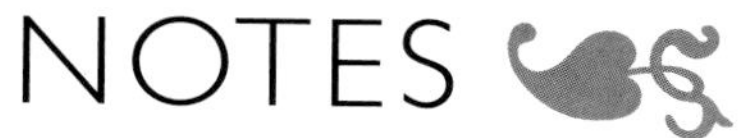

For details of works cited in shortened form, see the Select Bibliography, p. 173

Introduction (pp. 9–19)
1 Morris, 'The Beauty of Life, Delivered before the Birmingham Society of Arts and School of Design, February 19, 1880', in *Hopes and Fears for Art*, in *Collected Works*, 22:53.
2 Quoted in MacCarthy, *William Morris*, 598.
3 *The Letters of Henry James*, ed. Leon Edel (Cambridge, Mass.: Harvard University Press, 1974), 2:352.
4 Morris, 'Some Thoughts on the Ornamented Manuscripts of the Middle Ages', reprinted in *William Morris: The Ideal Book*, ed. Peterson, 1.
5 Morris, 'Art and the Beauty of the Earth', in *Lectures on Art and Industry*, in *Collected Works*, 22:164.
6 Morris to Cormell Price, July 1856, in *Collected Letters of William Morris*, 1:28.
7 See *Guide to Literary Manuscripts in the Huntington Library* (San Marino, Calif.: Huntington Library, 1979); and Sara S. Hodson, 'A Checklist of Pre-Raphaelite Manuscripts in the Huntington Library' and Shelley M. Bennett, 'A Checklist of Pre-Raphaelite Works of Art in the Huntington Library and Art Collections' in *The Pre-Raphaelites in Context* (San Marino, Calif.: Henry E. Huntington Library and Art Gallery, 1992) for more complete listings.
8 Quoted in Nicholas A. Basbanes, *A Gentle Madness: Bibliophiles, Bibliomanes, and the Eternal Passion for Books* (New York: H. Holt and Co., 1995), 444.
9 Ibid., 452.
10 Morris, 'Art and the Beauty of the Earth', in *Collected Works*, 22:168.
11 *Collected Letters of William Morris*, 2:207.

William Morris: A Life in Design (pp. 21–31)
I am extremely grateful to Alan Crawford, Stacey Loughrey and Johanna Brenner for comments on the manuscript and for help in other ways, and to Diane Waggoner, Anne Mallek and Shelley Bennett who have made working on this project such a pleasant experience. I am indebted to many people who have written about William Morris, the Firm, and the Arts and Crafts movement, particularly Fiona MacCarthy, Linda Parry, Paul Thompson, Gillian Naylor, Peter Cormack, Peter Faulkner, Raymond Watkinson, Charles Harvey, Jon Press, Peter Stansky, Robert Winter, Lynne Walker, Wendy Kaplan, Alan Crawford, Anthea Callen and the late Edward Thompson. I thank them all.

1 Morris, 'The Beauty of Life, Delivered before the Birmingham Society of Arts and School of Design, February 19, 1880', in *Hopes and Fears for Art*, in *Collected Works*, 22:76.
2 Oscar Wilde, 'The English Renaissance of Art', lecture, New York, 1882. Quoted in Harvey and Press, *William Morris: Design and Enterprise*, 1.
3 Quoted in Linda Parry, 'Introduction', in *William Morris*, ed. Parry, 19.
4 Ibid.
5 Charlotte Gere, 'Morris and Company, 1861–1939', in *Morris and Company*, ed. Gere (London: The Fine Art Society, 1979), 6; and Lesley Hoskins, 'Wallpaper', in *William Morris*, ed. Parry, 204.
6 W. R. Lethaby, *Ernest Gimson: His Life and Work* (London: E. Benn, 1924), 2–4.
7 The best account of Morris's early life is in MacCarthy, *William Morris*.
8 Morris, 'A Rather Long-Winded Sketch of my Very Uneventful Life', in *William Morris: Selected Writings*, ed. Briggs, 29.
9 *William Morris by Himself*, ed. Naylor, 7.
10 A. W. N. Pugin, *The True Principles of Pointed or Christian Architecture* (London: J. Weale, 1841), 1.
11 Margaretta Lovell, 'Introduction', in *William Morris: The Sanford and Helen Berger Collection*, exh. cat., The Bancroft Library and the University Art Museum, University of California, Berkeley, 1984, 8.
12 Kelmscott Press edition, cited in *William Morris by Himself*, ed. Naylor, 10.
13 Morris, 'A Rather Long-Winded Sketch', in *William Morris: Selected Writings*, ed. Briggs, 29–30.
14 Lecture to Bard Graduate Center, Bard Term Abroad course, Victoria & Albert Museum, June 2000.
15 Quoted in MacCarthy, *William Morris*, 209.
16 Ibid.,. 210.
17 Ibid., 279.
18 The phrase is taken from the title of E. P. Thompson's book, *William Morris: Romantic to Revolutionary* (London: Lawrence and Wishart, 1955).
19 Morris, 'A Rather Long-Winded Sketch', in *William Morris: Selected Writings*, ed. Briggs, 31.
20 Ibid., 32.
21 MacCarthy, *William Morris*, xi.
22 For Morris's socialism see E. P. Thompson, *William Morris: Romantic to Revolutionary*; MacCarthy, *William Morris*, especially 462–640; and Nicholas Salmon, 'The Political Activist', in *William Morris*, ed. Parry, 204.
23 E. P. Thompson, *William Morris: Romantic to Revolutionary*, 792; MacCarthy, *William Morris*, 543–46.
24 E. P. Thompson, op. cit., 801 and 795. I am aware that 'alienation' is used in different ways within Marxism but, like Thompson, consider that Morris's understanding of 'alienated sensibility seems permissible and consonant with some passages of Marx' (815, n. 78).
25 Morris, 'Useful Work versus Useless Toil', in *William Morris: Selected Writings*, ed. Briggs, 121–22.
26 E. P. Thompson emphasizes the importance of Morris's SPAB work, 'which demanded a solution in practice and theory', to his role in transforming the Romantic tradition (*William Morris: Romantic to Revolutionary*, 273).
27 Ibid., 626.
28 Tony Benn, Lecture, *William Morris Reviewed* symposium, Victoria & Albert Museum, 22 June 1996.
29 E. P. Thompson, *William Morris: Romantic to Revolutionary*, 632.
30 Quoted in MacCarthy, *William Morris*, vii.
31 *Clarion*, 10 October 1896. Quoted in Paul Thompson, *Work of William Morris*, 56.

The Firm: Morris & Company (pp. 33–63)
1 Harvey and Press, *Art, Enterprise and Ethics*, 176.
2 MacCarthy, *William Morris*, 167.
3 William Burges was a key figure, and Holman Hunt and Millais painted furniture as early as 1851. See MacCarthy, *William Morris*, 120, and Frances Collard, 'Furniture', in *William Morris*, ed. Parry, 169.
4 MacCarthy, *William Morris*, 130.
5 Paul Thompson, *Work of William Morris*, 17–19.
6 For the history of the Firm see Harvey and Press, *William Morris: Design and Enterprise*; and by the same authors *Art, Enterprise and Ethics*; and 'The Businessman', in *William Morris*, ed. Parry; Paul Thompson, *Work of William Morris*; and MacCarthy, *William Morris*.

128 Designed by William Morris for Morris & Company

Lea printed fabric, first issued 1885 (detail)

Indigo-discharged and block-printed cotton, printed at Merton Abbey, full area 25 x 18¼ (63.5 x 46.4)

7 They argued that they had been technically financially liable had the business failed. In the early years Rossetti and Brown were key players with important contacts and there was some substance to their sense of entitlement. Distressed by what he considered their excessive demands, Morris settled out of court, offering each partner £1,000; Burne-Jones, Webb and Faulkner refused to take anything.
8 Harvey and Press, *William Morris: Design and Enterprise*, 177.
9 For Morris and machinery see E. P. Thompson, *William Morris: Romantic to Revolutionary*, 649–54, and Harvey and Press, *William Morris: Design and Enterprise*, 97, 104, 112, 152–53.
10 For a commentary on Morris's discussion of these issues in his lecture 'Art under a Plutocracy', see Faulkner, *Against the Age*, 113–19.
11 For this and the discussion that follows see Pat Kirkham, *The London Furniture Trade, 1700–1870* (Leeds: Maney Publishing, 1988), and Raphael Samuel, 'The Workshop of the World: Steam Power and Hand-Technology in mid-Victorian Britain', *History Workshop* 3 (1977): 6–72.
12 Samuel, 'The Workshop of the World', 6–72.
13 For linoleum see Parry in *William Morris*, ed. Parry, 276, cat. no. M93; and Harvey and Press, *William Morris: Design and Enterprise*, 95–96; for dress fabrics see MacCarthy, *William Morris*, 445.
14 Morris, 'Some Thoughts on the Ornamental Manuscripts of the Middle Ages', reprinted in *William Morris: The Ideal Book*, ed. Peterson, 1.
15 Walter Crane, 'The English Revival in Decorative Art' (1911). Quoted in 'Morris and Company, 1861–1939', in *Morris and Company*, ed. Charlotte Gere (London: The Fine Art Society, 1979), 6.
16 Parry, 'Domestic Decoration', in *William Morris*, ed. Parry, 138–39.
17 Ibid., 140.
18 Gere (cit. at n. 15), 26.
19 MacCarthy, *William Morris*, 169.
20 Parry, 'Domestic Decoration', in *William Morris*, ed. Parry, 144.
21 Part of Morris's letter to Horsfall, 1881, is reproduced in *Morris on Art and Design*, ed. Christine Poulson (Sheffield: Sheffield University Press, 1996), 125–28. See also Parry, 'Domestic Decoration', in *William Morris*, ed. Parry, 144.
22 MacCarthy, *William Morris*, 163.
23 Frances Collard, 'Furniture', in *William Morris*, ed. Parry, 155.
24 Ibid., 172, cat. no. J18.
25 Ibid., 170, cat. no. J14.
26 Ibid., 176–77.
27 Ibid., 161–62.
28 Juliet Kinchin, 'Interiors: nineteenth-century essays on the "masculine" and the "feminine" room', in *The Gendered Object*, ed. Pat Kirkham (Manchester: Manchester University Press, 1996).
29 An 1898 article in *The Artist* attributed to him eight chair designs for the firm. The only one illustrated is extremely similar to the widely popular faux-bamboo chairs of the Regency period (Gere (cit. at n. 15), 8).
30 Collard, 'Furniture', in *William Morris*, ed. Parry, 168. The washstand is that discussed above in the main text in the paragraph on the worker's cottage.
31 Ibid., 178.
32 See Mark Girouard, *Sweetness and Light: The Queen Anne Movement, 1860–1900* (Oxford: Clarendon Press, 1977).
33 Collard, 'Furniture', in *William Morris*, ed. Parry, 179. A plainer version was also produced. It cost 60 guineas whereas the marquetry one cost 98 guineas. At least seven versions are extant.
34 Morris, 'The Lesser Arts of Life', in *Lectures on Art and Industry*, in *Collected Works*, 22:260. Most of the information about wallpaper is taken from Lesley Hoskins, 'Wallpaper', in *William Morris*, ed. Parry, 198–223. See also Paul Thompson, *Work of William Morris*, 98–131; and MacCarthy, *William Morris*, *passim*.
35 Hoskins, 'Wallpaper' (cit. at n. 34), 200–202, 206.
36 Ibid., 202, 209–10, 213.
37 Ibid., 202–04, 217–23.
38 Parry, 'Textiles', in *William Morris*, ed. Parry, 226. For Morris textiles see also Parry, *William Morris Textiles*.
39 Rozsika Parker, *The Subversive Stitch: Embroidery and the Making of the Feminine* (London: Women's Press, 1984).
40 Parry, 'Textiles', in *William Morris*, ed. Parry, 235.
41 For May Morris, see *May Morris, 1868–1938*, exh. cat., The William Morris Gallery, London, 1989. For Jane Morris and May Morris see Marsh, *Jane and May Morris*.
42 Parry, 'Textiles', in *William Morris*, ed. Parry, 243. It also indicates the depth and breadth of Morris's knowledge. The correspondence between Morris and Holiday is now in The Huntington Morris Collection.
43 Ibid., 242.
44 MacCarthy, *William Morris*, 401.
45 William Morris, 'Textiles', in May Morris, *William Morris: Artist*, 1:245.
46 Quoted in *William Morris: The Sanford and Helen Berger Collection*, exh. cat., The Bancroft Library and the University Art Museum, University of California, Berkeley, 1984, 14.
47 Lovell, in *William Morris: The Sanford and Helen Berger Collection*, 14.
48 MacCarthy, *William Morris*, 444, and Parry, 'Textiles', in *William Morris*, ed. Parry, 26.
49 Morris to Thomas Wardle, 13 April 1877, in *Collected Letters of William Morris*, 1:365.
50 Quoted in 'The Morris Exhibit at the Foreign Fair', reprinted in Harvey and Press, *Art, Enterprise and Ethics*, 125.
51 Parry, 'Textiles', in *William Morris*, ed. Parry, 277.
52 Ibid., 276–77, and Paul Thompson, *Work of William Morris*, 270.
53 The phrase is Morris's. Quoted in Martin Harrison, 'Church Decoration and Stained Glass', in *William Morris*, ed. Parry, 106. For Morris and stained glass, see also Martin Harrison, *Victorian Stained Glass*; Paul Thompson, *Work of William Morris*, 132–50; Sewter, *Stained Glass*; and MacCarthy, *William Morris*, *passim*.
54 Harrison, 'Church Decoration' (cit. at n. 53), 107.
55 Paul Thompson, *Work of William Morris*, 142.
56 Harrison, 'Church Decoration' (cit. at n. 53), 108.
57 Ibid., 115.
58 Ibid., 123.
59 Paul Thompson, *Work of William Morris*, 134.
60 MacCarthy views these windows in a similar way: see *William Morris*, 647.
61 Ibid.
62 Paul Greenhalgh, 'Morris after Morris', in *William Morris*, ed. Parry, 364.
63 Harvey and Press, *William Morris: Design and Enterprise*, 222; for Morris & Company after 1905 see pp. 222–24. See also Parry, 'Morris and Company in the Twentieth Century', *Journal of the William Morris Society* 6.4 (1985–86), 11–16.
64 Parry, 'Morris and Company in the Twentieth Century', 12.
65 Ibid., 13.
66 Morris, 'The Lesser Arts, Delivered Before the Trades' Guild of Learning, December 4, 1877', in *Hopes and Fears for Art*, in *Collected Works*, 22:16.
67 See Morris & Company catalogue, *Specimens of Upholstered Furniture: Decoration*, n.d. [before 1917], The Huntington William Morris Collection.
68 'Catalogue of Designs used for Windows Executed' (1916–40), The Huntington William Morris Collection.
69 Designed by Lady Chilston, it adapted the legendary life of St George to that of an imaginary Eton schoolboy called to serve his country. See Linda Parry, 'The Revival of the Merton Abbey Tapestry Works', *Journal of the William Morris Society* 5.3 (1983), 16–22.
70 Parry, 'Morris and Company in the Twentieth Century' (cit. at n. 63), 21.
71 Ibid., 14.
72 *Morris And Company Art-Workers, Ltd.* Catalogue, n.d. [1930s].

Stained Glass and Church Decoration (pp. 65–75)

1 Harrison, *Victorian Stained Glass*, 12. See Sewter, *Stained Glass*, for a full catalogue of Morris & Company stained glass.
2 Morris, 'Glass, Painted or Stained' (1890), reprinted in *William Morris on Art and Design*, ed. Christine Poulson (Sheffield: Sheffield Academic Press, 1996), 44.
3 George Wardle, 'Memorials of William Morris', in Harvey and Press, *Art, Enterprise and Ethics*, 86–87.
4 According to the accounts of the Minute Book, Powell & Sons supplied the Firm with £50 worth of coloured glass in 1863.
5 Entry in Morris, Marshall, Faulkner & Company Minute Book, 18 March 1863, The Huntington Morris Collection.
6 These quarries appear in at least two stained glass windows for domestic commissions.
7 Harrison, 'Church Decoration and Stained Glass', in *William Morris*, ed. Parry, 132.
8 See Alan Crawford, 'Burne-Jones as a Decorative Artist', in Wildman and Christian, *Edward Burne-Jones*, 5–24, for an excellent survey of Burne-Jones's stained glass designs.

9 Wardle, 'Memorials of William Morris' in Harvey and Press, *Art, Enterprise and Ethics*, 96.
10 *The Works of John Ruskin*, ed. E. T. Cook and Alexander Wedderburn, vol. 37, *The Letters of John Ruskin* (London: George Allen, 1909), 436.
11 Georgiana Burne-Jones, *Memorials of Edward Burne-Jones* (London: Macmillan & Co, 1904), 2:129.
12 Morris to John Ruskin, 15 April 1883, in *Collected Letters of William Morris*, 2:186.
13 Quoted in ibid., 2:187, n.1.

The Decoration of Houses (pp. 77–87)
1 Morris, Marshall, Faulkner & Company, 'Prospectus', 1861. Quoted in Mackail, *Life*, 1:151.
2 Morris to Andreas Scheu, 15 September 1883, in *Collected Letters of William Morris*, 2:229–30.
3 Morris, 'The Beauty of Life, Delivered before the Birmingham Society of Arts and School of Design, February 19, 1880', in *Hopes and Fears for Art*, in *Collected Works*, 22:77.
4 See Jennifer Hawkins Opie, 'Tiles and Tableware', in *William Morris*, ed. Parry, 180–97; and Richard and Hilary Myers, *William Morris Tiles*.
5 Morris, 'The Lesser Arts of Life', in *Lectures on Art and Industry*, in *Collected Works*, 22:262.
6 Parry, *William Morris Textiles*, 47. Parry points out that the fabric has since been proved to be a fake.
7 Morris to Thomas Wardle, 24 December 1875, in *Collected Letters of William Morris*, 2:282–83.
8 George Wardle, 'Memorials of William Morris', in Harvey and Press, *Art, Enterprise and Ethics*, 91–93.
9 Morris, 'Textiles' (1888), in May Morris, *William Morris: Artist*, 1:249.
10 Morris to Jenny Morris, 28 February 1883, in *Collected Letters of William Morris*, 2:160.
11 See Parry, *William Morris Textiles*, 65–66 and 160.
12 Wardle (cit. at n. 8), 96–98.
13 For a photograph of the finished decorative scheme, see *Collected Letters of William Morris*, 4:166.
14 Quoted in Caroline Dakers, *Clouds: The Biography of a Country House* (New Haven and London: Yale University Press, 1993), 9.
15 Morris, 'The Beauty of Life' (cit. at n. 3), 22:53.
16 See Parry, *William Morris Textiles*, 130.

The Art of the Book (pp. 89–97)
1 Morris to George Bainton, 1889–May 1890?, in *Collected Letters of William Morris*, 3:154.
2 Interview with William Morris, 'The Poet as Printer', *Pall Mall Gazette*, 1891, reprinted in *William Morris: The Ideal Book*, ed. Peterson, 89.
3 'A Note by William Morris on His Aims in Founding the Kelmscott Press', 1896, in *William Morris: The Ideal Book*, ed. Peterson, 75.
4 See *The Kelmscott Press*, ed. Peterson, for a comprehensive history of the Press.
5 See John Nash, 'Calligraphy', in *William Morris*, ed. Parry, 296–309.
6 George Birkbeck Hill, *Letters of Dante Gabriel Rossetti to William Allingham 1854–1870* (London: T. Fisher Unwin, 1897), 193–94.
7 May Morris, *William Morris*, 1:401.
8 Morris to Jenny Morris, 16 October 1889, and Morris to Jane Morris, 17 October 1889, in *Collected Letters of William Morris*, 3:114–15.
9 Morris to Emma Shelton Morris, 21 November 1889, in *Collected Letters of William Morris*, 3:127.
10 Mackail, *Life of William Morris*, 2:227.
11 Morris to F. S. Ellis, 21 January 1889, in *Collected Letters of William Morris*, 3:14.
12 W. R. Lethaby, *Morris as Work-Master: a lecture delivered by W. R. Lethaby at the Birmingham Municipal School of Art on the 26th of October, 1901* (London: J. Hogg; Birmingham: Cornish Bros., 1901), 20–21.
13 'The Poet as Printer', reprinted in *William Morris: The Ideal Book*, ed. Peterson, 89.
14 'The Kelmscott Press: An Illustrated Interview with Mr. William Morris', *Bookselling*, 1895, reprinted in *William Morris: The Ideal Book*, ed. Peterson, 112.
15 Ibid., 110.
16 Edward Burne-Jones to Charles Eliot Norton, 8 December 1894. Quoted in Paul Needham, *William Morris*, 139.

John Henry Dearle (pp. 99–107)
1 Day, 'A Disciple of William Morris', 84–89.
2 Ibid., 88.
3 Ibid., 88–89.
4 Wardle, 'Memorials of William Morris', in Harvey and Press, *Art, Enterprise and Ethics*, 101.
5 Edward Payne states that Dearle 'had been trained up from a student apprentice by Morris in all the crafts'. Payne, 'Memories of Morris & Co.,' *Journal of the William Morris Society* (Summer 1981), 4.3:2–3.
6 Day, 'A Disciple of William Morris', 86.
7 Morris to the Editor of the *Journal of the Derbyshire Archaeological and Natural History Society*, 5 April 1893; and William Morris to Marion Edith (Waugh) Hunt, 17 March 1894, in *Collected Letters of William Morris*, 4:27, 4:142–43.
8 Morris to Emma Shelton Morris, 27 December 1885, in *Collected Letters of William Morris*, 2:506.
9 See Parry, *William Morris Textiles*, 18.
10 William Morris to Jenny Morris, 28 December 1888, in *Collected Letters of William Morris*, 2:845.
11 The *McCulloch* carpet is reproduced in Parry, *William Morris Textiles*, 98. See also *William Morris*, ed. Parry, 284.
12 The carpet is reproduced in Parry, *William Morris Textiles*, 82.
13 Payne, 'Memories of Morris & Co.' (cit. at n. 5), 2.
14 Morris to Thomas Wardle, 14 November 1877, in *Collected Letters of William Morris*, 1:409–10.

The Things That Might Be: British Design after Morris (pp. 109–133)
1 *William Morris by Himself*, ed. Naylor, 27.
2 F. R. Leavis, quoted in Gillian Naylor, 'Morris as a Pioneer of Modern Design', in *William Morris Today*, 81.
3 *The Journal of William Morris Studies*, published twice a year, contains an annual Annotated Bibliography by David and Sheila Latham. Issue 14:3 (Winter 2001), covering 1998–99, included five categories: General, Literature, Decorative Arts, Book Design, and Politics; 121 entries were listed.
4 Heaton in *Hobby Horse*, 11 (1887), 158–60. Quoted in Harrison, *Victorian Stained Glass*.
5 For information on Whall, consult the William Morris Gallery, London, and material on stained glass exhibitions collated by Peter Cormack. See also 'Recreating a Tradition: Christopher Whall (1849–1924) and the Arts and Crafts Renascence of English Stained Glass', in *Art and the National Dream*, ed. Nicola Gordon Bowe (Dublin: Irish Academic Press, 1993), 15–42.
6 Christopher Whall, 'Stained Glass Past and Present', notes for lectures, Victoria & Albert Museum Special Collection 80.QQ.22, p. 24.
7 Ibid., 17.
8 Edward Payne, 'Memories of Morris & Co.,' *Journal of the William Morris Society* 4:3 (Summer 1981).
9 Quoted in Peter Rose, *James Powell and Sons and Design Reform in England 1830–1918*, 15. See also *Whitefriars Glass: The Art of James Powell and Sons*, ed. Lesley Jackson, exh. cat., Manchester City Art Galleries / Museum of London, 1996.
10 Quoted in Parry, *William Morris Textiles*, 29.
11 Ibid., 142.
12 See Sara E. Haslam, 'Ruskin and the Lakeland Arts Revival 1880–1920' (PhD diss., University of Manchester, 2001), 78.
13 'Home Arts and Industries', *Transactions of the National Association for the Advancement of Art and its Application to Industry, Edinburgh Meeting, 1889* (London, 1890), 422.
14 See Alan Powers, *Modern Block Printed Textiles* (London: Walker Books, 1992), and Tanya Harrod, *The Crafts in Britain in the Twentieth Century* (published for the Bard Graduate Center for Studies in the Decorative Arts, Yale University Press, 1999), *passim*.
15 Peterson, *The Kelmscott Press*, 65.
16 First published in *Modern Art*, a Boston magazine, in 1896. Reprinted by S. C. Cockerell at the Kelmscott Press as *A Note by William Morris on his Aims in Founding the Kelmscott Press* (1898), with wood-engravings, and a frontispiece by Burne-Jones.
17 Quoted in Colin Franklin, *The Private Presses* (London: Studio Vista, 1969), 110. Cobden-Sanderson's *The Ideal Book or Book Beautiful* was published by the Doves Press in 1901.
18 Quoted in Franklin, *The Private Presses*, 95.
19 Quoted in Peterson, *Kelmscott Press*, 285.

20 Carl P. Rollins, 'Since Gutenberg (part II 1800–1940): A Highlight Review of 500 years of Printing', *Print: A Quarterly Journal of the Graphic Arts*, 1.2 (September 1940), 59.
21 Betty Miles, *At the Sign of the Rainbow: Margaret Calkin James 1894–1995* (Alcester, Warwickshire: Felis Scribo, 1996), 11–12.
22 Jan Tschichold, 'New Typography', *Circle* (London: Faber & Faber, 1937), 249–55. Tschichold's book, *Die Neue Typographie*, the source of these ideas, was first published in Germany in 1928. Tschichold was forced to emigrate to Switzerland in 1933, and he contributed to the Swiss typographic revival in the pre- and post-war period. He also worked for Penguin Books from 1947 to 1949, redesigning the cover format for the Penguin and Pelican ranges, his work at this stage seeming to complement rather than confront what he described as the 'New Traditionalism'.
23 Hermann Muthesius, *Das Englische Haus* (1904; New York: Rizzoli, 1979), p. 14.
24 W. R. Lethaby, 'Design and Industry', first written for the Design and Industries Association in 1915, reprinted in his *Form in Civilization* (Oxford: Oxford University Press, 1922), 48.
25 Harold Stabler, a goldsmith, also designed glass, ceramics and metalwork. He joined Poole Pottery (Carter, Stabler and Adams) in 1922.
26 Information on these early DIA members comes from Nikolaus Pevsner, 'Patient Progress Three: The DIA' (reprinted from the *DIA Yearbook* 1964–65), in *Studies in Art, Architecture and Design*, II, *Victorian and After* (London: Thames & Hudson, 1968), 226–42.
27 *Reports of the Present Position and Tendencies of the Industrial Arts as indicated at the International Exhibition of Modern Decorative and Industrial Arts, Paris* (London: Department of Overseas Trade, 1925), 94.
28 Holbrook Jackson, *Dreamer of Dreams* (London: Faber & Faber Ltd, 1948), 164.
29 The 1949 edition of *Pioneers of Modern Design from William Morris to Walter Gropius* was published by the Museum of Modern Art, and subsequent editions by Pelican Books, Harmondsworth. The fact that Pevsner credits Philip Johnson, Edgar Kauffmann, Henry Russell Hitchcock and Alfred H. Barr in 1949 indicates the credit then given in the United States to the international message of the post-war *Pioneers*.
30 Nikolaus Pevsner, *An Enquiry into Industrial Art in England* (Cambridge: Cambridge University Press, 1937), 3.
31 Ute Engel, 'The Formation of Pevsner's Art History in Germany 1902–1933', lecture at the Centenary Conference, 'Reassessing Nikolaus Pevsner', Birkbeck College (University of London), July 2002. The papers will be published by Ashgate Press in 2004.
32 Nikolaus Pevsner, *Academies of Art, Past and Present* (Cambridge: Cambridge University Press, 1940), viii.
33 Morris to the editor of The Manchester Examiner, 14 March 1883, in *Collected Letters of William Morris*, 2:173
34 Pevsner, *Industrial Art* (cit. at n. 30), 3.
35 Quoted in *William Morris By Himself*, ed. Naylor, 315.

Two Sides of the River: Morris and American Arts and Crafts

(pp. 135–167)
1 MacCarthy, *William Morris*, 603–4.
2 Quoted in Eileen Boris, *Art and Labour: Ruskin, Morris and the Craftsman Ideal in America* (Philadelphia: Temple University Press, 1986), 56.
3 James F. O'Gorman, *Living Architecture: A Biography of H. H. Richardson* (New York: Simon & Schuster, 1997), 10.
4 Ibid., 137–39.
5 H. H. Richardson to Julia Richardson, 11 July 1882; Archives, Shepley, Bulfinch, Richardson and Abbott, Boston; see Lindsay Leard-Coolidge, 'William Morris and Nineteenth-Century Boston', *William Morris: Centenary Essays*, ed. Peter Faulkner and Peter Preston (Exeter: University of Exeter Press, 1999), 160.
6 William Morris, *Hopes and Fears for Art* (Boston: Roberts Brothers, 1882), 168.
7 James Mavor, *My Windows on the Streets of the World* (London and Toronto: J. M. Dent & Sons; New York: E. P. Dutton & Co., 1923), 1:193.
8 Morris to Ogden Codman, 11 April 1883. Preservation Society of Newport County, Newport, Rhode Island.
9 Morris to Catherine Lorillard Wolfe, 15 April 1883. Preservation Society of Newport County, Newport, Rhode Island.
10 *The Earthly Paradise*, ed. Lochnan et al., 28.
11 Edward R. Bosley, *Greene & Greene* (London: Phaidon Press, 2000), 140.
12 I am deeply grateful to Yoshiko Yamamoto for sharing information from her archives of early magazine articles related to Morris.
13 Irene Sargent, 'William Morris: Some Thoughts upon His Life, Art and Influence', *The Craftsman* 1 (October 1901), 1.
14 Ibid., 9–10.
15 Charles Sumner Greene to James A. Culbertson, Kenilworth, Ill., 7 October 1902; Mikado Copying Book, pp. 9–11, recently acquired by the Greene and Greene Archives at The Huntington. My thanks to Kori Capaldi and Ann Scheid.
16 This is according to Tiffany's secretary, William J. Fielding. I am grateful to Michael Burlingham, great-grandson of Louis C. Tiffany, for sharing this information, which is also mentioned in Hugh McKean, *The 'Lost' Treasures of Louis Comfort Tiffany* (New York: Doubleday, 1980).
17 Quoted in Gillian Naylor, *The Arts and Crafts Movement: A Study of its Sources, Ideals, and Influence on Design Theory* (2nd ed., London: Trefoil Publications, 1990), 103.
18 I am grateful to Albert Tannler of the Pittsburgh History & Landmarks Foundation for generously sharing his research on Harry Goodhue.
19 Peter Cormack, *The Stained Glass Work of Christopher Whall, 1849–1924: 'Aglow with Brave Resplendent Colour'* (Boston: Trustees of the Public Library of the City of Boston, 1999), 13–15.
20 Lecture by Peter Cormack, 20 June 2002, for New York University's conference on the Arts and Crafts movement, 'Sources and Inspiration: Boston as a Beacon for the American Arts and Crafts Movement', Boston, Mass., 19–23 June 2002.
21 I am deeply grateful to the late Walter W. Judson, of Judson Studios, for his willingness to discuss his family and firm's history with me on 25 November 2002, in Los Angeles and Pasadena, California, not long before his sudden and untimely death.
22 Jane Apostol, *Painting with Light: A Centennial History of the Judson Studios* (Los Angeles: Historical Society of Southern California, 1997), 29.
23 Marianne Carlano, 'May Morris in Context: British Needlework and its Influence on European Embroidery, 1862–1902', in Marianne Carlano and Nicola J. Shilliam, *Early Modern Textiles: From Arts and Crafts to Art Deco* (Boston: Museum of Fine Arts, 1993), 14.
24 Ibid.
25 Amelia Peck and Carol Irish, *Candace Wheeler: The Art and Enterprise of American Design, 1875–1900* (New York: The Metropolitan Museum of Art, 2001), 22. I am grateful to Ann Chaves for her help on the subject of Candace Wheeler.
26 Ibid., 28.
27 Ibid., 102.
28 Ibid.
29 Jan Marsh, *Jane and May Morris*, 251–52. Thanks are due to Anne Mallek for referring me to this quotation.
30 Margery Burnham Howe, 'Deerfield Blue and White Needlework', *Bulletin of the Needle and Bobbin Club* 47.1 and 2 (1963), 47. Quoted in Nicola J. Shilliam, 'Emerging Identity: American Textile Artists in the early Twentieth Century', in Carlano and Shilliam, *Early Modern Textiles* (cit. at n. 23), 29.
31 Lecture by Suzanne Flynt, 22 June 2002, for New York University's conference on the Arts and Crafts movement (cit. at n. 20).
32 Susan Otis Thompson, *American Book Design*, 5. This is the standard work on the subject of Morris's influence on American printing and typography, with an excellent Foreword, in the 1996 edition, by Jean-François Vilain.
33 Quoted in ibid., 30.
34 'A New Era in English Printing', *Inland Printer* 10 (March 1893), 518.
35 Susan Otis Thompson, *American Book Design*, 35.
36 George L. Harding, *D. B. Updike and the Merrymount Press* (San Francisco: Roxburghe Club, 1943), 10. Quoted in Susan Otis Thompson, *American Book Design*, 78.
37 W. Irving Way, 'Books, Authors and Kindred Subjects', *Inland Printer* 14 (Jan. 1895), 345. I am grateful to André Chaves for bringing this passage to my attention.
38 From 'A Description of The Merrymount Press, Boston, 1893–1917', n.d., p. 16; a privately printed pamphlet brought to my attention by Bruce Smith, to whom I am grateful for this and many other helpful suggestions.

SELECT BIBLIOGRAPHY

Banham, Joanna, and Jennifer Harris *William Morris and the Middle Ages* (Manchester: Manchester University Press, 1984)

Boris, Eileen *Art and Labour: Ruskin, Morris and the Craftsman Ideal in America* (Philadelphia: Temple University Press, 1986)

Briggs, Asa, ed. *William Morris: Selected Writings and Designs* (Harmondsworth: Penguin Books, 1962)

Carlano, Marianne, and Nicola J. Shilliam *Early Modern Textiles: From Arts and Crafts to Art Deco* (Boston: Museum of Fine Arts, 1993)

Day, Lewis F. 'A Disciple of William Morris', *The Art Journal* (March 1905)

Faulkner, Peter *Against the Age: An Introduction to William Morris* (London: George Allen & Unwin, 1980)

—, and Peter Preston, eds. *William Morris: Centenary Essays* (Exeter: University of Exeter Press, 1999)

Harris, Jennifer, ed. *William Morris Revisited: Questioning the Legacy*, exh. cat., Whitworth Art Gallery, Manchester, Crafts Council Gallery, London, and Birmingham Museum and Art Gallery, 1996–97

Harrison, Martin *Victorian Stained Glass* (London: Barrie and Jenkins, 1980)

Harvey, Charles, and Jon Press *Art, Enterprise and Ethics: The Life and Works of William Morris* (London: Frank Cass, 1996)

——, *William Morris: Design and Enterprise in Victorian Britain* (Manchester: Manchester University Press, 1991)

Institute of Contemporary Arts *William Morris Today* (London: Institute of Contemporary Arts, 1984)

Lochnan, Katherine A., Douglas E. Schoenherr, and Carole Silver, eds. *The Earthly Paradise: Arts and Crafts by William Morris and His Circle from Canadian Collections* (Toronto: Key Porter Books, 1993)

MacCarthy, Fiona *William Morris: A Life for Our Time* (London: Faber and Faber, 1994; New York: Alfred A. Knopf, 1995)

Mackail, J. W. *The Life of William Morris* (New York and London: Benjamin Blom, 1968)

Marsh, Jan *Jane and May Morris: A Biographical Story, 1839–1938* (New York and London: Pandora Press, 1986)

Menz, Christopher *Morris & Company: Pre-Raphaelites and the Arts & Crafts Movement* (Adelaide: Art Gallery Board of South Australia, 1994)

Morris, May *William Morris: Artist, Writer, Socialist* (Oxford: Basil Blackwell, 1936)

Morris, William *The Collected Letters of William Morris*, ed. Norman Kelvin (Princeton, N.J.: Princeton University Press, 1984–96)

— *The Collected Works of William Morris* (London: Longmans Green & Co., 1914)

Myers, Richard, and Hilary Myers *William Morris Tiles: The Tile Designs of Morris and his Fellow-Workers* (Shepton Beauchamp, Som.: Richard Dennis, 1996)

Naylor, Gillian, ed. *William Morris by Himself: Designs and Writings* (London: Macdonald & Co., 1988)

Needham, Paul *William Morris and the Art of the Book*, exh. cat., The Pierpont Morgan Library, New York, 1976

Parry, Linda *William Morris Textiles* (New York: Viking Press, 1983)

—, ed. *William Morris*, exh. cat., Victoria and Albert Museum, London, 1996

Peterson, William S., ed. *William Morris: The Ideal Book* (Berkeley and Los Angeles: University of California Press, 1982)

— *The Kelmscott Press: A History of William Morris's Typographical Adventure* (Berkeley and Los Angeles: University of California Press, 1991)

Pevsner, Nikolaus *Pioneers of Modern Design from William Morris to Walter Gropius* (New York: Museum of Modern Art, 1949)

Salmon, Nicholas, with Derek Baker, *The William Morris Chronology* (Bristol: Thoemmes Press, 1996)

Sewter, A.C. *The Stained Glass of William Morris and his Circle* (New Haven and London: Yale University Press, 1974)

Stansky, Peter *Redesigning the World: William Morris, the 1880s, and the Arts and Crafts* (Palo Alto, Calif.: The Society for the Promotion of Science and Scholarship, 1985)

Thompson, E. P. *William Morris: Romantic to Revolutionary* (London: Lawrence and Wishart, 1955)

Thompson, Paul *The Work of William Morris* (1967; rev. ed. London: Quartet Books, 1977)

Thompson, Susan Otis *American Book Design and William Morris* (2nd ed., London and New Castle, Del.: The British Library and Oak Knoll Press, 1996)

Wildman, Stephen, and John Christian *Edward Burne-Jones: Victorian Artist-Dreamer*, exh. cat., The Metropolitan Museum of Art; New York, 1998

The Journal of William Morris Studies publishes annually an Annotated Bibliography of Morris-related books

INDEX 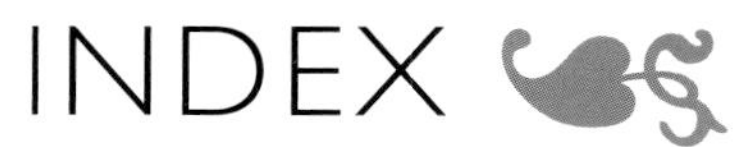

Adamson, Mabel 143
Aldrich, Thomas Bailey 165, *165*
Altar Book, The *166*, 166–67
Arroyo Guild of Fellow Craftsmen 143–44
Art Journal, The 116
Art Workers Guild *110*, 117
Ashbee, Charles Robert 110, 120, 122, 136, 143, 148
Ashendene Press 122–24, *125*

Barron, Phyllis 120
Bauhaus 114, 122, 130
Beardsley, Aubrey 124, *124*
Benson, William 39, *59*
Berger, Sanford and Helen 13–15, 16, 130
Blacker, Robert R. *144*, 146
Blatchford, Robert 31
Blunt, Wilfred Scawen 52
Bodley, George Frederick 57, 66, 70
BOOKS AND PRINTING 88–97, *88–97*, 122–28, *123–28*, 161–67, *162–66*
  illumination 21, *88*, 90–91, 94
  Kelmscott Press *11*, 13, 15, *19*, 21, 31, 59, 90,93–97, *93–97*, 122–23, 124, 161, *162*, *Aims in Founding the Kelmscott Press* 122; typefaces 93, *93*, 94, *123*, 122, 126–28, 161; Froissart's *Chronicles* 94, *96*; *The History of Reynard the Fox* 93, *94*; Kelmscott Chaucer 10, 13–15, 21, 30, 52, 97, *97*,164, 166, 167; *Le Morte d'Arthur* 10; *Recuyell of the Historyes of Troye* 93; *The Story of the Glittering Plain* 93, *95*, 97, 161
  translations by WM: *Aeneid* 21; *Beowulf* 21; *Odyssey* 21; *Volsunga Saga* 21, 23, *23*
  writings by WM: *A Dream of John Ball* 161; *The Earthly Paradise* 10, 13, 21, *90*, 91, (*Cupid and Psyche*) 91; *The Flowering Orchard* 158; *Hopes and Fears for Art* 26, 139; *The House of the Wolfings* 122; *Love is Enough* *90–91*, 91; *News from Nowhere* *11*, 12, 30; *The Roots of the Mountains* *92–93*, *92*, 122; *Sigurd the Volsung and the Fall of the Niblungs* 21; *Some Hints on Pattern-designing* 152; *The Story of Gunnlaug the Worm-Tongue* 122; *The Story of the Glittering Plain* 93, *95*, 97, 161; *Two Sides of the River* 134; *Useful Work v. Useless Toil* *28*, 29
Booth, George 61–63
Bowles, Joseph M. 164
Bradley, Will 13
Brown, Ford Madox 10, *14*, 26, 33, 34, 35, 36, 43–44, 48, 57, 58, 66, 67, *68*, *69*, 104, 147
Browning, Robert 16, *88*, 89, 90
Bryn Athyn, Pa. 137
Burden, Bessie 35, *35*, 51
Burden, Jane *see* Jane Morris
Burges, William 139
Burne-Jones, Edward 13, *26*, 40, *40*, 75, *78–79*, 124, 139, 140
  and WM 9–10, 25, 26, 27, 30, *31*, 33, 35, 60, 97
  books *23*, 91, *97*, 167
  furniture *26*, 34, 41, *41*
  stained glass 16, *17*, *18*,19, 34, 52, 56, 57, 58, 59, 66, 67, 70, *71*, 72–73, *72*, *73*, *101*, 104, 106, 112, 113, 114, *139*, *141*, *142*, 148, 151
  tapestry and embroidery designs 48, 51, *52*, *53*, 63, 86, 151, 152, *153*
Byrdcliffe, N.Y. 137

Campfield, George 35, 66, 70, *70*
Carlyle, Thomas 29, 89, 135
carpets *see* TEXTILES
Carrow Hall, Norf. 52
Castle Howard, Yorkshire 40, 139
Caxton, William 93
Central School of Arts and Crafts 110, 124
Century Guild 110
Chaucer, Geoffrey, and Kelmscott Chaucer 10, 13, 21, 30, 52, 97, *97*, 164, 166, 167
Chicago, Hull House 137
Chiswick Press 92, *92*, 122
Clarke, Harry 114
Clarke, William 135
Clayton & Bell 65
Cobden-Sanderson, T. J. 110, 124
Cockerell, Sydney 124
Codman, Ogden 140
Colman family 52
Colman, Samuel 153
Connick, Charles J. 115, 148, *149*, 151
Copeland & Day 164
Coronio, Aglaia 16
Craftsman, The *145*, 145–46
Cram, Ralph Adams 148, 151, 162
Cranbrook, Mich. 61
Crane, Walter 13, 27, 39, *41*, 51, 93, 101, 140, 152
Crawford, Alan 26
Culbertson, James A. 146
Curwen Press 127

D'Arcy, William Knox 40–41, 86
Day, Lewis F. 99, 101
De Morgan, William 27, 38, *38*, 39, 59, 80, 139
Dearle, John Henry 15, 19, 37, *50*, 52, 59, 60, 61, 63, 77, 83, 84, 86, *87*, 93, 99–107, 151
  stained glass designs 73, 74, 75, 112, *114*
  tapestry designs 41, *53*, 54
  wallpaper designs *15*, 46, *49*, *156*
Deerfield Society of Blue and White Needlework 158, 159, *160*, 161
de Forest, Lockwood 153
Design and Industries Association (DIA) 128–29
Deutscher Werkbund 128–29, 130
Dickens, Charles 29, 89, 136
Ditchling, Sussex, Guild of St Joseph and St Dominic 120
Doves Press 124, 125, *126*
Drury, Alfred 114

Elliot & Bulkley 138
Elliott, Charles Wyllys, *The Book of American Interiors* 137
embroidery *see* TEXTILES
Eragny Press 124
Essex House Press 122

fabrics *see* TEXTILES
Fairfax Murray, Charles 13
Faulkner, Charles 10, 27, 33, 36, 77
Faulkner, Kate 41, 46
Faulkner, Lucy 77, *78–79*
Fleming, Albert 119
Floud, Peter 133
Foster, Myles Birket 39, 58, 77
Friar Jerome's Beautiful Book 165, *165*
Froissart, *Chronicles* (manuscript) *35*, 48, (Kelmscott Press edition) 94, *96*
FURNITURE 26, *26*, 34–35, 39, 41, *41*, 42–46, *43*, *45*, *46*, *51* ,63, 129, 146
  post WM 46, 60–63, *61*, *62*
  influence in United States 146
  'Morris chair' 44, 146; St George cabinet 42, *43*; Sussex chair 40, 43, *44*, 45

Garnett, Annie 119
Gaskin, Arthur J. 167
Geddes, Wilhelmina 114, *115*
Gere, C. M. *11*
Gill, Eric 120–21, 124, 126
Glasgow School of Art 119
Glessner, John and Frances 140
Goodhue, Bertram Grosvenor 162, *163*, 166
Goodhue, Harry E. 148
Greene & Greene 6, 13, 143, *144*, 146
Grolier Club 161
Gropius, Walter 13, *131*
Guild of Handicraft 110, *111*, 120, 136, 143

Heal, Ambrose 129, *129*
Heath, Aldham 39
Heaton, B. J. Aldam 112, 113
Hewitt, Graily 124, 127
Hobby Horse, The 112, 113, 164
Holiday, Catherine 16, 51, 80, 151
Hollyer, Frederick *31*
Home Arts and Industries Association 120
Horsfall, Thomas 42
House Beautiful, The 136, 144
Howard, George, Earl of Carlisle 40, 139
Howells, William Dean 137
Hubbard, Elbert *164*
Hunt, William Holman 13
Hunter, Dard 164
Huntington, Henry E. 13

indigo 52, 54, *55*, 82, 83, 120, *168*
Industrial Art League 143
Ionides, Alexander 40

Jack, George 41, 44–46, *46*, 59
James, Henry 10

James, Margaret Calkin *127*
Jeffrey & Co. 47
Johnston, Edward 124, 126
Judson Studios *150*, 151
Judson, Walter Horace 151

Keeler, Charles 144
Kelmscott House *see* London
Kelmscott Manor, Oxfordshire 10, *11*, 12, 48
Kelmscott Press *see* BOOKS AND PRINTING
Keswick School of Industrial Arts 119
Knight Errant, The 162, *163*
Kropotkin, Peter 29

La Farge, John 147, *147*, 151
Ladies Home Journal 136,144
Langdale Linen Industry 119
Larcher, Dorothy 120, *121*
Lazarus, Emma 19
Lethaby, W. R. 94, 110, 113, 126, 128, 148
Liberty & Co. 117, *117*
London: Central School of Arts and Crafts 110, 124
1 Holland Park 40–41
Kelmscott House 59, 85, 86, 90, 112
Liberty & Co. 117, *117*
London County Council Technical Education Board *111*
1 Palace Green 40, *41*
Queen Square 35, 52, 77, 83, 86, 101
Red Lion Square (8) 35, 66, 77, (17) *26*
Royal Academy of Arts 110
Royal College of Art 113, 126
St James's Palace 27, 39–40
Victoria & Albert (formerly South Kensington) Museum 22, 48, 51, 54, 58, 80, Green Dining Room 39, *40*, 146
Longfellow, Henry Wadsworth 140–41
Longyear, Mrs J. Munro 158
Lowndes, Mary 114

Macbeth, Ann 119
MacCarthy, Fiona 29
McCulloch, George, work for 103–4
Macdonald, Margaret and Frances 119
Mackmurdo, A. H. 110, 112, 164
Mairet, Ethel 120–21
Malory, Sir Thomas, *Le Morte d'Arthur* 34, *124*
Marillier, Henry *5*, 60–63
Marshall, Peter Paul 10, 33, 36, 66
Marx, Enid 120
Marx, Karl 29
Mason, J. H. 124
Merrymount Press 13, 166, *166*
Merton Abbey, Wimbledon *12*, 19, 36, *50*, 52, *53*, *55*, 77, 80, 85, 93, 102, 103, 116, 139
dye book 15, 19, 82, *84*
stained glass 72, 113, 114
tapestry 51, 101
Millais, John Everett 13
Miller, Ellen 158–61
MORRIS & COMPANY (1875–1940) 15, 18
founded 19, 27
general history 36–63
interior decoration 77–87
showrooms 36, *62*, 146
stained glass 15, 65–75
post-WM *59–63*, *132*, 133
in United States 137–61
closure 63
See also J. H. Dearle; Henry Marillier; Merton Abbey
Morris, Jane *10*, 26, 34, *35*, 36, 51, 66–67, 92
Morris, Jenny 26, 51, 92
Morris, May 26, 37, 46, 51, *59*, 91, 101, 119, 151, 158, *159*
MORRIS, WILLIAM 9–13, 21–31
early life 24–25
attitude to United States 135, 143
as businessman 27, 33, 35–36, 72, 77
craftsman's qualities 106
drawings 15, 67, (*Iseult*) *34*, (*Liberty*) 17, (*Mary of Bethany*) 70, (*Mary Virgin*) *16*, (self portrait) *22*, (drawing method) 94
dyes, views on 52, 80–82
early studies of carpets 54, 85
embroidery 48, 80
stained glass *56*, *57*
tapestry 51, 86
friendship (Burne-Jones) 9, 25, *31*, 33, 59, (Dearle 99), (Richardson) 139
Iceland travel 24, 27
industrialism, attitude to 12, 24, 26, 37–38, 80
lectures 26, 91, ('Art and the Beauty of the Earth') 16, ('Beauty of Life') 9, 86, (*Hopes and Fears for Art*) 26, 139
literary interests 21, 27, (fine books) 89–90, (Norse literature) 21, *23*, 27, 91
medieval and gothic 9, 13, 24, 25, 34, 48, 86, 90, 136
political activism and socialism *8*, 12, 13, 22, 26, 27–31, 37, 85, 109, 136
religious influences 24–25, 26, 56, 65
Ruskin's influence on 25, 34
South Kensington Museum 22, 48, 51, 54, 80
MORRIS, MARSHALL, FAULKNER & COMPANY (1862–74) 10, *14*, 22, 33–36, *36*, *40*, *43*, *64*, *66*, *68–71*, *78–79*, *81*; Minute Book 15, 18, 19; in United States 137
Morte d'Arthur, Le see Malory
Mosher, Thomas B. 164, 165
Muthesius, Hermann 128, 129

New England Magazine 135
Newbery, Jessie 119, *120*
Norton, Charles Eliot 137

O'Connor, Jerome 164
Oxford University 21, 25, 33, 90; Union 34

Payne, Edward 113, 114
Peach, Harry 129
Pevsner, Nikolaus 129–30, *131*
Pissarro, Lucien 124
Powell, Harry 116, *116*
Powell, James & Sons 38, 56, 57, 65, 66, 116
Prince Who Did Not Exist, The 167
printing *see* BOOKS AND PRINTING
Prior, E. S. 148
Pugin, A. W. N. 25, 56, 65, 135

Red House, Bexleyheath, Kent 10, 34, 39, 47, 48, 67, 116, 143
Richardson, Henry Hobson 138–40, *140*
Roberts Brothers printers 161
Rogers, Bruce 164–65, *165*
Rollins, Carl P. 127
Rooke, Noel 124
Rose Valley, Pa. 137
Rossetti, Dante Gabriel 10, 13, 26, *26*, 33, 34, 35, 36, 91; furniture *26*, 34, 43; stained glass *14*, 34, 57, 58, 66, 67, *68*, *69*, 147; *Hand and Soul* 162, *162*
Royal Academy of Arts 110
Royal College of Art 113, 126
Roycroft Printing Shop 164, *164*
Royal School of Art Needlework (RSAN) 51, 119, 152–54, *153*
Ruskin, John 13, 21, 34, 89, 116, 137; general influence 112, 119, 138, 161, 167; influence on WM 24, 25, 33, 109, 135, 151; and Whitelands College 72, 75

Sanderson & Sons Ltd 47, *132*
Society for Checking Abuses of Public Advertising (SCAPA) 30
Schreiner, Olive 164
Scott, George Gilbert 66, 67
Scott, Walter 24, 58
Sedding, J. D. 148
Shakers 137
Shaw, George Bernard 21, 37
Simons, Anna 124
Smith, Frank and Robert 37, 93
Society of Decorative Arts 152–54
South Kensington Museum *see* London, Victoria & Albert Museum
Society for the Protection of Ancient Buildings (SPAB) 13, 22, 72
Sparling, Henry Halliday *8*, *23*
Stabler, Harold 129
STAINED GLASS 16, 56–59, 61, 65–75, 104–6, 112–16; 147–51
quarries 57, *58*, *70*
windows and window designs: Acocks Green, War., St Mary the Virgin *73*, 75; Ashmont, Mass., All Saints *149*, 151; Bishop's Tachbrook, War., St Chad's *64*, 67; Boston, Mass., Trinity Church *139*, 139–40, *141*, 147, *147*; Bradford, Yorks., St Peter's (later Bradford Cathedral) 39, 67, *68–70*; Cambridge, Peterhouse College, Combination Room 58; Compton, Leek, Staffs., All Saints *114*; Folkestone, Kent, 6 Earls Avenue *142*; Godmanchester, Hunts., St Mary the Virgin *74*, 75; Guernsey, Channel Islands, St Stephen's *14*; Haywards Heath, Sussex, St Wilfrid's 70, *71*; Henley-on-Thames, Oxon, Convent of the Salesian Sisters *141*; Heywood, Lancs., Unitarian Chapel 16, *17*; Langton Green, Kent, All Saints *66*, 66–67; London, Holy Trinity, Sloane Street *112–13*; London, Whitelands Training College Chapel 72, *72*; Newport, R. I., Vinland 140, *142*, 143; Ottawa, St Bartholomew's *115*; Oxford, Manchester College Chapel *17*; Pasadena, Calif., All Saints *150*, 151; Rugby, War., Rugby School Chapel 104, *106*, *107*; Weybridge, Surrey, St James's *18*
Stanhope, Spencer 39
Stanmore Hall, Middlesex 40–41, *41*, 85–86, *87*
Stepniak, Sergius 29, 30
Stickley, Gustav 143–44, 146
Street, George Edmund 9, 26, 48, 59, 66
Studio,The 117
Summerly's Art Manufactures 33
Swinburne, Charles Algernon 13, 34

tapestries *see* TEXTILES
Taylor, Warington 27, 44
Templeton, Frances Mary *119*
Tennyson, Alfred, Lord 21, 27, 164
TEXTILES (Morris circle)
dyeing and printing *12*, 52, 80–83, 120
carpets 15, 16, 19, 38, 41, 54–56, *56*, 63, 82, 85, *85*, 86, *87*, 103–4, *104*, *105*
embroidery 15, 18, 19, 34, 35, *35*, 37, 39, 47, 48–51, *51*, 58, 67, 80, *81*, *100*, *101*,

101–2, 151–52, 158, *159*
printed fabrics 15, 19, *50*, *52–54*, *54*, *55*, 60, *76*, 80–83, *82–83*, 104, *105*
tapestry 10, 15, 19, 39, 41, *41*, 48, 51–52, *53*, 60, 61, 63, 82, 86, 101, 138
woven 15, 19, 41, 48, 54, *55*, 80, 83–85, *84*
designs *Acanthus* 63; *Anemone 100*, 101; *Angeli Laudantes* 52, *53*; *Angeli Ministrantes* 52; *Apple Tree 101*; *Bird* 54, *55*, *133*; *Bird and Vine* 140; *Blue and Yellow Kennet* 83, *84*; *Brother Rabbit* 54; *Cabbage and Vine* 86; *Carbrook* 41; *Cherwell 50*; *Columbine* 52, *54*; *Daisy 35*, 48; *Flora* 52; *Forest* 41, 86; *Fruit* 155; *Fruit Garden* 159; *Golden Lily 132*; *Goose Girl* 51, 101; *Grapevine 101*; *Green Lea* 83, *84*; *Greenery* 86, *87*; *Helena* 83–85, *84*; *Holland Park* 41; *Holy Grail 41*, 52, 86; *Honeysuckle* 51, 52, *92*; *Iris 76*, 80; *Lea* 154, *168*; *Lily 56*; *Little Tree 85*; *Lodden 82–83*; *Marigold* 52; *McCulloch* 104; *Musicians* 51; *Passing of Venus* 61; *Peacock and Dragon* 140; *Peony 100*, 101; *Plum 101*; *Pomegranate 101*; *Pomona* 52; *Rose and Thistle* 140; *Rosebud 105*; *Scroll* 155; *Snakeshead 82–83*; *Strawberry Thief* 54, *55*; *Tulip* 52; *Tulip and Lily* 56; *Willow* 155
TEXTILES (non-Morris)
American 151–61, *160*
British 116–22, *118–21*, 152, *153*
Tiffany, Louis Comfort 147, 151, 153, 154
tiles 7, 38, *38*, 77–80, *78–79*
Tschichold, Jan 127–28, *128*

Updike, Daniel Berkeley 13, 165–67, *166*

Vale Press 124
Victoria, Queen 24
Vinland, Newport, R.I. 140, *142*, 143
Voysey, C. F. A. 117, *118*

Walker, Emery *8*, 93, 122, 124, 158, 161, 165, 167
WALLPAPER 15, 18, 36, 37–38, 39, 46–48, 52, 80, 102; *Acanthus* 46, 48; *Apple* 155, *156*; *Compton 49*; *Daffodil 98*, 104; *Daisy* 47, *137*; *Fruit* 48; *Golden Lily 102*; *Granville 15*; *Iris* 86; *Jasmine 2*, 48, 91; *Larkspur* 91; *Marigold* 91; *Peony* 155, *156*; *Pimpernel* 48; *Pink and Rose 18*, *47*; *Pomegranate* 48; *Poppy* 140; *Rosebud* 104–5; *Seaweed* 102–3, *103*; *Sunflower* 140; *Trellis* 48; *Vine* 48
Wardle, Elizabeth 119
Wardle, George *65*, 72, 80, 82, 85, 101
Wardle, Thomas *52*, *65*, 80, 82, 117, 118–19
Warner, Samuel 164
Warren, Edward Perry 167
Watts, G. F. *9*
Way, W. Irving 162
Way & Williams 162, *162*, 165
Webb, Philip 10, 27, 33, *34*, 35, 36, 40, *40*, 41, 42, 43, *43*, 44, 59, 60, 66, 86, 151; stained glass *14*, 38, 57, 67, *68*, *69*, 70, *71*, 112, table glass 116
Whall, Christopher *112–13*, 113, 148, 151
Wheeler, Candace 152–54, *155*, 158, 161
Wheeler, Dora 153, 155, *157*
Whitefriars Glass 116, *116*
Whiting, Margaret 158–61
Wilde, Oscar 21, 138
Wilson, Frederick 151
Winston, Charles 56, 65, 66
Wolfe, Catherine Lorillard 140, 143
Woman's Exchange 153
Wyndham, Percy 86

CONTRIBUTORS

DIANE WAGGONER is Andrew W. Mellon Foundation Curatorial Fellow in the Art Collections at The Huntington. She holds a PhD in art history from Yale University and has published on Lewis Carroll's photography. She is the curator of the special exhibition, *'The Beauty of Life': William Morris and the Art of Design*, at The Huntington.

EDWARD BOSLEY is James N. Gamble Director of The Gamble House (Pasadena, California), a National Historic Landmark operated by the University of Southern California School of Architecture. Among his publications on the American Arts and Crafts movement is *Greene & Greene* (2000), the definitive scholarly work on the subject.

PAT KIRKHAM is Professor of Design History at the Bard Graduate Center for Studies in the Decorative Arts, Design, and Culture, New York. Her PhD is from the University of London. She has written several books and many articles on design, film and gender. Among her publications are *Charles and Ray Eames* (1995); *Women Designers in the USA, 1900–2000* (2000), *The Gendered Object* (1996), *The London Furniture Trade* (1988) and 'William Morris's Early Furniture' (1981).

GILLIAN NAYLOR was Professor (and Visiting Professor) of the History of Design at the Royal College of Art in London. She helped to initiate the History of Design MA which is run jointly by the RCA and the Victoria & Albert Museum. She has published widely on nineteenth- and twentieth-century design, including books on William Morris, the Arts and Crafts movement and Hector Guimard. Her most recent work has been on Nikolaus Pevsner and on Art Nouveau.